DATE DUE

NO 20 '01			
AP 9 03			

DEMCO 38-296

CAUGHT BETWEEN
ROOSEVELT & STALIN

CAUGHT BETWEEN ROOSEVELT & STALIN

America's Ambassadors to Moscow

DENNIS J. DUNN

THE UNIVERSITY PRESS OF KENTUCKY

made possible in part by a grant
nent for the Humanities.

Editorial and Sales Offices: The University Press of Kentucky
663 South Limestone Street, Lexington, Kentucky 40508-4008

98 99 00 01 02   5 4 3 2 1

Library of Congress Cataloging-in-Publication Data

Dunn, Dennis J.
  Caught between Roosevelt and Stalin : America's ambassadors to Moscow /
Dennis J. Dunn
    p.   cm.
  Includes bibliographical references (p.   ) and index.
  ISBN 0-8131-2023-3 (cloth: alk. paper)
    1. United States—Foreign relations—Soviet Union. 2. Soviet Union—Foreign
relations—United States. 3. Ambassadors—United States—History—20th
century. 4. Ambassadors—Soviet Union—History—20th Century. 5. United
States—Foreign   relations—1933-1945. 6. Roosevelt, Franklin D. (Franklin
Delano), 1882-1945. 7. Stalin, Joseph, 1879-1953. I. Title
E183.8.S65D86 1998   97-23033
327.47073—dc21

For Margaret, Denise, and Meg

Contents

Illustrations follow page 178

Preface

On November 16, 1933, President Franklin D. Roosevelt and Soviet Commissar of Foreign Affairs Maxim Litvinov signed the Roosevelt-Litvinov Agreement, which established for the first time diplomatic ties between the United States and the Soviet Union. Two days later Roosevelt named the first of ultimately five ambassadors whom he would place in Moscow between 1933 and 1945: William C. Bullitt, 1933-36; Joseph E. Davies, 1936-38; Laurence A. Steinhardt, 1939-41; William C. Standley, 1942-43, and W. Averell Harriman, 1943-46. The ambassadors' chief advisers were George F. Kennan, Loy Henderson, Charles Bohlen, and Philip Faymonville.

This book examines these men and their relationships to Roosevelt and Stalin for four distinct but overlapping reasons. First, such a study provides a biopsy of Roosevelt's policy toward Stalin and the motivation behind that policy. Roosevelt as foreign policy leader has remained a sphinx for historians. Winston Churchill described Stalin's Russia as "a riddle wrapped in a mystery inside an enigma," but the description also seems to fit Roosevelt's foreign policy toward Stalin's Russia. Few books have been published on his foreign policy and even fewer on his policy toward Stalin's Soviet Union. He did not leave scholars many records with which to work. Warren Kimball, Robert Dallek, Daniel Yergin, John Lewis Gaddis, Lloyd Gardner, Robert Divine, and others have helped put him into perspective, but, in Kimball's words, he continues to be "disingenuous, deceptive and devious."[1] There seems to be general consensus that he pursued a policy of accommodation toward Stalin, especially during the war years, but there is no agreement on whether this was beneficial, harmful, or necessary, nor is there any agreement on his motivation.

Some historians hold out that FDR's deteriorating physical condition led him to appease Stalin. This view, however, is insufficient; the concessionary policy was consistent from the very beginning of FDR's relationship with Stalin, and he was not in bad health throughout his entire presidency. Others vouchsafe that Roosevelt had no choice but to cater to Stalin because of the Nazi threat, the restraining power of U.S. public opinion, and/or the geopolitical realities of

World War II. These views, too, lack force because FDR did have a choice at the beginning of the relationship, between 1939 and 1943, and especially in certain matters between 1943 and 1945, and he was, after all, the master molder of public opinion and the leader of the most powerful country on earth.[2]

Historian Daniel Yergin believes that FDR was a "renegade Wilsonian," a president who believed in spheres of influence but who was restrained by a Wilsonian public opinion from declaring it, although not from acquiescing in it.[3] This view, however, does not explain why FDR appeased Stalin other than to say that he was a realist, a practitioner of realpolitik. It does acknowledge that FDR harbored certain beliefs about Stalin, including that he was no longer a revolutionary but rather a suspicious ruler of a Russian state who was looking for security in the face of German and Japanese threats, but it neither sheds light on the reason for such beliefs nor assesses the evidence in support of a nonrevolutionary Stalin. The recent publication of Stalin's personal letters to his foreign minister and confidant Viacheslav Molotov and of other archival sources, especially *Dokumenty vneshnei politiki 1939 god* and *Komintern i vtoraia mirovaia voina*, reveal that he remained committed to revolution and never viewed Soviet interests and revolution in "either-or terms."[4] In addition, Stalin's actions are consistent with a commitment to revolution, albeit a careful position, always ready to expediently and temporarily compromise in the face of a perceived threat.[5]

Historian David Mayers believes that FDR was simply casual or careless in foreign policy.[6] This was certainly true, but FDR was also consistent and rather single-minded when it came to relations with Stalin. Casualness in his case is an indication of someone who has already made up his mind and moves along as so much flotsam on the surface of a powerful stream. George Kennan argues that Roosevelt was naive and simplistic, and although this characterization might arguably describe some of the consequences of FDR's Soviet policy, it fails to note that there was method to his action.[7] Warren Kimball argues that Roosevelt saw Stalin as a powerful, suspicious leader who had to be courted and persuaded by a concessionary policy to join "The Family Circle" of liberal democracies and to develop the American model of liberal democracy within his region of influence and within his own country.[8] This view seems to be correct except that it does not emphasize the element of inevitability within FDR's ideology that explains his nonchalance in the face of Stalinism's abject evil. A study of Roosevelt's ambassadors in Moscow and their advisers helps provide an answer to the conundrum of FDR's Soviet policy.

A second reason for studying Roosevelt's ambassadors in Moscow and their advisers is to open a window on Stalin's policy toward FDR and the United States. The Soviet dictator's attitude toward the United States has been little understood because the Soviet archives were closed for most of this century. Now, however, with the opening of some of the Soviet archives, a fuller picture of him and his policy toward the United States is possible.[9] In effect, the Moscow embassy is a microcosm of American-Soviet relations before World War II, during the war, and at the advent of the cold war. It also touches on the triangular relationship between Roosevelt, Churchill, and Stalin during World War II.

Third, this book provides a unique gauge to examine the value of the institution of ambassador. Since 1933, twenty envoys have represented the American people at the Kremlin, including Thomas R. Pickering, the appointee of the Clinton administration. In the wake of recent presidential campaigns, where it was charged that American ambassadors are anachronistic and should be replaced with business and trade experts, it is important to examine the history of a group of ambassadors in a critical post during a momentous period to determine if the position of ambassador does indeed play a useful role in advancing and maintaining America's foreign policy interests.

Finally, this is a story of significant individuals at a pivotal place during a crucial time, and it deserves to be told. This is not true of ambassadors and advisers generally. The chief function of an ambassador and a regional specialist is to carry out policy and provide political analysis and reporting. American ambassadors in Russia before the Bolshevik Revolution and after the Roosevelt era basically did that. Ambassadors in other countries with which the United States has had relations have generally done that. FDR's ambassadors in Moscow and their advisers were different.

FDR named as his ambassadors men who were both close to and independent of him and who could affect policy by influencing him or public opinion. This was especially true of Bullitt, Davies, and Harriman, but even Standley and Steinhardt could shape policy because of their strong personalities and independence. The advisers, in turn, helped develop the views of the ambassadors. This is not to say, of course, that FDR turned over the direction of foreign policy to the representatives in Moscow. He actually held a tight grip on America's Soviet policy, bypassing from the onset even the State Department. But it is to say that there were influential envoys in Moscow, much more so than in most diplomatic posts, whose stature and independence of mind allowed them to go beyond policy execution and political reporting to actually affect policy, at least to the point where FDR had to deal with them because he wanted their approbation and feared their contumacy. Precisely because FDR ran America's Soviet policy, the Moscow post takes on special significance. It was the front line in the diplomatic and military alliance that set the stage for the destruction of Nazism and Japanese militarism in World War II, oversaw the alteration of the political boundaries of Europe and Asia, forced domestic policy to take a backseat to national security, and changed forever the history of the United States, Europe, and Asia. It witnessed the consolidation of Stalinism in the Soviet Union, the Second World War, the start of the cold war, and the advent of the atomic age.

This is the first history of the ambassadors and their advisers that extensively uses Soviet archives and focuses in detail solely on all of the American observers in Moscow during the Roosevelt era—who they were and why they were selected and dismissed, their background, their experience in Moscow, what advice they gave Roosevelt—and the debates, arguments, and deliberations that not only framed American policy toward Moscow but determined the politics of Europe to this day. Most studies of a personal American experience in Stalinist Russia focus on newsmen, travelers, disillusioned intellectuals, and disappointed workers. Few concentrate on the personalities who were at the Moscow post.[10]

Transliteration of Russian words follows the Library of Congress system with a few modifications. Generally, I omitted the soft sign and rendered the ending of family names with *y*. Some words were already well known in another form, and so I adopted that form. In translating the heading of Russian documents, I preferred to give a specific indication of the persons involved rather than a more general but also more literal rendering of the text. For example, I used "Notes of Conversation between Molotov and Standley," rather than "Notes of Conversation of the People's Commissar of Foreign Affairs of the USSR with the Ambassador of the United States."

I am indebted to many individuals in the writing of this book, but probably none more than the librarians and archivists at the Library of Congress; the Franklin Delano Roosevelt Library in Hyde Park, New York; Southwest Texas State University; the University of Texas at Austin; the Kennan Institute for Advanced Russian Studies; the Public Records Office in London; the State Archive of Russian Federation (Moscow); the Russian Foreign Ministry Archive in Moscow; and the Russian Center for Preservation and Study of Contemporary Historical Documents in Moscow. I am grateful to my friend Professor Mikhail Matskovksy of the International Center of Human Values in Moscow for arranging access to Russian archives and to Professor Vladimir Pozniakov of the Russian Academy of Sciences for his assistance in locating the key documents relating to this study in the relevant Russian archives. I am indebted to Steven Merritt Miner of Ohio University and Amos Perlmutter of American University for their perceptive comments and criticism of the original manuscript. I thank my colleagues in central Texas for their stimulating discussions and insights, especially Dr. T. Theodore Hindson and Dr. Oliver Radkey. I also wish to thank my wife, Margaret, for putting up with extended retreats to my study.

Dates of Service for American Ambassadors in Moscow, 1933-1946

	Date of appointment	Credentials presented	Departure from post
William C. Bullitt	November 21, 1933	December 13, 1933	May 16, 1936[a]
Joseph E. Davies	November 16, 1936	January 25, 1936	June 11, 1938[b]
Laurence A. Steinhardt	March 23, 1939	August 11, 1939	November 12, 1941
William H. Standley	February 14, 1942	April 14, 1942	September 19, 1943
W. Averell Harriman	October 7, 1943	October 23, 1943	January 24, 1946

Source: U.S. State Department, *Principal Officers of the Department of State and Chiefs of Mission, 1778-1988* (Washington, D.C., 1988), and *New York Times*

[a] Recommissioned after Senate confirmation and reappointed on January 15, 1934
[b] Recommissioned after Senate confirmation and reappointed on January 23, 1937

Prologue: Early 1943

Not long after the Battle of Stalingrad turned in favor of the Red Army, William C. Bullitt entered the Oval Office. Behind a large, wooden desk in a wheelchair sat a vexed Franklin D. Roosevelt. Bullitt and Roosevelt had been close friends since 1932. Bullitt served FDR as the first ambassador to Stalin's empire from 1933 to 1936, ambassador to France from 1936 until June 1940 when the Nazis arrived, ambassador at large from 1940 to 1942, and, finally, special assistant to the secretary of the navy from 1942 until 1944 when Bullitt resigned to accept an officer's commission in the Free French Forces of General Charles DeGaulle. Bullitt was sharp, analytical, and especially knowledgeable about international affairs and European politics, and Roosevelt enjoyed and benefited from his expertise and analysis. The relationship had cooled somewhat in 1941 when they disagreed over Assistant Secretary of State Sumner Welles (Bullitt wanted him dismissed), but FDR still valued Bullitt's opinions and friendship.

Roosevelt was now disturbed over a lengthy report that he had asked Bullitt to prepare on "the machinery of preparation for civil administration in occupied territories." Bullitt's report, dated January 29, 1943, bothered Roosevelt because it was a searing critique of his view of and policy toward Stalin. It also directly clashed with the opinions of two of his chief advisers, Harry Hopkins and Joseph Davies. Hopkins was Roosevelt's closest friend and adviser. Hopkins met Stalin for the first time in Moscow in July 1941 as the Wehrmacht was bearing down on the city. His sole ambition in life, especially after his operation for stomach cancer in 1937, was to serve Roosevelt, whom he called "the Boss." Davies, like Bullitt, was a former ambassador to the Soviet Union. Unlike Bullitt, though, he had a very favorable opinion of Stalin. He now informally served Roosevelt as liaison between the White House and the Soviet embassy in Washington. FDR also relied on him as a key adviser on Soviet affairs and, when he was willing and well enough to travel, as a special representative.

For over three hours Roosevelt and Bullitt argued about Stalin's intentions. In his report Bullitt reviewed the incontrovertible record of Stalin's malevolence, brutality, and treachery and what would happen in Eastern and Central

Europe if FDR persisted in his policy of appeasement. He stressed that Stalin was a dictator, an imperialist, and a Communist ideologue intent on spreading the Communist revolution around the world, but that he could be brought to heel if FDR would take forceful steps, including involving the Soviet Union in war with Japan, using wartime aid to extract concessions from Moscow, attacking the Axis from the Black Sea and Balkans, preparing plans to organize the Eastern European states into a democratic coalition, developing ways to put American troops in Eastern Europe, streamlining the American government bureaucracy to focus on the development of democratic governments in Eastern Europe, and tactfully using the promise of postwar reconstruction aid to attenuate Stalin's behavior.

Roosevelt finally said: "Bill, I don't dispute your facts, they are accurate. I don't dispute the logic of your reasoning. I just have a hunch that Stalin is not that kind of man. Harry says he's not and that he doesn't want anything but security for his country, and I think that if I give him everything I possibly can and ask nothing from him in return, noblesse oblige, he won't try to annex anything and will work with me for a world of democracy and peace."

Bullitt reminded the president that "when he talked of noblesse oblige he was not speaking of the Duke of Norfolk but of a Caucasian bandit whose only thought when he got something for nothing was that the other fellow was an ass, and that Stalin believed in the Communist creed which calls for conquest of the world for Communism."

Roosevelt shot back: "Bill, . . . it's my responsibility and not yours; and I'm going to play my hunch."[1]

The debate of February 1943 echoed the first disagreement between Franklin Roosevelt and William Bullitt nine years earlier. Roosevelt, in the second year of his first term as president, was committed to friendly relations with Stalin. Bullitt, in Moscow for less than two months, was attempting to carry out Roosevelt's commitment. Roosevelt had bucked domestic criticism to recognize the Soviet government, and he wanted Bullitt to provide evidence of the shrewdness of his move. Bullitt tried but could find nothing redeeming about Stalin or his cold, xenophobic policy toward the United States. Bullitt wanted Roosevelt to adopt a quid pro quo policy toward Stalin to make him more reasonable, but Roosevelt refused, preferring instead to excuse Stalin's behavior. The difference in approach between Roosevelt and the embassy hardened as the years slipped by, until Roosevelt replaced Bullitt in late 1936 with Joseph Davies, who conjured up the policy that the president demanded.

The Roosevelt-Bullitt polarization foreshadowed the two main divisions in American policy toward Soviet Russia that developed between Roosevelt and his advisers, on the one hand, and all of his ambassadors in Moscow, except Davies, and their advisers, except for Davies's adviser Faymonville, on the other hand. The Roosevelt group and the embassy/State Department group shared the hope of seeing Russia become a friend of the United States and evolve into a pluralist society, but each had a different understanding and approach on how to attain those goals. The division was general rather than absolute, and occasionally Roosevelt or one of his group would state a reservation about Stalin, and one of the embassy/State Department coterie would see value in appeasing Stalin, but in terms of overall policy, particularly Roosevelt's, the division was clear.

The Roosevelt contingent espoused a remarkable amalgam of idealism, Machiavellianism, and social convergence that we can call Rooseveltism. Its leading proponents were Hopkins, Davies, and a host of lesser lights who revolved around the Roosevelt White House. They accepted generally the idealism of Woodrow Wilson or Wilsonianism, which held that democracy was the future of the world and that United States foreign policy should be devoted primarily to the support of democracy, human rights, national self-determination, and some form of collective security. They opposed imperialism and generally distrusted European or Old World strategies for keeping the peace, like spheres of influence, balance of power, and the art of diplomacy. They thought that human nature was innately good and that many of the world's problems, especially the bane of war, would be solved automatically as nations adopted democracy. They concluded that a "collective security" organization like the League of Nations, with all the world's nations as members, particularly the new major powers—the Soviet Union and the United States—could arbitrate disputes, resolve conflicts through discussion and compromise, and guarantee justice for all nations. The cause of war would be removed, the world would be at peace, and democracy would flourish everywhere.

The Rooseveltians, however, added a revolutionary and paradoxical twist to Wilsonianism when dealing with the Soviet Union. They subsumed the Wilsonian legacy into the pseudoprofound theory of convergence. This theory held that Soviet Russia and the United States were on convergent paths, where the United States was moving from laissez-faire capitalism to welfare state socialism and the Soviet Union was evolving from totalitarianism to social democracy. The Great Depression seemed to indicate that democratic capitalism—the idea of the unfettered individual who in seeking self-profit generated benefits for the whole nation—was anachronistic. The times called for a larger role for government to curb the excesses of unrestrained capitalism and to redistribute the nation's wealth to guarantee the social well-being of the nation as a whole. Instead of democratic capitalism, the times called for democratic socialism. In addition, the Bolshevik Revolution seemed to indicate that the drive toward socialism was part of a worldwide movement, another stage in the inevitable advance toward progressive society whose earlier stages included the American and French Revolutions. The Rooseveltians looked at Stalin and saw a man of the people. The hope of convergence persuaded them, despite evidence to the contrary, to tolerate and excuse Stalin's extreme measures because Stalin was attempting to modernize a "backward" country and was moving ineluctably toward democracy. The inexorable quality of such an outlook tended, not unlike other competing ideologies of the twentieth century, to blur, attenuate, or undo objective morality. It rejected or overlooked the fact that in order to develop and maintain democracy, there must be sacrifice, hard work, careful planning, firm laws, and sufficient strength and resolve, especially within the citizenry itself, to control the antisocial tendencies of human behavior. It dismissed the Judeo-Christian view of man's proclivity for self-destruction and hubris, and assumed that the world was evolving toward pluralism. Winston Churchill and his breed, of which Hitler was an extreme example, were representatives of a passing era that was noted for its aggression, imperialism, and balance of power machinations, and Stalin and Roosevelt were precursors of the New World—dedicated to peace, justice, and social progress. In fact, the disjunction with traditional morality ended up being the defining difference between Roosevelt and his aides and the ambassadors/ State Department group.

Roosevelt was convinced, like many western intellectuals in the 1930s, that the Soviet Union was no longer a revolutionary state but, rather, a traditional power, albeit suspicious and insecure, and that Stalin was not a genocidal megalomaniac guided by the higher power of revolutionary inevitability and intent upon revolution at home and abroad but an evolving democrat who was simply making hard and defensive decisions to quickly industrialize and protect his country. It disturbed FDR that Stalin persecuted religion, but he assumed, according to Rexford Tugwell, a leading theorist of the New Deal, that the hand of friendship would slow religious persecution.[2] He similarly assumed that Stalin's expansion into Eastern and Central Europe in 1943-45 would help spur the growth of democracy in the Stalinist empire, and thus the confusion and apparent contradiction in Roosevelt's Soviet policy are explained, where one moment he is publicizing the four freedoms and the Atlantic Charter and the next moment he is giving quiet approval to Stalin's control of parts of Eastern Europe and northeast Asia. There was really nothing sinister about Stalin. He was the voice of progress for countless "backward" peoples who were trying to improve their lives.

FDR shared some of the beliefs of such western political pilgrims as H.G. Wells, Theodore Dreiser, Walter Duranty, Paul Robeson, Louis Fischer, George Bernard Shaw, Sidney and Beatrice Webb, and Harold Laski, who saw the Soviet Union as building Paradise.[3] Even William Bullitt before he became ambassador held out hope that the Soviet Union represented a step forward in human social development, and he declared that Roosevelt and he agreed with John Reed, the young author of the moving account of the Bolshevik Revolution called *Ten Days That Shook the World*, who argued that the Soviet Union constituted "a pillar of fire for mankind forever."[4] For Roosevelt, the Soviet Union certainly represented new models, new initiatives, and "new deals" that aimed at solving the social and economic crisis of the Depression and generally improving society.

He thought that the United States and the Soviet Union had much in common: progressive states that aimed at social justice and an improvement in the condition of the common man, albeit by vastly different methods and in strikingly different circumstances.

Stalin intrigued Roosevelt. He knew him to be a brutal dictator, but he also thought he was a man of the people. He knew that he was a shrewd politician, for he not only survived and mastered the bloody intrigues of Communist politics but he was also known, in Walter Duranty's phrase, as "a man of steel."[5] Roosevelt told Bullitt in 1943 that he believed Stalin was not really a brutal dictator but a man who "will work with me for a world of democracy and peace." At the same time he told Harriman "that after the War American and Soviet societies are going to converge."[6] He also explained his view to Undersecretary of State Sumner Welles, arguing that the Soviet Union under Communism had "a modified form of state socialism" and that the United States since World War I had a greater degree of "true political and social justice."[7] He told Ambassador Constantine Oumansky in 1939 that he wanted "evidence for American public opinion that the USSR is on the road to democracy and therefore spiritually evolving toward the USA."[8] Forrest Davis, a reporter for the *Saturday Evening Post* who had a close relationship with Roosevelt and who often submitted his writing to the White House for approval, reported in 1943 that FDR believed that "the revolutionary currents of 1917" are spent and that the future would see "progress following evolutionary constitutional lines."[9] Undoubtedly, too, the fact that Stalin wanted a partnership flattered Roosevelt. It was a high form of diplomatic adulation, and such flattery was not lost on Roosevelt. It was proof that Stalin considered him to be a world-class leader and the United States to be a pivotal player in international politics, despite its policy of isolationism.

The direction of American and Soviet society seemed to be set and irreversible, so the order of the day for American policy toward the Soviet Union was patience, avuncular detachment, and permissiveness—all intended to reduce Stalin's suspicion of the United States, produce a cooperative partnership between the United States and the Soviet Union, and spur on the development of democracy in the Soviet Union. Since social democracy was inevitably Russia's future, it also made sense to try to smooth Russia's way to democracy, even if such smoothing included sacrificing the independence of Russia's smaller neighbors to its security needs because of the "greater good" of possibly accelerating the growth of democracy in the huge country of Russia, which would also invariably lead to the stable development of democracy in those very countries that slipped within the Soviet Union's security orbit. The paradox of trying to promote democracy by such undemocratic means was resolved by the belief that Russia would eventually be democratic.

The addition of the theory of convergence to Wilsonianism thus produced a double standard in American foreign policy. On the one hand, the Rooseveltians abhorred spheres of influence and imperialism as Old World snares and pro-scribed such temptations from entangling the United States and from reentangling other western democracies like Great Britain. On the other hand, they tolerated and supported the expansion of the Soviet empire in Eastern Europe and north-east Asia because they believed that such expansion was advancing the cause of democracy and collective security. The double standard, in turn, introduced an enervating moral relativism into American foreign policy, such that Roosevelt seemingly could determine that Stalin was a protean democrat and a worthy ally of the United States in building a new world order. In the view of his biographer, Robert Tucker, Stalin was one of the two greatest criminals in world history, the other being Hitler.[10]

To implement the double standard, the Roosevelt School had to mislead public opinion and circumvent the foreign policy professionals for much of the relationship with Stalin. When FDR was running for president in 1932, there was no broad-based support for befriending the Soviet Union. The Communist government of Russia had wanted a diplomatic relationship with the United States virtually from the time it came to power in 1917. It saw a relationship with the United States as a way to prevent the creation of an anti-Communist coali-tion of capitalist states and to build bridges to a young, powerful capitalist state that could provide economic and technical assistance to the Soviet Union as it built itself into a formidable military and industrial power. The United States, however, shunned the Communists. Every American administration since the Bolshevik Revolution in 1917, from Wilson to Hoover, had steadfastly refused to exchange ambassadors with Soviet Russia. The reason was that the Soviet government supported international revolution and the overthrow of the Ameri-can government through the Communist International, or Comintern, openly persecuted religion, confiscated American property in Russia without compen-sation, balked at paying the debt owed to the United States by earlier Russian governments, and, in general, was unfriendly, xenophobic, and secretive.

Soviet interest in a tie with the United States increased markedly in the early 1930s. Japan invaded Manchuria on the Soviet border in 1931, and Germany named Hitler, a vehement anti-Communist, chancellor in January 1933. Worse still, these threats emerged at a time when Stalin had weakened the Soviet Union by making war against the peasants with the policy of forced collectivization. Stalin hoped that diplomatic recognition would strengthen the perception that the Soviet Union had friends and was not isolated as it faced a surging aggressor in Japan and an inchoate threat in Hitler. He was apparently willing, in the opinion of Secretary of State Cordell Hull, to make some concessions on the problems in American-Soviet relations to gain American recognition.[11] But by then the issue of recognition was further complicated by a more profound ob-stacle from the American point of view: Stalin's policy of collectivization was causing the deaths of millions of peasants, especially in Ukraine, through starva-tion, deliberate terror, and violence.[12]

FDR determined before he was elected president that he had to change public opinion on Stalin and the Soviet Union. During the 1932 presidential campaign he held a well-publicized meeting with Walter Duranty, the Pulitzer Prize-winning reporter for the *New York Times*, whose support of Stalin and his policies was well known. Duranty denied that there was a "terror-famine" in the Soviet Union and, in line with the convergence school, countered those who produced evidence of the tragedy with the argument that one had to break a few eggs to make the omelet of modernization. The implication of the meeting was that there was no genocide in Soviet Russia, and if some peasants were dead, it was the inevitable result of Stalin's understandable effort to develop the Soviet Union quickly, especially in the face of Japanese threats. Roosevelt did not discuss the terror-famine with Duranty but simply asked some chatty questions about Soviet gold production and Soviet reliability as a trading partner.[13]

After winning the presidency, FDR increased support for recognition and further improved Stalin's image by arguing that diplomatic relations with the Kremlin would quiet the winds of aggression in Asia and Europe and open the vast Russian market to American goods, although he never explained how, and just about in everyone's mind those goals were more a hope than an expectation. By November 1933 he finally won over public opinion in favor of recognition and simultaneously frustrated the Russian experts in the State Department, who wanted to extract concessions from the Soviets in exchange for recognition, by lumping all of the earlier obstacles to recognition into an agreement with Foreign Minister Litvinov wherein the Soviet government promised that Americans could practice religion freely in Soviet Russia, that Moscow would not interfere in American domestic affairs through the Comintern, and that the Kremlin would settle the unpaid debt and compensation for nationalized property issues *after recognition*. The Russian experts in the State Department, most notably Robert Kelley, the head of the small East European Division, wanted all issues resolved *before recognition* because the Soviet government had a clear record of recalcitrance when it came to such matters, but he and the other experts were totally outmaneuvered by Roosevelt. Not only did they not get these problems resolved before recognition, but for whatever reason they did not even bring up the more fundamental issue of possible genocide in the Soviet Union. Indeed, by focusing on the secondary issues, the U.S. government, in the view of historian David Mayers, "came near to being a passive accomplice to Stalin in the Ukraine."[14] Of course, it is doubtful that FDR, given his meeting with Walter Duranty, would have brought up the issue of the terror-famine even if Kelley and the State Department had recommended it.

FDR, of course, did not have to be so accommodating. He held the whip in his relationship with Stalin, since the Soviet Union was much more menaced than the United States by Japan and Germany but was not yet so pressed that delays or tough bargaining would adversely affect the balance of power or American geopolitical security. Roosevelt could have driven a moderate bargain, but instead he demanded nothing from Stalin. His initial approach toward the Soviet Union in 1933—a penchant for misleading public opinion and hamstringing the State Department—became emblematic of his policy toward Stalin for the duration of his tenure as president.

During World War II, the policy came into full bloom. FDR orchestrated a public relations effort on behalf on Stalin in Washington and set up a lend-lease mission in Moscow, independent of the embassy and the ambassador, under General Philip R. Faymonville, the so-called Red General. From late 1941 until late 1943 General Faymonville, who reported directly to the Lend-Lease Administration in Washington and thus to Harry Hopkins, provided not only massive supplies but also invaluable intelligence information to Stalin's government. He never knew where or how the equipment and information were used, and he never received any worthwhile information in return. In many ways, he simply became an agent of the Red Army and represents the personification of the Rooseveltians' uncompromising support of Stalin. When Faymonville was eventually removed on suspicion of treason in late 1943, Roosevelt disowned him and said Faymonville had been "too friendly with [the] Russians."[15] Faymonville, however, was simply following Roosevelt's directives, and the president did not alter the pro-Stalin policy when the general departed.

Standing against FDR's policy of accommodation with Stalin were the ambassadors and experts who, with the exception of Davies and Faymonville, did not accept the theory of convergence. We might call them the Traditionalists. They all shared Roosevelt's goal of good relations with Stalin's Russia, but their experience in dealing with the Soviet Union disabused them of utopian theories. They desired, like Roosevelt, to see a better world and to work with governments that sought an improvement in their citizens' lot. They wanted the positive benefits of the American and French Revolutions to extend everywhere. However, they tended to believe that progress resulted from leadership, national effort, education, and absolute morality. They rejected out of hand the convergence view that pluralism was inevitable and the Machiavellian view that the end justifies the means. They looked at Stalin close up. They saw a murderer, a liar, and a vicious opponent of the United States and of pluralism generally. They, too, saw elements of Russian nationalism in Stalin's policy, but they also saw aspects of Marxism-Leninism. They refused to accept the "either-or" dichotomy that the Rooseveltians assumed, that because Stalin was a Russian nationalist, he could not also be a Communist ideologue. They found nothing redeemable in Stalin other than an expedient cancer to help kill off the Nazi virus. They refused to close their eyes to Stalin's crimes, and they demanded that Roosevelt's policy change to meet the Stalinist threat.

The Traditionalists desired American policy to be reciprocal, forceful, demanding, and objectively moral. They hoped that the Soviet Union would adopt pluralism, but found little evidence, as opposed to theoretical assumptions, to support that hope. They determined that a policy of concessions would be counterproductive, since it would not encourage the development of character necessary for pluralist society. If the Soviet Union had any chance of changing into a democratic state, they believed that it would come about as a result of external pressure that demanded that the Soviet Union be responsible for its actions, act reciprocally, and live up to the minimum standards of moral behavior that were outlined in the world's principal religions and moral codes. Consistent and relentless external, diplomatic, political, and economic pressure, backed by the example of the United States growing in power as a result of a free and market-driven society, had the best chance to produce in Soviet Russia the conditions necessary for the government and citizens to work together on reforms and a new value system to ensure the development of pluralism. They believed that American policy could encourage democratic change in Soviet Russia, but not by excusing or accepting outrageous behavior. They did not think that American-style pluralism or democracy were directly exportable. In fact, they believed them to be fragile movements that had been fostered by unique conditions in the West and that constantly had to be safeguarded against external threats and internal ennui. But they did not rule out the possibility of a Russian or Eurasian-style democracy, that is, a pluralist society built around law and human rights and supported and seasoned by the moral codes of Christianity, Judaism, and Islam. In their mind, the best policy for the Americans to follow, in order to have any hope of stimulating a democratic evolution in Soviet Russia and to live in accord with their own moral code, was to give to and demand from Moscow, on a reciprocal basis, respect and high standards of behavior. The United States had to adopt stands that promoted and protected the objective morality underlying democracy and that were defensible on the basis of experience as opposed to theory. American policy, in their view, had to be guided by the actual behavior and attitude of Soviet Russia, traditional diplomacy, common interests, experience, periodic testing, and practices that had in the past proved effective in maintaining peace and stability in the short term, including balance of power and spheres of influence. They did not support the type of sphere of influence that the Rooseveltians conceded to Stalin, which was of a type that Chamberlain allowed Hitler—hypocritical and encouraging of further expansion—but of a type that, say, Undersecretary of State Sumner Welles demanded from Stalin in Eastern Europe in 1942—principled and limiting of further expansion. They wanted to preserve and spread the American experience, but they saw Stalin as a threat to that experience and its growth.

All of Roosevelt's ambassadors except Davies objected to his policy of uncritical friendship toward Stalin. Their relationship with Roosevelt and Stalin became a story of intense drama, including bruising arguments over the policy. The arguments were often bitter, with Bullitt accusing Roosevelt of being a dupe of Stalin and Harriman complaining that Roosevelt was losing Eastern and Central Europe. Standley told FDR that the Soviets considered him Santa Claus, and Steinhardt wrote that Stalin interpreted Roosevelt's policy of concessions as a sign of weakness to be exploited. Davies alone applauded Roosevelt's genuflection before Stalin.

None of the ambassadors except for Davies and, to a degree, Harriman got on well with Stalin. The Soviet dictator detested Bullitt, Steinhardt, and Standley because they urged the United States to take a firm stand against him. Stalin hated any opposition, but he could not employ his usual tactic of arrest and execution against this group. All he could do was lobby Roosevelt to get rid of them, which he did with consistent success. He liked Davies because he had an unusual gift for putting a positive spin on whatever Stalin did, including murder, and in 1946 he awarded him the Order of Lenin, the Soviet government's highest honor. Stalin was leery of Harriman because he was very close to Roosevelt, so he treated him carefully, always holding out some ray of hope that Roosevelt's policy of concessions was paying off, but inevitably he showed his true hand, as in his refusal to help or allow the Allies to aid the Poles in their uprising against the Nazis in Warsaw in August 1944. Stalin would have undermined Harriman, too, with Roosevelt, but Harriman wanted to be a believer, and so dissimulation had a chance of succeeding or, at least, of confusing. Stalin did what he wanted, but then he explained that this atrocity or that aggression was the result of a misunderstanding, Kremlin intrigues, or British imperialism. Harriman accepted such feckless reasons until late 1944. Then he began to call for a strong hand in dealing with Stalin, eventually agreeing with Bullitt in 1945 that a "new barbarism" was sweeping across Eastern and Central Europe.

Part 1

William C. Bullitt
1933-1936

1

Stalin's Kiss

On Wednesday, December 20, 1933, William C. Bullitt was beaming. He had arrived in Moscow to officially begin America's first diplomatic mission to the Soviet Union on December 11, and finally he was to meet Stalin, the reclusive khan of Soviet Russia's workers and peasants and the would-be ruler of the world's toiling masses. Marshal Kliment Voroshilov, Stalin's commissar of defense, had invited the ambassador to dine in his apartment in the Kremlin and to meet Stalin and the Communist "inner gang." Bullitt took along George Kennan, his able specialist on all matters dealing with Russia, as his interpreter. Voroshilov's military aide picked them up at the National Hotel at the dinner hour.

The Soviets clearly had high hopes for this initial encounter with the first representative of the United States since DeWitt Clinton Poole, accredited to the provisional government, left in 1919 during the Russian Civil War. They had so far received Bullitt with extreme warmth. When he arrived in Moscow a large group of high officials met him at the train station, whisked him off to the National Hotel, the entrance of which was draped with a American flag, and put him up in the same room that he and his mother had stayed in when they visited Moscow on the eve of World War I in 1914. *Pravda* reproduced favorable but hitherto unpublished statements that Lenin had putatively made about Bullitt when Bullitt earlier visited Soviet Russia in 1919 as the head of a fact-finding mission that Woodrow Wilson and Lloyd George had tacitly approved during the Versailles treaty negotiations. They also told Bullitt that Lenin really liked him "and expressed his liking many times." In a compliment that was uniquely Stalinist, one Soviet official told him, "You cannot understand it, but there is not one of us who would not gladly have his throat cut to have had such things said about him by Lenin." Every evening between December 11 and 20 there were special dinners and parties. It was a wonderful time for the new ambassador. He was told that he was special, that Roosevelt was a magnificent leader as far as capitalists went, and that the United States and the Soviet Union would have a special relationship.

As proof of the unique tie G.F. Grinko, the commissar of finance, informed Bullitt that the Americans would be able to exchange American currency for rubles at a fair rate without resorting to smuggling rubles into the USSR or buying them on the black market, practices in which most of the other embassies had to engage. As further evidence of the unusual relationship, Stalin himself wanted to meet and dine with Bullitt. Bullitt was so impressed by this gesture that he told Litvinov that the press release should simply say that he was having dinner with Marshal Voroshilov and that Stalin had "dropped in," lest the envy of the other ambassadors in Moscow be aroused. As Bullitt confided to FDR, "It is valuable to have the inside track, but it seems to me not desirable to emphasize the fact to the world."

The military chauffeur drove Bullitt and Kennan to the Kremlin and then led them through "lines of soldiers" to Voroshilov's residence. There waiting for them were the Communist elite, including Stalin, Marshal and Mrs. Voroshilov, Mikhail Kalinin, Vyacheslav Molotov, Maxim Litvinov, Lazar Kaganovich, Sergo Ordzhonikidze, N.N. Krestinsky, Lev Karakhan, G.Y. Sokolnikov, Alexander Troyanovksy, Yuri Piatakov, Valerian Kuibyshev, V.I. Mezhlauk, and Marshal Alexander Yegorov.[1]

Stalin, of course, was the supreme dictator, but he had no government position. His job title was general secretary of the Communist Party, which gave him control of the Party and its executive arm, the so-called Politburo. The Party controlled the state, the Politburo commanded the Party, and Stalin ruled the Politburo. The legitimacy of the Party's and thus of Stalin's power was the revolutionary ideology of Marxism-Leninism, which maintained that economic relationships and class struggle were the engines of history and socioeconomic development, and that the Communist Party alone knew the future and could successfully lead the masses of Russia to the promised land of a classless society where there would be no economic exploitation. The Party's and Stalin's claim to exclusive control of the state was enhanced by Russia's legacy of absolutism. There was no democratic tradition, and although the people wanted land and a measure of freedom, they had lived for centuries as serfs under the brutal autocracy of the czars. Stalin ably exploited their ignorance and the lack of a democratic tradition to fashion a totalitarian state. He controlled the news media, the judiciary, education, the civil bureaucracy, the secret police (NKVD), the Red Army, the Comintern, and all forms of property. Farms were collectivized and industries nationalized. He concentrated all the resources of the state in his hands. In addition, the NKVD had extralegal authority to engage in terror, violence, surveillance, agitation, and propaganda. He himself was portrayed throughout the country as the infallible leader of the unerring Party, the "Great Genius of All Times and All Peoples," and the "Great Helmsman."

Stalin's path to power was violent, conspiratorial, calculating, dissembling, and dangerous. Before the Bolshevik Party took power in 1917, he specialized in criminal activity, especially robbery, which was a major source of funding for the illegal Marxist group. Lenin liked his brutality, efficiency, and willingness to do whatever was necessary to advance the Communist cause. He also valued him, since Stalin was a Georgian and not a Russian, as a credible spokesman for the Bolshevik Party's campaign to win the support or at least temper the opposition of the vast number of oppressed non-Russian nationality groups in the Russian empire. In 1913 Lenin helped Stalin write a pamphlet, *Marxism and the National and Colonial Question,* which promised the non-Russians that the Bolsheviks would support their desire to set up their own national states. Once in power, however, the Bolsheviks or, as they called themselves after 1918, the Communists fought the non-Russians who tried to set up independent states on the grounds that only exploiters would want to secede from a socialist empire, and exploiters had to be oppressed, not liberated. A few of the non-Russian nationalities—the Finns, Poles, Lithuanians, Latvians, and Estonians—were able to realize their desire for independent states because of western support and Soviet weakness, but most of the minority nationalities did not escape the clutching hand of Communist imperialism. Moscow did appease the remaining large nationality groups, including Ukrainians, Belorussians, Georgians, Armenians, Azerbaidzhans, Kazakhs, Kirghiz, Tadzhiks, Uzbeks, and Turkmenians, by eventually granting them the status of republics tied to the Russian Republic in the Union of Soviet Socialist Republics. However, there was no freedom for the republics or the people.

After Lenin's death in January 1924, Stalin came to the top of the Soviet empire following a bitter struggle with other leading Bolsheviks, including Lev Trotsky, Nikolai Bukharin, Lev Kamenev, Grigori Zinoviev, Karl Radek, and Yuri Tomsky. All of these old Bolsheviks still lived in the Soviet Union at the time of Bullitt's visit except Trotsky, who was exiled by Stalin in 1929 and living in Europe and soon Mexico. The old Bolshevik guard, however, had no power and Stalin suspected each of them of disloyalty to him. He was unusually paranoid, even for an underground revolutionary and a survivor of the savage scheming that followed Lenin's death. What made him especially crazed was the opposition and criticism that he encountered, even from people like Sergei Kirov, the head of the Leningrad Soviet, whom he thought was his ally, when he launched the policies of collectivization and industrialization under the so-called First Five-Year Plan in 1929. Using the police and the army he determined to implement the Communist idea of taking away all private property. Many peasants had actually been able to gain control of the land during the turmoil of the civil war. By the time the Communists won the civil war in 1921 the peasants were too entrenched, and the Communists too weak, to change the status quo. Instead, the Bolsheviks bided their time and consolidated the Party's control of politics and the coercive institutions of the state, the army, and the police.

By 1929 Stalin had the power to force the Communist economic plan on the peasantry. With all the delicacy of a butcher he started hacking away at the corpus of Soviet Russia, reshaping it to fit some phantasmagoric future. The peasants resisted, and suddenly Soviet Russia found itself bleeding in a flagellating frenzy. Stalin was unrelenting and brutal. Soon the great gray glacis of the Russian peasantry began to move. Many on the outside thought the direction was toward modernization and eventual democracy. To many on the inside the road seemed to point backwards toward the serfdom of the czars, except the signposts were written in the modern script of Marxism-Leninism and the roadway was wet with blood.

Stalin said that he was preparing Soviet Russia for modern times, that through collectivization the peasantry would become rural workers of the state, instead of independent and greedy landowners, and that the state would obtain the capital it needed to quickly industrialize the economy, so that it could defend itself against the industrialized capitalist states and lead the world to socialist nirvana. A number of his close colleagues, though, and quite a few of the old Bolshevik leaders whom he had already beaten and isolated, thought he was going too far, that the violence was unnecessary and too extreme. They criticized him, and he hated them for it and suspected them of plotting to overthrow him and possibly replace him with one of his supposed allies, probably Kirov, or, worse still, with his avowed enemy, the exiled Trotsky. Stalin had surrounded himself increasingly with clones by the time of Bullitt's arrival, but he was already coming to the conclusion that he would probably have to turn his butcher's ax against his fellow Communists. For Stalin, no one could stand in the way of the revolution. If there was opposition, it was evidence of bureaucratism and flagging faith in the inevitable revolution that he was privileged to lead. He had to act resolutely and ruthlessly to cut out such weakness and apostasy.[2] A brief note that Stalin sent to Molotov around August 6, 1930, reveals the miasma of insensate violence that gripped Soviet Russia: "It is important to (a) fundamentally purge the Finance and Gosbank bureaucracy, despite the wails of dubious Communists like Briukhanov-Piatakov; (b) definitely shoot two or three dozen wreckers from these apparaty, including several dozen common cashiers."[3]

Toward the world beyond the Soviet Union, Stalin's views were shaped fundamentally by Marxism-Leninism. He believed that Communism would eventually spread around the globe and that capitalist states were implacably hostile to Communist Russia but often hamstrung in effecting a concerted and uniform policy toward Moscow because of their own competition for colonies and markets. He also was suspicious of foreigners and was determined that as the Communist movement spread, he would control the foreign Communists and demand that they subordinate their interests, national and otherwise, to the Soviet Union through the institution of the Comintern and, after the Comintern was dismantled, through the International Department of the Central Committee of the Communist Party of the Soviet Union. Stalin was, in addition, a student of

Eurasian history, geopolitics, and realpolitik. He was ignorant of distant countries, including the United States, but he was quite familiar with Russia's traditional, geopolitical rivals for power and influence on the Eurasian plain: Turkey, Poland, Iran, Germany, China, and Japan. He was also knowledgeable about smaller countries like Romania, the Baltic States, Finland, and Afghanistan. His perception of reality was shaped by Marxism-Leninism, which made him essentially an expansionist, but an expedient retreat in the face of a more powerful threat was always a much exercised option. Expansion, however, in the face of weakness was also a much used alternative, and the weakness could be one of character that effectively neutralized a militarily superior power.[4]

In the room with Stalin were Stalinist loyalists and other Communists who stood with Stalin but who had an independent streak and about whose loyalty Stalin could not be absolutely certain. Around each of their necks Stalin had a firm noose. As Bullitt looked the crowd over, he knew Stalin was in charge, but he had no idea of the tension and fear that stalked the Communist "inner gang." His mood was expansive and gay. He found them to be "intelligent, sophisticated, vigorous human beings" who "cannot be persuaded to waste their time with the ordinary conventional diplomatist."[5]

Molotov was Stalin's man through and through.[6] He was a member of the Politburo and since 1930 had held the post of premier. He was not an intellectual but a sort of robot who barely spoke and who acted solely on Stalin's command. Nikita Khrushchev, the Ukrainian Party boss who eventually succeeded Stalin after his death in 1953, thought Molotov was "just plain thick" and "always in the dark on whatever the issue was."[7] Bullitt, on the other hand, clearly wanting to be positive, thought after this initial meeting that Molotov had "a magnificent forehead and the general aspect of a first-rate French scientist, great poise, kindliness and intelligence."[8] Stalin trusted him implicitly and used him to carry out his will. Correspondence from Stalin to Molotov between 1925 and 1936, which Molotov selected and gave to the Center for the Preservation and Study of Contemporary Historical Documents in Moscow in 1969, has recently been published and testifies to the warm, intimate relationship between the two men.[9]

Mikhail Kalinin held the title of president of the Soviet Union, which meant that he had to perform the ceremonial tasks of state, including receiving ambassadors and conversing officially with other heads of state. He was a member of the Politburo and a key ally of Stalin. Bullitt presented his credentials to him on Wednesday, December 13, and was expecting to find "a simple-minded old peasant." Instead, he met a man with a "delightful shrewdness and sense of humor." Bullitt informed FDR that Kalinin said everyone in Russia had a very high opinion of Roosevelt and considered him "completely out of the class of the leaders of the capitalist states" and a man who "really cared about the welfare of the laboring men and the farmers" rather than "the vested rights of property."[10]

Maxim Litvinov was the commissar of foreign affairs. He was Jewish and rather cosmopolitan. Of all the people around Stalin he was the most strong-minded and had an independent flair. He was no fool, however, and he knew that survival meant absolute and unquestioned loyalty to Stalin. The Soviet dictator did not entirely trust him and occasionally was critical of him, but he found him useful for contacts with the outside, especially capitalist, powers.[11] Litvinov had met Bullitt in Washington during the negotiations leading up to the Roosevelt-Litvinov Agreement and now was his guide through the labyrinth before him.

Marshal Kliment Voroshilov, one of Stalin's key lieutenants, was described by Bullitt as "one of the most charming persons that I have ever met." Bullitt thought he was in great physical condition, too.[12] He took Trotsky's place as commissar of war. Like Molotov, Stalin had broken his spirit and he was a virtual clone of Stalin. As a military leader, he was totally incompetent.

Lazar Kaganovich was a member of the Politburo and the head of Party organizational affairs. Like Litvinov, he was Jewish, but he lacked the foreign minister's independence and urbanity. He was Stalin's man, body and soul, like Molotov and Voroshilov.

Sergo Ordzhonikidze, commissar of heavy industry, was also a Politburo member. A Georgian, like Stalin, he was strong, independent, and familiar with Stalin's early life and career. He was a close friend of Sergei Kirov, the head of the Leningrad Soviet and Stalin's most likely successor. Valerian Kuibyshev was another ally of Kirov and Ordzhonikidze. He was the chief of Gosplan, the Soviet bureaucracy in charge of economic planning. Yuri Piatakov was an old Bolshevik and a former close associate of Trotsky. Piatakov now held the job of chief of industrialization under the five-year plans.

Lev Karakhan, N.N. Krestinsky, and G.Y. Sokolnikov were all deputy foreign ministers. They were prominent old Bolsheviks and closely tied to Lenin and Trotsky. V.I. Mezhlauk worked for the Heavy Industry Commissariat and Marshal Alexander Yegorov was the chief of the newly resurrected General Staff. Alexander Troyanovsky was an ex-Menshevik, the Marxist political group that split from the Bolsheviks in 1903, but he had repented his errors. He was Stalin's choice for ambassador to the United States.[13]

As Bullitt looked over the assembly, Litvinov told him, "This is the whole 'gang' that really runs things—the inside directorate."

Bullitt shook hands with Kalinin and Molotov and then was introduced to Stalin. They exchanged a few words, but Bullitt decided not to engage him in conversation, thinking it best to allow Stalin to come to him. He drifted to one side of the room, and Stalin to the other.

His first impression of Stalin was one of surprise. He wrote Roosevelt, "I had thought from his pictures that he was a very big man with a face of iron and a booming voice." Bullitt and many others held that view because Stalin's propaganda and cult of personality made him appear bigger than life.

Instead of finding a giant, Bullitt discovered that Stalin was "rather short, the top of his head coming to about my eye level, and of ordinary physique, wiry rather than powerful. He was dressed in a common soldier's uniform, with boots, black trousers and a gray-green coat without marks or decoration of any kind. Before dinner he smoked a large underslung pipe, which he continued to hold in his left hand throughout dinner, putting it on the table only when he needed to use both knife and fork."

Stalin's eyes, Bullitt continued, "are curious, giving the impression of a dark brown filmed with dark blue. They are small, intensely shrewd and continuously smiling. The impression of shrewd humor is increased by the fact that the 'crow's feet' which run out from them do not branch up and down in the usual manner, but all curve upward in long crescents. His hand is rather small with short fingers, wiry rather than strong. His mustache covers his mouth so that it is difficult to see just what it is like, but when he laughs his lips curl in a curiously canine manner." "The only other notable feature about his face," Bullitt went on, "is the length of his nostrils. They are unusually long. With Lenin one felt at once that one was in the presence of a great man; with Stalin I felt I was talking to a wiry Gipsy with roots and emotions beyond my experience."[14]

Bullitt's physical description of Stalin matched that of the Mongolian nomads who ravaged and ruled Eurasia for centuries before the Russian czars replaced Mongolian despotism with an omnipotent autocracy built around a modernized army. The ambassador's psychological portrayal of Stalin as a "wiry Gipsy with roots and emotions beyond my experience" suggested the essence of Stalin's conspiratorial twist of mind and his lack of elementary human feelings except for anger, for which he was already famous. Bullitt had entered the dark world of Stalin, a cosmos where bloody perversions, conspiracies, and atrocities were a normal way of life, where raw, blunt power in its most primeval form swirled through and around the heavy pillars and oriental festoons of the Kremlin, so that nothing—love, lust, money, comradeship, family—mattered in the end except power and the glory that came from exercising power in the name of the revolution.[15] Bullitt had come face to face with a dark force. Neither his western education and upbringing nor his attachment to the ideals of the American and French revolutions had prepared him for this. He knew he was dealing with someone from another world, but he did not yet know which world.

After the group had eaten "a tremendous hors d'oeuvre, consisting of every conceivable kind of caviar and crab and other Russian delicacy and every conceivable kind of vodka and other aperitif," they sat down to dinner. Bullitt was seated "at Madame Voroshilov's right at the center of one of the long sides of the table. Stalin was at her left. Immediately opposite her was Voroshilov with Kalinin on his right and Molotov on his left." Litvinov was on Bullitt's right, and Marshal Yegorov was on Stalin's left.

As soon as they sat down, Bullitt reported, "Stalin rose, lifted his glass and proposed a toast 'To President Roosevelt, who in spite of the mute growls of the Fishes dared to recognize the Soviet Union.'" Everyone, according to Bullitt, drained his glass and erupted in laughter over Stalin's reference to Congressman Hamilton Fish, a key opponent of recognition and the representative of Roosevelt's home district in New York.[16]

Stalin, of course, was right to salute Roosevelt's temerity in recognizing the Soviet Union. No American government had dared legitimate the Communist regime of Russia since it came to power in 1917. During World War I the United States briefly and unenthusiastically supported czarist Russia against Germany and Austria-Hungary, but when a democratically leaning provisional government replaced Nicholas II in March 1917, the Americans immediately recognized and allied with it. Dismay and shock set in when the Communists overthrew the provisional government in November 1917 and quickly made peace with the Central Powers. Not only did the Communists relieve Germany of the eastern front and thus allow it to concentrate on the stalled western front where American troops were just beginning to arrive, but the new rulers of the Kremlin were dedicated to revolution and to the overthrow of capitalist governments like that of the United States. They set up the Comintern to organize and coordinate Communist parties around the world in the struggle against capitalism. Civil war broke out in Russia in 1918 between the Communists and their opponents, and the Americans briefly intervened with the other Allies with the intention of reactivating the eastern front, preventing stockpiles of arms sent to the czar and provisional government from falling into German hands, and protecting the so-called Czech Legion, a group of some 40,000 Czech soldiers who were allied with the West against Austria and who were caught on the eastern front in the wake of the Russo-German cease-fire.

World War I ended in November 1918, the United States pulled out of Russia in 1919-20, and the Communists won the civil war in 1921. Because of its refusal to back away from the promotion of revolution, attacks on bourgeois morality, cancellation of debts, and nationalization of property without compensation, the United States decided against recognizing Lenin's government. It hoped that it would soon collapse.

The Soviet government, though, was still standing when Franklin Delano Roosevelt won election in 1932. By then some opinion makers in the United States, Roosevelt among them, had come to believe that the Soviet Union was only acting defensively and, beneath its rough and spiny exterior, there was ticking a heart sympathetic, not antipathetic, to mankind's drive for freedom. Roosevelt was not a specialist on the Soviet Union, but he had by then, in the wake of the depression that still had the world in its choking grip, come to accept the semisociological theory of convergence, which held that the evolution of social democracy in Soviet Russia was irreversible and which, by implication, devalued and set aside traditional standards for judging what was right and wrong.

Historian James MacGregor Burns described this condition of Roosevelt as a case of divergence between goals and means. FDR wrote, "I dream dreams but am, at the same time, an intensely practical person." He thought that his compromises in the name of practicality would never undermine his dreams because he believed his dreams were inevitable.[17]

Born into wealth and the famous Roosevelt family at Hyde Park, New York, in 1882, Franklin devoted himself at an early age to public service. Educated at Groton School, Harvard College (B.A., 1904), and Columbia University School of Law, he initially tried his hand at law, but soon determined to try to follow the path of his famous cousin, Theodore Roosevelt, who was the twenty-sixth president of the United States (1901-1909). In 1905 he married a distant cousin, a niece of Theodore Roosevelt, Eleanor Roosevelt. Elected state senator of New York in 1910, he moved to Washington, D.C., to join the administration of Woodrow Wilson as assistant secretary of the navy in 1913. The appointment was political rather than professional, and Roosevelt never did develop into a military expert. He soon emerged as a leading advocate of the Wilsonian ideology of reform, progress, and the growth of democratic ideals internationally. He was forceful, persuasive, charming, and politically shrewd. Both friends and enemies viewed him as a future leader of Wilsonianism and the reform wing of the Democratic Party.

With the criticism of idealism that followed Wilson's inability to transform the world and make it safe for democracy in the wake of the treaties ending World War I, Roosevelt started to mask his reform vocabulary. He was still a Wilsonian idealist, but in the 1920s he concluded, particularly after his defeat as a vice presidential candidate in the 1920 election, that Wilsonianism, although ineluctable, could be more easily achieved, at least in his lifetime, by the use of un-Wilsonian tactics. By 1921 he stopped using the word *reform* entirely, admitting that it now conjured up "visions of pink tea artists who dabbled in politics one day a week for perhaps two months in the year."[18] In 1928 he won election as governor of New York by a narrow margin. In 1930 he won reelection by a landslide and was now positioned to lead Wilson's disciples back to the White House. With the Great Depression, Roosevelt knew that American-style capitalism had to change, that government had to play a much larger role in the economic and social life of the republic, that reform was back in vogue. His election as president in 1932 opened the door not only to Wilsonianism but to the Soviet Union.

In the darkest days of the Great Depression, Roosevelt saw a beacon of hope in Stalin's Russia, a government that was dealing with the drawbacks of capitalism directly and essaying to improve the life of the whole community rather than enrich a few. Roosevelt did not know much about the Soviet Union, but he did think a relationship might be mutually beneficial. Many American intellectuals and reformers, dismayed by the suffering of the depression, agreed with him. John Dewey saw the Soviet experiment as applied Christianity, and Edmund

Wilson praised the Soviet utopia. Politicians also concurred. Henry Wallace, the secretary of agriculture and later the vice president, vouchsafed that Soviet Russia was an economic democracy. William Bullitt also shared FDR's belief. So did John Reed. Reed was the young American who participated in the Bolshevik Revolution and wrote the stirring, idealized account of the Bolshevik takeover, *Ten Days That Shook the World.* He personified that part of American intellectual opinion that found in Soviet Russia "a new vision of human life" tied "to an unbounded dream of freedom for all mankind." In November 1917, only thirty years old, Reed wrote from Petrograd, the seat of the Bolshevik revolution, that "this proletarian government will last . . . in history, a pillar of fire for mankind forever." He soon returned to the United States, helped organize the American Communist Party, and in 1919 published *Ten Days.* Bullitt in 1933 told Louis Fischer, an American correspondent in Moscow, "The President, Jack Reed, and I are of the same strain."[19]

Harry Hopkins was also of that genre. He was the man closest to Roosevelt, his chief adviser, alter ego, confidant par excellence. The son of an Iowa harness salesman, Hopkins made his way to New York where his activities as a social worker in the slums of New York City caught the attention of Franklin and Eleanor Roosevelt. He went to work for Roosevelt when he was governor of New York and then went to Washington as head of the Federal Emergency Relief Administration during FDR's first term as president. His loyalty to Roosevelt was absolute. An explosive, emotional apostle of Wilsonianism, Churchill once described him to Stalin as a man on fire for democracy. Hopkins helped shore up Roosevelt's view that Stalin and the Soviet Union were friends and not enemies of pluralism.

Most Americans, however, did not share Roosevelt's view of Stalin in 1933. Congressmen like Hamilton Fish, the leaders of the American labor movement, and most of the major Christian churches, especially the Catholic Church, held Stalin's Russia to be an abomination. Changing minds was FDR's specialty. He was a gifted orator and took justifiable pride in his ability to move the people. He was also a charming person and he used his charm to win over political opponents or to gain influential endorsements for a new initiative. He persuaded, for example, Reverend Edmund Walsh, the vice president of Georgetown University, to give his blessing to the Roosevelt-Litvinov Agreement. After visiting one-on-one with Roosevelt, most political leaders were putty. Still, though, recognizing Stalin's Russia on grounds of shared, albeit latent, values would have proved a daunting task even for Roosevelt's charm and oratory, so he did not push that reason for recognition in the United States. Instead, he argued that a diplomatic tie would help check aggression in Asia and Europe and open up the vast Russian market to American goods. Those were publicly acceptable reasons for recognition, and the majority of Americans favored relations on these grounds by 1933.[20] This is not to say that FDR was insincere in offering those reasons for recognition, but they simply were not his most important motivation. He also helped turn public opinion in favor of recognition by meeting with Walter Duranty, the Pulitzer Prize-winning journalist from the *New York Times,* who told Americans that Stalin's government was a progressive force of modernization.[21]

Bullitt touched on Roosevelt's deeper thinking when he presented his credentials to President Kalinin on December 13: "Today each of our nations in its own manner is seeking with the same indomitable will and limitless energy, but by different methods, to promote the welfare of its people. This simultaneous effort, rather than a source of conflict, offers an opportunity for creative collaboration."[22]

What Roosevelt wanted from Bullitt was resounding testimony that Stalin's Russia harbored Wilsonian principles. That would stymie future Hamilton Fishes and confirm his view of the direction of world history.

After Stalin's toast to FDR, Bullitt toasted President Kalinin. A whole series of toasts then ensued. The vodka flowed freely for the rest of the evening. Molotov soon toasted Bullitt as "one who comes to us as a new ambassador but an old friend."

Following the tenth or so toast, Bullitt recalled, "I began to consider it discreet to take merely a sip rather than drain my glass, but Litvinov, who was next to me, told me that the gentleman who proposed the toast would be insulted if I did not drink to the bottom and that I must do so, whereupon I continued to drink bottoms-up. There were perhaps fifty toasts and I have never before so thanked God for the possession of a head impervious to any quantity of liquor. Everyone at the table got into the mood of a college fraternity banquet, and discretion was conspicuous by its absence."

Litvinov leaned over and whispered to Bullitt, "You told me that you wouldn't stay here if you were going to be treated as an outsider. Do you realize that everyone at this table has completely forgotten that anyone is here except the members of the inner gang?"

Bullitt, clearly pleased and beaming in his unique status as an intimate of the Soviet government, agreed that that certainly seemed to be the case.

Stalin did his part, too. He toasted Bullitt's health several times and kept up a running conversation "across Madame Voroshilov." Bullitt toasted Stalin's health once. Stalin again stood up and "proposed the health and continued prosperity, happiness and triumph of the American Army, the American Navy, the President and the whole United States." Bullitt then jumped up and toasted "the memory of Lenin and the continued success of the Soviet Union."[23]

Bullitt's main interpreter for the seemingly endless rounds of toasts was George F. Kennan, a brilliant foreign service officer who was one of the few American diplomats who actually specialized in the study of Russia. A midwesterner who studied at Princeton, he brought common sense and scholarly insight to his task. The State Department trained him under Robert Kelley, the gentle and scholarly head of its small East European Division since 1926, and then sent him in 1931 to spend two years at the American embassy in Riga, Latvia, which was known as America's "window on Russia" during the period of nonrecognition. There Kennan met many Russian émigrés who had fled Soviet Russia. Emotional and romantic, with an intense interest in Russia stimulated by a cousin of the same name who pioneered American studies of Siberia and the czarist government's penal system in the nineteenth century, Kennan developed a deep attachment to Russia and the Russian people. He was particularly impressed by the continuities between the czarist and Soviet empires.[24] Once recognition was given he was a logical choice to assist the new ambassador. The Soviets, according to Bullitt, were quite impressed with Kennan, and Bullitt thought he was worth two regular analysts. He eventually became known as "Bullitt's bright boy."[25] But Kennan was not alone. Bullitt soon had two other sharp-eyed Russian specialists at the new embassy: Loy Henderson and Charles Bohlen. They, like Kennan, were fluent in Russian and familiar with Russian history. Henderson, twelve years older than Kennan and Bohlen, was tactful, firm, and able. He was the senior economic officer at the embassy, the third in command after Bullitt and the embassy's counselor, John C. Wiley, and greatly respected by Bullitt and his superiors at the State Department. He, like Kennan, had worked for the East European Division in the State Department under Robert Kelley and he had experience as a member of the American Red Cross distributing humanitarian assistance in Russia and the Baltic after World War I. Bohlen was carefree, charming, witty, and intelligent. Kennan liked Bohlen's insouciance and states that he held "a leading place in [his] formative influences." Entering the Foreign Service in 1929, for two and a half years he studied the Russian language, history, economics, and culture at the Ecole Nationale des Langues Orientales Vivantes in Paris and spent two summers in a Russian environment in Tallinn, Estonia, sampling the beaches and nightclubs. For the remainder of Roosevelt's time as President these three men, as they rotated between Moscow and Washington, were the nucleus of America's Russian experts.[26] There were others, of course, like Bertel Kuniholm who was a third secretary like Kennan and Bohlen, and the tireless Elbridge Durbrow who worked in the consular section, and Robert Kelley himself who trained virtually all of America's Russian experts. But Kennan, Henderson, and Bohlen were the key advisers. John Wiley, a tough-talking, aristocratic personality, who was married to a Polish émigré, certainly would have emerged as a major adviser on Russia, but his haughtiness tended to disturb the egalitarian equilibrium among the American group, and Bullitt had him replaced in 1935 with Henderson.

The military attaché in the first diplomatic delegation was Lt. Colonel Philip R. Faymonville. His interest in Russia was virtually as old as that of Bullitt. Graduating ninth in his class from the military academy in 1912, he shortly decided that war was likely between the United States and Japan and that the natural ally of the United States in such a conflict was Russia. On his own he took up the study of Russian and soon became fluent. He showed great ability with languages and by middle age was also fluent in Japanese, German, Spanish, and French. At first, his interest in Russia had more to do with geopolitics than any quixotic belief in Russia's democratic destiny, but eventually he become the tool and symbol of Rooseveltism in Moscow.

Once Bullitt was properly primed, Stalin got around to the central issue: Japan. By December 1933 the Japanese army was bunched against the Soviet Union's border with Manchuria, which the Japanese had invaded and renamed Manchukuo in 1931. The army was directly opposite the maritime provinces of Soviet Siberia, which Japan had occupied as part of the Allied intervention during the Russian civil war in 1918 and from which it only reluctantly departed under American pressure in 1922. A debate raged in Tokyo between those who wanted to follow a northern strategy and attack the Soviet Union and take the mineral-rich and population-poor maritime provinces of Siberia, and those who wanted to pursue a southern plan and drive against the Chinese heartland. A northern campaign meant war with the Soviet Union, whereas a southern attack translated into war with China and, eventually, since its interests and territories were in the southern region of the Pacific, with the United States.

Stalin wanted to convince the Japanese to go south. He met the threat on the border by putting the Red Army there to let Tokyo know that it would be a difficult fight. He also agreed to bribe the Japanese by turning over for a pittance Soviet economic interests in Manchuria. Furthermore, he was trying to reestablish ties with Chiang Kai-shek's Kuomintang (KMT). The KMT had been allied with the Comintern and the Chinese Communist Party in the mid-1920s, but since 1927 it had been waging war against the Chinese Communist Party (CCP). The Soviets broke with the KMT over this, but they had been wooing Chiang since the Japanese invasion of Manchuria in 1931. The CCP declared war on Japan in 1931, but since it was a small, isolated force, it made no impact on the Japanese, not enough at least to entice the Japanese to invade China proper and go after it. The more immediate purpose of the CCP's declaration of war was to pressure Chiang, the self-proclaimed leader of the Chinese nation, to go to the defense of Manchuria by declaring war on Japan. Chiang, however, wanted to annihilate the CCP before he went after the Japanese.

Stalin's final strategy for containing the Japanese threat was to establish diplomatic recognition with Washington to show the Japanese that Moscow was not isolated. Of course, he wanted to see if he could also squeeze more direct assistance out of the United States on the Japanese menace. His ideology told him that these two capitalist states, Japan and the United States, were natural rivals for markets in the Pacific. The key was to enflame their imperialist greed, then stand aside and watch the capitalists go to war and drain themselves. His model was World War I, which saw the major capitalist states bleed themselves white in a long war of attrition that gave the Communists an opportunity to come to power. Stalin was intensely interested in international affairs, but his analysis was always from a Communist point of view. He could not separate domestic and foreign policy—they were simply two parts of the same revolutionary stream. Although he was attempting to build socialism in Russia through his collectivization and industrialization policies, he was doing so only to advance the revolution, and if the pursuit of a particular foreign policy would advance the cause of socialism under his control, then he would pursue it. On September 9, 1929, he wrote Molotov a revealing letter regarding Soviet policy toward capitalist states (in this instance the subject was relations with England): "Remember we are waging a struggle (negotiations with enemies is also struggle), not with England alone, but with the whole capitalist world."[27]

Stalin talked to Bullitt at great length about the Japanese threat and the coming war between Moscow and Tokyo. He told Bullitt that Marshal Yegorov "is the man who will lead our Army victoriously against Japan when Japan attacks." He then proposed a toast to Yegorov and the Red Army. Near the end of the dinner Stalin turned to Bullitt and said, "There is one thing I want to ask of you. The second line of our railroad to Vladivostok is not completed. To complete it quickly we need 250,000 tons of steel rails at once. They need not be new rails. Your rails are so much heavier than ours that the rails you discard are good enough for us. Your railways, I understand, are reequipping themselves and will have many old rails to dispose of immediately. Cannot you arrange for us to purchase the old rails? I do not ask that they should be given to us, but only that our purchase of them should be facilitated."

Bullitt replied that he would be "glad to do anything" that he could to help. When he asked Stalin where the rails should be sent, he was told "Vladivostok." Stalin then went on to say, "Without those rails we shall beat the Japanese, but if we have the rails it will be easier."

Stalin had a difficult task. He wanted to impress Bullitt with the strength of the Soviet Union, but at the same time he wanted U.S. help against Japan. Bullitt understood the Soviet dilemma, but he knew the United States, in the throes of the depression, would not take any major action to help control the Japanese menace. He reported to Roosevelt, "I repeatedly emphasized to all with whom I talked that the United States had no intention whatsoever of getting into war with Japan but that our participation in any Far Eastern difficulties would be confined to the use of our moral influence to maintain peace."

After dinner the whole group moved to an adjoining drawing room. There Stalin, according to the ambassador, "seized Piatakov by the arm, marched him to the piano and sat him down on the stool and ordered him to play, whereupon Piatakov launched into a number of wild Russian dances, Stalin standing behind him and from time to time putting his arm around Piatakov's neck and squeezing him affectionately."

When Piatakov finished playing, Stalin came over and sat down next to

Bullitt. The full press was now on. Stalin said that he hoped Bullitt "would feel . . . completely at home in the Soviet Union; that he and all the members of the Government had felt that [Bullitt] was a friend for so long, that they had such admiration for [Roosevelt] and the things [he was] trying to do in America that they felt we could cooperate with the greatest intimacy."

Bullitt wanted that, too, and he knew that Roosevelt felt the same way. Bullitt sympathized with Stalin's plight of trying to improve the life of the Soviet people while being threatened with war, especially by the Japanese. Bullitt stressed to Stalin that FDR "sincerely hoped that war might be prevented in the Far East and that the Soviet Government might work out its great experiment in peace."

Stalin replied, "I know that that is what President Roosevelt wants and I hope you will tell him from me that he is today, in spite of being the leader of a capitalist nation, one of the most popular men in the Soviet Union."

When Bullitt reported this compliment to Roosevelt, he added, "Stalin was feeling extremely gay, as we all were, but he gave me the feeling that he was speaking honestly. He had by this time made the impression on me of a man not only of great shrewdness and inflexible will (Lenin, you know, said of him that he had enough will to equip the entire Communist Party), but also possessed of the quality of intuition in extraordinary measure. Moreover, like every real statesman I have known, he had the quality of being able to treat the most serious things with a joke and a twinkle in his eye. Lenin had that same quality. You have it."

Bullitt was obviously feeling gay himself, but his observation that Roosevelt, Stalin, and Lenin shared a public image of nonchalance and indifference in the face of "serious things" was perhaps attributable to the fact that the three of them were ideologues. Stalin, like Lenin, was guided by Marxism. He thought the future was with socialism, and thus the United States, a capitalist nation, would eventually give way to a Communist society. Roosevelt, on the other hand, was a believer in the theory of convergence who thought the future was with democratic socialism, and thus the Soviet Union and the United States were going to converge somewhere down the political-economic continuum into similar forms of social democracy where the government played a dominant, possibly the decisive, role.

When Bullitt finally got up to leave, Stalin turned to him and said, "I want you to understand that if you want to see me at any time, day or night, you have only to let me know and I will see you at once." Bullitt reported, "This was a most extraordinary gesture on his part as he has hitherto refused to see any Ambassador at any time."

After Bullitt bid farewell to the "inner gang," Stalin walked him and Kennan to the door of the apartment and asked, "Is there anything at all in the Soviet Union that you want? Anything?"

Bullitt confided to FDR that there was one thing that he desired, namely, some fifteen acres of land in the Sparrow Hills overlooking the Moscow River to build a new embassy. However, he was reluctant to ask for it because Litvinov had already told him that it was not available. Therefore he said to Stalin, "Everyone has been more than kind to me and I should hesitate to ask for anything in addition, except that the intimate relations we have begun tonight may continue."

Stalin, however, pushed him. "But I should really like to show you that we appreciate not only what the President has done, but also what you yourself have done. Please understand that we should have received politely any Ambassador that might have been sent us by the Government of the United States, but we should have received no one but yourself in this particular way."

Bullitt concluded that Stalin "seemed moved by a genuinely friendly emotion. Therefore, I thanked him and said that there was one thing that I should really like to have, that I could see in my mind's eye an American Embassy modeled on the home of the author of the Declaration of Independence on that particular bluff overlooking the Moscow River, and that I should be glad to know that that property might be given to the American Government as a site for an Embassy."

Stalin answered, "You shall have it."

Bullitt told FDR that Stalin then startled him. "I held out my hand to shake hands with Stalin and, to my amazement, Stalin took my head in his two hands and gave me a large kiss! I swallowed my astonishment, and, when he turned up his face for a return kiss, I delivered it."

The "evening with Stalin and the inner circle of the Soviet Government," the ambassador wrote FDR, "seems almost unbelievable in retrospect, and I should have difficulty convincing myself that it was a reality if I had not on returning to my hotel awakened my secretary and dictated the salient facts to him."[28]

The next day, December 21, Bullitt had a long meeting with Litvinov. The foreign commissar picked up where Stalin had left off on Japan, plus he mixed Germany into the equation. He told Bullitt that "he and all other members of the Soviet Government considered an attack by Japan in the spring so probable that everything possible must be done to secure the western frontier of the Soviet Union from attack; that he did not fear an immediate attack by Germany or Poland or both combined, but that he knew that conversations had taken place between Germany and Poland looking toward an eventual attack on the Soviet Union if the Soviet Union should become embroiled in a long war with Japan; that he feared that a war with Japan might drag on for years and that after a couple of years Germany and Poland combined might attack the Soviet Union, Poland with the hope of annexing the Ukraine and parts of Lithuania, and Germany with the hope of annexing the remainder of Lithuania as well as Latvia and Estonia."[29]

Germany was clearly a concern, but in 1933 Hitler seemed to be more a tool of the capitalists than an independent agent. Furthermore, his bellicosity promised war in Europe, and war was the environment in which the Communists came to power in Russia and which they believed would jump-start the stalled, but ineluctable, worldwide Communist revolution. The Soviet attitude toward Hitler thus was ambivalent. Stalin saw him as a potential problem, but for the foreseeable future he was emerging as an icebreaker that could smash the congealed rigidity of the capitalist world order.[30] That is unquestionably why Stalin did not bring up Hitler to Bullitt at dinner. Stalin admired Hitler and was particularly impressed by the way he dealt with his political rivals or potential rivals, commenting at a Politburo meeting in 1934, after Hitler had purged Ernest Roehm and the Brown Shirts, that Hitler was "some fellow" who "knows how to treat his political opponents."[31]

To help contain the Japanese menace, Litvinov suggested a nonaggression pact between the United States and the Soviet Union or, in Bullitt's words, to do "anything that could be done to make the Japanese believe that the United States was ready to cooperate with Russia, even though there might be no basis for the belief." Would it "not be possible," Litvinov pleaded, "for an American squadron or an individual warship to pay a visit during the spring to Vladivostok or to Leningrad?" He also wanted to know if the West would deny Japan credit so that it could not continue to build up its war machine.[32]

To harness the German threat, Litvinov informed Bullitt that "France had offered to make a defensive alliance with the Soviet Union providing that if either party were attacked by Germany the other party should at once declare war on Germany, but France felt that this could be done only within the framework of the League of Nations because of the difficulties caused by the Locarno agreements, and that in order to obtain this defensive alliance with France it would be necessary for the Soviet Union to enter the League."

When Bullitt noted that Russia and Germany lacked a common border, Litvinov laughed and said, "Germany is quite close enough."

Bullitt wondered if the Red Army would march against Germany to support France.

Litvinov said, "It would be easy compared with the difficulty of getting the French Army to march against Germany to support the Soviet Union."

Litvinov's expressed fears of Germany and Japan convinced Bullitt "that there is almost nothing that the Soviet Union will not give us in the way of commercial agreements, or anything else, in return for our moral support in preserving peace."[33]

The Soviets, though, desired more than moral support.[34] Stalin had written Molotov on June 19, 1932, that ties with the United States were "a complicated matter," but "insofar as they want to use flattery to drag us into a war with Japan, we can tell them to go to hell."[35] He wanted the United States to do something directly about Japan, but the United States was in no position then to engage Japan. Eventually, in 1941, the United States did fulfill the Soviet hope, but domestic affairs concerned the Americans in 1933-34. As soon as Stalin concluded from this initial contact with Bullitt that the United States was not going to go beyond "moral support" and "flattery" regarding Japan, he put relations with the United States on the back burner. The Soviets did not dismiss the United States the way Hitler did—there was no way their ideology could allow them to discount a country with the industrial power of America—but they wasted little time on the Americans.[36] They determined that they got as much benefit out of recognition as they could in terms of checking threats to them. They now looked increasingly to China as a brake on Japan and to Collective Security, the Popular Front, and the League of Nations as a curb on Germany.

Bullitt believed that the intimacy of the first encounter would continue. He had experienced a Russian bear hug. He liked it. His appetite was now aroused. His hope for a quick settlement of minor problems like the Soviet debt obligation and then the development of a strong friendship between the Soviet Union and the United States was firm and growing firmer. He left Moscow on the afternoon of December 21, 1933, basking in the belief that American-Soviet relations were about to flourish. His plan was to return to the United States, put his affairs in order, collect his full staff, and then come back to Moscow in early 1934.

Before he left Moscow Bullitt selected the buildings to house the embassy temporarily until a new embassy could be built. Spaso House, a dilapidated mansion built in 1914 by a "merchant who traded vodka for furs" and about a fifteen-minute walk from the Kremlin, became the residence of the ambassador. The chancery was installed in a seven-story building under construction on Mokhovaia Street, near the Kremlin. Eventually, the younger members of the delegation rented a dacha about twenty miles from Moscow for rest and recreation.[37]

2

Russia and the State of Grace

Everything in Bullitt's life seemed to have prepared him to be the United States representative to the country that was apparently carrying on the revolutionary cause of liberty. Born in Philadelphia on January 25, 1891, into a distinguished and wealthy family, Bullitt had ties that stretched back to the American Revolution. His father's grandmother was the niece of Patrick Henry, and his father's grandfather was the son of a French Huguenot who came to Maryland in 1685 from Nimes, France, a city which gave Bullitt honorary citizenship in 1937. His father was a staunch member of the Democratic Party, a lawyer, and a businessman who gave up a promising career in Philadelphia politics to make a fortune "supplying smokeless 'Pocahontas' coal to the Navy and the transatlantic steamship lines." From his paternal ancestors, Bullitt inherited an interest in politics, a love of France, a rebellious nature, and the financial wherewithal to pursue a life in public service in the tradition of noblesse oblige.[1]

On his mother's side, Bullitt was descended from a cultivated line of lawyers and surgeons who mingled Episcopalianism and Lutheranism. His mother was charming, affable, witty, and arrogant—traits she passed on to her son. He admired her strength, sophistication, and intelligence. After his service as ambassador she often stayed with him at his estate in Ashfield, Massachusetts. No woman ever quite measured up to his mother.

Bullitt had an excellent education. After attending DeLancey School in Philadelphia, he went to Yale University where he was admitted to Phi Beta Kappa, named editor of the *Yale News,* and elected president of the dramatic association and the debating association. After graduating from Yale and being voted "most brilliant" by his fellow classmates, he started at Harvard Law School, but dropped out after one year because he did not feel he could "reconcile" himself to the law. By then he was proficient in French and German and had developed a fascination with international politics.[2]

Sophisticated, articulate, flamboyant, witty, visceral, willful, and rich, Bullitt impressed everyone he met, some favorably, others unfavorably. Elbridge Durbrow, who worked with Bullitt in Moscow in the 1930s, called him "the most brilliant man whom I have ever been in contact with on a continuing basis."[3] George Kennan, who also worked for Bullitt in Moscow, remembered him as "brilliant, well-educated, charming, self-confident, and sophisticated." Kennan, however, also observed a certain recklessness and impatience in Bullitt's character. When he first met him in 1933, on the SS *President Harding,* which was taking America's first diplomatic mission to the Soviet Union, Kennan wrote that the ambassador was charming, confident, spirited, but at the same time egocentric, proud, sensitive, and filled with "a certain dangerous freedom—the freedom of a man who, as he himself confessed to me on that occasion, had never subordinated his life to the needs of any other human being."[4]

The introverted Kennan might have been envious, but others also agreed that Bullitt was strong-willed and uncompromising. Charles Bohlen, another of Bullitt's Russian specialists, found him at times to be too exuberant and inclined to extremes.[5] Bullitt's brother, Orville, stated that once Bullitt "was disappointed in another's character or deeds he would never return to the former intimacy."[6] Eugene Lyons, an American journalist, described Bullitt's visit to John Reed's grave in Moscow in 1932: "Sentimental to the core . . . I saw him place the flowers on the stone and stand there with bowed head for many minutes. When he returned to the car, tears were rolling down his cheeks and his features were drawn with sorrow."[7] Reed's book, *Ten Days That Shook the World,* found a broad audience and was favorably reviewed in the liberal and conservative press, including the Philadelphia *Public Ledger* where Bullitt worked.[8] Reed was a hero to Bullitt and to reform-minded Americans everywhere, including the aristocratic Franklin D. Roosevelt of Hyde Park, New York. He tapped into the Wilsonian ideology that had taken hold of the Democratic Party and that demanded a larger role for government in order to correct what appeared to be the abuses, failings, and injustices of finance capitalism.[9]

Bullitt, like Roosevelt, was a silk-stocking Democrat who, according to his brother, had a "deep feeling for the rights of man and an intense dislike for the rigidity of the ruling classes and of the status quo."[10] He decided early on that he was going to change the world, overturn tradition, and get on with the business of "liberty, equality, and fraternity." He identified with democratic rebels, men of action, and dreamers. He abhorred bureaucracy and the age-old tradition of paying one's dues. His brashness was both a strength and a weakness: it often opened doors to him, but once inside the inner circle he tended to alienate the power brokers when they did not agree with him and when they did not move at a pace that suited him. In many respects, Bullitt thought of himself as a modern Patrick Henry—a dazzling, rakish rebel who stood ready to sacrifice his very life for the progress of mankind.

George Kennan believed that the "great electrifying experience" of Bullitt's life was World War I.[11] That was true, as Kennan stated, of many men of that remarkable generation of Americans born just before the turn of the century (men like Ernest Hemingway, Cole Porter, John Reed, James Forrestal—many of them friends of Bullitt). They were sure that man was perfectible, that he was capable of solving all problems in time, including war, and that war was irrational and, in an age of rationalism and progress, simply impossible. The harrowing and ruthless brutality of World War I forced men like Bullitt to reexamine their faith in progress. He did, but like so many American intellectuals, he decided that the war was the tawny remains of the decaying old order rather than an ominous harbinger of the looming new order.

When World War I broke out, Bullitt was in Moscow with his mother, staying at the National Hotel. This visit with his mother was Bullitt's first contact with Russia. He was interested in the country, but his attention was soon focused on the war. Curious and excited, Bullitt and his mother left Moscow and made their way to Paris, Berlin, and London to examine firsthand the war effort in Europe. After he tried unsuccessfully to get hired as a correspondent for the *New York Times* in London, mother and son quickly returned to Philadelphia where the family's connections landed Bullitt a job as a reporter for the Philadelphia *Public Ledger*. In the spring of 1916 he married Aimee Ernest Drinker, the daughter of the president of Lehigh University and a woman Bullitt's brother described as "a striking beauty with dark hair, brilliant eyes, . . . a slender figure . . . a quick wit . . . and a fluent conversationalist."[12] In May 1916 Bullitt and his new wife went to Europe at their expense to cover the war for the *Ledger*. During their five-month stay, Bullitt developed many valuable contacts, especially in France.

Upon his return to the United States, the *Ledger* placed him in charge of its Washington office. Here he befriended Colonel Edward M. House, Woodrow Wilson's close friend and adviser. Using the contacts that he had made during his five months in Europe, Bullitt now began to feed information to House, and House told him that his information "was sometimes the best he received."[13] Shortly after the Bolshevik coup d'état in November 1917, House got Bullitt a position in the State Department's Western European Division under Joseph C. Grew.

Once in the State Department, Bullitt's interest in Europe waned in the face of the momentous revolution in Russia. Here Bullitt found justification for his persistent faith in progress and democracy. He saw in the Communist coup the continuation of the great American experiment in freedom. For him, as well as for many other American intellectuals, "Russia represented brotherhood, a spiritual conversion, indeed a state of grace." Bullitt soon began to urge Wilson's government to grant diplomatic recognition to the Communists, a position that he argued in and out of government until Roosevelt actually granted recognition in 1933. He wrote House in January 1918 that, although he did not yet have all the facts, it was clear that Trotsky "is a good deal ahead of us in the march toward world liberalism."[14] A month later, he told House, "It is obvious that no words could effectively stamp the President's address with uncompromising liberalism as would the act of recognizing the Bolsheviki."[15]

Throughout 1918 Bullitt pushed for some understanding with the new Communist government. He was flabbergasted when Wilson approved American participation in the Russian civil war, but his faith in the president was restored when Wilson made it clear in a speech in September 1918 that the interests of weak states would be protected at the peace table. Bullitt took this to mean that Bolshevik Russia would get a fair shake.[16] In December 1918 he was named to the American Commission to Negotiate Peace and left with Wilson for Europe. His job was that of chief of the Division of Current Intelligence Summaries, and it entailed daily briefings for each of the commissioners on the latest military and political information. Bullitt, however, was more interested in Russia. When a fact-finding mission to Russia was suggested, Bullitt pounced on the idea and convinced House that it should be undertaken. House and Secretary of State Robert Lansing eventually agreed, and apparently so did Wilson and the British prime minister, Lloyd George, but none of them thought of it as much more than a side trip to gather information and background. Not surprisingly, Bullitt had a different idea, and he was thrilled when he was chosen to go in February 1919.

Unquestionably, Bullitt felt that he was playing a pivotal role in Allied diplomacy. He was anxious and enthusiastic to be going to Moscow to meet with the leaders of the Bolshevik Revolution. In his romantic view, perhaps he saw himself being transported back in time to 1776, involved in a rare opportunity to meet the founding fathers of a new state dedicated to erasing exploitation, the rigid ruling class, and the debilitating status quo. It is clear, in retrospect, that he was operating on emotion and imagination. He had no understanding of Marxism-Leninism, Lenin, conditions in Russia, the dynamics of the civil war, or the attitudes of the European leaders and Wilson toward that conflict.

Once in Russia, Bullitt did not restrict himself to a simple fact-finding mission but negotiated with Lenin the terms for an armistice in the civil war. He found Lenin to be "a very striking man—straightforward and direct, but also genial and with a large humor and serenity." He found that "there is already a Lenin legend. He is regarded almost as a prophet."[17] Indeed, Bullitt concluded that Lenin was a fiery leader and statesman, beloved by his people and worshiped in the Soviet Russia like "Jesus Christ in the Christian church."[18]

The cease-fire to which Lenin agreed was, in fact, a very positive step, and Bullitt was congratulated by House when he returned to Versailles with the news.[19] George Kennan later concluded that Bullitt "had returned with Soviet proposals which were not ideal but which did offer the most favorable opportunity yet extended, or ever to be extended, to the Western powers for extracting themselves with some measure of good grace from the profitless involvement of the military intervention in Russia and for the creation of an acceptable relationship to the Soviet regime."[20] Bullitt's proposals, though, were never seriously considered by the Versailles Conference. Both Wilson and Lloyd George disclaimed

Bullitt and any responsibility for his mission. Not only did a strong anti-Communist opinion in the West influence their decision, but they, along with many military analysts, calculated that the conciliatory nature of the Bolshevik proposals was evidence that the Reds were weak and that the Whites would soon pummel them.

At any rate, Bullitt was repudiated. He never forgot the experience, and he never forgave Wilson or Lloyd George. He resigned from the American delegation at Versailles and returned home to deliver damaging testimony against American participation in the League of Nations and, years later, to collaborate with Sigmund Freud on a psychoanalytical study of Wilson that portrayed him as a superficial idealist.

For the next thirteen years, Bullitt went into self-exile, living most of the time in Europe. He developed many friends in France and England, and he mingled easily with the political elite. His private life, however, was in constant turmoil. He divorced his wife in 1923 (his impetuous and hot-blooded temperament and her reserved and cool demeanor never did find common ground) and within the year he married Louise Bryant, the widow of John Reed. She was an earthy eccentric who was just the opposite of his first wife. Their marriage produced one child, Anne, many storms of growing intensity, and finally divorce in 1932.

Fortunately for Bullitt, just when his private life lay again in a shambles, a new opportunity for foreign service appeared with Franklin Delano Roosevelt's election as president. Bullitt was taken by the sweeping, saviorlike speeches of Roosevelt, a man who seemed to promise a rekindling of the spirit of the American revolution.

Bullitt's entrée to Roosevelt was via Colonel House, with whom he had remained close, and Louis B. Wehle, a New York lawyer who knew both Roosevelt and Bullitt personally. Wehle considered Bullitt to be witty, penetrating, and knowledgeable, particularly about European and Russian affairs. Wehle enthusiastically agreed with Bullitt that the United States should recognize the Soviet Union. He worked closely with Bullitt on preparing a background document laying out the case for recognition.[21] At the same time, Wehle told Roosevelt about Bullitt and encouraged him to take advantage of Bullitt's expertise in foreign affairs, an area in which FDR was weak and uninformed.

Bullitt helped his own cause when, on September 14, 1932, he sent Roosevelt a campaign contribution of one thousand dollars and wrote him that his speech in Topeka, Kansas, on domestic policy "was the most inspiring address that I have heard since Wilson's speeches in 1918. You not only said the right things but also said them with a 1776 spirit. That is the thing I care most about in American life and that is what we need in the White House." As with Lenin, the only figure to whom he could compare Roosevelt was Christ.[22]

Roosevelt saw Bullitt on October 5, 1932, and, according to Wehle, "in that first talk the two men became warm friends." They were "an ideal team," according to Wehle, bound together by "a certain community of social background" and "a temperamental congeniality heightened by the fact that both were brilliantly and boldly intuitional." In addition, Bullitt "had the capacity for prodigious, sustained toil, for critically selecting relevant facts, and for resolving them into a plan for action. Yet he could swiftly and vividly make available to Roosevelt his scholarship in history and also his familiarity with Europe and its current leaders." At his own expense but with Roosevelt's approval, Bullitt undertook two fact-finding missions to Europe, one immediately after Roosevelt's election in November 1932 and the other in mid-January 1933. It was a way of putting his contacts to use to obtain current information for Roosevelt on outstanding foreign policy issues, including the problem of World War I debts owed to the United States, the rise of the Nazis in Germany, Japanese militarism, and recognition of the Soviet Union. While in Europe on the second trip Hitler became chancellor on January 30, 1933, and Japan left the League of Nations in February. Bullitt returned to the United States prematurely because of congressional criticism that he was conducting foreign policy negotiations as a private citizen—a chargeable offense under the Logan Act. With FDR's formal inauguration in March the criticism died down, and Bullitt stood ready to serve Roosevelt in any way that the new president wanted.[23]

Shortly after the election, Wehle suggested to Roosevelt that Bullitt be given the ambassadorial post in Paris and, upon learning that it had already been promised to someone else, stated, "Well, if we should recognize Russia, he would by all odds be your best man as the first ambassador." Wehle recorded that Roosevelt readily agreed.[24] Upon taking office, Roosevelt named Bullitt to the post of special assistant to the secretary of state over Hull's objection.

His first task was to study the general debt problem and the second was "the various questions involved in the recognition of Russia." In picking up the question of recognition, he joined a distinguished committee that was set up for that purpose and included Secretary Hull, Assistant Secretary of State R. Walton Moore, Undersecretary of State William Phillips, Henry Morgenthau of the Farm Credit Administration (and soon treasury secretary), and Robert Kelley, the head of the East European Division. Utilizing studies prepared earlier by Kelley and his staff, the committee recommended recognition on the condition that the Soviet Union and the Comintern halt Communist propaganda and activities in the United States, that Americans in the USSR be guaranteed civil and religious rights, that some agreement be reached on the repayment of loans, and, finally, that there be some form of compensation for the expropriation of property owned by American citizens or companies in the USSR. Under Kelley's influence, the committee suggested that these issues be resolved *before recognition* was given.[25]

Surprisingly, the State Department experts, although very aware of the "terror-famine" in Ukraine, did not recommend that Roosevelt also discuss this issue with the Soviets as part of the process of establishing relations, understanding Soviet society, and, perhaps, helping a new friend in need.

Of course, it was highly unlikely that Roosevelt would have acted on any recommendation to explore the issue of possible genocide in the Soviet Union. He had already signaled his sympathy for Stalin's firm action in Ukraine when he held a well-publicized meeting before the 1932 election with Walter Duranty, the Pulitzer Prize-winning reporter for the *New York Times*, who denied that there was a famine and further argued that in the process of modernization "you can't make an omelet without breaking eggs." Duranty dismissed the reports of famine as "an eleventh-hour attempt to avert American recognition by picturing the Soviet Union as a land of ruin and despair." Indeed, FDR did not even accept the State Department's recommendation that the secondary problems of debt, religious rights, Comintern activities, and compensation be resolved before recognition. Instead, he and Foreign Minister Litvinov signed the Roosevelt-Litvinov Agreement on November 16, which officially established relations, and then exchanged letters in which they agreed that the State Department concerns would be worked on *after recognition*, which was tantamount, as Kelley foresaw, to inviting tension in the relationship, particularly given the legalistic penchant of the American mind and the Soviet Union's patronizing attitude toward capitalist states and its disregard for normal diplomatic and civic behavior. In any event, it is difficult to disagree with historian David Mayers, who believes that the exclusive focus on side issues, no matter whether they were resolved before or after recognition, instead of the more profound problem of the "terror-famine," led Roosevelt and the State Department to being a "passive accomplice to Stalin in the Ukraine."[26]

Roosevelt, of course, did not have to be so accommodating to Stalin. The Soviet Union was more threatened than the United States by Japan and Germany. The threat, though, was not yet so menacing that it would affect the balance of power or American vital interests. The Soviets would have made some concessions, in Secretary Hull's view, even if they would not have done anything that the United States wanted them to do. There was no good reason, as Assistant Secretary of State Moore stressed, for unconditional recognition.[27]

Naturally, both powers hoped the relationship would give aggressors pause in Asia and Europe and would lead to economic opportunities. But for Roosevelt the relationship with Soviet Russia went beyond politics and economics. He thought that Stalin and the Soviet experiment were worth examining closely. They might have some answers to the political, social, and economic problems confounding the world, including the United States, in the wake of the depression, and the Soviet Union very likely was a country in transition to social democracy. He was intrigued by Stalin and pooh-poohed the State Department's hoary fears of Communism.[28]

For his part, Stalin wanted any relationship to help break Soviet isolation, but a tie to the United States was especially desirable because it was deemed a young capitalist state and, unlike mature capitalist states such as England, not yet voraciously imperialist and exploitative. The United States was also a Pacific power and a logical counterweight to Japan. However, Stalin remained a revolutionary, convinced that the future belonged to Communism under his brilliant leadership. He was contemptuous of the capitalist states and preferred to have little to do with them. His view was revealed in a letter to Molotov in January 1933: "Today I read the section on international affairs. It came out well. The confident, contemptuous tone with respect to the 'great' powers. The belief in our own strength, the delicate but plain spitting in the pot of the swaggering 'great powers'—very good. Let them eat it."[29]

Of all the people attached to Roosevelt's circle, Bullitt stood out as the natural choice for the job of ambassador to Moscow. The president, of course, wanted a good beginning with the Soviet government, and what better way to ensure that end than to send a sympathetic emissary to Moscow who was also his personal friend.

Bullitt shared Roosevelt's faith about the future direction of the Soviet Union. They both believed that the Communist Revolution was an event that fitted in with the general advance of mankind toward a democratic world. They were convinced that the Soviet Union had abandoned its goal of world revolution and the expansion of Communism, and was now basically trying to industrialize quickly, so that its people could enjoy the benefits and security of an industrialized society. Roosevelt told his secretary of labor, Frances Perkins, during the war that there was something unusual about the Communists of Soviet Russia. "They all seem really to want to do what is good for their society instead of wanting to do for themselves. We take care of ourselves and think about the welfare of society afterward."[30]

Both Roosevelt and Bullitt realized that the Soviet government was hostile and defensive, but they believed that this attitude was a result of economic "backwardness" and international isolation, made worse by the Great Depression and the growing militarism of Japan. Indeed, they felt the United States shared some of the responsibility for Soviet Russia's condition because of the United States' position during the Russian civil war and its refusal to sanction diplomatic and commercial ties with Moscow. They believed that Soviet Russia was a country that needed understanding and patience. They also concluded that the United States had a special obligation to help it become a fully integrated member of the community of nations.

Bullitt's selection as ambassador was enhanced by the fact that his burgeoning friendship with Roosevelt allowed him to communicate directly with the president rather than through a potentially unsympathetic bureaucrat in the State Department.[31] Roosevelt thought the Russian specialists in the State Department were too rigidly anti-Communist.[32] Stalin shared this bias against foreign policy experts with Roosevelt, except his fear was that contact with capitalists might dilute their commitment to Communism and world revolution.[33] It also did not hurt Bullitt's candidacy that the Soviets apparently liked him. Maxim Litvinov, the Soviet foreign minister, signaled early that Moscow would be pleased to receive Bullitt as the new American ambassador, and *Izvestiia* praised his selection.[34] Of course, the Soviets wanted a relationship and probably would have accepted anyone. Traditionally, they were suspicious of such ardent Russophiles as Bullitt—and for good reason.[35] It was difficult to fulfill high expectations, particularly in Stalinist Russia, whereas an anti-Communist curmudgeon would expect little and receive little.

After the Roosevelt-Litvinov Agreement was signed on November 16, Roosevelt named Bullitt to be America's first ambassador to the Soviet Union. Bullitt was ecstatic over the appointment and set off for the Soviet Union in early December, full of enthusiasm and determination to improve American-Soviet relations, with George Kennan in tow. He had been waiting for this opportunity for fifteen years, yearning to prove that he was right in 1919 and that Wilson was wrong. His reception in Moscow, as we have seen, was surrealistic. He and Stalin even slobbered one another with kisses. He was ecstatic over the possibilities of the new American-Russian relationship. Leaving Kennan in Moscow to serve as a continuing contact with the Soviets, he returned to the United States to collect the rest of his staff. He returned in March 1934 with John C. Wiley, Loy Henderson, Charles E. Bohlen, Bertel Kuniholm, Lieutenant Roscow H. Hillenkoetter, and his private secretary, Carmel Offie. In addition, eleven men were employed in the consular section, including its head, George Hanson, and his two key assistants, Elbridge Durbrow and Angus Ward. All told, there were about forty members of the team. An equal number of Russians were hired to serve as chauffeurs, mechanics, translators, and gophers.[36] He was now ready to build the alliance that would stir the world and push forward the great drive for human freedom.

The War Department assigned Lt. Colonel Philip R. Faymonville as the military attaché in Moscow in June 1934. Like Bullitt, he had a long-standing interest in Russia and was an admirer of the Soviet experiment. During the American intervention in the Russian Civil War, Faymonville served as chief ordnance officer of American Expeditionary Forces in Siberia. Later when the Soviet government set up the Far Eastern Republic in that part of Siberia from which Japan refused at first to withdraw, the War Department sent him as military observer to the Republic. When the Far Eastern Republic was dismantled and absorbed into the Soviet Union following Japan's withdrawal in 1922, he served as assistant military attaché in Japan. He impressed his superiors with his language abilities and intelligence reports, and soon moved up the career ladder. By the end of 1933 he was at the Army War College near Washington and serving as military aide in the Roosevelt White House. He was thrilled over the Roosevelt-Litvinov Agreement and pleased that the Army had nominated him for its military attaché in Moscow because of his "faculty of getting along well with Russians."[37] He would soon become the Roosevelt School's point man in Moscow.

3

"The Donkey, the Carrot, and the Club"

When Bullitt returned to Moscow on March 7, 1934, he expected the special relationship that characterized his visit in December 1933 to continue. He wanted to quickly resolve the problems of the debt, housing, and money exchange. He was anxious to arrange credits for the Kremlin as soon as it paid the debt. He also desired to modify a ridiculous regulation on use of an airplane that he brought with him when he returned to the Soviet Union. The Soviets reacted to this innovation by restricting the plane's use to Bullitt and his pilot and to a flying distance of only 15 kilometers. Bullitt asked the Soviets to allow others in the embassy to use the plane and to increase the flight distance to 150 kilometers.[1] Bullitt thought all such matters were routine and could be resolved quickly. He wanted to get on to the serious business of international affairs and a warm working partnership between Roosevelt and Stalin.

The Soviet government, however, did not react favorably to Bullitt's routine requests. They found his overtly friendly disposition to be presumptuous and his curt manner to be arrogant. In a memorandum dated March 12, Ivan Divilkovsky, the secretary general of the Soviet Commissariat of Foreign Affairs, reported, "Bullitt asked me about the time of dinner and supper adopted in Moscow, stating that he wished to accommodate his mode of life to that of ours and hoped that we would frequent his home as his guests. I'm afraid he is somewhat spoiled by the good welcome that he has met here and that in the future he might become an obtrusive person."[2] Ambassador Troyanovsky wrote Litvinov on March 3 that Bullitt "wishes to present himself as a very hard personality and wants to obtain the maximum results in negotiations with us."[3] It was not so much a question of obtrusion or of a hard personality as a question of high expectations. Bullitt wanted a special relationship, and he thought that Moscow desired one, too.

The Soviets did not wait long before informing Bullitt that there would be no special tie and that the issues he wanted resolved speedily were not so easily dealt with. In late March the Soviet government told Bullitt that the choice land that Stalin had promised for the building of an American embassy was not available.[4] In early April the Politburo apprised Litvinov to inform Bullitt "that we cannot provide him with any other rate of exchange save for the official one" and that the United States' "conditions related to credits . . . are to be rejected." He also was to be told that the Soviet Union would only accept a scheme of debt repayment that included a loan double the amount of the debt. "The overall amount of credits," the Politburo stipulated, "should be two times bigger than that of claims, i.e., $150 million in credits versus $75 million of claims, and $200 million versus $100 million of claims."[5] The Soviet government also refused to change "the air regime invented for him." On July 7, 1934, Deputy Foreign Minister Nikolai Krestinsky reported to Troyanovsky that Bullitt was finally "reconciling himself to the regime, and also, it seems to me, after the accident with his plane during his last flight in Leningrad, has rather lost a taste for air transportation." Bullitt did have a near fatal accident in his plane, but he really had not lost his enthusiasm for flying or for allowing others in the embassy, particularly the military attaché, to use the plane.

Bullitt was rather amazed at the difference in treatment and at the positions which the Soviets now took on many of the problems that had prevented diplomatic recognition for some sixteen years. He found them to be unbelievably unfriendly and uncooperative. Bullitt was inclined to treat the Soviets in kind. In March he wrote Secretary Hull, "The misunderstanding is so wide that perhaps it would be best to bring all commercial and financial relations to a standstill until it can be clarified."[6]

On Easter he wrote FDR, "Moscow has turned out to be just as disagreeable as I anticipated." Soberly, he concluded, "The honeymoon atmosphere has evaporated." Bullitt at first attributed the change in the Soviet attitude to Japan. "The Russians are convinced," he informed FDR, "that Japan will not attack this spring or summer and, as they no longer feel that they need our immediate help, their underlying hostility to all capitalist countries now shows through the veneer of intimate friendship."[7] He was right in looking for the explanation in the context of Soviet-Japanese-American relations, but it seems more likely that the Soviets were dismissing the Americans not because the Japanese threat had ebbed but because Bullitt was telling them that the Americans were not going to help stymie the Japanese threat. Before he left Washington, Bullitt reiterated to Troyanovsky that the United States would not send an American flotilla to Vladivostok. Troyanovsky reported to Litvinov that Bullitt believed a flotilla visit would be "too strong and dangerous a demonstration" and would provoke the Japanese. Bullitt, according to Troyanovsky, "considers it to be better to send a smaller squadron to Leningrad."[8] After he returned to Moscow and saw the Soviet approach, Bullitt did not even want an American ship to sail into Leningrad harbor. In June he recommended to Secretary of State Hull that no American warships visit Vladivostok or Leningrad to show support for the Soviet Union in the face of Japan's hostility.[9]

One month earlier he had stressed to Evgenii Rubinin, the chief of the Third Western Department in the Soviet Foreign Ministry, that the United States "had no reason to wage war against Japan." Bullitt knew, of course, that the Soviet government wanted a more forceful commitment on Japan, but he was not going to recommend that the United States go beyond its act of recognition as its initial contribution to the problem of controlling Japan. He believed that the ball was now in the Soviet court, and he wanted Moscow to resolve, above all, the debt issue. He told the Soviet government that some payment scheme could be worked out, but that a relationship does not start by granting loans or credits before foreign debts are paid. After the debt issue was resolved, relations could move forward.[10]

In response to the Soviet government's unvarnished hostility, Bullitt now recommended to FDR a position combining sweetness and firmness, which was a move away from the policy of openness and friendship. "We shall have to deal with them," he advised, "according to Claudel's formula of the donkey, the carrot, and the club." The United States should "maintain the friendliest possible personal relations with the Russians but let them know clearly that if they are unwilling to move forward and take the carrot they will receive the club on the behind." The ambassador then provided Roosevelt with a concrete example of what he meant: "The next time I discuss the payment of debts and claims with Litvinov, I shall allow him to derive the impression that if the Soviet Union does not wish to use the credits of the Import-Export Bank the Japanese Government will be eager to use the facilities of the Bank to finance large purchases from certain American heavy industries."[11]

Roosevelt certainly wanted to clear up such problems like the Soviet debt obligation to fend off domestic critics of recognition, help out American debt holders, and prove to Americans that good relations were possible. He did not like Bullitt's new approach, however, and he did not encourage him to pursue it. But as long as the ambassador continued to stress "the friendliest possible personal relations," the president tolerated it.[12] FDR attributed Bullitt's change of heart to homesickness, the plebeian ambiance of Moscow, and disappointment that he no longer rubbed shoulders with the inner circle. The president consoled his ambassador with the thought that he was missed and the hope that things would get better by the spring.[13]

Bullitt himself soon shrugged off his disenchantment. He was still too much of a Russophile to believe that the sulfurous attitude was endemic. He continued to show friendship and cordiality to his Soviet hosts to the point where Krestinsky informed Troyanovsky on July 7 that "Bullitt is very friendly, as he was before." But at the same time, while he understood the Soviet position on Japan, he knew there had to be some other explanation for Soviet hostility and aloofness. He was only beginning to comprehend the nature of Stalinism, so he did not search for that explanation in the nature of the Soviet government. Instead, he persuaded himself that it was a question of personalities, that there was a division in the Kremlin, and that Stalin did not know what was happening to American-Soviet relations. He singled out Litvinov as the main culprit in the deteriorating relationship.

As Soviet hostility continued to persist, Bullitt confided to FDR on July 14, "I got word from the Kremlin a few days ago that Stalin had chided his intimates for not seeing more of me."[14] Two weeks later, he told Undersecretary of State Judge Moore, "I suspect that Litvinov has not reported to Stalin with any accuracy our side of the dispute about claims and indebtedness and I have the past few days seen to it that other gentlemen who have access to Stalin should be informed as to our point of view."[15] Bullitt suspected that Litvinov's Jewishness made him obstinate. He similarly viewed the head of press relations for the Soviet Foreign Ministry, Constantine Oumansky, who was also Jewish and who eventually took Alexander Troyanovsky's place as Soviet ambassador in Washington in 1939. He thought Oumansky went out of his way to make life difficult for the American envoys.[16]

Moore shared Bullitt's opinion. He wrote Bullitt on July 9, 1934, that Troyanovsky could not figure out why he was not getting instructions to settle the debt question. Moore speculated that "perhaps Litvinov, who seems to be without any conscience whatever, is deceiving him just as he deceived the president and yourself when he was here and precisely as he has ignored all of his promises in his conversations with you at Moscow."[17] Moore, however, attributed Litvinov's contrariness not to his Jewish background but to a fear that he might lose influence with Stalin if he agreed to make concessions to the Americans.[18] Troyanovsky, of course, was not being candid with Moore. He already knew that the Soviet Foreign Ministry alone would negotiate the debt issue. On March 3 he wrote Litvinov, "I consider the decision to transfer the negotiations to Moscow to be absolutely right."

Bullitt, always creative, decided to go around Litvinov. He tried to develop a close relationship with Voroshilov by teaching the Red Army cavalry to play polo. Charles Thayer, then a clerk in the chancery, was Bullitt's polo coach. The Communists decided, though, that polo was a bourgeois game and that the rules were too restrictive for fast galloping cavalrymen. On one occasion, an excited Mongolian horseman rode off with the ball and was only halted three miles from the playing field. Bullitt also attempted to befriend members of the Moscow Soviet by teaching them baseball. The subtleties of the game, however, were lost on the Russians when one of them was beaned by a fast pitch.[19]

In July, Bullitt organized an extravagant ball at which "practically everyone who mattered in Moscow turned up," except, of course, the only person who did matter, Stalin. By August he was convinced that he had turned matters around. "We have dozens of indications lately," he optimistically wrote FDR, "that Stalin, Voroshilov and Molotov are most anxious to develop really friendly relations with us." In fact, he added, "I got word from the Kremlin the other day that all the leaders of the Government, including Stalin, would be glad to see a great deal more of me than they have been seeing and in the end I think we shall be able to beat down Litvinov's resistance."[20] In a letter to Moore in early September he reiterated his charge that Litvinov was the main problem in relations: "I am convinced that the chief obstacle both to a successful conclusion of the negotiations with regard to debts and claims and to the establishment of really frank and friendly relations between our two Governments is Litvinov himself." However, on September 15, Karl Radek disabused Bullitt. He told him that he had seen the file on the debt issue in Stalin's office and that Litvinov had accurately and thoroughly informed Stalin "without noteworthy distortions."[21]

The news was disquieting, but it did lead Bullitt back to a more accurate barometer of Soviet-American relations: Japan. "If a Japanese attack should again seem likely, or if we should begin to develop any sort of a real understanding with Japan," he told FDR in late September, "it would not take the Soviet Government very long to discover that our demands with regard to debts and claims were most reasonable." In a letter dated September 8 to Moore, Bullitt actually outlined his view of Soviet policy. Litvinov "seems to believe," he said, "that he can afford not to make any effort to maintain warm relations between the Soviet Union and the United States. . . . He is convinced that we will not enter into any special agreements with the Soviet Union directed against Japan or obliging us to take any action in the Far East and that he believes further that in case of war between Japan and the Soviet Union we would inevitably be drawn in on the side of the Soviet Union, and that it would make no difference whether our relations with the Soviet Union prior to such an event were warm, tepid or cold. His entire attitude is based on the belief that any real rapprochement between the United States and Japan is impossible."[22]

Roosevelt was amused by Bullitt's battles with Litvinov and his various gimmicks for breaking the ice in Moscow. He heartily approved of the extravagant ball, although he advised Bullitt not to put on a second in the near future because of the physical strain. What was central in FDR's concern was that Bullitt continued to believe that "good relations" were possible and necessary. That is what FDR wanted. He could not criticize Bullitt for complaining about the Soviet attitude and "the physical discomforts which make life hellish" in Moscow as long as the ambassador was convinced that good relations were needed and worth the effort to develop them.[23]

The Soviet analysis of the new American embassy and its cast of characters in 1934 was ambivalent. On the one hand, Deputy Foreign Minister Krestinsky concluded in July 1934 that "generally speaking, the American embassy is a kind of nonpolitical one. Neither Bullitt nor his subordinates show any special interest about the foreign and domestic policies of the Soviet Union and live a rather private life—focusing on their domestic lives—settling into their homes at Spaso-

Peskovsky Lane and Mokhovaia Street and preparing themselves for the construction of the Embassy building." On the other hand, Soviet officials thought that the consular services of the embassy, especially the issuance of visas for Soviet officials, did not meet "very elementary consular" standards. They found Bullitt to be "suspicious but generally interesting," Wiley to be difficult because "he raises issues in a more strongly worded manner and sometimes even allows himself some hints of threat to establish in America similar rules for us," and Lt. Colonel Faymonville, the military attaché, to be very friendly. Bullitt was clearly allowing Wiley to implement the quid pro quo approach for him. There was also an implied distinction between Bullitt, who was friendly but clearly seeking a mutually advantageous relationship, and Faymonville, who was just plain friendly. They dismissed Wiley's hard-nosed approach on the grounds that "he is under the influence of his wife . . . who is a daughter of a factory owner in Poland, a Pilsudskiite." As for the other embassy officials, including Kennan, Henderson, and Bohlen, none apparently made an impression in 1934, although Rubinin observed that Bullitt employed "several specialists interested in the inner life of the USSR."[24]

In the middle of October 1934, Bullitt left Moscow for Washington via Japan and China. He arrived in Washington on December 15, met with Roosevelt, and rehashed the problems in American-Soviet relations. He also met with B. E. Skvirsky, an official at the Soviet embassy in Washington, on January 7, 1935, and reviewed the panoply of American-Soviet relations. Bullitt discussed his recent trip to the Far East and pointed out that in Japan he had "heard many conversations about an inevitable conflict between the USSR [and Japan] in the future." Skvirsky wanted to know if an "Anglo-American front would develop to cut off Japan." Bullitt replied that at the present time it "was seemingly impossible." He did reassure Skvirsky that the United States knew the Soviet predicament in the Far East and watched the situation closely. He informed Skvirsky that if the Japanese entered into a "race" with the United States on building naval ships, the United States "would build a fleet far swifter than Japan's." Bullitt also stressed that he continued to "have faith in the necessity and desirability of relations" with the Soviet Union.[25]

A virus infection kept Bullitt in the United States in January and February 1935, but on March 22 he set sail for Europe. Once he reached the continent, he stopped in Paris, Berlin, and Warsaw before returning to the Soviet Union. From Paris, on April 7, 1935, he wrote FDR that the Soviets wanted France to sign an agreement for mutual assistance and that they had intimated that if the French did not agree, "the Soviet Union would begin to develop as close relations as possible with the German Reichswehr which has always been . . . pro-Russian and anti-French." Bullitt went on to report to Moore at the State Department that "the French have no illusions about the Russians and do not expect any real help from the Soviet Union. If they make the alliance, they will make it merely because they are afraid that, if they do not, the Soviet Government will turn to Germany." The French were convinced, Bullitt reported, that such a pact "will keep the Soviet Union out of Germany's arms." Bullitt, however, dissented. He argued that "the Soviet Government will make the mutual assistance pact with the French and then begin to flirt with Germany as well as France and succeed in getting Germany and France bidding against one another for Soviet support, and that the only country which will derive any real benefit from the present maneuvers will be the Soviet Union."[26]

Nonetheless, when Bullitt reached Moscow in mid-April, he immediately had a meeting with Krestinsky and offered to assist with "refining" the details of a Soviet-French agreement. He believed that his connections in France could be of assistance to the Kremlin. Krestinsky told him that the impending agreement between Paris and Moscow needed no refinement and that Litvinov and the French foreign minister, Pierre Laval, would officially announce it in Geneva.[27] On May 2, a mutual assistance pact was signed, but it contained no military protocol, so its significance was primarily indicative of a changing mood toward the mounting threat of Nazi Germany rather than a substantive treaty with real teeth aimed at stopping Germany.

Bullitt met with Litvinov on May 4 and complained that it was not possible to have good working relations with the bureaucracy of the Soviet Foreign Ministry because it could not answer serious questions but referred them to Litvinov. The foreign minister told Bullitt that he could not respond to such a general charge but that the Soviet government did not proceed on this or that issue with lightning speed, that all questions were carefully studied, and that it did not stray from this procedure.[28] The ambassador also thought it was important to make sure that the Soviets understood American society. On May 6 he "acquainted" T. Arens, a Soviet Foreign Ministry official, with some of the finer points of American democracy. He told Arens that the United States was not a feudal state but a vigorous democracy, that its economic system was in a temporary crisis but still had the support of the people, and that it was essential in comprehending the American mind to read the "provincial press" and not just rely on the *New York Times*. He further stressed that the United States would not be inclined to make foreign loans again because no one wished to repay the loans that had already been extended. Bullitt also stated that because "I have not been able to come quickly to an agreement with the NKID [Soviet Foreign Ministry] about full consulates in the USSR, there are those in Washington who wish to restrict your [Soviet] full consulates in the USA—New York for the state of New York, San Francisco for the state of California." Bullitt added that he had asked that this not be done. Arens objected that such a consulate policy would be "discrimination" against the USSR. Bullitt, according to Arens, agreed and concluded the meeting by saying that the Americans would need only the consulate in Moscow for the time being because "there is not much work here."[29]

By the time Bullitt reached Moscow in mid-April 1935, the purges were well under way. In December 1934 Sergei Kirov, the Leningrad Party leader, was assassinated. Stalin, who apparently ordered the murder, was ready to wield his bloody ax against the Communist elite. He used Kirov's murder as an excuse to launch an investigation into possible conspiracies against him, the Communist Party, and the revolutionary course of Communism. He and the secret police soon found "evidence" of a most extraordinary, far-reaching conspiracy that implicated the Communist leadership in counterrevolutionary activity, including sabotage, espionage, and collaboration with Soviet Russia's enemies, Japan and Germany. Over the next five years a shocking, unprecedented bloodbath of Communist officials ensued, both in the bureaucracy and in the military. Initially, the friends and supporters of Kirov in the Leningrad Soviet were summarily arrested and executed. Then Stalin moved against the old Bolsheviks and other Party members whom he suspected of disloyalty to him. "The terror, always present," Bullitt wrote to FDR on May 1, "has risen to such a pitch that the least of the Muscovites, as well as the greatest, is in fear. Almost no one dares have any contact with foreigners and this is not unbiased fear but a proper sense of reality."[30]

Ivan the Terrible in his bloody rampage against the boyars whom he suspected of opposition to his autocratic government in the sixteenth century had nothing on Stalin. In fact, Stalin criticized Ivan for not being thorough enough in rooting out political opposition.[31] Bullitt chalked up the rising tide of executions to Stalin's paranoia. He watched in disbelief as thousands of Soviet citizens, many of whom he knew to be loyal, disappeared.[32] The public purges went on until 1939 when Stalin finally ended them because he evidently realized that a regime which publicly shot its political and military leaders projected an image of weakness at a time when weakness invited attack. He continued secret purges, though, right through World War II.

In a letter to Judge Moore in March 1936, Bullitt described the arrests and disappearance of thousands of people as "unbelievable." Not only were the numbers striking to Bullitt, but in the cases of which he had personal knowledge, the "persons were without question loyal to the Soviet regime."[33] By then, of all the Communists whom he had met at the dinner with Stalin in 1933, only Molotov, Kaganovich, Kalinin, Litvinov, Yegorov, and Troyanovsky were still standing outside the growing ring of suspicion. The others—Ordzhonikidze, Krestinsky, Karakhan, Sokolnikov, Piatakov, Kuibyshev, and Mezhlauk—were soon arrested, tried, and executed or pressured to commit suicide. Prominent old Bolshevik leaders—like Bukharin, Tomsky, Kamenev, Zinoviev, and Rykov—were tried publicly and forced to confess to specious charges of treason in 1936, 1937, and 1938.[34] Trotsky was tried in absentia in 1937 and sentenced to death. In 1940 the execution was carried out in Mexico when a Soviet assassin infiltrated Trotsky's inner circle and rammed an ice pick through his cranium. Pavel Sudoplatov, the NKVD official responsible for Trotsky's assassination as well as many key projects related to American-Soviet relations throughout World War II and the cold war, published his memoirs in 1994 and gave the world the first insider's view of Stalin's espionage and police operations. Historian Robert Conquest called Sudoplatov's book "the most sensational, the most devastating, and in many ways the most informative autobiography ever to emerge from the Stalinist milieu."[35]

The beginning of the purges in 1935 left Bullitt limp. He saw the hope for the development of freedom and real change drown in a sea of blood and terror. As devastating as the advent of the purges was to the ambassador's dream of Russia becoming a leader in mankind's democratic development, an even more shocking blow to his hope for the flowering of American-Soviet friendship took place in July and August 1935. It was then that Stalin decided to call a meeting of the world's Communist parties in Moscow, the seventh time they had met and the first time since 1928. Stalin wanted the Seventh Comintern Congress to change the marching orders of the Communist parties.

In 1928, at the Sixth Comintern Congress, Stalin told them that they must wage war against all socialist parties because capitalism had seemingly stabilized itself and was not about to collapse and give way to Communism as the Communists had thought immediately after World War I. When the Great Depression of 1929 seemed to indicate that capitalism had indeed run its course, Stalin did not change the direction of the world Communist movement. He determined that now it was more essential than ever to get rid of all competitors of the Communists on the left side of the political spectrum. Capitalism was about to collapse entirely, so it was pointless trying to undermine it. The best action for the Communists was to prepare to take power worldwide once capitalism had given up the ghost by eliminating the socialists who were the Communists' chief rivals for the workers' support. The violent attacks by the Communists on the socialists helped the radical Right gain support in a number of countries, but nowhere with more strength and enduring consequences than in the coming to power of Hitler and the Nazis in Germany in 1933.

Stalin, however, was not particularly disturbed by Hitler's ascension to power. He saw Hitler as capitalism's last gasp of life before death. To be sure, he knew Hitler was a virulent anti-Communist and had laid out a fantastic plan of conquest and expansion in *Mein Kampf* that included the annexation of Ukraine and the reduction of the Slavic peoples to the status of slaves serving the Teutonic master race. However, Hitler seemed to be the puppet of the large industrialists in Germany and thus not an independent actor. When he clearly showed that he was in charge by the end of 1933, he still did not seem to be an immediate threat to the Soviet Union, but actually more of a hope for finally nudging the capitalist world into the grave through all-out war with the West. Hitler promised war against the West before war against the East because he was determined to violate the Treaty of Versailles, which the French and English were committed to enforce. Stalin and the Communists thought that war would help advance Communism, providing, of course, that the Soviet Union was not dragged into it prematurely, that is, before the capitalist states had drained themselves and before Stalin had put his own house in order with the purges and the industrialization/collectivization program.

By 1935 Hitler seemed more of a threat to Stalin. He was still the Communists' great hope for an intercapitalist war, but at the same time his passionate anti-Communism put pressure on Stalin. His growing cooperation with Japan and Italy was also worrisome. The Communist dictator decided that it was not prudent to be isolated when aggressors were on the march in Asia and Europe. He launched two policies to try to control and deflect the burgeoning threats from the USSR. One was Collective Security, which had two parts: to attempt to persuade the Western Powers to stand up to Hitler and, second, to end Soviet isolation by establishing diplomatic relations with the United States and other states, joining the League of Nations in 1934, and signing a bevy of treaties of nonaggression and friendship with many states, including the Baltic States, Romania, France, and Czechoslovakia. The Soviet foreign minister, Maxim Litvinov, became a famous personality at the League of Nation meetings in Geneva and ultimately personified Stalin's policy of Collective Security and his attempt to collaborate with the West. From Bullitt's point of view, however, Soviet attempts to align with the West were cynical and expedient. On April 20, 1936, he wrote Secretary Hull that it was Communist policy to befriend "democrats in order the better eventually to lead those democrats to the firing squad."[36]

The other policy was the so-called Popular Front, which was the replacement of the world Communist movement's war against socialist parties with a policy that sought to forge a common alliance between Communists and socialists against the growing tide of the radical Right. The strategy of tolerating the radical Right for purposes of cultivating an intercapitalist war had to be carefully balanced by a concomitant policy that kept the radical Right from expanding beyond its main bases in Germany and Italy. The times called for the containment of the Nazi/Fascist threat, not its elimination. An alliance between the Communists and the socialists could help the extreme Left stave off further expansion of the extreme Right but at the same time keep the latter alive for purposes of breaking up the world capitalist order.

The purpose of the Seventh Comintern Congress in Moscow was to officially inaugurate the policy of the Popular Front. For Bullitt this event was an outrage. It not only proved that the Communists still pursued the goal of world revolution, but it also proved that they were breaking their promise made in the letter exchange between Roosevelt and Litvinov in November 1933, which stipulated that Moscow would have nothing to do with the American Communist Party. To the bitter disappointment of Bullitt, the American Communist Party attended the Seventh Comintern Congress and, worse, assumed a major role during the proceedings. Both Earl Browder and William Foster, the general secretary and chairman of the American Communist Party, respectively, were elected to the presidium of the Congress.

Bullitt wasted no time protesting the Americans' role at the Congress. He met with Litvinov on a number of occasions in early July and demanded to know the exact dates of the Congress and the names and addresses in Moscow of the Americans who would participate in the event. Litvinov sarcastically answered that such ignorance could be removed by consulting the proper Soviet authority, that Bullitt had no special "liberty" to make such demands at the diplomatic level, and, finally, that Bullitt might know more about events if he had worked for more than six months out of the year in the Soviet Union instead of spending four months traveling around the United States. Litvinov added that the tone of Bullitt's requests were threatening and "these threats will not be accepted." Bullitt replied that Litvinov avoided threats by telling lies. Litvinov was surprised at Bullitt's animus over the Congress and concluded, in a note to Troyanovsky, that Bullitt "either is actually anxious about the outcomes of the Congress or he is exaggerating the matter for his own purposes."[37]

In fact, the ambassador interpreted the involvement of American Communists in the Congress as a repudiation of the Roosevelt-Litvinov agreement and a reaffirmation of the Soviet goal of world revolution. On July 19 he wrote Secretary Hull: "It is my conviction that there has been no decrease in the determination of the Soviet Government to produce world revolution. Diplomatic relations with friendly states are not regarded by the Soviet Government as normal friendly relations but 'armistice' relations and it is the conviction of the leaders of the Soviet Union that this 'armistice' can not possibly be ended by a definite peace but only by a renewal of battle. The Soviet Union genuinely desires peace on all fronts at the present time but this peace is looked upon merely as a happy respite in which future wars may be prepared." When Bullitt complained to Karl Radek that he feared the Comintern Congress might break the Roosevelt-Litvinov Agreement, Radek shouted, "We have lived without the United States in the past and we can continue to live without the United States in the future and we shall never permit you or anyone else to dictate to us what we shall do in Moscow." Bullitt was flabbergasted at the reaction, he told Hull, particularly by someone whom Stalin had demoted and held in suspicion. It was for Bullitt an object lesson in the hold that ideology had on many of the old Bolsheviks. Pavel Mikhailsky, a writer and a longtime Bolshevik who overheard Radek's rebuke to Bullitt, explained to the ambassador, "You must understand that world revolution is our religion and there is not one of us who would not in the final analysis oppose even Stalin himself if we should feel that he was abandoning the cause of world revolution."[38]

The tragedy, of course, of such passionate myopia was that Stalin was the Party and the Comintern, and no sincere Communist could object to his will, including an order to incriminate oneself as a deviationist, or, if one did object, proving by that very objection that one was a deviationist, which in either case was a crime punishable by death according to Party canons. In fact, since there was no objective morality, there was no way for a committed Communist to oppose Stalin, which, along with his absolute ability to threaten family members, helps explain why so many Communists incriminated themselves and meekly accepted the sentence of death during the purges. The average citizen was swept along by a simple but, under the circumstances, effective propaganda campaign that blamed all problems on wreckers and saboteurs—class enemies—and attributed all positive developments to the Party and Stalin.[39]

Bullitt, at any rate, was clearly abandoning his optimistic view, which he had shared with Roosevelt, that the USSR was advancing the cause of liberated man and continuing the American experiment in democracy. Charles Bohlen, who returned to the State Department to work in the East European Division in spring 1935, commented, "It was not long before these and other disappointments produced a very marked change in the attitude of Ambassador Bullitt, who was for the rest of his life a consistent and at times violent opponent of the Soviet Union."[40]

Bullitt informed the Soviet government that the United States was outraged by the Comintern meeting, especially by the American Communist Party's participation. He was realistic enough to know that the Soviets did not give a tinker's damn what the United States thought, and he relayed that message to Roosevelt. Thinking that the president agreed with his change of view, he also advised FDR against breaking diplomatic relations with Moscow even though the Congress was an egregious affront to the United States. Instead, he urged the president either to overlook the meeting or, if that proved impossible, to issue a forceful protest. However, "if the Bolsheviks should become so violent before this Congress is over that you decide to break diplomatic relations," he wrote FDR on August 3, "please let me have a personal and strictly confidential intimation well in advance so that I can send out of the country by courier our code books, confidential despatches [*sic*], and telegrams before our Soviet friends grab them. They are entirely capable of behaving like Bolsheviks." Bullitt was now clearly moving into a different orbit than FDR. The president had no intention of severing relations. Roosevelt tried to dampen his friend's anger and disillusionment with humor. "Since you wrote on August third," Roosevelt answered, "there is no violent news of *your* Congress so I take it I shall not have to send an ambulance for you."[41]

As the Congress progressed, Bullitt became increasingly disturbed over the rather significant role that the American Communist Party played. He now urged the American government to retaliate to this affront by cutting Soviet representation in Washington, reducing the number of visas for Soviet citizens, and having FDR make a speech on Soviet intentions to overthrow the American government. However, he still advised against breaking off diplomatic relations.[42] Bullitt's new approach was summarized in a telegram to Secretary of State Hull at the end of August: "The Soviet foreign office does not understand the meaning of honor or fair dealing, but it does understand the meaning of acts."[43] Robert Kelley, the head of the East European Division at the State Department, heartily agreed with Bullitt's tough stand, but Roosevelt and Hull did not. They did order him, however, to protest to the Soviet Foreign Ministry the participation of the American Communist Party in the Comintern Congress.[44]

Bullitt did not allow his shock over the purges and the Seventh Comintern Congress to distract him from his concern with Soviet foreign policy. In the Far East, he told Hull in July 1935 that Moscow hoped for a war between the United States and Japan, and then it would move in and take Manchuria and spread Communism into China at the war's end. The ambassador also believed that war in Europe was a central goal of the Kremlin. There Moscow's plan was to precipitate war between Germany and France, avoid involvement itself at first, and then, when the Europeans had drained themselves and when the Soviets had built up their strength, "to intervene successfully in such a war, and . . . protect and consolidate any Communist government which may be set up as a result of war and ensuing revolution in any European state."[45]

Bullitt reported in November that Litvinov was enthusiastic over the British decision to enforce the League of Nations' sanctions against Italy for invading Abyssinia. "He expressed once more the conviction that the British had decided to eliminate Mussolini. . . . Litvinov said that he believed the British would blockade the Suez Canal if and when necessary. . . . He felt that as soon as the British had finished Mussolini they would finish Hitler."[46] Bullitt reinforced Litvinov's optimism by informing A. F. Neiman at the Soviet Foreign Ministry that he believed the Abyssinian crisis would lead to a broad war involving the major powers within fourteen months. He did not think that the United States would support the sanctions, but Henderson did and so informed the Soviets.[47]

When the British failed to enforce the sanctions against Italy and when Italy conquered Abyssinia, the Soviets began to doubt that the West European powers were going to take a stand against the growing aggression by Germany and Italy. Litvinov's optimism quickly gave way to the gnawing reality that western appeasement might lead Hitler to the door of the Soviet Union. Complications to Stalin's foreign policy soon developed in the wake of the Abyssinian crisis. In March 1936 Germany remilitarized the Rhineland. The French, who were most threatened by this violation of the Treaty of Versailles, did nothing. Suddenly, the French military commitment to East Central Europe, especially Czechoslovakia, was worthless. France no longer had a way to pressure Germany. The French now sought security behind the Maginot Line and in alliance with the appeasers of England, Neville Chamberlain and Lord Halifax, who personified that segment of British intellectual opinion which believed that Versailles was unjust, that France was the destabilizing country in Europe, and that Germany should be allowed to redress its grievances stemming from Versailles. As for the new countries of Eastern and Central Europe, they soon found themselves facing Germany alone. Hitler's approach was shrewd and calculating. He abandoned the Weimar government's preoccupation with the territory that Germany lost to Poland at the end of World War I—the so-called Polish Corridor—and instead concentrated on establishing a political hegemony over the Carpatho-Danubian countries of the former Hapsburg Empire, in particular Austria and Czechoslovakia. He worked for union with Austria by promoting the economic and political benefits of Anschluss and for isolation of Czechoslovakia by portraying it as "Bolshevism's Central European aircraft carrier," because Prague had signed the Czechoslovak-Soviet agreement of May 16, 1935, which supplemented the Franco-Soviet Mutual Assistance Treaty of May 2, 1935, to defend itself against German threats.[48] At the same time, Germany enticed all of the countries of Eastern and Central Europe, some quite reluctantly, into its economic orbit by setting up a system of bilateral trade whereby Germany paid above market prices for the agricultural products of Eastern and Central Europe, and the latter used their profits to buy German industrial goods. Even Czechoslovakia, which had a relatively mature industrial sector, could not resist the Germans because the West, particularly after the Great Depression, had closed its markets to the countries of Eastern and Central Europe. All the new Eastern European states—Poland, Hungary, Czechoslovakia, Bulgaria, Yugoslavia, Romania, Albania, Lithuania, Latvia, Estonia—had tried to set up democratic governments after World War I, but found themselves, with the exception of Czechoslovakia, veering toward authoritarianism of one type or another because of a host of paralyzing domestic and foreign problems that included irredentism, ethnonationalism, boundary disputes, chauvinism, uneven and incomplete land reform, and the disruption and destruction of prewar trade patterns and infrastructure. Hitler soon swept all of these beleaguered countries into his orbit.

Bullitt realized that appeasement of Germany was quite threatening to the Soviet Union because it gave Hitler a free hand in Eastern and Central Europe, which directed him on an easterly course increasingly toward a confrontation with the Soviet Union. Appeasement might also contain the seeds of de facto coalition of capitalist states, led by Germany and arrayed against the world's one oasis of Communism. The Soviets, Bullitt understood, wanted to redirect Hitler toward the West and prevent a capitalist coalition at all costs. Their policy, he told Judge Moore on March 30, 1936, was "to keep Europe divided, and the Soviet Government can be counted on to do anything necessary to maintain a hearty hatred between France and Germany." Collective Security and the Popular Front were two strategies to arouse the West and keep the Soviet Union from being isolated. Stalin, however, pursued yet another course: an alliance with Nazi Germany. As early as April 1935 Bullitt wrote FDR that the Soviets were threatening to play their German card if the French were not more aggressive in lining up against the Nazis.[49] The French, to be sure, were aware of that possibility and they did eventually sign the Franco-Soviet Mutual Assistance Treaty, but the treaty had no teeth because it lacked a military protocol.

The fact of the matter was that the Western Powers considered the Soviets to be too weak to be an effective balance and ally because of collectivization and the purges. Moreover, the Soviet threat to fashion a modus vivendi with Nazi Germany was unconvincing because they believed, as did Roosevelt but not Bullitt, that the ideological antagonism between Nazism and Communism made an alliance between Berlin and Moscow highly unlikely, if not totally impossible. To a certain extent, the assumptions of the western leaders were correct. Hitler despised the Communists and also had a low opinion of their military strength. Furthermore, the lack of interest by the English and French in an alliance with Moscow gave Hitler even less reason to take the Soviets into consideration since it meant that he did not have to be concerned about the possibility of a two-front war. So Hitler did not respond to Soviet initiatives for an alliance. How-ever, the western statesmen miscalculated when they assumed that ideological antagonism would be more important than security and political expediency. Bullitt, on the other hand, was convinced that Stalin would do "anything neces-sary" to start war in the West and to keep peace in the East.

By the spring of 1936 American-Soviet relations had deteriorated signifi-cantly, despite Bullitt's efforts to halt the decay. In April 1936 he sent Hull a telegram summarizing his views. It was a mixture of hard-boiled advice and lingering idealism. He told Hull that the United States could not break diplo-matic relations with the Soviet Union since "it is now one of the Greatest Powers and its relations with Europe, China, and Japan are so important that we can not conduct our foreign relations intelligently if we do not know what is happening in Moscow." But, he emphasized, the United States "should not cherish for a moment the illusion that it is possible to establish really friendly relations with the Soviet Government or with any Communist party or Com-munist individuals." Furthermore, "it is difficult to conduct conversations with the Soviet Foreign Office because in that institution the lie is normal and the truth abnormal and one's intelligence is insulted by the happy assumption that one believes the lie."

On the other hand, he informed Hull, the United States must be patient and "should never threaten" the Soviets. "Above all, we should guard the repu-tation of Americans for business efficiency, sincerity, and straightforwardness. We should never send a spy to the Soviet Union. There is no weapon at once so disarming and effective in relations with the communists as sheer honesty."[50]

Basically what Bullitt was suggesting was that the United States stop being "soft" on Moscow and start adopting a "hard" line until "the atmosphere is favorable."[51] He advised FDR to swing away from friendly accommodation to a policy of quid pro quo because the Russians viewed concessions as a sign of weakness. He was more convinced than ever that this was the only way to deal with Moscow. Although he knew Moscow was displeased over American inaction toward Japan, he also knew after the purges, the ongoing collectivization drive, the massive terror, and the Comintern Congress that Stalin's hostility toward and suspicion of the United States had deep roots in Communist ideology. For Bullitt, Stalinism was inherently and irrevocably anti-American, and this ideology not only was at the center of Soviet antipathy toward the United States but also virtually voided the possibility of cooperation and partnership except in cases of extreme mutual peril.

Under the influence of Charles Bohlen and George Kennan, Bullitt also concluded that Soviet animosity was exacerbated by a Russian cultural tradition characterized by xenophobia, secrecy, surliness, chauvinism, and a propensity to seek security through expansion and authoritarianism. In a cable to Washington, Bullitt admiringly quoted the impression of the American minister to czarist Russia in the 1850s, the Honorable Neil S. Brown of Tennessee, who wrote:

One of the most disagreeable features that [an American] has to encounter [in Russia] is the secrecy with which everything is done. He can rarely obtain accurate information, until events have transpired, and he may rely upon it, that his own movements are closely observed, by eyes that he never sees. The Russian mind seems naturally distrustful, and this is especially so with the Government officials. Everything is surrounded with ceremony, and nothing is obtainable, but after the most provoking delays. Nothing is more striking to an American here on first arrival than the reign of the police. It would seem that the capital was in a state of siege; and among all the astringents put into requisition for the preservation of peace and order none is so abhorrent, as the censorial power. As a proof of the extent to which it is carried I may mention, that the late message of the president of the United States, was not regarded in all its parts as a safe document for Russian readers, and came to their hands scathed with the censors' knife.

It is difficult in many instances to see the reason of the application of this power, and no doubt it is often capricious. . . . There is a strong anti-foreign party in Russia, whose policy would exclude all foreigners, except for mere purposes of transient commerce. They conceive that the motive which induced Peter the Great to open the door to traders and artisans, has been answered, and that they have learned sufficiently the lessons of civilization to maintain its craft and its maxims by themselves. And yet Russia cannot boast of a single invention in mechanics, that has been practical or copied out of the Country. All they have is borrowed, except their miserable climate, and even upon that, they are paying an enormous rate of usury, in the defences, and privations of winter. They fight their battles on borrowed capital, and make loans to build their railways. Their best vessels are built in England and the United States. And all their arts and pursuits, though cultivated and pressed, with commendable diligence and a good degree of success, are the products of foreign genius, and duplicates of inventions and discoveries of a people wiser than themselves. No nation has more need of foreigners, and none is so jealous of them.

Bullitt went on to stress that nothing much had changed in Russia since Brown's time.[52] In a later cable to Secretary Hull he stated, "Russia has always been a police state. It is a police state today. The authority of the Kremlin rests on the strength of its army and the omnipresence of its secret police, no less than on the fervor of the convinced Communists."[53] Kennan noted that he and Bohlen had "helped move Bullitt away from his optimistic view," although Kennan also realized that "the Soviet Government itself did the most to turn Bullitt off and dispel his ill-placed hopes."[54] Of course, Bullitt still rightly held that Stalin's reign of terror had less to do with Ivan the Terrible than with Marx and Lenin. Stalinism was incomprehensible, in his mind, outside of Communist eschatology.

The ambassador now favored a series of tough moves to gain Soviet attention. He recommended that the United States encourage France to follow a policy of appeasement toward Germany, so that the USSR would be isolated.[55] He also decided, on his own, to indulge in an anti-Soviet campaign in Moscow. He delivered protests, held press interviews where he disparaged the Soviets, and urged fellow ambassadors to adopt an anti-Soviet line. "I did all I could," he recalled, "to make things unpleasant."[56]

Bullitt obviously put himself in an untenable position. President Roosevelt did not agree with his quid pro quo policy, and he objected to the heavy-handed way in which Bullitt sought to implement it. George Kennan wrote that Roosevelt "had no intention whatsoever of adopting" Bullitt's new approach. "Not only did he have no intention of adopting it, but since the mere recommendation of it reflected an outlook on Soviet-American relations that did not fit with the general orientation of his policy, he soon sidetracked Bullitt altogether as an adviser on Russian matters, no doubt blaming Bullitt's personal pique and impatience."[57]

The Soviets, of course, knew that relations with Bullitt were worsening. Litvinov's meetings with Bullitt often turned into verbal battles. Litvinov rejected all discussions on the debt issue, and when Bullitt charged him in 1935 with reneging on a promise to purchase $30 million worth of American goods, he shot back that it was only an intention and not a duty to make such purchases. They argued about the Comintern Congress and about the unresponsiveness of the Soviet bureaucracy to American requests.[58] Bullitt even persuaded Roosevelt to utter a reservation about the American Communist Party's participation in the Comintern Congress. Bullitt also told the Soviets that they solved their unemployment problems by sending workers to Siberia and by keeping people on the collective farms.[59] Kennan complained about the high tariffs that the Soviets leveled on automobiles that members of the embassy brought into Moscow. He stressed that the foreign diplomatic communities were not "rich men's nests."[60]

From Washington, however, Troyanovsky informed the Soviet Foreign Ministry on September 28, 1935, that Roosevelt's objection to the American Communist Party's participation in the Comintern Congress was simply a campaign gambit to mollify voters who were "dissatisfied with us, indignant at us, and opposed to us." The Soviet ambassador went on to say that "relations with us" could not be considered "a trump card for Roosevelt and Bullitt in the coming election. On the contrary, many people do consider the restoration of relations with us to be a mistake." As for Bullitt's "cursing and losing his balance," Troyanovsky thought he was "reflecting Roosevelt's mood" in election mode.[61] Troyanovsky's report prompted the Soviet government to ask Bullitt in late 1935 if he thought that the argumentative state of American-Soviet relations would hurt Roosevelt's reelection bid. Bullitt answered that it would not be a significant factor in the campaign.[62]

The Soviet archives reveal that the Soviet government treated the American representatives with the arrogance of a self-righteous missionary dealing with a certified sinner. The Kremlin did not like Bullitt's friendliness and aggressiveness, and naturally it was disappointed that the Americans did not adopt a strong position against Japan. But Stalin's government was also certain that Communism was superior to capitalism, that the Soviet Union was going to triumph over the United States, and that there was no need to be civilized, reasonable, or accommodating to the American representatives. From Moscow's point of view, Soviet relations with the United States were normal, given the capitalist nature of the U.S. government and Bullitt's choleric personality. A modicum of reasonableness on the debt issue and of friendliness on the part of government authorities would have undoubtedly ensured that Bullitt remain an avid supporter of the Soviet Union, at least in international politics, instead of becoming a jilted lover. Of course, Stalinism did not allow for such policies when it came to the United States. And soon Stalin's drive for total control, based on terror and violence, ipso facto, stupefied, appalled, and polarized Bullitt and most of the other Americans at the embassy.

Bullitt left the Soviet Union in August 1936, never to return. After nearly three years in the Soviet Union he would have readily agreed with chargé d'affaires Loy Henderson's verdict, which was made in a communiqué to Secretary Hull on the third anniversary of the establishment of American-Soviet ties: "Relations between the American and Soviet Governments are not likely to be what might be regarded as cordial unless at least one of them displays a willingness to make several radical shifts in its general foreign policies and to abandon certain principles to which it has thus far steadfastly adhered." The basic problem, Henderson went on, was the Soviet government's commitment to "the establishment of a Union of World Soviet Socialist Republics." Further, in working toward this goal the Soviets expected the United States and all other states to cooperate with them in whatever measures they might take to stymie threats to their security, to acquiesce in their support of international revolution, and to provide them with all the technical and financial assistance that it might need to become a "self-sufficient world power."[63]

Henderson's report outlined Bullitt's central explanation of Soviet behavior, namely, its commitment to international revolution. Bullitt would have added another factor: that the Soviets were heirs of the czars and, as such, continued many traditional Russian attitudes.

No matter, though, because Bullitt was out of sync with Roosevelt. The president continued to believe that the Soviet Union had abandoned its support of world revolution and that it was now a normal, if introverted and defensive, state attempting to make a better life for its people in extremely difficult times. The best approach for the United States in its relations with the Soviet Union was still friendship, patience, flexibility, and understanding.

One man at the embassy who agreed with Roosevelt was Lt. Colonel Faymonville. He viewed the "individual instances" of violence against the peasantry during collectivization as an inevitable but transient aspect of "the transition toward socialized agriculture," but by 1936 clearly over and long since "forgotten in the prosperity of the kolkhoz movement and the rise in living standards of the peasant as a class." He also saw the political purges, according to Bohlen, as necessary to uproot "traitors and enemies of the people." Bullitt, Henderson, and Bohlen distrusted Faymonville. Bohlen thought of him as "the weak link in the staff," "a slender, pink-faced man with a fringe of white hair who had a definite pro-Russian bias." Bullitt and Henderson later voiced "serious doubts as to his judgment and his impartiality wherever the Soviets are concerned."[64] Faymonville, though, had the kind of outlook that Roosevelt wanted in Moscow. The Soviets liked his views, too. Faymonville criticized Bullitt behind his back to the Soviet government as early as July 1934, and by October 1934 Rubinin reported that a "most friendly attitude toward Faymonville on the part of our government agencies" was in place.[65] Soon the president found an ambassador who shared Faymonville's orientation—Joseph E. Davies. Loy Henderson, who took John Wiley's place as counselor in 1935, ran the embassy until Davies arrived.

Roosevelt still respected Bullitt and decided to name him ambassador to France in September 1936. From his position in France, Bullitt continued to criticize Roosevelt's policy toward Moscow as futile and counterproductive.[66] He argued that the Soviet Union was an ideological state that was inherently hostile to the United States, that the Soviet empire was a successor to the Russian empire and as such had tendencies that flew in the face of America's democratic tradition, and that Stalin was an omnipotent dictator who was not comprehensible or approachable by the standards of normal human behavior. Roosevelt, however, was listening to a new voice in Moscow.

Part 2

Joseph E. Davies
1936-1938

4

"His Brown Eye Is Exceedingly Kindly and Gentle"

Joseph E. Davies was "perfectly amazed and struck dumb with surprise."[1] He was not expecting to meet Stalin. Like his predecessor, William C. Bullitt, Davies knew that Stalin rarely saw any ambassador, indeed any foreigner. The "Great Helmsman," like the grand khans and autocratic czars of yesteryear, kept himself aloof for purposes of security and divine image.

Stalin did not greet Davies when he arrived in Moscow in 1937 to take Bullitt's place. It was a signal that Stalin was discounting the Americans. Now on June 5, 1938, as Davies was preparing to take up a new assignment as the American ambassador to Belgium, Stalin saw fit to drop by Molotov's apartment in the Kremlin where the envoy was saying farewell to the Soviet premier. It was a sign that Stalin liked Davies's view of the Soviet government and that he hoped his isolation of and unfriendliness toward the American mission had not so alienated Roosevelt that the Americans might stop kowtowing. The times were dangerous and friends scarce. Germany took Austria in a bloodless merger called the Anschluss in March 1938. Hitler was demanding the Sudetenland from the Czech government. In the Far East, Japan continued to probe Soviet defenses along the Manchurian and Mongolian borders. On that late spring day the rumble of war could be heard in the distance.

For two hours Stalin and Davies talked about the growing crises in Europe and Asia, the economy and industrial development of the Soviet Union, Davies's financial condition, the debt problem, and the Soviet desire to buy a new battleship and battleship technology from the United States. The discussions were general, in part because Davies knew very little about the geopolitical situation in Europe and Asia, and in part because time was short and Stalin's real intention was to convince Davies and the American government that American-Soviet relations were on course. Stalin blamed the British, particularly the government of Chamberlain, for the deteriorating situation in Europe. He said, though, that the policy of appeasement would "probably fail because the fascist dictators would drive too hard a bargain." As for Soviet Russia, Stalin told Davies, "It could defend itself."

Stalin complained to Davies that the Soviet Union was encountering delays in trying to contract an American shipyard to build a battleship for which the Soviets were prepared to "pay cash." Davies replied that he was familiar in a general sense with the problem and that he, too, found it difficult to understand the delay, but that he believed it would soon be cleared up. Stalin replied that "if the President of the United States wanted it done he felt sure that the Army and Navy technicians could not stop it." Davies countered that Roosevelt probably did not even know of the problem, since he was preoccupied with domestic issues.[2]

Stalin turned to the issue of the debt which had so strained American-Soviet relations during Bullitt's ambassadorship and which still had not been resolved. Stalin thought that it could be cleared up if the United States would loan Moscow the money to repay the debt. To think that such a scheme would fly is testimony to Stalin's own ideological bias and approach to dealing with wealthy capitalists. The fact that the ambassador thought it could work certainly encouraged Stalin in his predilection. In June 1932 Stalin told Molotov, "We would be foolish not to take money" from the Americans, providing there was no political compensation.[3]

During their conversation, Stalin and Molotov showed great interest in the wealth of the ambassador and his wife, Marjorie Merriweather Post Davies, the heiress to the General Foods fortune. For the Soviet leaders Davies and his rich wife were quintessential capitalists—greedy, hypocritical, narcissistic, indifferent to human suffering and need, inclined to measure life by ledgers, and, above all, naive about the revolutionary direction of society.

Davies, as was his custom, reiterated to Stalin and Molotov that he was a capitalist. Stalin laughed and replied, "Yes, we know you are a capitalist—there can be no doubt about that." Davies and his wife were sensitive about flaunting their wealth in the face of Russia's squalor and a Communist government that was dedicated to leveling society and taking away and redistributing among the masses the wealth of such obscenely rich people as themselves. Mrs. Davies, for example, chose not to wear her diamonds when Foreign Minister Litvinov hosted a farewell banquet for the couple on June 7. Proud of her and her sense of diplomacy, Joseph Davies told a friend, "Marjorie looked particularly beautiful in a white gown and with no jewels. She felt it was in better taste to wear none. She is in every way a great Ambassadress and a credit to our country."[4]

There were limits, however, to what the wealthy couple would do to show solidarity with the unwashed masses. They insisted on having their yacht *Sea Cloud* moored in Leningrad harbor for those weekends when they could while away the hours cruising the Gulf of Finland, like Russian nobility from one of Chekhov's plays, but protected from the envious workers and peasants by legions of Soviet secret police. They also frequently felt the need to leave the plebeian and saturnine atmosphere of Moscow to satisfy their acquisitive impulse and taste for high tea and high fashion in Paris, London, Vienna, Palm Beach, New York, and Washington. They also could not resist buying up at bargain prices truckloads of valuable Russian art, which Marjorie carted off to form the nucleus of the Hillwood Art Museum in Washington, D.C., and which Stalin permitted in order to reward Davies for his favorable reports on the purges.[5] So Stalin knew that Davies was a capitalist, though Davies had not yet had the opportunity to tell him personally.

In the discussion Davies emphasized to Stalin that capitalism was a way of life with him, a firm conviction, but that did not mean that he and "a great many other capitalists" in the United States were unsympathetic with what the Communists were trying to do. He stressed that the United States was committed, like Soviet Russia, to "a fairer distribution of wealth, but we were doing it better in the United States than [you] were doing it in Russia; that we were holding fast to the best and trying to eliminate the worst in the process of evolution; that we were doing a better job for the common man than [you] were; that we were holding on to those freedoms which we cherished and at the same time we were trying to bring about greater distribution of wealth and greater equality of opportunity, economically and socially, for the underprivileged."

Davies then gave Stalin and Molotov a concrete example. He asked them, "How much of all of Mrs. Davies's property do you think will go to the state and how much to her children and to her heirs?"

Before he answered his own question, Davies noted that Stalin came to life and manifested great interest. "More than 80 percent will go to the federal and state governments and less than one-fifth of her property will go to her children; that in my own case more than 50 percent would go to the state and less than 50 percent to my children."

Davies then asked Stalin, "How much do you suppose I pay to the government in income taxes alone every year, even including my salary as a government official—more than 60 percent, whereas Mrs. Davies pays more than 72 percent."

Davies noted that Stalin registered surprise and that he then "looked at Molotov with a smile and Molotov nodded."[6]

Stalin liked such simple-mindedness. It fit the Marxist textbook example of a capitalist. It confirmed his view of the world and, specifically, his perception of the United States and President Roosevelt. To appeal to the Americans, to make certain that they would continue the diplomatic relationship, he had to appeal to their greed. If Davies represented the top of the capitalist plutocracy, Stalin could feel certain that he could manage the Americans. Greed and an easy life clouded the judgment and common sense of such leaders. They were nothing compared with Trotsky and his ilk.

In the course of the conversation, which Davies termed "an intellectual feast," Stalin sought to dampen the imperialist ambition of the United States toward the Soviet Union, which he took as a given. He hammered home to Davies that there was nothing that the United States has that the Soviets could take and that there was nothing that they had that the United States would want to take, and so it was "just impossible that there would at any time ever be an armed clash between the two countries." Stalin was always alert to prevent the possibility of a capitalist coalition from being organized against Communist Russia.

Stalin also appealed to Davies's vanity and colossal ego in the hope that his kind of reporting on Soviet successes and Stalin's brilliant leadership would continue not only from Davies in his new post but also from the mouth and pen of Davies's successor. Stalin told Davies that he probably knew more about Soviet industrial developments "than any foreigner and probably as much as anyone in the Soviet Union." Davies was truly moved. He wrote his daughter that the Soviets "have been impressed with the objectivity of my viewpoint and the effort which I made to get the facts and base my conclusions on personal knowledge. They also have been impressed by my honesty." Davies said that the Soviets were telling everyone that they liked him. He reported to his daughter that a British socialite friend told him that the Soviet ambassador to England remarked, "We like Davies. He disagrees with us, but we believe him to be an honest man."[7]

Unlike Bullitt, who came to see Stalin as an enemy of the United States and a brooding, suspicious dictator who would kill or imprison any real or imagined opponent, Davies found Stalin to be a modern-day Marcus Aurelius—wise, thoughtful, kind, but pressed by conditions to act forcefully. When Stalin walked into Molotov's apartment through the very same door that Davies had used only moments before, Davies was awash with pride at having been singled out by Stalin for such an honor. Davies confided to his daughter that it was virtually "a historical event when he receives any foreigner."[8]

Davies said that Stalin greeted him "cordially with a smile and with great simplicity, but also with real dignity." Like Bullitt, Davies found him to be shorter than he had anticipated and "slight in appearance." He also thought he carried himself with "the sagginess of an old man," a view with which Bohlen concurred when he saw Stalin at a meeting of the Supreme Soviet in January 1938.[9] Davies's impression of Stalin's personality and demeanor, however, was a mirror image of the picture that Bullitt, Kennan, Henderson, and Bohlen had painted. He found that Stalin's "demeanor is kindly, his manner almost deprecatingly simple; his personality and expression of reserve strength and poise very marked." In general, he "gives the impression of a strong mind which is composed and wise. His brown eye is exceedingly kindly and gentle. A child would like to sit in his lap and a dog would sidle up to him. It is difficult to associate his personality and this impression of kindness and gentle simplicity with what has occurred here in connection with these purges and shootings of the Red Army generals, and so forth."[10]

Davies's image of Stalin was a far cry from the "wiry Gipsy" whom Bullitt had described. It was matched by an even more favorable view of life in the Soviet Union under Stalin. In many ways, Davies was unbelievable, even for

Stalin, but the Soviet leader was not one to look a gift apologist in the mouth. He was everything Stalin wanted in a foreign representative short of being an actual spy. He was also the perfect person from FDR's point of view. It is unfair to say that Davies was not concerned about reality, morality, or facts, but his romanticism and desire to please Roosevelt colored his outlook and interpretation of Stalin and the Soviet Union. Appearance was important to him. He was a dandy, a pompous showman who paraded as an expert on the Soviet Union and as a deep thinker who saw a direct parallel between Roosevelt's and Stalin's policies. A Rooseveltian through and through, he determined early on that all excesses and peculiarities in Stalin's Russia had to be excused because of the higher good of the Soviet Union's evolution toward democracy. He treated the American specialists on Soviet Russia as boys who played silly games of sleuthing, secrecy, and intrigue. He wanted to be wide open, to hide nothing from Stalin in order to show him that the United States was a friend and not an enemy. He did all of this to please Roosevelt, to give the president the kind of reports that he wanted. As historian Keith Eubanks said of Davies, "Eager to be loyal to Roosevelt, Davies often wrote reports that were misleading and biased."[11]

The son of an immigrant wagon-maker, Joseph Davies was born on November 29, 1876, in Watertown, Wisconsin. His father was an alcoholic Welshman who died when Joseph was ten, and his mother was a parsimonious, gentle minister of the Welsh Congregational Church. But the major influence in his youth was a wealthy paternal uncle who instilled in him the importance of industriousness and hard work.[12] He supported himself as a student instructor in gymnastics and graduated cum laude with a bachelor of arts degree from the University of Wisconsin in 1898. He received a law degree from the same university three years later. In 1901 he opened a law practice in Watertown, and in 1902 he married Emlen Knight, the daughter of a wealthy lumberman in Watertown. Davies's law practice did quite well, and before long he was on his way to realizing the American dream.

If there were a pivotal event in his life, it was undoubtedly his personal experience of seeing hard work, education, and the right social circle pay off. It made him a firm believer in the validity of democratic capitalism. In his mind there was nothing better than the American market system which rewarded hard work, education, and talent, regardless of status. Although his view was the product of personal experience, he tended to universalize it. Ultimately, it became his Weltanschauung, which even his time in Moscow could not shake. He told every Soviet official that while he appreciated the Soviet goal of trying to help the common man, the American method of distributing wealth and opening opportunities for the poor was vastly superior to the Soviet method. According to MacLean, he portrayed himself as "a liberal left of center, but committed wholeheartedly to the free enterprise system."[13]

By the time Davies was thirty-five, he was a rich man, and his interest increasingly turned to politics. He was ready to break in with the East Coast blue bloods. In 1912 he was elected to the Democratic National Committee and soon found himself fully engaged as chairman of Woodrow Wilson's presidential campaign in the western United States. When Wilson won, he joined Franklin D. Roosevelt in Washington as one of "Wilson's Young Men." He attended the right church, too: the Congregationalist Church.

Wilson appointed Davies commissioner of corporations in 1913 and then chairman of the Federal Trade Commission in 1915, a position which he held until his resignation in 1918. During the war he was also an ex officio member of the War Industries Board and served as Wilson's economic advisor at Versailles. Roosevelt, of course, was named assistant secretary of the navy, a position which he held from 1913 to 1919.

Davies and Roosevelt became fast friends. They were also neighbors and frequently played golf together. Davies reported that he was quite impressed with Roosevelt and that he and many of the Wilsonian Democrats viewed him as "the future great progressive liberal" who would lead the Democratic Party.

After Davies left the Wilson administration, he unsuccessfully ran for a Senate seat from Wisconsin. He then set up a law office in Washington, D.C., to represent banks and corporations, especially Standard Oil, before the Federal Trade Commission, the Interstate Commerce Commission, and the Court of Claims. In his most famous case he beat the U.S. Treasury Department in its $30 million suit against former Ford Motor Company stockholders and collected an unheard fee of $2 million for his efforts. He also served as counsel for the governments of Mexico, the Netherlands, Greece, Peru, and the Dominican Republic. His defense of Rafael Trujillo Molina, the Dominican dictator, as a New Dealer who needed more time to repay American bondholders earned him a scaled down fee of $300,000 and the suspicion of some State Department experts. He dramatically increased his fortune in the 1920s, but then lost 60 percent of it when the stock market crashed in 1929.[14]

When Roosevelt won the election in 1932, Davies was offered a position in the government, but he turned it down because he was determined to regain his fortune before taking up government service again. His wealth was restored by 1935, and he then made a move that forever guaranteed his economic security. He met Marjorie Merriweather Post, heiress to the General Foods fortune, wife of E. F. Hutton, the chairman of the board of General Foods, and according to the *New York Times* of December 16, 1935, one of the twenty-three richest women in the United States. They fell passionately in love, carried on a torrid affair, and divorced their spouses in September 1935. Davies shocked his wife of thirty-three years and Washington society with his divorce, but he did provide her with a generous settlement. In December the marriage of Davies and Marjorie Post became one of the social events of the year on the East Coast. She celebrated by decorating her sixty-two-room apartment in New York with one thousand chrysanthemums that were dyed pink to match her dress and the icing on a three-hundred-pound wedding cake that was topped with a "temple of love" nestled in doves and sugar roses. She also became a director of the board of General Foods Corporation, and shortly thereafter her erstwhile husband, E. F. Hutton, quietly resigned.[15]

Even though Davies had turned Roosevelt down in 1932, he remained active in Democratic politics. He contributed to various campaigns and served as vice chairman of the Democratic National Committee in 1936. He also made speeches for Roosevelt during the reelection campaign. He was now ready to take up government service, and Marjorie decided to help his career along with a huge contribution ranging from $17,500 to $100,000 to FDR's campaign treasury in 1936.[16]

In many ways Davies and Roosevelt were very much alike. Both held firm convictions about the benevolence of government, even though in their minds they were still advocates of capitalism. They had been rewarded by government, particularly Davies, and now in the wake of the Great Depression they were convinced that "progress" in the evolution of democratic capitalism demanded a more active role for government. Neither was brilliant or incisive, but they did understand politics in a democracy. They knew the importance of perception and thus of good publicity, and they cultivated the mass media. They generally avoided intellectuals, mistrusted experts, and really had no overall plan of action than to respond to the needs of the moment. Of course, they both shared a belief in the inevitability of democracy as a worldwide movement, a sort of simple faith that provided them and many other Americans with a certain benign arrogance. This view supported in both Roosevelt and Davies a certain nonchalance, even gullibility, regarding foreign affairs. For them, American foreign policy was simple: support democracies or embryonic democracies, that is, states that appeared to be evolving toward democracy even if they were currently ruthless dictatorships, and oppose imperialist or incipient imperialist states even if they contained democratic or representative institutions. Davies, especially, was suspicious of Europeans and Old World values.[17]

With Bullitt's resignation in one hand and Marjorie Davies's generous campaign contribution in the other hand, Roosevelt decided in late August 1936 to offer the ambassadorship in Moscow to Davies. With his fortune restored and he and his new wife anxious to go abroad, Davies was thrilled to enter diplomatic service, but he and Marjorie had hoped that their gift would buy them a post better than Moscow. FDR explained that Paris, Berlin, and London were all taken, but that Moscow would only be temporary until a more desirable place could be found.[18] "Please know, my dear 'Boss,'" Davies obsequiously wrote FDR a few months after accepting the post, "that I am deeply grateful to you for the privilege which you are giving me of being identified with your great administration. It means more to me than I can tell you and I shall always remember it."[19] The appointment was officially announced on November 21, 1936.

The announcement was a surprise to many observers because Davies had no background in Soviet Russia or in the foreign service. The Moscow post was crucial, and some foreign policy experts thought that Roosevelt would not include the Soviet Union on the list of ambassadorships that were available for political patronage.

Bullitt, for example, immediately informed Roosevelt of his opposition to the appointment.[20] The embassy staff objected, too, according to George Kennan, and considered resigning in a body to protest the nomination.[21] Roosevelt, in Kennan's mind, had sinned grievously for treating the Moscow post as "only another political plum."[22] The *Washington Post* objected that "Roosevelt has not seen fit . . . to appoint as Ambassador to Russia a man professionally qualified for that important and arduous post by long years of training and experience in the American Foreign Service."

But all protests were in vain. FDR told Bullitt that he knew Davies was not qualified for the Russian post but that Marjorie Merriweather Post Davies had donated to the reelection campaign, and she wished to be an ambassador's wife. Besides, Roosevelt informed Bullitt, Davies was a loyal supporter and was one of the "Roosevelt-before-Chicago" group whom FDR wanted to reward. The *Washington Post* added that Davies had promised a diplomatic post to Marjorie as a wedding present, and some newspapers even carried the appointment on the society page.[23]

Roosevelt, though, was not being entirely candid with Bullitt. He chose Davies for reasons other than money and friendship. Davies, as mentioned, agreed with the president's firm conviction that the United States and the Soviet Union shared a fundamental principle, namely, that each country was attempting to improve the lot of the common man, albeit by different methods. The best approach for American policy toward the Soviet Union in light of this belief in shared values was uncritical friendship that would prove to the Soviet leadership that the United States was not an enemy but a kindred spirit. From both the president's and Davies's point of view, this stand was in America's best interest. It would encourage the Soviets to open up and would assist the very process of evolution toward a type of state capitalism that both Roosevelt and Davies believed was the future of the United States and the Soviet Union.

Davies thought that the Soviets were essentially Russian-speaking Americans who were quickly developing into democratic capitalists. This was his view when he arrived in Moscow, and it was still his opinion when he departed in June 1938. This outlook coincided with FDR's own predisposition about the Soviet Union and his belief that the quid pro quo approach of Bullitt was counterproductive. What better man for the Moscow post than a friend whose money could take the sting out of Moscow's dullness and whose faith in progressive liberalism would insulate him against criticism à la Bullitt?

Roosevelt and Davies also agreed that Moscow could help maintain peace in Europe. The growing crisis in Europe in 1936 and 1937, which saw Hitler increase his threats to peace in direct proportion to English and French appeasement of those threats, persuaded them that a stronger American-Soviet nexus would help stabilize a world drifting toward war. Davies was to be midwife to that new relationship. He also assumed that he would be the president's chief European troubleshooter.[24]

Before Davies departed for Moscow, Roosevelt and Sumner Welles, the new undersecretary of state, briefed him on his role. He was to try to end the strained atmosphere that had developed during Bullitt's tenure. His official attitude, according to FDR, was "to be one of dignified friendliness." Second, he was to attempt to settle the debt question according to the formula worked out at the time of the Roosevelt-Litvinov agreement. He was not to be hard or threatening but, rather, he was to take the approach that the president and the secretary of state were deeply disappointed in the failure of the Kremlin to live up to the agreement and that it was now a problem for the Kremlin. Third, he was to negotiate a trade agreement that would allow the Soviet Union to make purchases in the United States. Fourth, he was to evaluate the military and economic strengths and weaknesses of the Soviet Union. Finally, he was to ascertain the Soviet position toward Hitler and its policy in the event of a European war.[25] Marjorie Davies only became enthusiastic over the Moscow post, according to her daughter, when it became clear that FDR wanted the couple to "befriend" the Russians. "Mother loved to entertain," and in Moscow "this was part of her job. She thought she'd died and gone to heaven."[26]

Ambassador Alexander Troyanovsky and his new assistant, Constantine Oumansky, also advised Davies. They hosted a lunch for him at the Soviet embassy just before he left Washington. They impressed upon the new ambassador that the "best opportunity for the development of friendly relations" was to "let bygones be bygones." Oumansky stressed that Foreign Minister Litvinov thought that the conduct of Davies "should be addressed to future relations and not to past controversial matters." At the same time, the Soviet government informed Henderson, who was still first secretary of the American embassy in Moscow, that "any irritations which may have arisen during the past three years are to be forgotten and a new book in the relations between the embassy and the Soviet Government is to be opened." It further stressed that it preferred an envoy "with a feeling of antagonism" to one "so full of sentimental friendliness" that expectations were unrealistic. In a clear reference to Bullitt, the Kremlin summed up that ambassadors "who have come to the Soviet Union with an attitude of sentimental friendliness have in the end become embittered when they have discovered that such an attitude is embarrassing to the Soviet authorities who can not afford to treat them in a manner markedly different from the manner in which it treats other Chiefs of Mission." Davies was being warned not to imitate Bullitt. It was an unnecessary warning, for Davies had no intention of copying Bullitt.[27]

Litvinov was relieved over the Davies appointment and the new ambassador's reputed ignorance of Soviet Russia. He noted in his journal the following evaluation: "I am glad that Washington has decided to send us Davies. Troyanovsky has supplied a full account of his talk with Davies at a lunch at our Embassy. . . . He affirms that Davies understands nothing about our affairs but that he is full of the most sincere desire to work with us in complete co-operation and to carry out strictly Roosevelt's instructions."[28] Oumansky, for his part, communicated to the Soviet Foreign Ministry that "Davies had been treated poorly by the press, owing, principally, to the nouveau riche ways and manners of his wife and to cheap and noisy publicity connected to 'their' appointment." He added in a note to Litvinov that many of Davies's friends called the appointment "historical" and "evidence of Roosevelt's determination to build a political relationship with the USSR."[29]

Davies inherited many of the people who had worked for Bullitt, including Loy Henderson, George Kennan, and Elbridge Durbrow. Alexander Kirk, a very competent foreign service officer who quickly adopted the Bullitt outlook, was also added and eventually took Henderson's place as chargé d'affaires. The Soviet Foreign Ministry's profile on Kirk was that he was prudent, intelligent, cultured, and multilingual.[30] Bohlen, who had been moved back to the East European Division in the State Department in Washington, changed places with Kennan in the summer of 1937, although he did not reach Moscow until late in the fall. All of these men eventually became ambassadors in their own right, and Kennan and Bohlen were ambassadors to the Soviet Union. They were intelligent, experienced, and professional, but each of them had come to the conclusion that the American policy toward the Kremlin in 1937 was too trusting, too optimistic, and too naive. They favored a policy that was balanced, tough, morally objective, reciprocal, and mutually beneficial.

The three dominant figures—Kennan, Bohlen, and Henderson—had come to the conclusion that Moscow was expansionist, suspicious of the United States by nature, and distrustful of the American policy of friendship, which it interpreted as a sign of duplicity. They believed that Moscow was xenophobic and expansionist because of its history and its immediate fear and suspicion of the capitalist states. In naming the chief motivation in Soviet foreign policy, Henderson gave primacy to ideology, whereas Bohlen and Kennan assigned prominence to deep-seated insecurity and a desire to control the home base, but they all agreed that the Rooseveltian belief about the future direction of the Soviet Union was unproven. From their point of view, the Soviet Union was not an evolving democratic state but a totalitarian empire that was attempting to modernize in order to squelch democratic countries like the United States, which Moscow saw as a threat. "The Kremlin," Bohlen stated in a cable on November 25, 1938, "does not envisage cordial relations with the capitalist governments on any permanent basis but rather as a temporary expedient dictated by the more immediate objectives of Soviet policy."[31] Bohlen stressed that the only workable approach for the Americans to adopt toward the Kremlin was one that was based on self-interest. Policies of friendship that were not based on shared principles would have no effect.

The outlook of the embassy staff members probably explains why Davies did not take advantage of their expertise. Additionally, of course, they knew much more about Soviet affairs than he did, and that fact may have grated on Davies's ego. He wanted to be in charge, and he felt confident that he knew where the Soviet Union was going. The major exception to the tough approach among the staff members was the military attaché, Lt. Colonel Faymonville, who adopted a friendly and trusting attitude toward the Kremlin. The other staff members considered Faymonville to be naive and untrustworthy, but Davies regarded him as his main ally in the pursuit of the policy of uncritical friendship. Davies and Faymonville saw collectivization as positive and the purges as necessary. When Faymonville's tour of duty was completed at the end of 1937, Davies successfully prevailed on the army to prolong his assignment because his departure would be an "irreparable loss" to the embassy.[32]

The departure of Kennan, on the other hand, in the opinion of Davies, would be a major plus for the embassy. Davies decided to remove Kennan shortly after he arrived in Moscow. He recommended in the spring of 1937 that Kennan, the leader of the putative anti-Stalin group in the embassy, be transferred. In a note to the State Department he praised Kennan's efforts, but he argued that he had been in Moscow "too long for his own good" and that he needed a break for reasons of health.[33] Kennan, unaware of Davies's recommendation, was soon removed and given Bohlen's job as the resident Russian expert in the State Department, and Bohlen was given Kennan's job in Moscow.

Immediately after Davies dumped Kennan, Roosevelt purged the anti-Stalin clique at the State Department.[34] Robert Kelley, the head of the East European Division, was sent to Turkey as a first secretary and his division was absorbed into a new European Division under J. Pierrepont Moffat. Bohlen, who was part of the clique, saved some of the East European Division's reference books, but most of its library was banished to "anonymity in the Library of Congress." Foreign Minister Litvinov believed that the division had better records on Soviet foreign policy than Moscow itself.[35] FDR also put in Sumner Welles as undersecretary of state, according to Bennett, because Hull, although supportive of the policy of friendly relations with Moscow, was generally too cautious and less optimistic about Soviet Russia. In effect, according to Robert Conquest, Roosevelt brought "the well-informed Soviet experts" of the State Department's "Eastern division under the control of the ignorant or pro-Stalin European division." That conclusion is an exaggeration. It is obviously true that the anti-Stalin East European Division in the State Department was dismantled as an institution. However, the new leader of the European Division, J. Pierrepont Moffat, was, unbeknownst to Roosevelt, almost as suspicious of the Soviets as Kelley. In addition, the chief political counselor on European affairs, James Clement Dunn, was critical of Moscow, and he made sure Hull's authority was not undermined.[36] And, of course, the leading Russian authorities—Bohlen, Kennan, and Henderson—were still involved in American-Soviet relations. Welles, too, was no apologist for the Soviet Union. He openly supported FDR's policy, but he was not a believer in the theory of convergence. He was a backer of democracy, to be sure, but above all he was a man of principle who refused to look at Stalin through rose-colored glasses.

Nonetheless, Roosevelt did try to purge and isolate the State Department's experts on Soviet Russia. His motivation has been the source of much debate.[37] It is difficult to say with precision why he did it, because he left no record. However, the purge was certainly tied to his belief that the department was incorrigibly anti-Stalin and the times called for an improved American-Soviet relationship. Nazism was the problem, not Communism. FDR wrote Undersecretary of State William Phillips on February 6, 1937, that "every week changes the picture and the basis for it all lies, I think, not in Communism or the fear of Communism but in Germany and fear of what the present German leaders are meeting for or being drawn toward."[38] Davies, of course, would have additionally been pushing to remove the anti-Soviet group at the State Department.[39]

Roosevelt also had an innate mistrust of diplomats and experts, preferring to trust his own common sense, intuition, and worldview. Demolishing the beehive of American expertise on Russia might give him a clean slate from which he could manage the relationship with Moscow either personally or through hand-picked ambassadors or special representatives. It might also have been related to domestic politics. Wilson never trusted the State Department because he thought it was a Republican stronghold. Perhaps Roosevelt continued that Democratic bias. Kennan suspected that there was Soviet influence involved in the changes because they so adversely affected American interests. The Soviets certainly wanted the State Department purged of its Russian experts, but Litvinov thought in July 1938 that it still had an anti-Soviet bias. He stressed to Henderson, who was actually departing Moscow to take up a position in the State Department, that "although the President of the United States was a great liberal and was anxious to further the cause of democracy and liberalism throughout the world, reactionaries in the State Department tried so to distort the policies laid down by the President as to give them an anti-Soviet and, sometimes, a pro-fascist bias."[40]

5

"The System Is Now a Type of Capitalistic State Socialism"

The new ambassador, his wife, and his daughter from his first marriage arrived in Moscow on January 19, 1937, in the dead of winter. Davies adopted a positive attitude from the beginning. He complimented everyone and everything. He found the lumbering Soviet trains to be efficient and the peasants to be like the friendly, sturdy farmers one found "in rural frontier districts of the United States." He was very impressed by the concluding session of the Constitution Congress on January 21, by what he described as its democratic deliberations and above all by the singing of the Communist national anthem which, for Davies, "was really a moving thing and left an impression of power and earnestness."[1] The Congress, he wrote Colonel House, "gave one some insight into the democratic professions of aspiration and effort of the Russian people." He drew parallels between the United States and the Soviet Union, seeing in the latter an agrarian United States, a nineteenth-century America just beginning its industrial revolution and struggling to give meaning to its democratic inspirations. Davies also found Spaso House to be an agreeable surprise. After six days in Moscow, he wrote a close friend, Roy Van Bomel, that the position of ambassador "promises to be an interesting experience and well worthwhile."[2]

The Davies family, however, did import part of their own food supply from General Foods Corporation. The Russians were mildly insulted that Davies brought in 2,000 pints of Birds Eye cream because of his fondness for ice cream, but the *New York Times* adopted a sympathetic position, pointing out that although there were cows in Russia, there was "nothing like so many cows as there were up to a half a dozen years before Stalin began to collectivize."[3] Unfortunately, the cream spoiled due to power failures caused by the twelve freezers that the ambassador installed in the basement of Spaso House, an early indication that he was out of touch with Russian realities.

Wishing to distance himself from Bullitt's acrimony, Davies stressed when he presented his credentials to Kalinin that he was not a professional diplomat and that he viewed the USSR "with an open mind." Kalinin replied that was good news because "too often professional diplomats were so steeped in prejudice and 'superiority' that their observations, if honest, were not accurate." What the Soviets wanted, Kalinin went on, "was an objective appraisal of what they were doing." They thought the new ambassador's training "as a lawyer and a capitalist would assure a fair report." Davies recorded in his diary that the Soviets preferred a capitalist rather than "the overzealousness of people who were too friendly in their approach and who frequently thereafter cooled off equally suddenly and were equally violent in unfair condemnation."[4] Bullitt was obviously the convenient scapegoat for why American-Soviet relations had floundered to date. In fact, Davies made it a hallmark of his tenure to follow a policy that was exactly opposite that of Bullitt's ambassadorship. He also painted an image of Stalin's Russia that Bullitt, Kennan, Henderson, Bohlen, and the other American experts on Russia strongly objected to in virtually every aspect.

It is not surprising then that Davies and the Soviet experts in the embassy did not get along. The experts did not respect the ambassador, and he had no use for their anti-Stalin disposition, despite their knowledge. Because of his predisposition against them, Davies came to rely upon Faymonville, the shortwave radio, the *Times* of London, and the foreign press reporters, especially the American correspondents, for information and advice.[5] His main companions, besides Faymonville, were Walter Duranty and Harold Denny of the *New York Times*, who were notoriously pro-Stalin, Joseph Barnes and Joseph Phillips of the New York *Herald Tribune*, Charles Nutter and Richard Massock of the Associated Press, Norman Deuel and Henry Shapiro of the United Press, James Brown of the International News, and Spencer Williams of the Manchester *Guardian*.[6] Kennan bitterly criticized Davies for relying on newsmen rather than the diplomatic experts, revealing, for example, that at the purge trials Davies sent him off for refreshments while he exchanged views with the press corps. Bohlen added that Davies and his wife treated the staff as hired help and rarely listened to their opinions. But even among members of the press, according to Bohlen, Davies was often out of his depth. He recalled an occasion when Davies asked Alfred Chollerton of the *Daily Telegraph* his opinion of the purge trials. The reporter sardonically replied, "Mr. Ambassador, I believe everything but the facts." According to Bohlen, Davies was oblivious to Chollerton's sarcasm.[7]

To be sure, Davies had another reason for embracing the newspapermen. He was competing for Roosevelt's attention and approval, especially against other notables like Joseph Kennedy in London and William Bullitt in Paris. He wanted good press coverage in the United States, and he got it by deliberately cultivating the American correspondents. His constant companion on the ship carrying him across the ocean to Europe was none other than Walter Duranty, Stalin's chief apologist among western correspondents, whom Davies described as a fount of Russian information. In Moscow, his chief adviser was Faymonville, whom the ambassador described as "one of our best sources of accurate information."[8]

Davies's treatment of the professional staff earned him their enduring re-sentiment and dislike. Bohlen's opinion of Davies was that he was "sublimely ignorant of even the most elementary realities of the Soviet system and of its ideology" and that "he was determined, possibly with Bullitt's failure in mind, to maintain a Pollyanna attitude." Elbridge Durbrow said, "I never worked with a more mentally dishonest man than Joe Davies."[9]

Davies simply refused to criticize, challenge, or confront the Kremlin. He actually seemed to adopt the position that Stalin's Russia was his client, and his obligation was to defend it, regardless of guilt. Rooseveltism could allow Davies to defend Stalin and concomitantly think that he was serving the interest of the United States. The ambassador's approach was epitomized by an episode that he described shortly after arriving in the Soviet Union. The embassy electrician uncovered a Soviet microphone hidden in the attic over Davies's desk. Staff members were outraged, but Davies dismissed their complaints with a patronizing sarcasm. "The youngsters," he wrote in his diary, "were all 'het up' over a possible diplomatic adventure. I cooled them off and 'kidded' them about their 'international sleuthing.' . . . My position was if the Soviets had a dictaphone installed so much the better—the sooner they would find that we were friends, not enemies."[10]

Similarly, when the British ambassador tried to have the foreign diplomatic community issue a joint complaint to the Soviet Foreign Ministry over the shabby treatment meted out to departing diplomats (mainly inconvenient searches and tax assessments by custom officials), Davies refused to get involved. He explained to Secretary of State Hull that he did not want the Soviets to think that there was a "'ganging up' of the representatives of capitalist nations against the Soviet Union." Besides, he maintained, the diplomatic corps was anti-Soviet.[11] He held this view despite the fact that American envoys and officials were subjected to, in the view of the State Department, "particularly obnoxious and unpleasant" searches and intrusions. Bullitt for one was so outraged over the way the Soviet custom inspectors treated him when he departed that he directed a note of protest to the Commissariat of Foreign Affairs. Two months after he left Moscow the Commissariat answered by publishing "rules" for departing diplomats, which it said had been established on February 16, 1933. The "rules" stated that all diplomats, including the ambassadors, unlike any other post in the world, had to submit to searches.[12]

When it came to the secret police, Davies thought of them as protectors for the diplomats. He said that he created "a sort of comradeship" with his surveillance team.[13] He was not disturbed by the constant surveillance of him and his staff or by the resulting isolation of the embassy both from the general Soviet population and from the Soviet government itself. Both Henderson and Kennan, however, found the secret police to be persecutors of the foreign diplomats. They found Stalin's antiforeign campaign to be menacing, the isolation of the embassy to be total, the xenophobia of the government and people to be ubiquitous, and the ideological attacks on capitalism to be incessant and inbred. Kennan noted that it was a mark of honor and heroism for a Soviet official to rebuff envoys from capitalist states and that all foreign representatives were treated as "accredited spies."[14]

Davies was also undisturbed by the welter of problems that had so exercised and infuriated Bullitt, including the purge trails, the Comintern, the debt issue, currency conversion, and the Soviet refusal to provide land for a new embassy. Davies's approach was to remain warmly aloof, to place the most optimistic interpretation possible on perplexing developments, and to drift along and react to Soviet indifference, arrogance, and hostility with a type of avuncular tolerance.

On the issue of the debt problem, which the Soviet government evidently thought was an irritant in American-Soviet relations, Davies was dismissive. The Soviets brought the issue up shortly after Davies arrived, and Davies informed them that it was a Soviet problem. He told them that he had "no expressed instructions from my government to initiate any debt discussions or to project any plan." He informed them, further, that "the attitude of my government was that it was up to the Soviet government in view of the commitments made; that the problem was in their lap; that my disposition was friendly; that I was here and available for use by them if they saw fit to take the matter up."[15]

This approach, which Roosevelt encouraged, was rather disingenuous. The Americans clearly thought the debt issue was important, and the Soviets thought that the debt issue was critical to the Americans, but then Davies informed the Soviets that the issue was more important to the Soviets than it was to the Americans. The Soviets presumably were puzzled by Davies's tact, but they did not broach the subject again until Davies was ready to leave Moscow, and then Stalin told him that the USSR would retire the debt with one total payment of $50 million if the United States would first loan the Soviet Union $200 million. Davies concluded that the key for resolving the debt problem was finally revealed: what was needed was a banker who would make a loan to the Soviet Union.[16]

On the matter of Communism as a working system, Davies was ambivalent. He admired the Soviet industrial development. He told Stalin that the Soviet Union's industrial achievement was unparalleled and that "history would record Stalin . . . as a greater builder than Peter the Great, or Catherine" because he was building "for the practical benefit of the common man." He also thought that the new industrial base could "support a long war." Furthermore, he was very impressed with collectivization and recorded in his diary that he had heard that in some parts of Russia the new farming system was producing "millionaire farmers."[17]

On the other hand, Davies faulted the huge bureaucracy and waste of the Soviet system. He also concluded that the price of industrialization and collectivization was too high in human terms. He modified this criticism, though, by implying that any deaths were the result of a clash between a modernizing government and a recalcitrant peasantry, a view that Lt. Colonel Faymonville also held.[18] Davies was abysmally ignorant of the famine and terror that reigned in the countryside, but he also refused to brook any criticism or objective analysis of Stalin's government from his staff members who knew what was going on in the Soviet Union. Some western journalists supported Davies's idyllic view and deliberately portrayed a false image of Stalin's Russia in the United States.[19]

Davies was also convinced that religious persecution, one of the hallmarks of Communism in the eyes of Americans, was exaggerated and was, at any rate, declining. He reported in March 1937 that the new "Stalin" constitution provided for freedom of "religious worship and antireligious propaganda" and that he had heard that membership in the League of Militant Atheists was dropping. In addition, he understood that Stalin served as a buffer against antireligious extremists.[20] In fact, religious persecution was reaching a crescendo.

The ambassador also believed that Communism would not produce a new Soviet citizen, that nationalism was rearing its head, but he assumed that the only significant national force was Russian nationalism. He knew there were other nationalities in the Soviet empire, but he thought of them as quaint variations of the Russians. Generally, he thought of everyone as a Russian and referred to the Ukrainian city of Kiev as "the most interesting Russian city I have seen."[21]

True to his faith in capitalism, Davies thought Communism would not last, that self-interest would win out over egalitarianism. He argued that by 1937 wage differentials and the profit motive were already appearing throughout the system. He also provided what was unquestionably part of the real explanation for why the Soviet Union was still able, despite its uncompetitive and inefficient system, to achieve impressive industrial goals: it was an enormously wealthy country that was willingly to waste its wealth to maintain Communism.[22]

The experience of living in the Soviet Union did not dampen his belief that Stalin's Russia was on the path to capitalism. In April 1938 he wrote to Steve Early, Roosevelt's press secretary, that the Soviet Union "is in the position of economic development, in my opinion, that corresponds with the situation that the United States was in sixty years ago and the possibilities here are enormous." The forces of capitalism, he went on, are awesome and "it doesn't make any difference who is in the Government, these forces will not be denied. This Government is not communism. It is socialism. And this socialism has been modified and is being compelled to accede more and more to the methods of capitalism and individualism to make the machine work."[23]

In a telegram to Secretary Hull on April 1, 1938, he reiterated his point: "Many fine things are being done under the present regime. Many noble enterprises have been projected which arouse sympathy and inspire intense admiration. . . . This country's present position, economically and industrially, appears to me to be now at a point of development where the United States was about sixty years ago. . . . Great forces exist here and still greater forces are here in the making." Again in June 1938 he told Hull that "Communism will fail here" because "human nature cannot be changed in two generations. The system is now a type of capitalistic state socialism." Furthermore, he emphasized, even though the Soviet Union is a dictatorship, "the fact of dictatorship is apologized for here. It is justified on the ground that it is a realistic expedient, resorted to only to protect the masses of the people, until they can themselves rule under a system where ideologically the individual and not the state shall be supreme." Indeed, Davies also thought that Stalin was the closet democrat among the Soviet leaders. He was the one, Davies told Hull, who insisted that "secret and universal suffrage" be included in the 1936 Constitution. And even though the purges had placed a cloud over the government, Davies stated, they had not been attributed to Stalin. All the citizens liked and respected him. He was "a clean-living, modest, retiring, single-purpose man" who was "fast becoming, along with Lenin, the 'superman' ideal of the masses."[24]

Davies was also impressed with Stalin's subordinates. He found Voroshilov to be a "man of intellectual power that grasps the elementals of a situation that sweeps the nonessentials aside." Andrei Vyshinsky, the chief prosecutor at the purge trials, was compared to Homer Cummings, the American attorney general and a close friend of Davies. Davies described Vyshinsky as "calm, dispassionate, intellectual, and able and wise" who "conducted the treason trial in a manner that won my respect and admiration as a lawyer." Anastas Mikoyan, a member of the Politburo and an Armenian whom Davies misidentified as a Georgian, was described as "swarthy, prominent nose, high cheekbones, strong chin, and quick as a rapier." Molotov was depicted as "an exceptional man with great mental capacity and wisdom."[25]

Henderson, Kennan, and Bohlen had a completely different view than Davies and Faymonville of Stalin's subordinates and the likelihood of democracy or capitalism emerging in the Soviet Union. Henderson called Soviet elections "a gigantic dumbshow," and Bohlen referred to them as "a farce." They found Stalin's Russia to be a brutal, aggressive totalitarian dictatorship wrapped in propaganda myths of democracy, peace, and proletarian brotherhood. They saw Stalin surrounded by toadies and chanters who had to be told by Stalin when to stop singing his praises. Bohlen described the meetings of the Supreme Soviet as burlesque. At one such meeting in January 1938, Bohlen recalled that Stalin sat onstage looking bored while the assembly hailed him until Stalin, "with an impatient gesture of his hand, signalled to the presiding officer to cut short the demonstration in his honor." Throughout the proceedings, Bohlen reported, Stalin's subordinates tried to sit near him. Andrei Zhdanov, who took Kirov's place as Leningrad Party secretary, was Stalin's new favorite for "the moment," so he sat closest to Stalin. Voroshilov, who was trying to get closer, kept "changing his seat to be near him" and "to engage him in conversation." Nikita Khrushchev, the Ukrainian Party secretary and a coming attraction in Stalin's charade, was also trying to get near Stalin, but, according to Bohlen, he was "less obviously 'boot-licking' than Voroshilov." Finally, Kaganovich and Molotov did not sit far from Stalin, although Kaganovich sat by himself and rarely spoke and Molotov preoccupied himself with speech writing.[26]

On the problem of the purge trials, Davies and Faymonville held a unique position. Most independent observers, inside and outside the Soviet Union, believed that the purge trials were judicial shams and a source of weakness for the Soviet Union. Ambassador Davies and Lt. Colonel Faymonville, however, argued that the purge trials were fair and just, and later they actually maintained that they strengthened the Soviet Union by removing "fifth columnists" or "traitors."[27]

The Trotsky-Radek trial was concluding when Davies arrived, and he attended the final sessions of what was a watershed in the massive purge that Stalin launched following the death of Sergei Kirov in 1934. The accused all pleaded guilty (except Trotsky, of course, who was in exile and was tried in absentia for espionage, sabotage, and terrorist activities), although very little evidence was offered. Davies wrote Hull that "viewed objectively . . . and based upon my experience in the trial of cases and the application of the tests of credibility which past experience had afforded me, I arrived at the reluctant conclusion that the state had established its case, at least to the extent of proving the existence of a widespread conspiracy and plot among the political leaders against the Soviet government, and which under their statutes established the crimes set forth in the indictment." Davies then went on to say that "assuming . . . that basically human nature is much the same everywhere, I am still impressed with the many indications of credibility which obtained in the course of the testimony. To have assumed that this proceeding was invented and staged as a project of dramatic political fiction would be to presuppose the creative genius of a Shakespeare and the genius of a Belasco in stage production. The historical background and surrounding circumstances also lend credibility to the testimony."

The ambassador concluded that "on the face of the record in this case it would be difficult for me to conceive of any court, in any jurisdiction, doing other than adjudging the defendants guilty of violations of the law as set forth in the indictment and as defined by the statutes." Faymonville defended the ambassador's position, except in the case of the military purges, which he thought were politically motivated.[28]

George Kennan, however, believed that Davies was wrong, that the guilt of the defendants was not proved. He filed a somewhat turgid report with the State Department in which he argued that while it was probable that the defendants had engaged in political "opposition activity," no real evidence was produced to show that they had "any real connection with specific acts of wrecking and sabotage."[29]

The new ambassador, however, kept his own view and, in a letter to Judge Moore, revealed the basis for his judgment. The purge trial of Trotsky and Radek, he explained, was a natural state in the revolution. It was a question of the "outs" taking up against the "ins" and failing. The same thing, he assured the judge, happened in the French Revolution. In a letter to Colonel House two days later, he continued his analogy and stressed that "the French Revolution is repeating itself here, only on a greater scale."[30]

Davies bundled up copies of the transcripts of the court proceedings and shipped them off to his friends because he was sure that they would be of great value in the future. When he conveyed his view of the trial to Winston Churchill during a visit to London in May 1937, Churchill replied sarcastically that the ambassador "had given him a completely new concept of the situation." When Davies revealed his view at a diplomatic dinner in London in May 1937, he said it "was a great surprise to the diplomatic guests" because "so violent is the prejudice" against the Soviets in England.[31] Davies's opinion of the British as anti-Soviet was an important part of his outlook. He did not trust the British or other Europeans, thinking of them in part as purveyors of Old World abuses, as desirous to embroil the United States in their sordid affairs, and unwilling to give the Soviet Union the benefit of doubt. The Kremlin would later exploit his axiomatic anti-British disposition.[32]

The trial and execution of the Red Army officers, including Marshal Mikhail Tukachevsky, in the summer of 1937 took Davies and Faymonville by surprise. They thought that the Soviet Union was deliberately weakening itself at a time when the German and Japanese dangers were growing. As arrest followed arrest, as people whom Davies knew were incarcerated, in some cases tried, and then executed, his journal entries noted surprise, shock, and confusion. The ambassador groped for an explanation. He decided that they must be Trotskyites, that is, opponents of Stalin who wanted Trotsky as the leader of the world Communist movement. He admitted, though, that "ordinary psychology does not apply in this situation." "I confess," he lamented, "the situation has me guessing." Faymonville attributed the execution of the military officers to their opposition to the reintroduction of political commissars into the army, and thus he saw politics rather than treason as the explanation.[33]

Davies broke with Faymonville on the military trials. He eventually waded through the initial shock and confusion to a characteristic conclusion. "In all probability," he wrote to Sumner Welles on June 28, 1937, "there was a definite conspiracy in the making looking to a coup d'état by the army—not necessarily anti-Stalin, but antipolitical and antiparty, and that Stalin struck with characteristic speed, boldness, and strength." Soon Davies fitted the event into his French Revolution framework. The arrested army officers, he wrote Roosevelt in July 1937, were all "Bonapartists." Stalin actually strengthened his regime, Davies now argued in a telegram to Hull, "for the danger of the Corsican for the present has been wiped out." And, he added, the loyalty of the Red Army had not been shaken.[34] Henderson, Bohlen, and Kennan all disagreed with this assessment. They concluded that the purges were a consequence of Stalin's paranoia and had the effect of wounding the Soviet Union militarily and politically.[35] Faymonville decided that the army purges delivered "a serious blow" to morale but that the Red Army was still an effective defensive force and could, if called upon, repel an attack.[36]

The Bukharin trial in early 1938 was viewed by Davies and Faymonville as they had evaluated earlier political trials: essential surgery against treason and conspiracy. "It is my opinion," Davies informed Secretary Hull, "so far as the political defendants are concerned sufficient crimes under Soviet law . . . were established by the proof and beyond a reasonable doubt to justify the verdict of guilty of treason and the adjudication of the punishment."[37] He noted in his diary on March 5 that it was exciting to be in the Soviet Union where history was evolving. Bohlen, who was assigned to observe the Bukharin trial, gave his assessment of Davies's analysis of this and other trials: "He had an unfortunate tendency to take what was presented at the trial as the honest and gospel truth. I still blush when I think of some of the telegrams he sent."[38] Faymonville, in Bohlen's opinion, showed the same willingness to accept the accusations of the purge trials at face value. Marjorie Davies found the purges to be unsettling partly because they made planning a dinner party so uncertain.[39]

There is one other dimension to the purges that relates to Davies. He and his wife were able to buy at bargain prices, as mentioned, a whole museum of rare Russian art during the trials. What they apparently did not understand, according to one scholar, was that Stalin allowed them to do this in order to obtain good press coverage in the West during the brutal purges. According to Robert Williams, Davies and his wife did not comprehend "that they were, in part, pawns in a deadly game, a game in which Stalin was eager to manipulate Western opinion while destroying real and imagined enemies at home."[40]

Russian scholarship since Mikhail Gorbachev's relaxation of censorship in the late 1980s has uniformly condemned Davies's view of the purges. They are now seen the way most astute observers, including Kennan and Bohlen, viewed them in the 1930s, as extensions of Stalin's sadistic, narcissistic, and neurotic personality and as debilitating attacks on the Soviet state.[41]

6

"Less Objective and More Friendly"

As the purge trails progressed, the international situation became foreboding. Of course, the two major foci of concern had not changed since Bullitt's time: Germany and Japan. Following the German remilitarization of the Rhineland, the Spanish Civil War erupted in July 1936. Germany and Italy assisted Franco, and the Comintern swung behind the Republic. The Nazis portrayed the conflict as a struggle between international Fascism and international Communism.

With Trotsky still available as a rival for leadership of the international Communist movement, Stalin evidently felt constrained to order the Comintern into Spain to show that he was exercising leadership and to conduct a purge of Trotskyite forces among the soldiers whom the Comintern had conscripted from around the world. Stalin, however, wanted to avoid the possibility that the Comintern's effort in Spain might lead to a war between Germany and the Soviet Union. As a result, the Soviets took no credit for the Comintern effort. They acted as if the Comintern were an independent agency that just happened to have its headquarters in Moscow.

It was not surprising then that the Kremlin rarely discussed the issue of the Spanish Civil War with Ambassador Davies other than to complain about English and French inaction and about pending American neutrality legislation that would adversely affect the position of the Spanish Republic and, beyond Spain, would do nothing to dampen the "dangers of war in Europe." Davies responded to such criticism by stating that the Western European governments were not yet ready to act and that the neutrality legislation aimed to prevent war and, if war were to come, to prevent American involvement.[1] As it turned out, the Comintern's involvement was largely counterproductive and ended up being enmeshed in Stalin's purges in the Soviet Union. Constantine Oumansky, who succeeded Alexander Troyanovsky as Soviet ambassador to the United States in April 1939, accused the State Department of sabotaging Roosevelt's plans to assist the Republic. The civil war dragged on until 1939 when Franco finally won and established a right-wing military dictatorship.[2]

In November 1936, Japan and Germany signed the Anti-Comintern Pact in which they agreed to work against Communist expansion in Europe and Asia. When Davies visited Litvinov for the first time on February 4, 1937, the Soviet foreign minister quickly brought up Japan. Davies said that the United States had no problem with Japan, but Litvinov disagreed, stating that isolationism did not equal security.

Litvinov also revealed two other major fears of the Soviet government: Hitler's "lust for conquest" and for the "domination of Europe" and, second, the possibility of "some composition of differences between France, England, and Germany." Davies did not comment on Litvinov's fears of Germany and the possibility of rapprochement between the European capitalist states, but he did faithfully report them to Secretary Hull. On February 15 Davies invited Litvinov to a luncheon at the embassy. The Soviet foreign minister reiterated his fear to Davies that England and France might be trying to reach some kind of accord with Germany, and he again complained about American isolationism. Davies thought that Moscow and Berlin should simply stop their propaganda campaigns against one another. Litvinov dismissed the suggestion by stressing that "Germany was concerned solely with conquest." Davies reported to Hull that "some of the diplomats who have been here longest" thought that Soviet Russia and Nazi Germany, despite their ideological differences, "would compose any difficulty if there were advantages to be gained." The ambassador gave no indication of his opinion.[3]

In March 1937 Japan invaded China proper and thereby relieved the Soviet Union of the immediate danger that Japan might invade the maritime provinces of Siberia. Japan, of course, kept massive numbers of troops along the Sino-Soviet border in Manchuria (Manchukuo) and Mongolia, and constantly challenged the Red Army with forays and pitched battles, but the advance into China certainly reduced the possibility that Tokyo would open another front against Soviet Russia in the near future. Soviet aid to China strengthened after this and remained strong until the Molotov-Ribbentrop Pact opened up an opportunity to trade reduced aid to China for reduced tension with Japan.[4] At the same time, Germany continued its rearmament and increased its pressure against Czechoslovakia by complaining about Czech mistreatment of Germans living in the Sudetenland. Hitler also shrewdly and successfully sought to isolate Czechoslovakia by claiming that its treaty of May 1935 with the Soviet Union, which it signed as a defensive measure against Germany, made Czechoslovakia an advanced base for Communism in East Central Europe.

On March 26, Litvinov tried to entice the United States to support the Soviet policy of "collective security." He met with Davies and encouraged the United States to join the Soviet Union and others in issuing a declaration in favor of peace which, in Litvinov's mind, would be directed against Germany and Japan.

Davies answered that the United States had "no serious apprehension with reference to Japan" and had no desire to become "embroiled or entangled in European troubles." He also gave Litvinov a word of advice on how to solve the German issue: England, France, Germany, Italy, and Russia should guarantee the territorial integrity of all European states, and then the others should "provide Germany with raw materials and thereby the assurance that she could live, which would relieve the peoples of Europe and the world of these terrific burdens of armament and the fear of catastrophic war." Litvinov did not think that Hitler would accept such a solution.[5]

The Soviet foreign minister again brought up the issue of American participation in "collective security" in July 1937. The Americans were not yet ready to take that step, but Roosevelt did approve a visit to Vladivostok by an American warship in late July 1937 when Soviet-Japanese clashes along the Manchurian and Mongolian borders mounted. Henderson reported to Secretary Hull that *Izvestiia* and *Pravda* were lavish in their praise of this American initiative, but that, unfortunately, the praise was not accompanied by "a noticeable change in attitude of the Soviet authorities towards this Mission or towards American citizens in general."[6]

The United States continued to show support for the Soviet Union as pressure between Tokyo and Moscow grew. Throughout July the embassy worked to renew a commercial treaty that was finally signed on August 4, 1937.[7] Then Roosevelt agreed to sell the Soviet Union a battleship that because of opposition in the Navy Department was stalled during Davies's tenure, but even Robert Kelley, the putative leader of the anti-Stalin group in the State Department, supported this sale.[8] The president also ordered Davies and Faymonville in spring 1938 to develop in conjunction with the Soviets a plan whereby the United States could supply the Soviet Union in the event of a Japanese-Soviet war, but Davies was reassigned before any plan was worked out.[9] In November 1937 Litvinov informed Davies that the Soviet Union was considering supplying the Chinese through Manchuria. In fact, the Soviets had been doing that for some time. Litvinov also expressed his fears about German pressure against Austria and Czechoslovakia and the lack of an Anglo-French response.[10]

In March 1938 Hitler took over Austria. The Anschluss, or union of Germany and Austria, was viewed warily by the Soviets. For some western intellectuals, however, it was a natural process of resolving some of the contradictions and injustices perpetrated by the Treaty of Versailles at the end of World War I. The new government of Neville Chamberlain and Lord Halifax in England represented this viewpoint. For them, appeasement would not only prevent war; it would achieve justice and thereby prevent war. When German pressure on Czechoslovakia mounted after the Anschluss, there was concern in England and France that Hitler might be going too far, but the policy of appeasement continued to prevail. Moscow, of course, felt increasingly threatened as

Germany seemed to be moving in an easterly direction and the Western Powers seemed to simply abet and encourage him. In addition, tension between Soviet and Japanese troops along the Soviet border with Manchuria and Mongolia escalated in the spring of 1938.

Litvinov met again with Davies on March 23, 1938, and told him that English appeasement of Hitler was responsible for Austria's plight and for the death of the League of Nations. He also thought that the Germans would move against Czechoslovakia in the summer and that Prague "might voluntarily yield to Germany because she had no confidence in France and because she was completely surrounded." In addition, he stated that in "a very short time" Germany would take the Polish Corridor and Danzig without compensation to Poland. Litvinov also informed him that the Japanese had 300,000 troops in Manchukuo but that Moscow did not expect an attack by Japan because "the Chinese were putting up a remarkable fight and causing Japan much trouble."[11]

The Soviet foreign minister wanted to increase American and western interest in Moscow. The way to do that was to emphasize that the Soviet Union was strong enough to take care of itself, that the purges had not weakened Soviet Russia, and that the Western European states would be isolated vis-à-vis Germany without an ally in the East. He also hoped to imply that there was a growing possibility of a Russo-German alliance, that Berlin was taking Moscow as a serious power, and that the Soviet Union would come to terms with Germany if the West Europeans and Americans did not act quickly. He wanted the United States to abandon isolation and take a more forceful stand against Germany and Japan or, failing that, at least to encourage the English and French to attenuate their hostility to Moscow and form some sort of anti-Nazi alliance.

Davies eventually concluded that the Soviet policy of Collective Security with the English and French was nearly dead and that Moscow might attempt to develop "a union . . . with Germany in the not distant future." He was also convinced of the Soviets' "ability to take care of themselves from an attack from either the east or the west." On April 1, 1938, he cabled Secretary Hull that Moscow believed that it was surrounded by enemies and confronted with "the hostility of all capitalist states."[12]

Davies was disturbed that the English and French were underestimating the Soviet Union. If Moscow were to reach an accommodation with Berlin, Davies argued in a memo to Roosevelt, it would do so only because of its security needs and British and French unwillingness to accept the Soviet Union as a serious power and a member of the concert of states that were opposed to aggression. The Soviets, Davies asserted, were honorable men who were being foolishly isolated by the English and French, a view which he expressed to both the American and the Soviet governments. Davies even suggested in April 1939, after he had been reassigned to Brussels, that he be sent back to the Soviet Union on a special mission to effect a Russo-British nonaggression agreement.[13]

Although the Soviets had not paid much attention to Davies and certainly found some of his views puzzling, they liked his uncritical approach. Indeed, when Davies abruptly announced in early 1938, after he had returned from a visit to Washington, that he was being reassigned to Brussels, the Soviets evidently wondered if their indifference to the Americans had needlessly alienated them.

At any rate, a flurry of activity, more activity than in the whole of Davies's duration in Moscow, erupted during the final months of his appointment. Litvinov asked Davies if the United States government thought that its "diplomatic mission here had not received proper consideration from this government." He told Davies that he reviewed the American-Soviet relationship and that he had concluded that "with the exception of the debt question, practically all the other matters were either trivial or matters that had already been disposed of to the satisfaction of the United States." He added that the Kremlin "felt particularly aggrieved" because of "the exceptional manner in which the Soviet Union and his department had gone out of its way to show the highest consideration for the United States." Litvinov also organized a farewell dinner for Davies and his wife and lavishly praised the ambassador as a fair and objective observer. Stalin himself visited Davies, as described earlier—a rare event which the ambassador fully appreciated. Stalin wanted to clear up the debt problem with a loan and obtain an American-built battleship and the blueprints and expertise for duplicating the battleship. Kalinin also received Davies and stressed that the Soviet government was sorry to see him leave.[14]

The Soviet ambassador in Washington, Alexander Troyanovsky, followed up Litvinov's, Stalin's, and Kalinin's efforts by visiting Secretary Hull and informing him that, thanks to Davies, the Soviet Union was now ready to move forward on a number of outstanding issues, including the debt problem. He also told him that American-Soviet relations were better than ever and that peace would be served by the strengthening American-Soviet friendship.[15]

Secretary Hull was surprised. He thought American-Soviet relations were still strained and that Davies had accomplished very little. Now, however, Hull changed his opinion. He told Davies, when he returned to the United States at the end of June 1938, that he had caused a tremendous change in Moscow and that the new outlook "was a very important thing for the future in these hazardous days of international threat from the 'aggressor bandits' in the world."[16]

The Soviets, though, did not understand Davies's reasons for leaving. He was not alienated or disturbed by what Kalinin called the isolated "condition" of the diplomatic community. Everyone else was distressed, but not Davies.[17] Davies believed that the Soviets were "fair to the United States, which is a unique position in their attitude toward foreign states."[18] Although Davies's time in Moscow was tense because of his relations with the embassy staff and the normal stress of living in Moscow and dealing with the Soviet government, he wanted out of Moscow for a more mundane and personal reason: his wife was unhappy.

Moscow was not Paris or Palm Beach. After the newlyweds visited Tretyakov Art Gallery, attended the ballet and opera, and sat through some of the purge trials, there was little to do. There were no fashion shows, no boutiques, and very little social life. For her, it was like being sent to the moon. She simply could not tolerate Moscow.

Davies attempted to pamper his wife by redecorating Spaso House, importing her favorite dishes from General Foods, and mooring *Sea Cloud* in Leningrad where on summer weekends they could sail the Baltic Sea under the protective eye of the secret police. He also took her on extended trips. After just ten weeks in Moscow, the couple returned to the United States for a long break. They returned to Moscow in late June 1937 and then left again in early August for an extended tour of Europe, including a planned sailing of the Black Sea on their yacht. Marjorie, however, took ill with some flulike infection that she called "Moscow malaria," and sailed back to the United States with her daughter in September. Davies made his way back to Moscow alone and anxious, but left again for Washington in late November when Roosevelt informed him that he was moving him to the post in Brussels. Davies wanted Berlin, but accepted Brussels when informed that sending a presidential friend there would send the wrong message to the Nazis. In mid-January 1938 the ambassador and his wife returned to the Soviet Union for a few months for the purpose of saying good-bye, but the German annexation of Austria in March 1938 forced the disappointed couple to stay on in Moscow longer than planned. They finally departed Moscow on June 10. According to Elbridge Durbrow, Davies spent a total of nine months out of eighteen at the Moscow embassy.[19] His absence stirred enough adverse publicity early in his assignment that FDR had to warn him indirectly to spend more time in Moscow.[20]

The fact was that the living conditions in Moscow were simply dismal compared with what the couple was used to and what they could obtain in Brussels. Davies was blunt with Kalinin. While he regretted leaving Moscow, he said, "Quite frankly, the living conditions that obtain in Belgium would be more agreeable." At a breakfast just before he left, he praised Stalin, hailed Soviet progress, promised to continue to work for American-Soviet friendship, expressed his regret at leaving, but candidly stated that in Brussels he would be able "to procure worldly pleasures" for his wife. Davies did reassure Kalinin, Stalin, and Litvinov that his departure was not a result of Soviet mistreatment. He told Litvinov, "I came here with an objective mind. I am leaving with an objective mind, but possibly less objective and more friendly because of the kindnesses which you and your government have extended to me as the representative of my country."[21]

Kalinin told Davies that the Soviet government liked his honesty and "objectivity." Litvinov encouraged him to "pass on the results of your study and observation and unbiased judgment to your government and to your countrymen." In this way, the foreign minister went on, "You will certainly contribute much more to the strengthening of friendly relations between our two countries than by any other purely diplomatic activities."[22]

Davies took Litvinov's advice to heart. He reported to Hull that Moscow regarded the United States "with friendly favor" and that all problems between the two countries could be resolved "in a spirit of tolerance, understanding, and friendliness." He carefully added, however, the proviso that the Soviets' "friendliness does not deter them in matters affecting their vital interests, as indicated by the debt and Comintern situations."[23]

In the summer of 1938, just as Davies was finishing up his assignment in Moscow, war clouds mushroomed over Czechoslovakia. He was gone by September when, at Munich, the British and French agreed that they would not stand in the way of Hitler's desire to take the Sudetenland from Czechoslovakia. Surprisingly, the Czechoslovak government, led now by Eduard Beneš, acquiesced in the Great Powers' decision. Czechoslovakia had a first-rate army, a superb armament industry, and a natural defensive wall in the Sudeten Mountains. The democratic government was also popular, except among the German minority, the Volkdeutsche, whom Hitler was manipulating, and some Slovak leaders. The large Czech population was ready to fight if Beneš had provided some leadership. He chose instead to prostrate the nation before Hitler, to blame the West for his capitulation, and to resign and leave in October 1938 in what historian Joseph Rothschild calls "a profound failure of political and psychological nerves." The Germans annexed the Sudetenland and took virtual control of the economy of the rest of Czechoslovakia. To please the Nazis, the new government denounced democracy, restricted the Jews, banned the Communists, gave special status to the remaining German minority, and implemented censorship.[24]

The Soviet Union watched nervously from the sidelines as Munich unfolded. There were some increasingly vociferous voices in the West, not the least among which was Winston Churchill, who demanded that Munich be the last concession, and in these the Soviets found some consolation, but, of course, they also had to avoid being drawn into the war and that could only be guaranteed through an alliance with Germany.[25] The Soviets had made overtures to Berlin as early as 1936 without a response, but after the Anschluss in March 1938 and the Munich Agreement in September 1938, they increased their efforts to tie Germany to some kind of nonaggression pact, but Hitler saw no advantage in alliance with a Soviet Russia weakened by collectivization and purges and isolated from France and England.

Nonetheless, the French were informed by Moscow of the possibility of a Nazi-Soviet agreement in the wake of the Munich conference. The French ambassador in Moscow, Robert Coulondre, visited Vladimir Potemkin, the deputy commissar of foreign affairs, on October 4, 1938, and was told: "My poor friend, what have you done? As for us, I don't see any other conclusion than a fourth partition of Poland."[26] Of course, as long as Germany was unresponsive, the French had nothing to worry about, and they undoubtedly concluded that the Germans were unresponsive for the same reason that they were not pursuing Soviet Russia: Stalin had so weakened his country that the Soviet Union no longer counted. Moscow naturally was attempting to change minds by maintaining that it was strong (Davies was convinced, for example) and by pressuring one of the western states to take it seriously, thus setting off a chain reaction that potentially would see them all take the Soviet Union seriously.

In March 1939 at the Eighteenth Party Congress Stalin stressed that the Soviet Union wanted good relations with Germany, but he also attacked the appeasement of the West European states.[27] Moscow was still fishing for some ally. Then suddenly, while the Congress was still in session, Germany moved in and took the rest of Czechoslovakia, setting up a protectorate over Bohemia and Moravia, establishing Slovakia as a satellite, and turning over the Carpatho-Ukraine to its new ally, Hungary. On March 23 Germany forced Lithuania to turn over the territory of Memel. The Soviet government mildly protested the German action, but clearly realized that Germany had strengthened itself by taking over Czechoslovakia's Skoda armament industry.[28]

The British finally decided to shake off appeasement and try to stop any more aggression. On March 31 Neville Chamberlain warned that England and France would go to war with Germany if the Germans threatened Polish or Romanian independence. Chamberlain also said that Moscow supported the ultimatum to Germany after Ivan Maisky, the Soviet ambassador to England, informed the British that the Soviet government understood the principles that underpinned the British-French action. Moscow clearly wanted to elicit the strongest possible commitment by Chamberlain because it meant that the West was finally abandoning appeasement. So Maisky indicated to Chamberlain that Moscow's name could be associated with the ultimatum, although Maisky was careful not to commit the Soviet government to it. Once London issued the declaration, the Kremlin expressed surprise and denied absolutely that it had taken a stand on the Polish problem. The message was rather blunt: If Berlin wanted an ally, the Kremlin was available. The Germans, however, remained impervious to the Soviet démarche.[29] The German representative in Moscow saw through the Soviet plan. He wrote his foreign ministry in April 1939 that the Soviets desire "a development which would preferably bring about war between Germany, France, and Britain, while they can, to begin with, preserve freedom of action and further their own interests."[30] Hitler, too, understood that if the ultimatum led to war between England and Germany, then the only beneficiary would be Moscow.[31]

London and Paris reacted to Moscow's gambit by appealing to the Soviets to work with them. They took no direct action, however, other than discussions at the ambassadorial level.[32] Lloyd George criticized the Chamberlain government for trying to threaten Germany by a two-front war that hinged on Poland instead of the Soviet Union.[33]

When there was no meaningful response to the Soviet stance on Poland, Stalin had his ambassador to Germany, Alexei Merekalov, meet with German's secretary of state, Ernst von Weizsacker, on April 17 and inform him that improved German-Soviet relations were a possibility.[34] When Germany failed to respond to this overture, Stalin decided to increase the pressure on the western states and to appeal to Hitler by replacing Litvinov—the architect of Collective Security and a Jew—with Molotov on May 3.[35] The implication was clear to England, France, and Germany: the pursuit of an alliance with Paris and London was being discarded in favor of the pursuit of an alliance with Berlin. The English and French were surprised by this development and finally decided that maybe Moscow, despite its weaknesses, could be useful as a pressure on Germany. In May they decided to send a military mission to the Soviet Union, but it did not arrive until July.[36]

The British and the French have been criticized for slowness, but they were not optimistic about an alliance with Stalin because they believed the Soviet Union was weak, untrustworthy, and ultimately intent on joining an alliance only if it were enticed to do so by bargaining over the independence of Poland and other East European states—a condition that the British and French found difficult to accept for political, military, and moral reasons, although they had done exactly that at Munich in 1938. Once the English and French decided to court Moscow, though, Germany, for obvious reasons, followed suit. By August 1939 Moscow was hosting English, French, and German delegations, each attempting to persuade Moscow to sign an alliance. Davies thought that the situation did not look good for Paris and London.[37]

The Germans wanted a nonaggression pact, guaranteeing Soviet neutrality in the event of war, and the English and French wanted a military alliance. The Soviets clearly wanted to sign a pact with the Germans that would keep them out of the war and would give them buffer territories against Germany and into which the Communist movement could be expanded, but they were hesitant because they wanted to make sure that the English and French went to war with Germany even if Moscow were aligned in a nonaggression pact with Berlin. It would be suicidal to sign a nonaggression pact if the western states simply pursued appeasement and allowed Hitler to move against Poland, the main bone of contention in 1939. Hitler clearly would not stop at Poland. *Mein Kampf* made clear that he wanted the Ukrainian breadbasket. He also was a vehement anti-Communist and held the Slavic people to be *untermenschens*. Such dispositions virtually guaranteed that, if Hitler got away with crushing Polish independence, he would attack the USSR next. If Moscow had signed a nonaggression pact with Hitler to allow him to fight the West over Poland and the West had refused to defend Poland, there was little likelihood that the West would then rush in to help the Soviet Union if it were Hitler's next victim. So in the summer of 1939 Moscow pursued a policy of temporizing, waiting for some clear-cut sign that the West would definitely go to war with Germany over the Polish issue.[38]

The enthusiasm that Secretary Hull had expressed in June 1938 when Davies returned to Washington soon gave way to the reality that nothing had changed from the American perspective. On January 13, 1939, Hull was complaining to Troyanovsky that the old problems were still afflicting American-Soviet relations. The irritants were listed in his memoirs: "These embraced the nonsettlement of Soviet debts and our claims; refusal to give us sufficient currency for the use of our Embassy in Moscow; cutting down our Moscow consular district; failure to provide the necessary currency exchange with which to build an Embassy in Moscow; inspection of the effects of American diplomats and restrictions on their movements; and detention for some days of drawings and papers of American engineers." Hull also objected strongly "to the arrest of Americans in the Soviet Union and their being held incommunicado without notification to American authorities, and to spying on our diplomatic representatives."[39]

Loy Henderson, who was now the assistant chief of the Division of European Affairs in the State Department, summarized in July 1939 his analysis as to why American-Soviet relations continued in the doldrums. He stated that Moscow was moved by the desire to expand Communism, to preserve itself, and to avoid capitalist encirclement. By July it had so positioned itself, he argued, that the German threat was reduced by the British ultimatum to guarantee Poland and the Japanese threat was reduced by the war in China. The Soviets were in the driver's seat and had no immediate need for the United States.[40]

The Soviets, however, discounted the complaints of the Hendersons and Hulls. They knew that there were anti-Soviet types in the United States. Ambassador Oumansky told Molotov, "We learned in our practical work about the possibility of anti-Soviet provocation" in capitalist countries. Oumansky readily identified some State Department bureaucrats (especially Loy Henderson), the Catholic Church, some "reactionary" Democrats and Republicans in Congress, and America's "economic royalists" as enemies of the Soviet Union.[41] For the leaders of the international Communist revolution, opposition was a fact of life, a measure of success. They did not expect and did not want a warm, open relationship with the United States. They wanted good relations, but on their terms. They hoped to take advantage of the United States, to get benefits from the relationship, and to have the Americans treat them as privileged individuals without giving any comparable privileges in exchange. This was fitting, since they were representatives of the new order and the Americans were defenders of the old order.

They liked President Roosevelt. He and key members of his administration worked to benefit the Soviet Union. He was a progressive and, after all, the man who recognized the Soviet Union. As Stalin told Bullitt in 1933, Roosevelt was, "in spite of being the leader of a capitalist nation, one of the most popular men in the Soviet Union."[42] Roosevelt, Treasury Secretary Henry Morgenthau, and Interior Secretary Harold Ickes met privately with Oumansky and emphasized that the anti-Soviet bureaucrats in the State Department would be thwarted.[43] The president also tried to beat down the isolationists, helped China against Japan, and openly backed England and France in the developing crisis with Germany. The Soviets liked all of those policies, and American support of London and Paris gave them a tool to increase pressure on Germany to come to terms.[44] Roosevelt told Oumansky that American-Soviet relations were "smooth," and the Soviet ambassador could not agree more. Oumansky informed Molotov that Roosevelt followed a policy toward the Soviet Union of "accentuated friendliness, even perhaps intimacy." He confessed that he believed the American relationship held out great promise for Moscow.[45]

Of course, the president was attempting to bolster the American-Soviet relationship during the summer of 1939 and he was undoubtedly fulsome in welcoming and engaging the newly appointed Soviet ambassador. But there was something more in Roosevelt's approach. True to his belief in the convergence of American and Soviet societies, he stressed to Oumansky on July 2 that Soviet-American relations in the immediate future hinged on two issues: "first, wiping out, once and for all, the issue of the debt; second, giving evidence for American public opinion that the USSR is on the road to democracy and therefore spiritually evolving toward the USA." Oumansky was clearly confused by the second point, but he told Molotov that he discussed with the president the different types of democracy and recalled for Roosevelt "the words of Stalin about the realization . . . of political democratic life in our state."[46]

The type of warm and friendly relationship which President Roosevelt wanted was not a priority of the Soviet Union. The United States was a capitalist, imperialist state and, from the Soviet perspective, an inherently incompatible ally for the long term. Even though the Kremlin desired Washington to abandon the policy of isolationism, it never considered bilateral "intimacy" as a means to achieve that goal.

The Soviets, in other words, despite the irritation of anti-Soviet people in the State Department, Congress, and the Catholic Church, thought that American-Soviet relations were harmonious. Of course, there were annoyances and they regularly complained about these, but relations with the United States were good, given the fact that the United States was a capitalist state.[47]

Davies, moreover, had assured the Soviet leaders that the relationship was fine. It was probably unsettling that a new ambassador was not named until March 1939 and then did not present his credentials until August 1939, but the Soviets had more important matters on their agenda. The Germans, English, and French had delegations in Moscow. The opportunity for an intercapitalist war was at hand. In Asia, the Chinese seemed to be preoccupying the Japanese.

The United States was on the periphery but still important. Moscow was interested in the American relationship for whatever economic and political benefit that it could obtain without actually addressing the concerns of Washington or the American embassy in Moscow.

Roosevelt, of course, had not abandoned his hope that American-Soviet relations might evolve into a special relationship. He carefully searched for a replacement for Davies. He and Davies thought the best man might be a banker who could help the Soviets with a loan to resolve the debt problem. FDR offered the job in July 1938 to Sidney J. Weinberg, a wealthy New York banker and a close friend of Davies, but Weinberg's business interests forced him to decline. After that Roosevelt had difficulty finding a suitable candidate for the Moscow post. In January 1939, with no nomination in sight, Davies wrote Hull that it was essential that someone who was committed to friendship with the Soviet government be found for the Moscow post and that, until that person was named, Lt. Colonel Faymonville should stay on in Moscow. Davies was trying to protect Faymonville, whose unfiltered sympathy for Stalin's government led to pressure from the War Department and the State Department to remove him.[48]

Roosevelt and Hull continued to focus their search for a replacement on the Jewish banking community in New York. Finally, the name of Laurence A. Steinhardt surfaced. He was a wealthy lawyer with extensive ties to the Jewish community in New York City and a man who had decided to make a career out of diplomacy. He was also the nephew of Samuel Untermeyer, another lawyer who was a close friend of Davies and Roosevelt and an ardent admirer of the Soviet experiment. It was actually Secretary Hull who recommended Steinhardt for the Moscow post. He seemed to be everything that Roosevelt and Davies were seeking. He was a liberal Democrat with extensive ties to the New York banking and legal community, and he was an accomplished diplomat. In addition, he wanted to go to Moscow and he had the financial wherewithal to soften the hardships of the Moscow post. He appeared to be a perfect blend of philosophy, experience, and dedication.

He was named ambassador to the Soviet Union on March 5, 1939, but he was allowed time to put together his personal affairs and he was told he did not have to report to Moscow until August. In the interim, the embassy was in the capable hands of Alexander Kirk who, according to Bohlen, lifted the embassy from the stupor of Davies's tenure "to a more serious routine." Lt. Colonel Faymonville, without Davies on the scene to protect him, was recalled in 1939. He returned to the United States in July 1939, and Roosevelt demonstrated his continuing commitment to the policy of unrequited friendship by publicly receiving Faymonville at the White House and going on a private fishing trip with him. However, Faymonville's pro-Soviet reputation ruined his career in the army, and his new assignments were unimportant. Eventually, he settled down "to an unofficial retirement" in his home town of San Francisco as an ordnance officer for the Fourth Army. Roosevelt, Hopkins, and Davies, however, were not through with Faymonville. The very reputation that compromised him with the War Department and State Department gave him high standing at the White House. He would soon reappear in Moscow as an essential cog in Roosevelt's Soviet policy.[49] As for Davies, he left Moscow in June 1938, but he also remained a major force in America's policy toward the Soviet Union. In fact, his pro-Stalin views helped firm up Roosevelt's chimerical views about the democratic nature of the Soviet Union and the trustworthiness of Stalin.

Part 3

Laurence A. Steinhardt
1939-1941

7

Old Testament Justice

L aurence A. Steinhardt was expecting to quickly present his credentials to Premier Kalinin and then depart immediately for a well-deserved vacation in Sweden where he had many friends and had been United States ambassador during FDR's first term. The ambassador, his wife, Dulcie, and their daughter, Dulcie Ann, sailed for Europe on July 12, 1939. They stopped in Paris to see Bullitt, in Brussels to see Davies, and then after a brief visit to Sweden they reached Moscow on August 11, shortly after the French-British military mission had arrived in Moscow.

The British and the French were there to persuade Stalin to join them in a military alliance against Germany. They were bidding against a German mission, which was there to convince Stalin to join Hitler in a nonaggression pact. Hitler wanted to spill Polish blood. He was in a frenzy, pushing the world relentlessly toward war. Ideology gripped his nation and blotted out sanity, common sense, prudence, and restraint. Demagoguery, racial hatred, and obsession with war stifled, slashed, and ripped away at the roots of Judeo-Christian civilization. Ideology was on the march everywhere. In Japan the militarists sought hegemony throughout East Asia. In Italy the Fascists sang blood chants. In Soviet Russia the Communists plotted for war among the capitalists and in their own country were savagely trying to sculpt a new society based on class hatred. In England, France, and Czechoslovakia the appeasers ran from justice, morality, and principle in order to avoid war, only to bring on war more quickly and more deadly because their weakness excited the aggressors. In the United States isolationism held sway, but Roosevelt seemed to be increasingly viewing international affairs from an untested and dogmatic paradigm that resulted from combining Wilsonian idealism and the sociological theory of convergence. The world seemed crazy, out of control, severed from its moral moorings, and headed ineluctably for mayhem and destruction.

The diplomatic jostling in Moscow was intense and ominous. The fate of the world had come down to this: conversations with Stalin. The Soviet government's diplomacy in 1939 aimed above all at keeping the USSR out of war. Second, it sought to cultivate war between the western states. These goals were a combination of realpolitik and ideology. War between Germany and England-France was the best way to check potential German aggression against the Soviet Union and to punish the English-French alliance for its policy of appeasement, which appeared, certainly from Moscow's vantage point, to have a pronounced anti-Soviet orientation.[1]

In addition, war between the capitalist states would undoubtedly open the door to Communist expansion. This was the case during World War I when the capitalist states had so weakened themselves through a long war of attrition that a profoundly anticapitalist state, the Soviet Union, was able to come into being and to maintain itself. For Moscow, the key to avoiding war and precipitating conditions likely to lead to a western war was to obtain a nonaggression pact with Germany that would guarantee Soviet neutrality and allow Germany a free hand to deal with France and England. Nonetheless, in August 1939 the Soviets were still talking to all suitors—the Germans, the English, and the French.

The United States favored the British and French position in the discussions with Moscow and had made this clear to Ambassador Oumansky.[2] After Steinhardt's departure, Roosevelt decided to reiterate the American position to Soviet Ambassador Oumansky and he cabled Steinhardt, who was in transit to Moscow, to inform the Soviet government of the American position.[3] The Soviets, however, alerted by Oumansky, publicly leaked the American position before Steinhardt had a chance to present it. Steinhardt completely understood that the Soviets did this to put pressure on the Germans, and he duly reported to Welles what to his mind was an example of Soviet duplicity and high-handedness.[4]

Because of close ties between Bohlen and a member of the German embassy in Moscow, Hans Heinrich "Johnny" Herwarth, Steinhardt soon found out that he had an extremely valuable pipeline into the developing German-Soviet relationship. He presented his credentials on August 16, and on that same day he informed Secretary of State Hull that the Germans and the Soviets were on the verge of signing a nonaggression pact.[5] The State Department, however, doubted the accuracy of the report, although Hull did pass the information along to the British and French ambassadors in Washington. Bohlen maintained later that the State Department's skepticism was a product of Washington's naive belief that Moscow would put its anti-Fascist views before "the preservation of the Soviet system."[6]

One week after Steinhardt had informed the State Department that a Nazi-Soviet agreement was about to be signed, the German foreign minister, Joachim von Ribbentrop, arrived in Moscow. Hitler made it clear that Ribbentrop had to leave Moscow within forty-eight hours, and the Soviet government knew that the deadline meant that Germany intended to go to war against Poland on August 26. The British and the French were shocked, but to Moscow's relief they did not back away from their commitment to Poland. On August 24 they reiterated their pledge, and now Hitler, surprised that the western states were actually going to fight, decided to postpone his planned attack on Poland. By September 1, he was again convinced that the western states would not fight, and even if they did, he believed a peace could be quickly arranged, so that in any event he would have a free hand to deal with the Communist menace. He ordered the Wehrmacht to strike Poland and start World War II on September 1. The Soviet attitude toward Hitler and Nazism changed overnight.[7]

Once the Molotov-Ribbentrop Pact was made public, Steinhardt reported on August 24 that there was a secret, unpublished protocol attached that divided up parts of Eastern Europe between Moscow and Berlin. He informed Hull, "Estonia, Latvia, eastern Poland, and Bessarabia are recognized as spheres of Soviet vital interest."[8] His information was incomplete because the Soviets, according to the agreement, were supposed to annex, rather than simply have a vital interest in, Estonia, Latvia, and eastern Poland. Finland was also included in the Soviet sphere.[9]

Nonetheless, Steinhardt's information, coming from Bohlen's contact in the German embassy, was essentially correct. He was quite surprised that the British and French ambassadors had not anticipated the Soviet move. "I have never quite been able to understand," he wrote a friend in December 1939, "the failure in London to appreciate that these negotiations were not carried on in good faith."[10]

At the end of September, the Germans and the Soviets revised the territorial protocol such that most of eastern Poland, excluding western Belorussia and western Ukraine, was allotted to Germany, and Lithuania, originally marked for Germany, was promised to Moscow.[11] Immediately after the Molotov-Ribbentrop Pact was announced, the Soviet and Japanese governments opened negotiations that led initially to a cease-fire and then to a full nonaggression pact in April 1941. When the negotiations started, Molotov told the Chinese ambassador in Moscow that Soviet assistance to China against Japan would be curtailed and that China should look to England for help.[12]

Steinhardt had not expected the crisis of war, but he was up to the task. He was a shrewd, balanced observer who analyzed the Communists on the basis of their actions, not their words, and certainly not on the basis of some unproven theory. He was a man of intelligence, principle, and deep moral conviction.

Steinhardt was born into a well-to-do Jewish family in New York City on October 6, 1892. He earned a B.A. in 1913 and an M.A. and LL.B. in 1915, all from Columbia University, and then worked for an accounting firm until the United States entered World War I. He joined the army as a private and was eventually named as associate counsel for the War Department. In 1923 he married Dulcie Yates Hoffman. In 1920 he joined the law firm of Guggenheimer, Untermeyer, and Marshall where his maternal uncle, Samuel Untermeyer, was a partner. His uncle was also a force in the Democratic Party in New York and a supporter and friend of Franklin D. Roosevelt, Joseph Davies, and many other prominent Democrats. Soon Steinhardt found himself contributing both time and money to Roosevelt's presidential campaign. In 1932 he was appointed to the preconvention committee and then to the Democratic Finance Committee.

Although Steinhardt was not an intimate friend of Roosevelt, the two were more than acquaintances. Steinhardt thought that FDR was both brilliant and prescient, "a year, as usual, ahead of the politicians." He also thought that Roosevelt was worthy of his loyalty, which for Steinhardt was the highest of compliments. He himself valued loyalty in his subordinates and amply rewarded it. He strove to be loyal to Roosevelt, in fact, to be the president's favorite, which in his mind was a noble goal bespeaking charm and personality rather than obsequiousness. Roosevelt, for his part, considered Steinhardt to be a loyal political supporter and competent diplomatic servant. He told Steinhardt in June 1940, "You have done a 100 percent job" in Moscow, and this assessment thrilled the ambassador. Steinhardt concluded that his hard work and loyalty were paying off.[13]

After the election in 1932 Roosevelt offered Steinhardt the job of ambassador to Sweden. He was independently wealthy and decided to take the position on a trial basis. He was not intending to make a career of the foreign service, but he and Dulcie fell in love with Sweden and the diplomatic service. They found Stockholm to be a beautiful, cultivated city where they fitted in comfortably and soon gathered about themselves many lifelong friends.

Steinhardt decided in Stockholm that he had found a job that he wanted to do for the rest of his life. He gave up his law career and numerous business opportunities in New York to devote himself entirely to diplomacy. He easily made the difficult transition from political appointee to professional envoy. His legal training helped, but he was also a careful and balanced observer and reporter of events. He was intelligent, analytical, witty, and concise. He was fluent in German, French, and Spanish, and eventually he developed a working knowledge of Russian. He proved to be well suited for diplomatic service.[14]

In 1937 Steinhardt was moved from Sweden to Peru. He found Peru's climate to be deenergizing, but he admired the Peruvian people and culture. As in Sweden he made many lifelong friends and did a fine job as ambassador.

In March 1939, with the Moscow post still vacant following Davies's departure in June 1938, he was offered the ambassadorship. His excellent record convinced Secretary Hull to recommend "to the President that he be transferred to the higher and more responsible post at Moscow."[15] Undoubtedly, his uncle's connections with Roosevelt and Davies played a role in his appointment. Untermeyer had been to Soviet Russia several times, and Davies had hosted him on one of those occasions.[16] In addition, of course, Steinhardt's connection to the banking and legal community in New York made him a logical choice. Roosevelt, in fact, had tried to tap the New York Jewish community to fill the post when Davies first resigned in June 1938. Sidney J.

Weinberg was offered the position first, but he turned it down. Steinhardt quickly accepted Roosevelt's offer.

Steinhardt brought to the Moscow post a complex outlook. He agreed with Roosevelt's optimism about the Soviet-American relationship, and that attitude certainly played a role in his selection. He was also sympathetic to the Soviet experiment. The traditional Jewish tie to the land of Eastern Europe predisposed him to like the Soviet Union, particularly after the Communists had removed the czar. His uncle, too, had given him a favorable image of Soviet Russia. Sam Untermeyer admired the Communist experiment in Russia because, along with others in the West, he believed that the Soviet Union was advancing the cause of human progress. He was persuaded that any government was better than the czarist regime, which had so consistently persecuted Jews. Steinhardt was also familiar with the Soviet Union. He had helped with the negotiations leading up to the Roosevelt-Litvinov Agreement and had visited the country in 1934.[17] Once he arrived in the Soviet Union, he informed the Soviets that he was not an apologist for capitalism. He had a liberal cast of mind, he was not biased against the Soviet Union, and he admired certain aspects of the Soviet system.[18]

On the other hand, Steinhardt was a pragmatist, a lawyer with a refined sense of justice, and a Jew with a developed sense of objective morality. He had no abiding faith that democratic capitalism was an inevitable movement around the world. He took life as it came. He dealt with people as they appeared and as they dealt with him. He was also sensitive and cared deeply about protocol, style, and behavior. He had an Old Testament sense of justice—an eye for an eye, and a tooth for a tooth—but was willing to compromise if there was evidence that the compromise would effect change for the better and would not undermine basic moral principles. He was far removed from ideologues like Roosevelt, Davies, and Hopkins. He favored the growth of democracy around the world, but he would never tolerate, whitewash, or rationalize Stalinism as some embryonic form of democracy or democratic capitalism. A predisposition for him was only tentative and would ultimately and quickly give way to reality.

Did Roosevelt know whom he was getting in Steinhardt? The evidence indicates that he did not know early on that Steinhardt was closer to a Bullitt than a Davies. He thought of him as a link to the banking community who might be able to solve at least the debt problem in American-Soviet relations. It does not appear that FDR gave the assignment much attention. He was content that Steinhardt was a loyal Democrat, had a reputation for competence, and had ties to Samuel Untermeyer and Joe Davies. Steinhardt was certainly in agreement with FDR's notion of good relations with Moscow, too.

Before Steinhardt left for Moscow, however, there was no doubt that FDR knew where he stood because Steinhardt made his position clear. Once he was free of the post in Peru in spring 1939, Steinhardt spent time in Washington poring over the correspondence between the Moscow embassy and the State

Department. He discovered that the Kremlin treated foreign representatives as spies and that diplomatic service in Moscow was truly a hardship. It surprised him that the Soviets refused to extend customary courtesies to the American delegation, especially since the United States government provided all normal amenities to the Soviet embassy in Washington.

The new ambassador eventually concluded that the imbalance in the relationship had to be addressed. He wanted the State Department to treat the Soviet delegation in Washington exactly the way the Soviet Foreign Ministry treated the Americans in Moscow. He also desired permission to adopt a policy of reciprocity in Moscow: if the Soviets treated the American representatives discourteously and offensively, he wanted to be able to retaliate. He was steeled in his conclusion by a personal affront immediately before he departed Washington. Personal mail that had been prematurely sent to him in Moscow was returned to him in Washington crudely opened.[19]

He made the case for a policy of reciprocity to the State Department just before he left for Moscow. His tactical argument was that this approach would lead to better relations. He was in agreement with FDR's basic approach of building a strong Soviet-American relationship in order to check Nazi and Japanese aggression and to preserve the peace. He was simply convinced, after reading the files and visiting with Henderson and Bullitt, that American policy should stress reciprocation more than conciliation. Steinhardt wanted concessions by Washington linked to concessions by Moscow. The record seemed clear to him: relations between Washington and Moscow had not improved after the American government had consistently made efforts to ameliorate them, so it was time to try a new strategy. He also talked with Davies, but he clearly determined that his fawning approach had not improved life at the embassy.

Evidently in reading the record Steinhardt chose to ignore or failed to notice that Roosevelt had dumped Bullitt because he had insisted on a reciprocal approach. Undoubtedly the president was surprised by the new ambassador's plan of action.

Nonetheless, Roosevelt eventually decided to sanction the new effort. He did so probably because he was irritated that the Soviets were talking to the Germans about an alliance. Steinhardt received backing from Sumner Welles, who agreed with the new envoy that normal "methods of persuasion" seemed to be ineffective with Moscow.[20] In addition, Steinhardt's appointment had been long in coming, and it would have been awkward both domestically and internationally to withdraw him on the eve of his departure. Steinhardt made his views known late, only after he had studied the files. Then, as soon as Steinhardt arrived in Moscow, the Soviets signed the Molotov-Ribbentrop Pact and, in quick order, invaded Poland, occupied parts of the Baltic States, and attacked Finland.

Roosevelt soon began to warm to Steinhardt's idea of reciprocity. In December 1939, after the Soviet attack on Finland, he told Secretary Hull and

Undersecretary Welles, "I think we should match every Soviet annoyance by a similar annoyance here against them." Those were revolutionary words coming out of Roosevelt's mouth, but he was getting fed up with Soviet behavior. He still saw no long-term alternative to seeking some accommodation with Moscow, if only to keep it from being pushed further into the German alliance, but for the moment the new ambassador's approach toward the Soviets suited him.[21]

The Soviets were disappointed in Steinhardt's appointment. They were hoping for another Davies, but after Oumansky twice talked with Steinhardt before he left for Moscow, they knew that they were not going to have another apologist. The Soviet ambassador wrote Molotov that the new American ambassador was egotistical, petty, bourgeois, and a "former active Zionist." His wife, Oumansky declared, was worse—"bourgeoisie to the marrow of her bones." In summary, Oumansky stated that Steinhardt is "between Bullitt and Davies, better than the first, worse than the second." The Soviet envoy took some consolation, though, from the fact that Steinhardt had not yet received his final instructions from Roosevelt. When he did, Oumansky hoped, he would be "set straight."[22] Oumansky made it a point to complain to Secretary Morgenthau about Steinhardt's exacting approach, specifically his demand that the Soviets make an effort to solve the debt problem. Morgenthau assured Oumansky that Steinhardt had no authority to deal with the debt issue and, furthermore, that Roosevelt was taking these types of issues out of the hands of the State Department experts and planning to resolve them under his "direct guidance." Oumansky broadened his attack in a conversation with Interior Secretary Harold Ickes. He maintained that there were anti-Soviet, reactionary officials in the State Department. Ickes guaranteed him that Roosevelt was determined to end that problem. The president himself also stressed to Oumansky that there were anti-Soviet types in the State Department. Such indiscretion by Roosevelt, Morgenthau, and Ickes undercut Steinhardt and the State Department at a time when the United States desperately needed a strong ambassador in Moscow and solid advice from its experts in the State Department.[23]

Steinhardt, it was clear, was being trivialized even before he arrived in Moscow. Once he did alight in the Soviet capital, he found himself surrounded, like Bullitt and Davies, by a brilliant staff including Charles Bohlen, Stuart Grummon, Walter Thurston (the embassy's counselor), Frederick Reinhardt, Llewellyn Thompson, Charles Thayer, and Angus Ward. Virtually all of these men admired him, and he respected them.[24] Thurston was new, and Oumansky characterized him as "of a breed" like Henderson. Henry Cassidy, the Associated Press correspondent in Moscow, reported that one of Steinhardt's fellow diplomats described him as "the best consul who ever came to Moscow." Steinhardt himself thought that he was very good. In a half-humorous, half-serious vein, he wrote a relative, "I am the outstanding member of the American diplomatic service."[25]

The ambassador's role, he felt, was one of service to country, government, and president, and not to self. When he was in the Soviet Union, he deeply resented the "public" ambassadorships of his more famous contemporaries in the foreign service: Joseph Davies in Belgium, William Bullitt in France, Joseph Kennedy in England, and Anthony Biddle Jr., the ambassador to Poland who was temporarily stationed in Paris. He chalked up their notoriety to an ability to buy public relations agents rather than to diplomatic skills. He simply did not think it was fair that they were getting so much attention from the press while he was getting so little despite the importance of his work.[26]

Steinhardt was pleased about the new appointment because he considered Moscow in 1939 to be "the pivotal post" in Europe, with the French, English, and Germans each attempting to work out some relationship with the USSR. At the same time, he suffered few illusions about the Soviet standard of living. Before he left for Moscow he took care to order a huge amount of canned goods to be shipped to the embassy "in view of the food problem there." He also showed a lack of faith in Soviet dental care. He wrote a friend in Stockholm that he would be visiting often if for no other reason than to have his teeth fixed.[27]

On the other hand, he did have a few illusions. He told Stuart Grummon, then the chargé d'affaires in Moscow, that he wanted him to hire a cook, butler, and chauffeur—"the best available." He also assumed that Spaso House would be fairly comfortable and clean. He sent two automobiles to Moscow, a Rolls Royce and a new twelve-cylinder Packard. He assumed that there would be ample gasoline and adequate roads to handle his luxury cars.

Once in Moscow he quickly discovered that he had assumed too much. He decided that most of the Soviet employees of the embassy were pitifully lethargic and wasteful. They assumed they could take whatever they wanted, he reported to Henderson, and that they could move their families "even unto the fourth generation" into Spaso House. He further found Spaso House to be virtually untouched since Davies's departure in 1938. It was well below standard, he told Henderson, and there was "not a wine glass in the house."[28] And as for his Packard, after a few months of gas shortages, potholed roads, and Moscow's daredevil drivers, he shipped it home with a list of fourteen required repairs.[29]

He also found daily living in Moscow to be stressful. When the Soviet ambassador to the United States, Constantine Oumansky, dismissed Steinhardt's complaints about visa problems, food shortages, and housing and transportation problems as "minor," Steinhardt retorted that because of Oumansky's "years of residence in the United States, he may no longer attach as much importance to freedom of movement, housing, transportation, and a modest food supply as those of us who reside in his native city." When his toilet broke down, he had the telephone operator "call up Vyshinsky [the assistant commissar for foreign affairs] and tell him that if my toilet isn't working in one hour, I'm going up there and use his!"[30]

He was easily irritated by the Kremlin's callousness and insensitivity to the needs of the ambassadorial community. "Generally speaking," he wrote Nathaniel P. Davis, chief of the Division of Foreign Service Administration, "the diplomats are treated worse in Moscow than the ordinary Soviet citizen." The lack of protocol and common courtesy drove him to take refuge in sarcasm. When he was told that he could expect an explanation for the Soviet delay in expediting the release and departure of an arrested American, he told Loy Henderson, now back at the State Department as the assistant chief of the Division of European Affairs, "I infer that it will be a typical piece of Soviet reasoning, commencing with a wrong premise and arriving at an idiotic conclusion by means of devious methods of circumlocution." Some two months after inviting Molotov to dinner, he wrote John C. Wiley, the American minister in Riga, Latvia, "I am still waiting for the august voice of the Kremlin to fix the date of my dinner for Molotov."[31]

His taste for high culture also suffered sorely. Not only was the foreign community kept isolated by the Soviets, he complained in a letter to a friend, but "there are no nightclubs or nightlife and no amusement other than the ballet and the opera which are rather good, but after you have seen all twenty of them you are through." Besides, he went on, the secret police make life absolutely miserable. "They are never more than two or three yards from me, and they follow me right into the barber shop."[32]

Steinhardt also had to deal with pleas from American relatives of Polish refugees and from the American ambassador to Poland, Anthony Biddle. When the Red Army moved into eastern Poland in mid-September 1939, it soon captured the remnants of the retreating Polish army, including over 15,000 Polish officers, millions of Polish refugees, and apparently the belongings of Ambassador Biddle. Soon the embassy was deluged with pleas from Polish citizens looking for information on relatives and friends. Steinhardt found it impossible to obtain conclusive information on the Poles because the Soviets refused to allow any diplomat or military attaché from Moscow to visit the occupied region. They also cut off all mail and telephone calls until the end of 1939. Steinhardt tried to impress the Soviets by telling them that Biddle was a political "friend of Roosevelt" and that his wife was one of the "wealthiest women in America who was nagging her husband very much" about the "immense property" that they had left behind in Poland.[33] In frustration, Steinhardt told Biddle, "It is necessary to live here to appreciate having to work under conditions where everything is topsyturvy from the world in which you and I have lived, in that morals and ethics simply do not exist as we understand them." He also informed him that the Soviets, when it came to his possessions, live by "the old adage that possession is nine points of the law." He advised the State Department to retaliate by seizing Soviet property in the United States.[34]

Steinhardt's comment to Biddle about moral relativism in Soviet Russia was a perception that he later elaborated on in letters to friends. He wrote his Swedish friend Carl Trygger, "There has been such a complete demoralization in standards since I was a young man." He wrote Alvin Untermeyer that Soviet Russia was "a combination of the arrogance of the old Russia and the political parvenu." It was a place, he went on, where power was so concentrated at the top that "a single individual sitting at a desk can isolate a whole community with a few words of command, and isolate them to such an extent that their complete disappearance from the face of the earth could neither be known nor established for years." The government, he told Untermeyer, had developed "a degree of truculence which cannot be conceived of in western countries, and there is still a great deal of the Oriental in the makeup of the higher Soviet authorities. They are utterly indifferent to outside opinion and do not follow the lines of reasoning of the west. Their standards of ethics are diametrically the opposite of those which prevail in occidental countries. As a result it is impossible to deal with them as one would deal with westerners. They only understand one language, the language of superior force, and unless and until force is applied they go their own way."

Shortly after he arrived in Moscow, Steinhardt had occasion to implement his strategy of quid pro quo. In late August, before the war broke out, Steinhardt and Henderson coordinated a plan to link the passage of the Soviet ship *Kim* through the Panama Canal with the unwillingness of the Soviet government to send a customs official to the apartment of Dr. Walter G. Nelson, the embassy's physician, who was returning to the United States. The Soviets wanted to force Nelson to pack his belongings, cart them to the Soviet customs hall, and then unpack them for the customs inspector.

The Soviets complained that there was no connection between the passage of the *Kim* through the canal and Dr. Nelson and that the Soviet government could not "grant special privileges to the American embassy without granting them to all diplomatic missions." Henderson replied that the American government "was not intending to connect the *Kim* and the customs inspection in Moscow. The fact seemed to be that the Soviet government was concerned regarding the passage of the *Kim* through the Canal and the Department was disturbed over the customs treatment accorded the members of our Embassy in Moscow." Henderson added, "The American Government took the point of view that the extension of courtesies was based upon reciprocity and international amenities, whereas the Soviet Government took the point of view that such extension was based entirely on the principle of the most-favored nation."[35]

In the end, the Soviets relented and sent a customs official to Dr. Nelson's apartment and the *Kim* sailed through the canal. Steinhardt wrote Hull on September 2, "I believe the successful outcome of the Nelson matter demonstrates that it is possible in specific cases to obtain a modification of Soviet *intransigence* in respect of the usual courtesies if a sufficiently firm attitude is displayed, and I desire to express my appreciation to the Department for its wholehearted cooperation in this matter." Andrei Gromyko, who would eventually become Soviet chargé and then ambassador in Washington, informed Molotov that Steinhardt was adopting "a firm and even quarrelsome attitude."[36]

The Soviet evaluation of the new American ambassador smacked of Marxist stereotyping and anti-Semitism. In a profile sent to Molotov on August 7, 1939, Oumansky announced that Steinhardt was "a wealthy, bourgeoisie Jew who was permeated with the foul smell of Zionism." He also reported that Steinhardt contributed ten thousand dollars to the Roosevelt campaign in 1932 and that he continued to be a major supporter of the Democratic Party. He also stated that he was a "personal friend" of Roosevelt.[37]

8

"A Silent Partner to Germany"

Once the Germans attacked Poland, the English and the French declared war on Germany, but no major fighting ensued in Western Europe—a development called the "phony war." The simple truth was that neither England nor France wanted to fight. They were not prepared to do battle, to put pressure on Germany from the West while Hitler attacked Poland in the East. Poland was doomed no matter what the western states did, but it probably could have held out somewhat longer if the English and French had helped. The Germany military machine marched through Poland with terrifying speed. The Polish government fled and set up a government-in-exile in London under General Wladyslaw Sikorski.

The Soviets watched the advance with excitement. When the Polish ambassador pleaded with Molotov to allow military supplies from other states to come across Soviet territory, he was told, "The Soviet Union does not wish to get involved in this war." The Soviet foreign minister was certainly telling the truth. The situation was fraught with danger, and it was clear that the western states were doing little or could do little immediately to halt the German Blitzkrieg. Steinhardt reported on September 9 that Soviet reserve troops were being called up. Since the Soviets already had more than enough troops to handle any major task, including the occupation of eastern Poland, the call up of reservists certainly revealed some anxiety about German intentions. Steinhardt also stressed, "There is nothing that the Soviets desire more than to avoid being involved in a European war at the present time."[1]

Undoubtedly the Soviets were relieved when the German juggernaut stopped close to the demarcation line agreed on in the Molotov-Ribbentrop Pact. It was reassuring evidence that the new allies could hunt and feed together on the weak and vulnerable countries of Eastern Europe. It would be imprudent, of course, to miss the feeding frenzy in Poland or to show any weakness before the Germans, so in mid-September the Soviets moved in and claimed their prize in eastern Poland. Steinhardt informed Hull on September 17 that Moscow had announced that its armed forces had crossed into Poland "to take under their protection the life and property of the population of the Western Ukraine and Western White Russia" and also "to extricate the Polish people from the ill-fated war into which they have been led by their unwise leaders and to give them the possibility of living a peaceful life."[2] Soon the NKVD was working with the German military and the Gestapo in developing administrative policies for the occupied lands. In the Soviet zone the NKVD nationalized communications, banks, and newspapers. It also arrested the members of the Polish army and so-called reactionaries. Counterrevolutionary parties were taken over.[3]

The Soviets stressed the protective role that their army was playing in the hope of avoiding war with England and France. By the end of the third week in September the Red Army had taken eastern Poland, capturing the bulk of the Polish officers corps and millions of refugees. The western states, for the moment, chose not to declare war on the USSR. The United States also decided not to extend its arms embargo, already invoked against Germany, against the Soviet Union.[4]

Steinhardt understood that the alliance between Germany and the Soviet Union was a marriage of convenience and not a relationship of equals. He informed the State Department at the end of September that the Soviets were acting as Germany's purchasing agent on the international market, including buying goods for Germany in the United States, and that they were "acting in fact, if not in law, as a silent partner to Germany in the existing conflict."[5]

On the other hand, Steinhardt believed that Moscow was in the alliance to create the conditions for all-out war between Germany and England and France and thereby achieve its goals of preserving and strengthening itself by initially staying out of the war and by taking new territory, and eventually of turning against Germany in order to spread Communism. He argued that eventually it would not be too surprising to see the Soviets play the double-game against Germany, that is, to maintain the alliance but simultaneously to use the Comintern to attack Germany. In a note to Secretary of State Hull, dated November 15, 1940, he observed that if the Comintern should start encouraging resistance to Germany, it should not be viewed as evidence of a deteriorating relationship but "as an interesting manifestation of the duality of Soviet conduct of foreign affairs."[6] Such a development was not out of the question in late 1940 or in 1941, even though the Germans had managed to dispel the western armies and were stronger than ever. Stalin informed the Politburo on August 19, 1939, that the proposed nonaggression pact with Germany would open the door to war in the West and would allow "us to stay out of the conflict, and we may hope [later] to be able to find our way advantageously into the war. [Our] experience of twenty years shows that, in time of peace, it is not possible to have a Communist movement in Europe [in any one nation] for the Bolshevik Party to take power." As absurd as a possible Soviet attack against Germany in 1941 may seem, it should not, ipso facto, be ruled out. Stalinism, as collectivization and the purges proved, followed its own logic.[7]

The Comintern's view was that this was an imperialist war where the filthy rich nations of England, France, and the United States were lined up against the "cheated" states of Germany, Italy, and Japan.[8] Officially, the Comintern was neutral, but it was neutral in favor of the Axis powers.[9] The start of the war between the capitalist states was a great moment for Stalin and Communists everywhere. It was the beginning of the end of the capitalist era, which would soon be followed by the Communist era under the aegis of the Soviet Union. "This is not a war between Fascism and democracy," the Comintern Executive Committee announced at the end of September 1939, "but *a war for world rule,* a war between exploiters for the evil enslavement of the working class."[10] The bourgeoisie of the wealthy empires did not wage this war "against Fascism, as Chamberlain and left social-democrats claimed. The war is waged between two groups of capitalist states for world rule. . . . The division of the capitalist states into fascist and democratic" camps is preparing the way for the advance of Communism.[11] Stalin himself announced in the Comintern executive directive to the world's Communist parties at the end of September that "the era of dying capitalism is manifesting itself together with the era of dying social-democracy in the workers' movement."[12] This was not a man who was an emerging democrat or who led a society evolving toward social democracy. This was an ideologue, but a deliberate, careful politician who understood that while the big picture was clear in terms of history's direction, it was also crucial to indulge in realpolitik to manage daily affairs, to prevent an erosion of position, to exploit contradictions and rivalries among near and distant enemies, and to use the knowledge of the past to protect oneself and to arouse, control, and exploit the national spirit. Precisely at the time that he was outlining the future to Communists around the globe, he was also looking after Soviet security needs. Aside from the events that transpired in Poland and would soon take place in the Baltic States, Finland, and Romania, Stalin also opened up negotiations with the Turks in October 1939 to encourage them not to sign an alliance with the British. In his discussions with the Turkish ambassador in Moscow, Stalin showed a keen understanding of realpolitik and geopolitics—a startling contrast to his Communist jargon.[13] And this was neither the first nor the last demonstration of his understanding and use of power politics. He was a blend of ideology and realpolitik, with the former as his primary vision and the latter as his daily guide to survival. Cautious and prodding, he was also aggressive and dangerous. Steinhardt understood the amoral, opportunistic, and ideological nature of Stalin's foreign policy.

The Soviet invasion of Poland was followed in October by a Soviet seizure of naval and air bases in Estonia, Latvia, and Lithuania, and by an attack on Finland at the end of November. Moscow was also openly assisting German aggression and negotiating with Japan. In October the Germans captured the American merchant ship *City of Flint* and sent it to Murmansk, where the Soviets received it over American protests.

Each Soviet aggression or pro-Axis stand was unsettling to the Americans, especially the Winter War. These events put Roosevelt in a quandary. He did not want to denounce the Soviet Union because it would feed his political opponents at a time when there was an election on the horizon and it might isolate the USSR and drive it irretrievably to Hitler's side. Of course, he also had high hopes that the Soviet Union would eventually become a democratic state. Accordingly, his response to the attack on Poland and the Baltic States was barely palpable.[14] For Finland he went further. He had Steinhardt warn the Soviets to leave Finland alone when Soviet threats surfaced in October 1939.[15] For his effort Roosevelt received a public rebuke from Molotov, who warned Roosevelt to curb American imperialism in the Philippines and Cuba before interfering in the Soviet Union's relationship with Finland, "which long ago received from the Soviet Union its freedom and state independence."[16]

Roosevelt was furious over the Soviet rebuke to him and mounting pressure against Finland, but he hesitated to publicly castigate Moscow. He decided to support Steinhardt's penchant for retaliation, at least on minor matters. On December 22 he told Hull and Welles, "I think we should match every Soviet annoyance by a similar annoyance here against them." But he cautioned, "When it comes to the larger questions of downright rudeness on the part of Stalin, Kalinin, or Molotov we cannot afford to repay such rudeness with equivalent rudeness over here."[17]

American public opinion, never pro-Soviet, was shifting against the Soviet Union in the wake of the Soviet attacks on Poland, the Baltic States, and Finland. Americans were also upset over Soviet aid to Germany, negotiations with Japan, and a decidedly anti-American stand in the *City of Flint* incident. The newspaper coverage of the *City of Flint* episode was extensive in the United States, and Steinhardt was quoted at length stating that the Soviet Foreign Ministry refused to see him and keep him abreast of the crisis.[18] A spate of minor anti-Soviet activity was discernible, at least to the Soviet eye, including ill feeling toward Soviet institutions in the United States, especially the Amtorg Trading Corporation, anti-Soviet press coverage over the *City of Flint* incident, and discrimination against Soviet buyers. Deputy Commissar of Foreign Affairs Vladimir Potemkin, joined by Ambassador Oumansky who was then in Moscow, complained bitterly to Steinhardt and Thurston on October 17 and sarcastically asked, "Is it possible that the U.S. government cannot be responsible for the appearance of the anti-Soviet activities?" Steinhardt was surprised by the charges and declared that he would look into it. Potemkin urged him to use his influence to curb the anti-Soviet campaign.[19] The Soviets were not really concerned about the minor American problems, however. Molotov informed the German ambassador, Friedrich-Werner von Schulenburg, on October 19 that the United States was mainly interested in taking advantage of the war to improve its economic position and in dragging the USSR into war against Japan.[20]

The Molotov-Ribbentrop Pact had stipulated that Finland belonged to the Soviet Union, but there was evidence that the Germans were hoping that they would not have to honor that commitment. Their hope, however, was based on the belief that the war with the western states would never materialize or, if it did, would be settled quickly. The Germans had offered peace terms to England and France after Poland's capitulation, but both had refused. It has been assumed by scholars that the Soviet Union was relieved over the western states' refusal to negotiate a peace treaty.[21] That view is probably correct, but it is also true that the Kremlin was warming to its political-military relationship with Germany and offered, whether sincerely or not, to serve as a mediator between Germany, England, and France. Perhaps the Soviet Union saw a negotiated peace as a step to consolidate its newly annexed holdings and to prepare for the next round of land grabbing. When Ribbentrop visited Moscow at the end of September, he was received as an old Bolshevik. In October when Ambassador Maisky reported that Parliamentary Foreign Undersecretary Richard Butler hinted at the possibility of peace between Germany and England, Molotov quickly informed Schulenburg and offered to serve as a mediator. He then pressed Maisky to obtain more specifics. He cabled him that his talk with Butler was "of greatest interest [regarding its] hints of peace."[22] Peace in the eyes of unprepossessed observers, like Steinhardt, would have been an unmitigated disaster for the Soviet Union because Hitler hated the Communists and was champing at the proverbial bit to attack them. However, Stalin had blinders on. He thought the end of the capitalist era was at hand and that Germany—national socialist Germany—and the Soviet Union could work together to plunder the bourgeoisie colonial empires, expand their totalitarian systems to surrounding lands, and create a powerful alliance. In the long run, of course, Communism would prevail even in Germany, but Hitler was the kind of amoral, forceful ally who was closer to Communism than to social democracy and who was ridding the Germans of their democratic scruples. Stalin liked Hitler. This is not to say, naturally, that he trusted him or that he believed Hitler would never turn against him. He believed that if he could project an image of strength, adhere fastidiously to the alliance, and keep the western states as a viable military balance, whether they were fighting or not, then he could hunt with Hitler. The relationship, after all, was already producing dividends from land conquests to Japan's willingness to reduce tension with the Soviet Union in Asia. When Hitler did break faith with Stalin, the Soviet dictator was shocked. Molotov plaintively asked the German ambassador, "What have we done to deserve this?" And Stalin complained to Hopkins that Hitler was not a man who kept his word.[23]

Hitler did not share Stalin's view of the future, but in November 1939 he was in no position to block the Soviet Union against Finland, and the Soviets moved to take what had been promised to them. The Soviets had another reason for wanting Finland. The Finnish border ran within twenty miles of Leningrad, and for defensive purposes the Soviets desired to obtain a larger buffer against the real possibility that Germany might tear up the Nazi-Soviet agreement and attack the USSR. Steinhardt understood this point clearly. In a telegram to Secretary Hull on December 1, 1939, he wrote that Moscow undertook the war with Finland "perhaps to strengthen its position vis-à-vis Germany."[24]

The Soviets knew that they were gambling when they moved against Finland because Finland had close ties to Germany—it supplied Germany with naval goods—and it also had excellent relations with England, France, and the United States. The Americans admired the Finns as the only people who had paid their debt to the United States from World War I. For the Americans the Finnish payment was not simply a matter of a good economic partner but even more a matter of integrity and justice. It was also an issue of politics, for there were, as Steinhardt told Molotov, some 2.5 to 3 million Finnish-American voters.[25]

Nonetheless, the Soviets thought that the benefit of attacking Finland outweighed the risk. In addition, they had it in mind that they would demolish Finland quickly and simply present the world with a fait accompli. Deputy Commissar of Foreign Affairs Potemkin told Steinhardt that the war would be over "in four or five days."[26]

The war started on November 29, and to the surprise of many, including the Soviets, the Red Army had a difficult time against the Finns. In addition, foreign reaction was universally opposed to Moscow. England, France, and the United States condemned the attack, and on December 14 the USSR was expelled from the League of Nations for a war of aggression. The United States particularly denounced Soviet bombing of the civilian population, a charge which Molotov told Steinhardt was "based on a misunderstanding."[27] Nazi Germany, with a powerful military machine positioned directly opposite the Soviet armed forces in Poland, also was not pleased. The Soviets knew that the war could not go on very long, for a protracted conflict implied that the USSR was weak—its army could not defeat even little Finland—and risked bringing in England and France against them.

Steinhardt fully understood the Soviet dilemma. "It is becoming increasingly apparent," he told Hull on December 18, "that the Soviet plans in respect of Finland have seriously miscarried and that the Soviet Government is now faced with the necessity of expending a far greater effort than had been anticipated." But, according to Steinhardt, it was not only the impotency of its military that was causing "the discomfiture of the Soviet Government," but also the fact that Moscow "did not anticipate the extent of foreign reaction against Soviet aggression or expulsion from the League."[28]

Steinhardt recommended to Henderson in December 1939 that the United States show its outrage over Soviet aggression in Finland by breaking diplomatic relations, expelling all Soviet citizens from the United States, closing American ports "and perhaps the Panama Canal" to all Soviet ships, embargoing all exports to the Soviet Union, and "by other steps of similar severity." He stressed, "These people here are not interested in gestures, morality, ethics, or anything else. The only language that they understand is that of action, retaliation, and force."[29] The ambassador's recommendation, bristling with tough language and a clear message to Moscow, was not accepted.

In early January the ambassador wrote Henderson and again urged strong action. "As you know only too well from your own experience," he went on, "the only way to deal with these people is to 'get tough'—stop talking about retaliation—and actually retaliate. . . . As they need us a great deal more than we need them and as the only language they understand is the language of force I think it high time we invoked the only doctrine they respect." He informed Sumner Welles a few days later that "the Communist Utopia is probably the greatest fraud perpetrated on mankind in all of recorded history."[30] In March he pointed out to Henderson that Moscow was openly supporting Germany with deliveries of foodstuffs and raw materials and was working as Germany's purchasing agent in neutral countries. If the Germans do not get what they want, he added, it will not be because of Soviet unwillingness to provide it but "merely the result of the customary Soviet inefficiency."[31] Steinhardt, of course, was absolutely right. The Soviets were directly abetting the German war against France and England. They were obtaining critical supplies for the German war machine.

Steinhardt's views and recommendations were too tough for Roosevelt. The president wanted to show a modicum of displeasure over the Soviet Union's attack on Finland and its continuing close relationship with Germany and warming ties with Japan, but he did not wish to abandon the policy of conciliation. Instead of implementing Steinhardt's suggestions, Washington imposed a "moral embargo" on Soviet dealings with American aeronautical companies; that is, these firms were told that they should not trade with the USSR. In addition, it reduced the number of Soviet engineers who were allowed to visit American factories, and it slowed the delivery of American goods that Moscow had purchased.[32]

Washington's initiatives were mild, but the Soviets reacted to them as if Roosevelt had ordered the bombing of Moscow. Ambassador Oumansky lit into Hull, and Molotov lay siege to the embassy in Moscow. Secretary Hull complained of the "vituperative tone and demeanor" of Oumansky, and Thurston in Moscow was shocked at the "bitter and patronizing talk of Molotov."[33] In addition, the Soviet government tightened the already suffocating pressure on the embassy. Police surveillance included following representatives into public restrooms, of which there were only a few in Moscow, and placing microphones in every crook and cranny of the embassy and Spaso House. Food supplies were cut, and it became nearly impossible to obtain gasoline, train tickets, and such normal commodities as shoes and haircuts. Snow was usually piled high in front of the buildings. Private American citizens were harassed, and Americans who had accepted employment in the USSR or Soviet women who had married

Americans found it nearly impossible to leave. Searches of departing representatives with diplomatic immunity amounted to intrusive assaults.[34]

Steinhardt assumed the policy was moving toward a hard line. Thus, when he suggested that the Finnish mission coming to Moscow to negotiate a peace treaty be put up in the American embassy, he was confounded by Hull's reply that such an action would show favoritism and align the United States too closely with Finland. That was precisely Steinhardt's point. He became suspicious that there was some kind of understanding between Moscow and Washington of which he had not been informed. He immediately asked Henderson if he were being told everything.[35] Steinhardt was assured that he was privy to all the facts. The ambassador was bewildered.

The Soviets and the Finns signed the formal treaty ending the Winter War on March 12, and the terms were relatively lenient. The Russians took the Isthmus of Karelia and some other territory, thus moving the border away from Leningrad. They also set up naval and military bases on Finnish soil. However, the Finns escaped with their own government, independence, and most of their territory intact. The Soviets were not pleased over the lenient treaty, but any prolongation of the war underscored Soviet military weakness and opened the door to western involvement.

As the Winter War was ending, the Kremlin announced that Molotov would finally accept Steinhardt's invitation to dinner at Spaso House on April 25. Steinhardt reacted diplomatically. On March 4 he visited with V. N. Barkov, the chief of the Soviet Foreign Ministry's Department of Protocol, and gave him the list of people who would be invited to the dinner. He tactfully left off the names of the representatives of the belligerent powers. He told Barkov that he and his wife were honored that Molotov had agreed to accept their hospitality. He then carried on at some length with fulsome praise of Molotov and the Soviet system. He told Barkov that he considered Molotov "to be a very sympathetic personality" with whom "it would be a great pleasure to discuss any issue." He also declared that he appreciated Molotov's sense of humor, which was so "characteristic of the Russian mind, and his ability to handle major state issues 'in a human way' in contrast to other statesmen who would handle the same issues in an abstract and dried-up manner." He further declared that "he felt good in Moscow, had become accustomed to the peculiarities of [the] country, and was very glad that he was on good terms with Mr. Molotov." He emphasized that he came to the Soviet Union "with no bias, with a liberal cast of mind, and as no absolute advocate of the capitalist system." In fact, in 1932 or 1933 he had even published a work directed against the capitalist system. Moreover, Steinhardt stressed that he studied the Soviet Union and its system in an "unbiased and objective way" and that his legal training gave him an objective mind that allowed him to see Soviet successes, especially in education and upbringing. Finally, he believed that the Soviet Union was immunized from all of the political and economic troubles that had led Europe into war and that disturbed the United States because of "its special ways."

Barkov found the discussion long and tedious with Steinhardt doing most of the talking, but the ambassador was performing his duty. He was trying to impress the Soviets that he was an advocate of bilateral relations and that now that the Winter War was over there was an opportunity to improve the American-Soviet relationship. He also had another agenda. He was being friendly and hyperbolic because he wanted the Kremlin to approve a two-week trip at a good price (since he was not as rich as his predecessors, Bullitt and Davies) that he wished to take to the southern part of the Soviet Union, and he hoped that the Soviet Foreign Ministry would accommodate the embassy on a number of secondary issues, for example, to expeditiously issue exit visas for the Soviet wives of American diplomats and to turn over Ambassador Biddle's possessions, which were hidden someplace in Soviet-occupied Poland.

Steinhardt succeeded in extracting a good price from Intourist for his trip, but he failed in altering even slightly the Kremlin's obdurate and arrogant approach toward the United States. On March 27 Deputy Foreign Minister Lozovsky called Steinhardt into his office at 11:30 P.M. and handed him a memorandum that was a litany of complaints against the United States and Steinhardt personally. It charged that the United States was discriminating against the Soviet Union because Washington was selling war materials to England and France and "placing obstacles in the path" of Soviet agencies that were attempting to fill prewar [Winter War] orders for raw materials and machinery. It complained that the Soviet Union and Ambassador Oumansky were criticized in the United States by the Dies congressional committee and by Assistant Secretary of War Johnson. Lozovsky claimed that no American ambassador had ever been subjected to similar attacks in Moscow. The memorandum also rejected as "lies" the charges found in the American press that the Soviet Union bombed women and children in Finland. Furthermore, it charged that Steinhardt had persuaded American furriers to leave the Soviet Union. Finally, it objected to the fact that the United States wanted to recall some American engineers and that it embarrassed Soviet engineers traveling to the United States by asking them if they were spies.

Although Steinhardt tried to answer the charges, Lozovsky proudly reported that he beat him down and that by the end of the conversation Steinhardt had "lost his self-confidence and realized that his defense lawyer's ways were making no impression." In fact, Lozovsky maintained that Steinhardt made an about-face and started to express his "sympathy for the USSR."

Nonetheless, Steinhardt advised the Soviets to withdraw the memorandum. He told Lozovsky that it was "ill advised to send the memo to Washington because it might only lead to a revival of an anti-Soviet campaign." He believed that "the anti-Soviet campaign was in decline and, since the war with Finland had ended, the campaign would eventually subside." He stressed to the Soviets that all of his activities have been aimed at improving relations between the United States and the Soviet Union and that this type of memorandum made the relationship more difficult. At minimum he demanded that all complaints about him and the embassy be removed. If not, he would not take the planned trip to the southern part of Russia on March 28, but would remain in Moscow to refute the Soviet charges. When Lozvosky reported this to Molotov, the Soviet foreign minister decided to cut out the complaints about Steinhardt. He was handed the revised memorandum at 9:00 A.M., March 28, the day that his trip was scheduled to start. Reluctantly, he dispatched it to Washington.[36]

Steinhardt proceeded on his scheduled trip with his wife, daughter, her tutor, and an embassy aide. They went by railway lounge car to Rostov on Don, Baku, Tbilisi, Sochi, Yalta, Odessa, and Kiev. When he returned to Moscow two weeks later, he reported to the Soviet Foreign Ministry that he was "really happy" with the trip and the work of Intourist in arranging and conducting it. As for his opinion of the Soviet Union's southern cities, he told the Soviets that he was impressed with the railroad transportation system and with the supply of consumer goods in every city except Odessa. In general, he thought everything was going well.

Nonetheless, nothing had changed in the Soviet attitude toward the United States. The dinner with Molotov went off as scheduled, but it produced nothing. Steinhardt's desperate efforts to obtain Biddle's possessions before he left for the United States two weeks later also ended in frustration.

When Steinhardt announced that he would soon be returning to the United States, the Soviet government did show some concern. He was asked if his trip was "somewhat unexpected." The ambassador told the Kremlin that it was routine, a simple vacation that was pushed ahead because he had some private matters to settle in the wake of his uncle's recent death. He told the Soviets that he expected to be gone about two months.[37]

As planned, Steinhardt left Moscow on April 28, 1940. He arrived in the United States at the end of May, after spending a month in Europe. After he took care of his personal business in New York, he decided to stay on and attend the Democratic National Convention in Chicago in July. By the time he returned to Moscow in August 1940, a number of critical events had taken place and, most important for Steinhardt, the policy of accommodation, which had been under some strain because of Soviet aggression in Eastern Europe and Finland, was back in full force, which meant that Steinhardt, the advocate of reciprocity, had become a liability.

The "phony war" on the western front ended in April 1940 when Germany wheeled about its army in Poland and attacked France and England. France fell to the Nazis in June 1940. Mussolini declared war on France and England just before France's capitulation. Japan soon demanded occupation rights in French Indochina, which the Vichy French government quickly agreed to. Hungary and Bulgaria strengthened their ties to Nazi Germany and joined in the partition of Romania. Hungary took part of Transylvania (a territory that contained nationals of both Hungary and Romania and that both countries wanted), and Bulgaria grabbed southern Dobruja. The Soviets annexed the Romanian territories of Bessarabia and northern Bukovina, to Hitler's great consternation. The rump of Romania, with its rich oil reserves, soon fell in with the Axis. England retreated from Dunkirk, beaten and bloodied, to its island fortress. A wisp of its former self, England was now alone in the war against Germany.

Winston Churchill, the new prime minister, desperate for any help, began in the summer of 1940 to offer friendship and potential alliance to Moscow. The Red Army was the only force that stood in the way of complete Nazi-Fascist domination of the Continent. The British prime minister detected strain in the Nazi-Soviet alliance after the Soviet occupation of the Baltic States and Bessarabia and Northern Bukovina in June 1940.[38]

The British were willing to overlook Soviet aggression in the hope that they could befriend the Soviet Union and break the Nazi-Soviet pact. In fact, their policy toward the USSR eventually evolved into what was essentially a version of the policy of appeasement that they had adopted toward Nazi Germany. They also hoped to use the United States as a means to draw the Soviets away from the Germans. The British, as Steinhardt understood, had cast the Americans in the role of "wet nurse."[39] The Soviets, however, caught up in the opportunity to take territory created by the German victories and simultaneously wanting to avoid German displeasure, shunned all British proposals. The British ambassador to the USSR, Sir Stafford Cripps, who was pro-Soviet, found Stalin to be "formal and frigid."[40]

With the fall of France to Germany and the Japanese advance into French Indochina, the Roosevelt administration was more intent than ever on befriending the USSR. Sumner Welles told the British ambassador, Lord Lothian, on June 18, 1940, that he "imagined that certain practical steps would have to be taken by this Government if the Soviet were to believe that *we were sincerely desirous of improving relations with Russia*."[41] Not even Soviet aggression against Lithuania, Latvia, Estonia, and the Romanian territories of Bessarabia and northern Bukovina in late June altered the view. Washington, to be sure, censured Moscow for its aggression and froze the assets of the Baltic States, but good relations were the order of the day. The Americans patiently endured Soviet complaints and insults over their Baltic policy. Oumansky told Welles, "The action taken by the Soviet should have been applauded by the United States since it had obliterated the growth of 'fascism' in the three Baltic republics and had made it possible for the suffering peoples of those three nations to come under the sheltering protection of the Soviet Government as a result of which they would obtain the blessings of liberal and social government." Furthermore, he stated, the Americans should not view "the freely expressed will of the Baltic peoples to come under Russian domination on a par with the military invasion and occupation by Germany of the small Western European nations."[42]

Welles, of course, was not so gullible as to believe Oumansky's explanation, but he was interested in trying to improve relations. Between July 1940 and April 1941, he met periodically with Oumansky to find out what had to be done to achieve that goal. Throughout these discussions, Oumansky was importunate and captious. He repeatedly warned that if the Americans wanted better relations with Moscow, they had better start making major concessions. He came to the first meeting with a list of fifteen complaints against the United States, which he eventually agreed, as part of his concessions and show of good faith, to cut back to nine demands.[43] The Americans soon gave in on all of his points, including lifting the "moral embargo," permitting purchase of American machine tools on low-interest credit, and allowing Soviet engineers to visit American plants.[44] In the course of the discussions with Oumansky, Welles asked for two things in return. He wanted approval from the Soviet government to send American planes to China by way of Siberia, and he wished the difficulties that American citizens were experiencing in Soviet-occupied Poland to be cleared up. Oumansky rejected both requests out of hand.[45]

Although Steinhardt was not asked his opinion about the Oumansky-Welles talks, despite the fact that he was in the United States between May and August, he naturally soon became aware of them once back in Moscow. He was confused by the policy of unilateral concessions and told Henderson that the policy makes "it difficult to orient our course here."[46] Eventually, Welles and Hull wearied of Oumansky—Hull described him as a "walking insult"—and, in frustration, ordered Steinhardt to carry on the discussions in Moscow because in view of "the non-cooperative aggressiveness, in spite of the concrete results attained, which Oumansky continues to display here, the Department feels that more positive results might be accomplished through the transfer for discussion and negotiation in Moscow of many of the existing problems." They confided to Steinhardt, "The Department is of the opinion that Oumansky, in an endeavor to strengthen his personal prestige by playing a lone hand, may well be working at cross purposes with his Government. There is reason to doubt that he has reported accurately to his Government on all that has transpired here, especially on the concessions already made and on how this Government has sincerely endeavored to cooperate in these recent conversations."[47]

Steinhardt believed that there was no such thing as a "lone hand" in Stalin's Russia. Nonetheless, he opened up discussions with Molotov and Vyshinsky, who now held the position of assistant people's commissar of foreign affairs. He soon discovered that the Soviets were happy to take concessions, but they were not about to concede anything in return to the United States and, above all, they were not going to alter their relations with Germany. Although Steinhardt attempted to impress upon the Soviets that they were being isolated, especially in view of the signing of the Tripartite Pact in September 1940, his arguments were dismissed. Vyshinsky informed him rather glibly that "the existing agreements between the Soviet Union and Germany had not isolated the Soviet Union from other countries nor as our conversation proved had it stood in the way of an exchange of views." At the end of October Steinhardt informed Hull, "I am more than ever of the opinion that any concessions made to the Soviet Union in administrative and commercial fields should be effected on the basis of strict reciprocity and with no expectation that they will in the slightest degree affect the political policy of the Soviet Government."[48] He confided to Henderson on October 20 that the American and British policies were viewed by Moscow "as signs of weakness." In addition, he reported to Henderson that the Soviets were trying to arrange a nonaggression pact with Japan that aimed at war between the United States and Japan. On January 11, 1941, he told Hull that the Soviets were still supplying Germany with essential goods.[49]

The Welles-Oumansky discussions were, in fact, hopeless from the beginning. The Soviets were not going to jeopardize their opportunity to take territory or their relationship with Germany and would not change their behavior toward the United States, obnoxious though it be, since it was being reinforced by American concessions. That reality seemed to escape the American government. In fact, the American leaders had reached the point where, as Welles summarized for Roosevelt, they believed that if they altered their conciliatory posture, the Soviets would take measures against the United States "which would render futile the efforts we are making . . . to remove some of the obstacles that might permit an improvement of relations between the United States and the Soviet Union."[50] Concessions, thus, were no longer simply a way to warm up the Soviets but now were necessary to prevent the Soviets from becoming colder.

Despite Soviet unresponsiveness and Steinhardt's arguments and protests, Washington continued on with its policy. It was now helped along by the mounting evidence of strain in the Nazi-Soviet alliance. The Tripartite Pact, signed on September 27, 1940, by Germany, Italy, and Japan, seemed directed against Moscow. The large Nazi troop movements in Eastern Europe plus the positioning of German forces in Finland in the fall of 1940 clearly menaced the Soviet Union. Hungary and Romania joined the Tripartite Pact on November 20 and 23, respectively. Hitler enticed the Hungarians and Romanians by opening up the issue of control of Transylvania, indicating that he would give it to the country that showed the most dedication to Berlin and its military plans. British and American intelligence had obtained evidence by the beginning of 1941 that a Nazi attack on the Soviet Union was imminent. The NKVD also had information on German troop movements into East Europe.[51]

Stalin did not think that the alliance was over. He sent Molotov to Berlin in November 1940 to demand that the Nazis reduce their military activity in Finland and Romania and agree to a Soviet sphere of influence in Finland, Bulgaria, and the Dardanelles. On November 25 he offered to join the Tripartite Pact under certain conditions. In early 1941 the Supreme Soviet Command completed a detailed theater-of-war survey of Iran. Clearly Stalin was still thinking of the Nazi-Soviet alliance as a viable, if troubled, relationship.[52]

Hitler, however, was not. The Nazis moved advisers into Bulgaria in late February 1941, and Bulgaria formally joined the Tripartite Pact on March 1, 1941. The Soviets were shocked, for they felt Bulgaria was their bailiwick. They publicly complained to Berlin but received no response. At a cocktail party Steinhardt's wife asked Ambassador Schulenburg if war were about to break out between Germany and the Soviet Union. He assured her that it was not, but the evidence from all quarters indicated otherwise.[53]

The Germans began overflights in March, photographing defense networks as far as one hundred miles into the Soviet Union. To show their displeasure with the German policies, the Soviets recognized and signed a pact of friendship on April 5 with Yugoslav leaders, who had overthrown a pro-Nazi government on March 25. On April 6 an awesome German force swept into Yugoslavia and partitioned the country among the Axis powers. Italy took Dalmatia, the Adriatic islands, and part of Slovenia. It also set up a protectorate in Montenegro, and its satellite government in Albania annexed the Kosovo region. Germany annexed the bulk of Slovenia into the Third Reich and set up a German satellite government in Serbia. It sanctioned a collaborationist government under the Fascist Ustasa Party in Croatia and Bosnia-Hercegovina. Hungary took lands that it had ruled before World War I, and Bulgaria annexed Macedonia. The Soviets quickly retracted their day-old pact of friendship and openly prostrated themselves before the Nazis in the hope of warding off the blow that now seemed inevitable to everyone with the exception of Stalin, who insisted that the evidence of an attack was a British provocation.[54] On April 13 the Kremlin signed a five-year neutrality agreement with Japan. It did not have a territorial protocol like the Molotov-Ribbentrop Pact, but it was a crucial agreement that prepared the way for a Japanese move to the south with its rich natural resources, especially oil, and toward conflict with the United States. For Stalin it was a small sign, perhaps, that the feared German attack might not be coming, for military logic would argue for a joint German-Japanese attack on the Soviet Union if an attack were planned. Of course, Tokyo and Berlin could be playing the card of deception, but it seemed unlikely. On the other hand, Stalin was not taking into consideration Hitler's racist ideology. The Nazi dictator proved himself quite willing to sacrifice military advantage to show that the Teutonic race needed no assistance from an Asiatic race to defeat the likes of the Russian Slavs, who could not even conquer little Finland. In that case, the nonaggression pact was a godsend for Stalin, for it allowed him to transfer troops westward from the borders of Siberia and Outer Mongolia to oppose the Germans in the winter of 1941. In any case, though, Stalin did believe that Hitler would give him an ultimatum and thus allow him an opportunity to negotiate and turn over some land to prevent a Nazi attack.[55]

Steinhardt was quite aware of the growing stress in Nazi-Soviet ties, but he still felt that the policy of uncritical accommodation was foolish. He informed the State Department that, despite the decline in Nazi-Soviet relations, the Soviets would literally do anything to avoid war with Germany.[56] No amount of concessions by the United States would break the Nazi-Soviet tie. The only way, he concluded, that Moscow would become an ally of the West would be if Germany attacked the Soviet Union.[57] And so it was. But Steinhardt's voice was increasingly being tuned out. Even when the Soviets signed the nonaggression pact with Japan on April 13, 1941, which Steinhardt correctly interpreted as directed against the United States, the Roosevelt administration did not react. Steinhardt's days were clearly numbered.

On June 22, 1941, Germany attacked the USSR. Stalin, writes General Dmitri Volkogonov in the first objective Russian biography of Stalin by a nondissident, "went into psychological shock." He "was so depressed and shaken that he ceased to be a leader."[58] Molotov, not Stalin, addressed the Soviet people on the day of the invasion and called on them to "fight the enemy."[59] Great Britain offered an alliance, the United States offered aid, and the Soviet people fought and died. Stalin must have been astonished by these events. He knew that he had unleashed Hitler against the West, and now the Western Powers were offering to help him. He also knew that he had done terrible things to his people, from collectivization to the purges, and the people and the army did not turn on him but fought tenaciously. Maybe they were not waging war for him or for Communism, but they were determined to protect their land, their homes, and their nation. The Orthodox Church particularly helped rally the people, beckoning to life the submerged nationalism of the Russians. The time was too critical to think about getting rid of Stalin. He was useful as a symbol of unity.

On July 3 Stalin finally addressed the Soviet people. His voice was dull and colorless, as if he were in a daze, according to Ivan Maisky, the Soviet ambassador to England. He told his fellow citizens, "Our war for the freedom of our fatherland joins with the struggle of the people of Europe and America for their independence, for democratic freedom."[60] It was a propaganda message that would play well in the West and perhaps in the Soviet Union, but in the latter case he made sure that such notions as democratic freedom would not grow. Once it was clear that the Soviet people were going to resist Hitler, he quickly moved to take leadership of the Soviet Union, to consolidate his power, and to insulate himself against any potential reprisals. He shrewdly downplayed Communism and Marxism-Leninism and started to play up Russian nationalism and the Russian Orthodox Church. The Russian people fought doggedly and proved themselves to be strong and brave and able to withstand incredible hardships.

Their vast land with its cold climate also assisted against the invader, as it had against Napoleon Bonaparte nearly 130 years earlier.

People and territory, however, were not enough this time. The Soviet Union and Stalin wouldn't have survived relying on space, climate, and nationalism. They desperately needed outside help. It came in part from the British and the Americans, but even that would not have turned the tide. The critical help ultimately came from the invaders themselves, from their excesses. Embarking on a crusade against Communism, Hitler proceeded to maintain its most grievous feature, the collective farms. He decided to keep the collective system because of its effectiveness as a way to control the people. He also put into effect a savage law of hostages, a ratio of 100 to 1; that is, for every German soldier killed by a guerrilla behind the lines, 100 Soviets were shot, regardless of whether they had anything to do with guerrilla action or not. The Nazis also mistreated prisoners of war, and no attempt was made to conceal this maltreatment. It was perpetrated right before the eyes of the population, so the harshness of the occupation sank in generally. Finally, of course, the Gestapo brought the holocaust to Soviet-occupied territory. Many Soviet citizens and especially the Jews were arrested, summarily sent to extermination camps, and in most cases cruelly murdered. Many Soviet citizens initially welcomed the Germans as liberators from the hated Communist system, but they were quickly disillusioned and turned against the Nazis. Ironically, the Nazi invasion and occupation strengthened Soviet totalitarianism. Steinhardt had predicted that many, especially in Ukraine, would welcome a foreign liberator and that probably "the Stalinist regime could not survive any invasion," but he had not factored in the absolute, alienating horror of Nazism.[61]

Roosevelt and Hopkins met with Oumansky on July 10. Roosevelt told him that the United States would assist the Soviets with credits and aid, but that he was concerned about the ability of the Red Army to hold out against the Germans. Oumansky, reflecting Molotov's instructions, assured him that it would survive. When the president expressed a fear that Japan might also attack the Soviet Union, Oumansky immediately declared that "it was critically important that the American government 'assist' the Japanese government by public and diplomatic pressure to find the course of peace and to realize that an attack on the USSR on land or at sea would lead to . . . concrete measures by the USA." When the president replied that the United States would set up an economic and financial embargo against Japan if it should attack the Soviet Union, Oumansky wanted to know what the United States would do to prevent such aggression as opposed to reacting after such aggression. FDR, according to Oumansky, was vague and defensive, but he did stress that the United States was already putting economic pressure on Japan. Hopkins, for his part, told Oumansky that the members of the Roosevelt administration were committed to the Soviet Union as it faced the German armies. For example, he told Oumansky that Secretary of the Navy Frank Knox and Secretary of War Henry Stimson had a "prejudice" against the Soviet Union, but they "quickly swallowed the pro-Russian pill" to support FDR's program.[62]

Whereas the United States promised aid, the British government offered an alliance. Stalin, however, did not accept the British offer of alliance until July 18, and then his acceptance was terse and for the first and last time he referred to the Molotov-Ribbentrop Pact by stating that it was only a temporary arrangement to which the Soviets agreed in order to gain more time to build their forces against Germany.[63] His explanation was an expedient, though shrewd, defense of his aggressive policy. It was accepted by western political leaders and curiously by western historians, even though all the evidence indicated that he was in the alliance with the Nazis for the long haul and for whatever territory he could conquer. After dismissing the Molotov-Ribbentrop Pact, Stalin started to list his demands. He wanted a second front in Western Europe immediately, and he wanted the Polish government-in-exile in London to establish diplomatic relations with the USSR without defining the Polish-Soviet border. General Sikorski, head of the Polish government, wanted the Soviets to guarantee Poland's 1939 borders, but under pressure from Churchill, he acquiesced in a treaty that simply did not mention territory.[64]

Given the precarious position of the Red Army, Stalin's demand for a second front was understandable, but England had just been beaten off the continent and was in no position to launch an offensive in Europe. A measure of Stalin's desperation might be gleaned from the fact that he was quite willing in 1941 and 1942 to have western troops on Soviet soil.[65] After the Battle of Stalingrad, he did not want them even in the Balkans, let alone the Soviet Union.

The great struggle that now raged across Eastern and Central Europe was not simply between Germany and the Soviet Union. The Eastern and Central Europeans themselves were caught up inevitably in the conflict as allies and victims. Although its army and country were devastated by the German advance, the Polish government did set up an effective guerrilla army called the Home Army, which eventually tied down roughly 500,000 German occupation soldiers and prevented one out of every eight German transports from reaching the eastern front. Over six million Poles, including three million Jews, were killed.[66]

In Yugoslavia the resistance movements, especially Tito's partisan guerrilla army, also preoccupied some 125,000 German soldiers by 1944. Roughly 1.75 million people died there as a result of the German occupation and internecine conflict among the different ethnic groups that populated Yugoslavia. Romania joined the invasion of the Soviet Union as a full partner, hoping to reclaim its lost territories of Bessarabia, northern Bukovina, and Transylvania. It provided grain and fuel to Hitler's invasion force and fielded itself twenty-seven divisions. The Romanians fought tenaciously against the Russians, ultimately suffering 500,000 casualties of whom 300,000 perished. On August 23, 1944, though, the Romanians did an abrupt about-face, declared war on Germany, and joined with the Allied Powers.

Hungary, under Regent Miklos Horthy, was an unenthusiastic ally of the Axis. It joined in the invasion of the Soviet Union in order to protect its claim on Transylvania, but it refused to implement the Nazi extermination campaign against the Jews and virtually maintained neutrality in the war between Germany and the West, even though it was officially at war with both England and the United States. The Allies did not bomb Hungary until Hitler actually occupied it in mid-March 1944, and Hungary did not fire on Allied overflights until 1944.

Bulgaria, the only country in Eastern Europe lacking a significant German minority that Hitler could manipulate as a fifth column, was even less involved than Hungary. It refused to declare war on the Soviet Union on grounds of Slav brotherhood, and it protected Bulgarian Jews against the radical Right. It declared war on the Allies on December 13, 1941, but it did no fighting against the West, and the West did not bomb it until the winter of 1943/44 when a strongly pro-Nazi government was set up.

The Czech regions of Bohemia and Moravia saw no significant resistance to the Nazis, and they collaborated with and were rewarded by the Germans. Slovakia, an autonomous satellite of the Reich, did eventually mount a formidable resistance effort against the Nazis and was subsequently occupied. Eduard Beneš, who had resigned as president in October 1938, set up in London a Czechoslovak government-in-exile in 1941 that was accorded recognition by England, the United States, and the Soviet Union.[67] He quickly developed a close working relationship with the Soviet government.[68]

In addition, of course, the Western Powers were fighting in the Pacific against Japan, and they soon opened up a massive bombing campaign against Germany and Italy. They also took control of the seas with their technology, convoys, and capital ships. The Soviet Union feared that Japan might launch an attack in the Soviet Far East, but it hoped that the United States would prevent such an invasion.[69]

9

"Comrade Stalin" Becomes "Mr. Stalin"

The Nazi attack on the Soviet Union brought relief to Roosevelt. Friendship now had a legitimate rationale. The USSR was in desperate straits, and the United States could now step forward without embarrassment and offer unconditional aid as proof of its desire for good relations and as a means to keep the Soviet Union in the war against the Nazis. The eastern front would be the quid pro quo for American concessions in the short run. By the time the need for the eastern front had diminished, Roosevelt believed that the Soviet government would be so moved by selfless American largess that it would voluntarily abandon its odd ways and move toward democracy. The president told Churchill on October 28, 1942, that he was "not unduly disturbed about our respective responses or lack of responses from Moscow. I have decided that they do not use speech for the same purposes that we do." But he emphasized, "I want us to be able to say to Mr. Stalin that we have carried out our obligation one hundred percent."[1]

When the war broke out in 1939, there was no doubt of Roosevelt's sympathy for the English and French. His actual policy, though, was cautious because of strong isolationist sentiment in Congress and among the voters and probably because he had no burning desire to prop up the European empires.[2] After the Nazi attack on the Soviet Union and the advent of the de facto alliance between England and Soviet Russia, aid to London and Moscow accelerated dramatically, and the Soviet Union's needs became America's top priority. Roosevelt promised, "We are going to give all the aid we possibly can to Russia." He did not fear, as some of the State Department experts did, Russian domination of Europe after Hitler's defeat.[3] Secretary Hull characterized the new policy succinctly as "all aid to the hilt."[4] Hopkins soon adopted the policy. There was no thought of making demands of the Soviets in return, such as a guarantee of the independence and borders of Poland and the Baltic States, so Steinhardt was soon bypassed by the American government.

The Soviets, for their part, immediately requested everything from bombers to pursuit planes. Molotov sent pleas to Oumansky to relay to the American government, and he also called in Steinhardt and complained that the United States was not being specific with its promise of aid. The ambassador reassured him and declared that all requests would be sent to Washington. He asked how and where the aid should be delivered, and Molotov told him that the Persian Gulf-Iranian route was open all year and there were also some airports in Siberia.[5] The offer of Siberian bases was unusual and reflected Soviet anxiety. Although Molotov initially worked through Steinhardt, it soon became clear to him that the American government discounted the envoy, so he, too, soon paid him little attention. On July 24 he again called in Steinhardt and this time attacked him for a saturnine evaluation of the Red Army's performance that the ambassador had given to Erskine Caldwell, who was writing an article for *Life* magazine entitled "Behind Russian Lines." After Molotov complained, Steinhardt agreed to remove his evaluation of the Red Army and to limit his interviews. Caldwell's article appeared on July 28 and made no mention of Steinhardt. However, Molotov was furious with Steinhardt and considered him to be out of step with Roosevelt and Welles, "who have shown a most generous assistance to the USSR in the struggle against Fascism."[6]

Despite the Nazi attack, though, Roosevelt faced two significant problems in delivering massive aid to Soviet Russia. First, the policy was not popular with the American public because of the Soviet Union's totalitarianism, attack on tiny Finland, and alliance with Nazi Germany. Senator Harry S. Truman from Missouri reflected public opinion when he announced on June 22, 1941, in the wake of the Nazi invasion: "If we see that Germany is winning we ought to help Russia, and if Russia is winning we ought to help Germany, and that way let them kill as many as possible, although I don't want to see Hitler victorious under any circumstances."[7] Former president Herbert Hoover put the public objection to aid in prescient terms: "Now we find ourselves promising aid to Stalin and his militant conspiracy against the whole democratic ideals of the world. . . . If we go further and join the war and we win, then we have won for Stalin the grip of Communism on Russia, and more opportunity for it to extend in the world."[8]

The second problem was that both the State Department and the War Department wanted to move slowly in assisting the Soviet Union. They were not sure that the Soviet Union could survive the attack and saw no point in wasting resources on a hopeless cause. They also did not trust Moscow, and they agreed with Truman and Hoover that there was little difference between Nazi and Communist totalitarianism.[9]

Roosevelt and Hopkins tried to solve the first problem by orchestrating from the White House a widespread propaganda campaign to persuade the American people that Stalinist Russia was a long-suffering, emerging democracy. Roosevelt, Hopkins, Davies, and Harriman all played critical roles in this image-altering effort, which was phased in over the course of the wartime alliance and is described incrementally below.[10] FDR proclaimed in 1942, "I am perfectly willing to mislead and tell untruths if it will help win the war."[11] The long-term consequences of that approach were cynicism, confusion of purpose, and an erosion of faith in the democratic ideals for which American society stood.

The Soviet government was aware of the popular opposition that Roosevelt faced in changing the image of the Soviet Union. Oumansky informed Molotov on the day of the invasion that the Roosevelt administration was very supportive of the Soviet Union but that the president had to overcome "isolationists like Hoover and Lindbergh" and to defeat "anti-Roosevelt fascist groups," who rejoiced in the start of the war between Nazis and Communists. He also had to deal with "groups of Republicans and independent Democrats plus groups of our professional enemies like Bullitt and Berle plus the Catholic hierarchy who were already criticizing the actions of Roosevelt and the dramatic efforts of Churchill."[12]

The second problem was more immediate and acute in the short term, and it related directly to the practical problem of fulfilling the Soviet Union's request for material assistance. Roosevelt and Hopkins created a super agency to handle aid to Britain and Soviet Russia, the Lend-Lease Administration and its allied Division of Defense Aid Reports. In the case of the Soviet Union, this agency soon took over the jobs of the State Department, the War Department, and the ambassador and embassy in Moscow. Roosevelt and Hopkins thought the State Department was too cautious on the Soviet Union, and Hopkins dismissed the War Department's reservations as so much "bunk."[13] On July 11 Hopkins told Oumansky that incorrigible anti-Soviet types like Adolph Berle would be removed from dealing with Soviet-American relations and that the president was drawing close to him people like former ambassador Joseph Davies, who was pro-Soviet. Oumansky reported to Molotov, "I immediately took advantage of this view and without naming Berle complained that there were several circles" of anti-Soviet sentiment in the American government. Hopkins assured him that this would change.[14]

The vehicle for the change was the Lend-Lease Administration, informally called the "Hopkins Shop," which came into existence shortly after the Lend-Lease Act became law in March 1941. Its actual, though unofficial, head was Hopkins and its key officials included General James H. Burns, former head of the Army Ordnance Department; W. Averell Harriman, who was appointed Lend-Lease expediter in London; Edward R. Stettinius, a friend of Hopkins and former chairman of the U.S. Steel Corporation; and Oscar Cox, a Treasury Department assistant who helped draft the Lend-Lease Act.

The man chosen to run the Lend-Lease Program in the Soviet Union was none other than Colonel Faymonville, who had been removed and put out to pasture by the War Department because of his exaggerated Sovietophilia. Summoned to Washington in July 1941 by the "Hopkins Shop," he immediately demonstrated that his pro-Soviet disposition had not changed. He escorted a visiting Soviet military mission around Washington and was roundly criticized for showing them classified documents and pressuring government agencies and factories to comply with Soviet requests for information and supplies. His role as guide "was viewed as such an extreme violation of military regulations," according to one report, "that the General Staff regarded it as treason and charges in writing, the basis for a trial, were actually on General Marshall's desk." The Lend-Lease Administration, though, was "as pleased as the army was upset" over Faymonville's guided tour.[15] It proved that he could be counted on to implement the president's policy of unilateral aid to Moscow. He would be the perfect tool for Roosevelt and Hopkins in their effort to demonstrate uncritical friendship toward Stalin and to nudge the Soviet Union along the path of democracy.

The Soviets, too, knew of Faymonville's importance to Roosevelt's policy. Burns told Oumansky on July 17 that he was appointing Faymonville to a commission that could provide "direct guidance" on Soviet supply needs to the Lend-Lease Administration. Oumansky was thrilled and wrote Molotov that Faymonville in all the topsy-turvy years of the American-Soviet relationship had maintained an "absolute friendship" with the Soviet government and alone among American military officials had pushed for assisting the Soviet Union. For his pro-Soviet positions, Oumansky went on, he "was denied a promotion to the rank of general."[16] Oumansky also had nothing but praise for Faymonville's help with the Soviet military mission.[17] Deputy Soviet Foreign Minister S. A. Lozovsky praised Roosevelt to Morris Hindus of the New York *Herald Tribune* on June 13, 1942, for having the foresight to send Faymonville to Moscow. Hindus agreed and told Lozovsky that when FDR learned that Colonel Faymonville thought that "the Red Army was strong and capable of defeating the Germans, Roosevelt summoned him from the province where he had been sent by the reactionary officials of the Department of State for his pro-Soviet reports and sent him to the Soviet Union."[18]

To assign Faymonville to Moscow, however, was a problem. The State Department and the War Department thought that he was a willing tool of the Soviets. Hopkins had to resort to subterfuge to sneak him into Moscow.

In late July Hopkins flew to Moscow to meet with Stalin. His job was to assess Stalin and find out if the USSR could hold out against the Nazis and, if it could, to reassure Stalin that massive American aid would be forthcoming. His onsite inspection would also serve as a counterpoint to those in the United States who were arguing that aid to Soviet Russia was a waste of resources because of the USSR's inevitable defeat. Churchill cabled Stalin that Hopkins was an extremely powerful man who was very close to Roosevelt with clout to get immediate assistance to the Soviet Union. He also told him that Hopkins hated Hitler and was on fire for democracy.[19] Roosevelt wrote Stalin that he was "to treat Mr. Hopkins with the identical confidence you would feel if you were talking directly to me." For the Soviets his importance was underlined by the fact that he lived in the White House.[20]

Steinhardt met Hopkins at the airport in Moscow on July 30. He briefed him about the situation in Soviet Russia and stressed that he believed the Soviet Union could hold out. That evening he escorted Hopkins to the Kremlin to see Stalin. The ambassador warned Hopkins that Stalin had a penchant for secrecy.[21] The Soviet dictator, however, was more talkative than usual. Steinhardt cabled Hull that Stalin talked to Hopkins "with a frankness unparalleled in my knowledge in recent Soviet history."[22] He realistically described the dire plight of the Soviet Union. He told the Americans that the USSR could hold on if massive aid were forthcoming. He requested machine guns, rifles, 20,000 antiaircraft guns, and reams of aluminum for building aircraft. He also emphasized the desirability of American involvement in the war and the need for accessibility to American military secrets.[23] He denounced Hitler for breaking his word. He told Hopkins that there must be "a minimum moral standard between all nations and without such a minimum moral standard nations could not co-exist." He declared, "The present leaders of Germany knew no such minimum moral standard and that, therefore, they represented an anti-social force in the present world." Agreements and treaties must be kept, Stalin emphasized, otherwise "international society will be unable to survive."[24] Apparently, Hopkins did not realize that Stalin was complaining that Hitler broke the Molotov-Ribbentrop Pact, which opened the door to World War II and was responsible for America's assistance to Great Britain and indeed for Hopkins's visit to Moscow. Hopkins, who emphasized to Stalin that "the most important thing to be done in the world today was to defeat Hitler and Hitlerism," seemed to be oblivious to the fact that Stalin admired Hitler, was his ally in the invasion and occupation of Eastern Europe, and was now hurt that Hitler had turned against him. Marshal Georgi K. Zhukov recalled in his memoirs that Stalin trusted Hitler to the end and refused to believe that the invasion of 1941 was sanctioned by his coconspirator in Berlin.[25]

Hopkins, of course, had no way of verifying whether or not the USSR could survive the Nazi attack, but he was of a mind to gamble, as was Roosevelt, that it could. Steinhardt advised Hopkins that he believed Soviet Russia could hold out, and his view undoubtedly strengthened Hopkins in his predilection to recommend to Roosevelt immediate and comprehensive assistance to the Soviet Union. Hopkins did not bring up the Nazi-Soviet alliance or the Soviet aggression against Poland, Finland, the Baltic States, and Romania, and neither did Stalin. He really did not care if Stalin was a totalitarian dictator. His touchstone was Hitler. "Whoever fights against Hitler," he stressed to Stalin, "is on the right side in the conflict and we intend to help that side." Roosevelt believed, he asserted, that "Hitler was the enemy of all peace." The president "gives his word and is prepared without delay to deliver every kind of assistance without any conditions." Hopkins did ask Stalin for two favors: to permit American military observers on the eastern front and to allow an American consulate at Vladivostok. Stalin rejected both requests. He also told Stalin that American experts would accompany the technical Lend-Lease aid, but Stalin never explicitly agreed to accept them.[26]

When the United States tried to obtain visas for the American technicians, the Soviet government refused to grant them, and Faymonville had to provide a face-saving solution for Hopkins. No one could accuse Stalin of essaying to curry favor with the Americans. He did not trust the Americans or, for that matter, the British. He harbored a profound animosity toward the western states. Stalin, as Walter Laqueur put it, "slightly preferred Hitler" to Churchill and Roosevelt. "The Western countries were considered to be the true enemies of the Soviet Union, whereas the attitude toward Nazi Germany was far more equivocal."[27]

Hopkins left Moscow with a favorable opinion of Stalin. He thought that he was an excellent administrator and a man of realism, confidence, determination, and power. He knew Stalin was in charge and alone had all the facts at his disposal. Even though Stalin was rather candid in describing Soviet needs, Hopkins was still bothered by the "secretiveness" that permeated his meeting. "I would hardly call Uncle Joe a pleasant man," he wrote General Hastings Ismay, the head of the British military mission to Moscow, "although he was interesting enough, and I think I got what I wanted, but you can never be sure about that." He also found Stalin to be strong, with big, sturdy hands and the small, muscular frame of "a football coach's dream of a tackle."[28]

Hopkins went to England to join Churchill, who was sailing to Placentia Bay in Newfoundland to meet with Roosevelt. The meeting took place on August 9-12. Its purpose was to plan military cooperation in the Far East and Europe, to offer aid to Stalin, and to enunciate the principles guiding the United States and Britain in the war. Hopkins was instrumental in persuading Roosevelt that the Soviets could hold out through the winter and, if aid were forthcoming, beyond that. He also informed Roosevelt that Stalin was not an imperialist whom the United States had to guard against in Eastern Europe or elsewhere. Roosevelt was unquestionably influenced by Hopkins's report on Stalin. He told Bullitt in early 1943 that he agreed with Hopkins's characterization of Stalin and that he had a "hunch" that Stalin was not an imperialist.[29]

Upon hearing Hopkins's report Roosevelt decided to send Stalin all the assistance that the United States could muster.[30] He immediately notified Steinhardt that aid would be coming and that an American-British delegation would soon be sent to work out the details. Steinhardt relayed the good news to Stalin on August 15. The ambassador reported that Stalin gave him a note for Roosevelt indicating that he accepted his generous offer. After Stalin read the note aloud and handed it to Steinhardt, the ambassador reported, Stalin took the note back and said with a smile, "I think I should change Comrade Stalin to Mr. Stalin," which, according to the ambassador, he did.[31] Clearly, Stalin was taking off the hat of anticapitalist revolutionary and putting on the chapeau of bourgeois ally. For him it was as easy as changing names, and he knew it would have a positive impact on Roosevelt and Hopkins. Oumansky told the State Department that the Soviet government deeply appreciated the offer of assistance against the German aggressor that "is threatening the security and independence of all freedom-loving nations."[32] Oumansky's statement fitted in nicely with the declaration of principles called the Atlantic Charter for which the Placentia Bay meeting is best remembered. Roosevelt and Churchill announced that their countries were involved in the war in order to guarantee the right of all nations to hold free elections and to be free from foreign pressure. The Soviet government was soon extended a $1 billion line of credit.[33]

W. Averell Harriman, a linchpin in the "Hopkins Shop," was dispatched to Moscow in September to ascertain the amount and type of assistance that the Soviets required. Lord Beaverbrook, Churchill's minister of aircraft production and later minister of supply and a leader of pro-Soviet sentiment in England, went along with Harriman to protect British interests and to make sure that the USSR received enough aid to stay in the war, even if it meant giving Moscow some of the aid already pledged by the United States to Great Britain.[34] Beaverbrook's influence in England rested largely on his ownership of the largest mass-circulation newspaper group, including the *Daily Express.*

The Beaverbrook-Harriman mission was a substantial undertaking, replete with military and naval experts. The American delegation was "a Hopkins creation" from beginning to end. Its job, under Harriman, was to carry out FDR's commitment of unconditional aid. Beaverbrook had no problem with that policy whatsoever. Laurence Steinhardt did, but Harriman paid no attention to him and, in fact, recommended his removal, which Hopkins had already set in motion. To neutralize the ambassador until he could be replaced and to guarantee that the president's policy of unquestioning and unilateral aid would be implemented, Hopkins had arranged for Harriman to outrank Steinhardt, and he had planted Colonel Faymonville in the delegation with the misleading title of secretary but, unbeknownst to Harriman, the War Department, and the State Department, with the actual intention of naming him Lend-Lease administrator after the mission had arrived in Moscow. When the Army objected to Faymonville's participation in the delegation because of his well-known sympathy for the Soviet Union, Hopkins showed that he was ready to fight for the colonel and bluntly informed the Army, "You might as well get his papers ready, because he's going over." The army evidently gave way because the mission was temporary and Faymonville's role appeared minor.[35]

On October 2, when the mission was about to return home, Hopkins announced the appointment. He shocked the War Department, the State Department, and Harriman. So strong were the objections of the embassy staff to Faymonville that Harriman had to ask another member of the delegation, economist Douglas Brown, to stay on temporarily as head of the Lend-Lease mission, so that it would not appear as if Faymonville were in charge. However, the economist soon left and it was absolutely clear that Faymonville ran the operation and reported directly to the "Hopkins Shop" in Washington, bypassing the embassy entirely. A storm of protest broke over Hopkins in Washington. The War Department and the State Department expressed their outrage and pushed for Faymonville's removal. Hopkins, however, was able to keep him in Moscow until late 1943. For Hopkins the risk of such underhandedness was well worth the reward of having in Moscow a person who would implement Roosevelt's approach without question.[36]

The Beaverbrook-Harriman discussions in Moscow amounted to a list of demands that Stalin and Molotov petulantly put forward. The talks also revealed some of the concerns and attitudes of the new Allies. First of all, of course, the Soviets wanted massive aid, including fighter and reconnaissance planes, anti-tank guns, tanks, barbed wire, medium bombers, and armor plate. Harriman readily agreed to fulfill their demands. He was interested in impressing Stalin with the openness and generosity of the United States. He pointedly did not ask for anything in return for the American aid. Stalin was alternately rude and friendly. He complained about being offered only a thousand tons of armor plate by the United States. Harriman had to explain the technical problems involved in production and distribution. Harriman offered five thousand jeeps, but Stalin demanded more. Harriman said that he might be able to obtain more armored cars, but Stalin rejected them. Harriman described the evening meeting of the second day "as pretty hard sledding."

Stalin also wanted a second front by Britain in 1941. When Beaverbrook told him that this was impossible, Stalin assailed him and charged that the British army did not know how to fight. He asked if Rudolph Hess was a guest of the British. He also wanted the British to bring Turkey into the war against Bulgaria and to blockade Finland. Beaverbrook said these issues had to be referred back to London. However, Stalin was pleased with the generosity of the British offer of assistance and aid, which was probably unexpected because, as Robert Conquest explained, he "no doubt thought that the hard-pressed British industrial base could not extend to such aid—or perhaps that the memory of the large-scale supply of material he himself had sent to Hitler right up to 22 June for his war against Britain might rankle and incline them [the British] to be niggardly." Beaverbrook, like Harriman, was very impressed with Stalin and thought him a "kindly man." Once back in England he used his influence to push "pro-Soviet (and anti-Polish) campaigns," an orientation which was already strong in the British Foreign Office.

General Hastings Ismay, who was part of the Harriman-Beaverbrook delegation and head of the British military mission in Moscow, had a decidedly different view of Stalin, one that matched Bullitt and Steinhardt's opinion. According to Ismay, Stalin "moved stealthily like a wild animal in search of prey, and his eyes were shrewd and full of cunning. He never looked one in the face. But he had great dignity and his personality was dominating. As he entered the room, every Russian froze into silence, and the hunted look in the eyes of the generals showed all too plainly the constant fear in which they lived. It was nauseating to see brave men reduced to such abject servility."[37]

Stalin also desired to discuss the political and territorial adjustments, especially the borders of the Soviet Union, which would be made when Hitler was finally defeated. Beaverbrook was noncommittal on this issue, and Harriman said that the political goals of the United States and Britain were already stipulated in the Atlantic Charter, a Wilsonian document that implied that small nations would be given their independence. Stalin was surprised that the British did not want to discuss politics, and, of course, the sonorous phrases of the Atlantic Charter were to him so much claptrap. He was a totalitarian dictator, not a democrat, and no words, edicts, or documents could square that circle. From his point of view, it probably appeared as if the western states were going to allow the Soviets to bear the brunt of the fighting and, at the same time, remain vague about what the Soviet reward would be. He certainly would not allow that to happen if he could stop it. In Stalin's mind, as historian Steven Miner observed, war was subordinate to political goals in accordance with Carl von Clausewitz's famous dictum, not vice versa.[38]

The British, for their part, were mainly interested in keeping the eastern front open but remaining, if possible, circumspect regarding the borders of the Soviet Union. They were not wedded to the Atlantic Charter, for if it were taken literally they would lose their empire.[39] If allied only with Moscow, they certainly would have arrived at spheres of influence and territorial adjustments, but Washington was part of the alliance. The United States was providing the wherewithal for Britain to continue in the war and would soon be doing the same for the Soviet Union. The Americans were spasmodically anti-imperialist and thought imperialism was the worst of sins. The British hoped to lead the Americans on this issue, but they were not totally independent agents and could not alienate or cross the Americans in any fundamental way.

Roosevelt was opposed to working out territorial agreements before the end of the war, and Harriman was simply reflecting that perspective. Now Roosevelt's stand could have been a brilliant maneuver if he were committed to using Stalin to stop Hitler, then blocking Stalin from duplicating what Hitler was trying to do, and ultimately protecting the independence and possible growth of pluralism in the East Central European countries and the Soviet Union itself. The stand gave no commitment to Stalin, other than to help him stay in the war against the Nazis. It did mean that armies would decide who controlled which land. Roosevelt would have had to plot out a Mediterranean campaign, which he did, but then an East European campaign. American and British armies would have to move into East Central Europe. Aid to the Soviet Union would be in proportion to the need to keep the Red Army engaged on the eastern front. Of course, this was not Roosevelt's plan, so his refusal to discuss territory was not part of a broader strategy to throttle both Nazism and Communism.

Was Roosevelt unwilling to reach an agreement on territorial issues because the Atlantic Charter was truly his position? If so, he should have been prepared to present Stalin with a fait accompli regarding the freedom of the Baltic States, Poland, Finland, and Romania, countries which Stalin had attacked and wholly or partially annexed into the Soviet Union in alliance with Hitler. Stalin was never weaker or more vulnerable than in the period up through the Battles of Stalingrad and Kursk, that is, while the Germans were on the offensive through the spring of 1943. But Roosevelt refused to made demands of Stalin, so it does not appear as if the Atlantic Charter were his real position.

He, of course, was influenced by public opinion and by Sumner Welles, who strongly advised him against recognizing Soviet annexation of the Baltic States on moral grounds. Ultimately, though, ideology guided Roosevelt's behavior. He believed that Stalin was a crystallizing democrat who would cooperate with him at the end of the war to set up a new world order of democratic governments operating under the protective cover of some type of collective security organization, so it was unnecessary to make political decisions at the outset of the alliance. When Stalin failed to accept this amiable fantasy and showed himself to be suspicious and hostile, FDR eventually concluded in 1943 that sacrificing parts of Eastern Europe to Stalin's control was worth the price to persuade him that the United States was a friend and an ally and, in addition, might spur the growth of democracy in the Soviet Union.[40]

Stalin, however, had his own misty dreams. He was, among other things, a Communist dictator who would have readily agreed to divide the world *temporarily* into spheres of influence or camps. The future belonged to Communism, but in the meantime he would hold power and build up his strength in his own camp against the capitalists. He never said that he was a western-style Democrat or gave anyone cause to think that he would set up democratic governments in the Soviet Union or elsewhere. In his relations with the West he was reasonably candid about his imperialist intentions and quite eager to show them "what the Bolsheviks are like!" This is what he told Molotov in 1929, when he rebuffed the offer of the United States, England, and France to mediate the strained relations between Soviet Russia and China.[41] He considered his capitalist allies to be hypocrites but also adept propagandists. The Atlantic Charter could be used very effectively against the Nazis, but certainly it should never be applied to those countries fighting the Nazis. He gave his opinion of Churchill and Roosevelt to Milovan Djilas, the Yugoslav Communist who visited Stalin during World War II. "Churchill," Stalin remarked, "is the kind who, if you don't watch him, will slip a kopeck out of your pocket. Yes a kopeck out of your pocket! By God, a kopeck out of your pocket! And Roosevelt is not like that. He dips in his hand only for bigger coins."[42] Khrushchev recalled that Stalin referred to Roosevelt as a clever politician with whom he could do business.[43] Of course, he was quite willing to use words like *democrat* and *constitutions* to confuse and disarm Roosevelt, but he consistently made it obvious that he believed in centralized Communist control.

Stalin, suspicious even of his fellow Communists, would never constitutionally be able to trust a capitalist leader like Roosevelt. FDR's unwillingness to accept territorial agreements simply enhanced, if that were possible, Stalin's mistrust of Roosevelt. FDR's eventual willingness to concede some territory did not dampen the suspicion, but made FDR appear to be a hypocrite. If FDR were unwilling or unable to pursue a military policy to support the Atlantic Charter, then working out a territorial agreement with Stalin at the beginning of an alliance would have made sense. Such an agreement might dampen aggression, ambition, and uncertainty, and it would establish the limits and parameters of the partnership. Stalin's actions throughout the alliance with the Nazis and the Allies indicated that he would have been minimally satisfied with controlling eastern Poland, the Baltic States, the Finnish lands that he annexed after the Winter War, and the Romanian regions of Bessarabia and northern Bukovina.[44] The rest of East Central Europe could theoretically have been free of Stalinism by prior agreement.

Stalin could not accept the Atlantic Charter or the initial lack of prior territorial agreements. He had to conclude that Roosevelt's position was hypocritical and manipulative. It was in line with Roosevelt and Harriman's posturing on the issue of religion in the Soviet Union. Before he left Moscow, Harriman told Stalin that Americans, especially Catholics, needed to be reassured that there was no religious persecution in the Soviet Union. Roosevelt made the same case with Oumansky.[45] Roosevelt and Harriman did not ask that the Soviet government stop persecuting religion but that it make some statement about religious freedom. Stalin did not seem to pick up at first on the political significance of what Harriman was saying, but on October 1, while Harriman was still in Moscow, Roosevelt held a news conference where he announced that Article 124 of the Soviet Constitution guaranteed freedom of worship. Two days later, the Kremlin, taking the cue, announced that Roosevelt's interpretation was accurate.[46] Clearly, there was a great caesura between the American government's words and actions. It was capable of expediency and manipulation, and thus the Atlantic Charter and all the American talk of democracy and of the rights of nations had to be taken with a grain of salt.[47]

Roosevelt, of course, knew there was no religious freedom in the Soviet Union, but as historian Robert Dallek has written, "His concern to associate the Soviets with the democratic principle extended beyond the question of aid to the problem of American involvement in the war. Convinced that only a stark contrast between freedom and totalitarianism would provide the emotional where-withal for Americans to fight, Roosevelt wished to identify the Russians, regardless of Russian realities, with Anglo-American ideals as fully as he could." The claim that Stalin's Russia allowed religious freedom was the first step in a massive pro-Soviet campaign that the White House coordinated for the duration of the war. The Vatican futilely informed the American government that there was no change in Soviet antireligious policy.[48]

In FDR's mind such hypocrisy, although employed in the short run to win the support of the American people, would not backfire because Stalin would change. FDR could be publicly Machiavellian, but if he determined that the American electorate would not support such a position, he would retreat while simultaneously trying to signal Stalin that he could have his way if he would just do it quietly or, better yet, with some "democratic" window dressing. In time, it would make no difference because Stalin's government would become democratic. The fundamental problem in the alliance remained, over and above the question of Stalin's revolutionary morality, that of Roosevelt's relative morality. Because the value systems of the United States and Stalinist Russia were diametrically opposed, the only way that Roosevelt could find common ground with Stalin and maintain trust with the American people was to compromise American values in private to Stalin while simultaneously upholding those same values in public to his constituency.

Poland, of course, was at the heart of the Soviet political-territorial concerns. Stalin wanted the Polish issue settled on his terms quickly because it was a Pandora's box. He knew that the British had gone to war to protect Poland, that the Poles would never willingly accept the loss of eastern Poland to the USSR, that there was a significant Polish community in the United States, and that the Soviet government had committed a horrible but still undetected crime against Poland: the massacre of over fifteen thousand Polish army officers whom the Soviets had captured in 1939 when they occupied eastern Poland.[49] The Polish government-in-exile hoped to recruit a large army from the two million Polish refugees in the USSR, using the Soviet-held Polish soldiers and officers as a core. Stalin, however, turned aside the Polish request and the supporting pleas of Harriman and Beaverbrook. He did not want a Polish army organized on Soviet soil or anywhere else. He also refused to tell the Polish government where its army officers were being held. All attempts by the Polish ambassador in Moscow to find them, of course, proved futile. Eventually, Stalin agreed to the departure of about sixty thousand Poles from the USSR to fight in the West, but that was all. The Polish army officers would not be found until April 1943 when retreating German forces discovered some of their bodies in a mass grave in the Katyn Forest near Smolensk, a major base of the Soviet secret police.

Stalin also did not want much contact with his new allies. He wanted their money and products but not their personnel or ideas. He particularly proscribed any independent, direct contact between Soviet military leaders and their western counterparts. The British military liaison in Moscow, Lieutenant General M. B. Burrows, reported that all contacts with Russians "are forbidden" and that "no Russian officer is allowed to accept unofficial hospitality; Russians who strike up an acquaintanceship with British or Americans are very apt to disappear and we have evidence of punishments of up to eight years in labour camps for familiarity with foreigners."[50] In *One Day in the Life of Ivan Denisovich*, Aleksandr Solzhenitsyn gave an example of exactly what Burrows was referring to. The novel, based on a true incident, tells the story of a Russian naval commander who was sent to a Siberian labor camp for simply accepting a gift from a British naval officer.

It was obvious that Stalin thought a warm, cooperative relationship between his soldiers and the soldiers of the West would be disastrous for him. Stalin's priorities, which the western leaders could not grasp, were to protect himself, then the Communist government, and lastly the Soviet empire. He had a very personal stake in the war, which FDR and Churchill did not share or understand. He knew that the Russian revolutionary movement of the nineteenth century, which eventually brought the Bolsheviks to power in 1917, started with close contact between Russian soldiers and western peoples. He was not about to allow history to repeat itself in his time.

Stalin's propensity for isolation from his allies ran afoul of a major American strategy, namely, the creation of warm personal ties between Roosevelt and Stalin. A personal relationship, the Americans felt, would go far in smoothing the rough edges of the American-Soviet alliance and would also give the Americans a tremendous advantage because of FDR's charming yet domineering personality. Harriman talked to Stalin at great length about the necessity of meeting and establishing a relationship with Roosevelt. Stalin agreed that such a meeting was desirable, but he refused to be specific on when and where.

Roosevelt, though, was eager to nail down a time and place for a meeting. He was convinced that he could exorcise Stalin's fears and suspicion and possibly open the door to fundamental change in the Soviet Union itself. He thought, according to Harriman, that the USSR was already changing, that its centralized bureaucracy was giving way to decentralization, that freedom was beginning to rear its head, and that its commitment to world revolution was dying. He wanted to step in and personally persuade Stalin that he had nothing to fear from the West, that the changes going on in the Soviet Union should be allowed to blossom, and that together they could build a better world.[51] Kennan added that Roosevelt believed that if only Stalin "could be exposed to the persuasive charm of someone like F.D.R. himself, ideological preconceptions would melt and Russia's co-operation with the West could be easily arranged." Unfortunately, Kennan lamented, "there were no grounds whatsoever" for this assumption and it was "of a puerility that was unworthy of a statesman of F.D.R.'s stature."

Bullitt sarcastically remarked that the president belonged to the "charm school of diplomacy."[52]

In his memoirs, Harriman called Roosevelt "a forerunner of the present-day convergence school."[53] He was an ideologue who was convinced that Stalin's Russia was a natural partner for the United States in building a world free of imperialism and flush with democracy. Roosevelt would be close to Churchill because of the joint war effort and shared traditions, but he would never embrace Great Britain, imperial England, as a fitting partner in the construction of a postwar democratic world. He wanted an exclusive and permanent relationship with Stalin, not Churchill. He did not want to cooperate with Churchill to prepare and present democratic faits accomplis for Stalin. Rather, he sought to entice Stalin through unconditional aid to become his partner. He was convinced of his ability to sway Stalin and bend him in the direction of democracy and of maintaining and protecting world peace and stability. "I know you will not mind my being brutally frank," FDR gratuitously wrote Churchill in March 1942, "when I tell you that I think I can personally handle Stalin better than either your Foreign Office or my State Department."[54] Robert Nisbet concludes that Roosevelt saw "the Soviet Union, its record of terror and slaughter, its omnipotent dictatorship and despotism notwithstanding, as containing a greater promise of democracy and freedom in the long run than Great Britain."[55] Of course, Churchill was no angel, and he would have readily worked out a territorial agreement with Stalin and used the United States to advance Great Britain's imperial interests. That is not the point. Roosevelt, if he used the gauge of objective morality instead of an unproved ideology, would have discovered Churchill to be a much more dependable ally in building democracy around the world than Stalin and would have used Great Britain to help stymie Soviet expansion and to promote American interests.

From this very first meeting, Harriman realized, as did Roosevelt, that Stalin was the only man to deal with in the Soviet Union, that his power was total. "Dealing with others," Harriman told Roosevelt and Hopkins, "was almost a waste of time." Harriman never abandoned that tenet, yet when it later became obvious that the Soviet Union was acting aggressively and inimically, Harriman and Roosevelt slipped into an inconsistency that excused Stalin of responsibility. Harriman explained Soviet atrocities or hostility in terms of unfriendly factions in the Politburo who were opposed to Stalin's desire for genuine friendship with the West, or he blamed Molotov or Vyshinsky for not giving Stalin full information. For example, in the wake of the Warsaw Uprising in 1944, Harriman wrote that "perhaps Molotov had never fully or accurately reported Clark-Kerr's [British ambassador] or my representations. Stalin may have been misinformed by his NKVD."[56]

Harriman and Roosevelt never managed to reconcile the inconsistency of their views. They seemed to know that they held mutually incompatible ideas, but they believed that totalitarianism was better than imperialism, which is doubtful but in any case did not apply to Stalin, who was both totalitarian and imperialist. The basic problem was that they could not admit that Stalin was behind the hostility of the Soviet government, for that would have contradicted the basic premise of their unconditional aid policy, namely, that Stalin could be changed and that the Soviet Union wanted to work with the United States in establishing a world where peace, freedom, and democracy would prevail.

When Harriman returned to the United States in October, he stated, "It is of the utmost importance that prompt action confirm the confidence the Russians now have in the sincerity of our aid."[57] He told Roosevelt and Hopkins that Stalin "had been frank with us and if we came through as had been promised, and if personal relations were maintained with Stalin, the suspicion that has existed between the Soviet Government and our two governments might well be eradicated."[58] Roosevelt took Harriman's advice to heart. In a letter to his special assistant, Wayne Coy, he stressed that he wanted aid sent to the Soviets quickly and smoothly in order to engender Russian confidence. He was fearful that the Russians might get the impression that the Americans were "using them." "Frankly," he told Coy, "if I were a Russian I would feel that I had been given the run-around in the United States." As for the threat that a reinforced Soviet Union might replace Nazi Germany as the main menace in Europe, he wrote Admiral William Leahy, "I do not think we can worry about the possibility of Russian domination [of Europe]."[59]

In Washington, Roosevelt resurrected the ambassadorial personification of the belief that the Soviet Union was evolving into a democratic, capitalist state: Joseph Davies. Davies did not hold an official position within the government at the time. He was offered jobs, including the post in Moscow following Steinhardt's resignation in 1941 and again in 1942 when Roosevelt became upset with Steinhardt's successor, Admiral William Standley, for criticizing Stalin, and yet again in 1943 following Standley's removal. But he turned down the president's offers, pleading poor health and, more important from his point of view, arguing that his effectiveness for Roosevelt would be impaired if he held an official post.

What job did he unofficially perform for FDR? In effect, he became the leader of the administration's campaign to convince the American people that the Soviet Union was trustworthy, to persuade the Soviets that the United States understood them and wanted to be their friend, and to relay to Washington what the United States really had to do to convince the Kremlin of America's sincerity and sympathy.

After the Nazi attack on the Soviet Union, Davies was enthroned at the White House as the expert on the Soviet Union.[60] He was in constant contact with Roosevelt, Hopkins, and the Soviet embassy throughout the war. Hopkins told Oumansky as early as July 11, 1941, that Davies would be a major participant in the Soviet-American relationship and would "manage and push through [Soviet] orders."[61] He played a critical role in convincing FDR that American aid should be sent to the Soviet Union.[62] Very likely he and Hopkins strengthened FDR's conviction that he, FDR, could mold Stalin to his will. He certainly reinforced Roosevelt and Hopkins's belief that Stalin's hostility was tied to insecurity over external threats and could only be removed by ceaseless goodwill efforts to reduce his suspicion and build his confidence.[63] Later Davies helped persuade them that a second front was critical to the alliance, that a second front in northern Europe was preferable to one in the Balkans, that the British could not be trusted, and that Eastern Europe was within Stalin's legitimate sphere of influence. As early as October 1941 he and Walter Duranty were pushing the British for a second front. He also told the Soviets that they could trust Roosevelt, that the supply effort was sincere and unconditional, that the British had their own agenda, and that Stalin should meet with Roosevelt.[64] "Davies was, in effect," Ambassador Litvinov declared, "an envoy of the Soviet Union in Washington."[65] When Davies published a book in 1941, *Mission to Moscow*, which portrayed Stalin as a freedom-loving democrat, Roosevelt scrawled on his copy of the book, "This book will last."[66] The State Department experts called it "Submission to Moscow."[67]

Davies's influence derived not so much from what he knew or from piercing insight and analysis but from the fact that he agreed totally with Roosevelt's predisposition about the Soviet Union and with whatever Stalin said about himself. In 1943 he frankly admitted that he knew little about the Soviet Union or Stalin's trustworthiness, but his reputation as an expert on Soviet affairs persisted.[68] Even Harry Truman sought him out in 1945 for advice on the Soviet Union and called him one of three Americans most knowledgeable about foreign affairs, the other two being Harry Hopkins and Cordell Hull.[69] He was at Truman's side at the Potsdam Conference and played a major role in putting together the package of concessions that Stalin wanted.[70] Davies was the only American ambassador ever to receive the Order of Lenin.[71]

Steinhardt did not believe that the United States and the Soviet Union shared fundamental principles, and he did not approve of the policy of unreciprocal concessions. He argued that the Soviets were naturally suspicious of the Americans and that granting them unconditional aid simply made them more demanding and ungrateful.[72] He wanted to take advantage of the Soviet predicament. He felt this was an opportunity that Americans should use to redress past grievances and lay the foundation for a new understanding. He was not opposed to aid. In fact, he agreed with Hopkins's optimistic view in July that the Soviets could hold out against the Germans. His optimism waned in October 1941 when the Soviet government and the foreign embassies were moved to Kuibyshev (present-day Samara), some five hundred miles southeast of Moscow on the Volga River, but he still did not oppose aid.[73] He simply wanted a more balanced approach and an end to what he saw as a policy of illusion, ignorance, and naïveté. His experience and observation convinced him that unconditional aid was counterproductive.

There was no room, however, for Steinhardt's approach. He no longer counted. Stalin, Harriman, Hopkins, and Roosevelt all wanted him out. Stalin denounced the ambassador, in Harriman's paraphrase, as "a defeatist, a rumormonger, a man chiefly interested in his own safety"—an attack that aimed to get Harriman to recommend that Steinhardt be removed and was probably more harsh because of Stalin's virulent anti-Semitism. Harriman defended Steinhardt and retorted by criticizing Ambassador Oumansky's work in Washington, but Steinhardt was not included in any of the discussions in Moscow during the Beaverbrook-Harriman mission and Harriman did recommend his removal.[74] He had been included at first, but Beaverbrook ordered the British ambassador, Sir Stafford Cripps, out of the first meeting, and Harriman followed suit. In Beaverbrook's words, he wanted to start with "a clean slate" in order to bridge over "a lack of mutual confidence."[75] Stalin had no objection to the pro-Soviet Cripps and so told Beaverbrook. The British leader, however, wanted to impress the assembly with the fact that he was in charge, a sophomoric exercise that created a lasting bitterness between Cripps and Beaverbrook.[76]

In a terse telegram Roosevelt notified Steinhardt of his termination on November 5, 1941. The president stressed that what was needed in Moscow was someone who would give the Soviets what they wanted without a hassle:

> It would now seem that Soviet-American relations in the immediate future at any rate will consist almost exclusively of matters pertaining to the furnishing of supplies and equipment to the Soviet Union in order to enable that country to continue its resistance to Germany.
>
> In conducting this type of relation it would be advantageous to have as ambassador in the Soviet Union someone who is fully acquainted with detailed problems of American production and supply. Such a background for ambassador may at once require the settling on the spot of problems of a highly technical nature.[77]

Steinhardt immediately offered his resignation. The search for a replacement had already started. Roosevelt wanted someone who would serve as an uncritical facilitator of aid. He did not desire analysis, criticism, understanding, or reciprocity. He wanted a supporter of unconditional aid who would work with Stalin in order to prove to the Soviet dictator that the United States was not only an ally but a friend. He knew Stalin was suspicious, but he assumed that he could touch Stalin's heart by unilateral aid, that Stalin would react in a normal human fashion and feel gratitude and warmth toward the United States. The problem with this analysis was that Stalin was not a normal human being. He was closer to what Churchill called him, "an unnatural man," and still closer to what Robert Conquest concluded in his biography of Stalin, "unnatural" and "unreal."[78] Stalin lived in a world devoid of normal human feeling. He was a ruthless murderer who had cut himself off or been cut off from all human institutions.

He believed that terror and violence were good and natural. He believed in the class struggle, in a world where there were only people who accepted his will and people who did not and where he alone defined morality and international law.[79] He was a vicious monster but extremely sly and an expert at dissimulation. He easily took in progressive ideologues like Roosevelt and Hopkins, who believed that he was a democratic leader facing incredible odds at home and against Germany. He also took in realists like Churchill and Harriman, who believed that even Stalin had a spark of humanity in him and deserved the benefit of a doubt because his people were fighting the Nazis.

Roosevelt was aghast at Steinhardt's hard-hitting but accurate portrayal of Stalin. He did not want to hear it, and he did not want Steinhardt's successor to continue it. He first offered the job to a man whom he thought would follow the pro-Stalin line, W. Averell Harriman. He demurred, admitting quite frankly that he had seen enough of Moscow to know that was not the place he wanted to be. It "was about as close to prison as anything outside of bars," Harriman recalled in his memoirs.[80]

FDR then offered the Moscow post to Joseph Davies, who also knew only too well what Moscow offered. He pleaded poor health and his importance in Washington as a liaison between Roosevelt and the Soviets.[81] Eventually the name of retired admiral William H. Standley came up. Standley had accompanied the Beaverbrook-Harriman mission to Moscow as the American naval expert. Both Harriman and Davies recommended him. Evidently, Standley had impressed them as someone who would meet FDR's specifications and who, because of his military background, could also tolerate the rigors of life in Moscow. He seemed to be a simple soul who worshipped FDR and who would do what he was told without blinking a critical eye.

Steinhardt, whose advice and observations were proven to be sound, left Moscow in semidisgrace. Gromyko summed up the sentiment in both Washington and Moscow: "To the satisfaction of both sides, Steinhardt did not remain long in Moscow."[82]

Standley, though, was not really the person whom Roosevelt and Hopkins planned to use to implement and carry out their Soviet aid policy. That person was Colonel Philip Faymonville. With Steinhardt's departure in November 1941, Faymonville became the key contact in Moscow between the White House and the Kremlin. His usefulness to Hopkins and Roosevelt was soon exhibited. Hopkins and Harriman were under the impression after their trips to Moscow that Stalin had no objection to allowing American technicians to enter the Soviet Union and service Lend-Lease equipment. However, the Soviet embassy rejected all visa applications for such technicians in October and November 1941. The rejection was doubly embarrassing to the "Hopkins Shop" because it "represented a breach of faith and it made it impossible to guarantee the proper maintenance of equipment." Hopkins and Harriman asked Faymonville why

Moscow turned down the applications. Faymonville provided a five-part explanation. First, the Soviets had had bad experiences in the past with foreign engineers. This was apparently a reference to the so-called Shakhty Trial of 1928 in which a few German technicians were found guilty of "wrecking." Faymonville evidently believed the story. Second, the Soviets resented the implication that their technicians could not maintain the equipment. Third, Moscow could not maintain the Americans as comfortably as they were used to, so it avoided problems by rejecting all visas. Fourth, Soviet standards for equipment use in battle were likely lower than American standards, and the Soviets were afraid that American technicians might keep the equipment out of battle. Finally, the Soviet government believed (and so apparently did Faymonville) that the Americans might come with "mixed motives"; that is, they might engage in espionage while providing technical assistance.[83]

Hopkins liked the analysis. It was just what he needed. He informed General Burns that he agreed with Faymonville's position. On November 21 the Lend-Lease Administration announced that American technicians were not needed in the Soviet Union. A telegram to Faymonville stressed that "the United States authorities have not the slightest desire to insist on supplying such services."[84] He saw no point, as he wrote later, in promoting "a lot of conversation . . . that will only irritate the Russians over something that is not really important to us."[85] In addition, unlike any other Lend-Lease recipient, the Soviet Union was not asked to file documentation or produce any evidence to justify need or ability to use requested equipment and aid. It was also not subject, unlike others, to reductions in assistance once the war turned in favor of the Allies.[86]

Not only did Hopkins prevail in the struggle to keep Faymonville in Moscow, but he and General Burns were so pleased with his performance that they convinced General George C. Marshall, army chief of staff, to promote Faymonville to the rank of brigadier general. With Steinhardt gone and a chargé heading the embassy, Hopkins argued that Faymonville was the only real contact the United States had with the Soviets.[87] General Marshall recalled that "Hopkins had power in representing the Russians" and that Hopkins's power could always override Marshall's because of his close friendship with Roosevelt.[88] With his promotion, Faymonville outranked the military and naval attachés at the embassy. His prestige with the Soviets increased, and he received the message that his apologetics for Stalin were right on course. He was riding the wave of Rooseveltism, but on the horizon was a crusty, old admiral who was determined to take command and change course.

Part 4

William H. Standley
1942-1943

10

The Secret Message

In early October 1942 Roosevelt and Hopkins received an urgent, disturbing request. Ambassador William Standley, who had been in the Soviet Union just seven months, asked to return to Washington for important consultations. FDR and Hopkins immediately granted permission. They concluded that Standley was carrying a secret message from Stalin, something so sensitive that it could not be cabled or entrusted to the diplomatic pouch. They decided that it was a warning from Stalin that he would sign a separate peace treaty with the Nazis unless aid were substantially increased. Of course, aid was already pouring into the Soviet Union through the Persian Gulf, Murmansk, and Archangel, and it was playing a major role in the Battle of Stalingrad, which had been raging since August 1942.

While Standley was en route to Washington, Roosevelt informed Churchill that Standley was returning home carrying an important message from Stalin that very likely warned of a separate peace with Germany if increased aid were not forthcoming. Roosevelt's conclusion made no sense to Churchill. The Soviets were holding out at Leningrad and Moscow and frustrating the German siege of Stalingrad. The situation for Stalin was not so desperate that he would sue for peace with the Nazis while the Red Army was holding the line against further German advances but with the Germans still occupying huge parts of the Soviet Union. On October 9 he cabled FDR that he was puzzled by what message Standley was bringing home to Roosevelt, "but I cannot believe it threatens a separate peace. So far, the Russian Campaign has been very adverse to Hitler, and though they are angry with us both they are by no means in despair."[1]

On October 26 Standley reached the White House after a long and dangerous journey via Iran, North Africa, and the South Atlantic. When he entered the Oval Office he found Roosevelt and Hopkins anxiously waiting and fearing the worst. To their utter bewilderment and eventual anger, Standley carried no message from Stalin other than an old request for more Airacobra fighter planes, which Roosevelt had already received on October 7.[2] Instead, his secret message came from himself, from his experience in the Soviet Union. It was straightforward and to the point: "Stop acting like a Santa Claus, Chief." It was a simple but devastating attack on Rooseveltism and unconditional aid.

Standley went on to explain his advice to a shocked Roosevelt and Hopkins. He desired Lend-Lease to be contingent on Soviet assistance, especially sharing intelligence and allowing Allied observers at the front. "Let's get something from Stalin in return," he counseled. "Faymonville agrees to give them everything in the world they ask for, from a darning needle to a tire factory, which they won't have operating ten years after the war. My advice is to treat Stalin like an adult, keep any promises we make to him, but insist that he keeps his promises, too." There is no alternative, Standley went on, because "the Soviets will take advantage of any other course of action."

"Is that why you asked to come home for consultation?" asked Hopkins.

That was not the only reason. Standley had two other problems. He demanded that General Faymonville be placed under his authority. He thought that Faymonville was serving the interest of the Soviet Union rather than the interest of the United States and that he was undercutting the leverage of the military and naval attachés to bargain for information because he was simply giving Moscow military and intelligence information without demanding reciprocity. He also requested that Roosevelt stop sending special representatives to Moscow rather than relying on him. He was referring to visits to Moscow by W. Averell Harriman and Wendell Willkie in August and September 1942, respectively. He complained to Roosevelt that "such by-passing by Special representatives and other American agencies in Moscow not under the Ambassador's control had proven to be so destructive to my prestige that I doubt my continued effectiveness in my mission. It must look to people in Moscow, as if I no longer enjoy the confidence of my Government."[3]

Standley did not find Roosevelt or Hopkins sympathetic to his point of view. They treated him as if he did not realize that there was a bigger picture than his authority and position. They did not like his criticism of unconditional aid. The last thing they wanted in their relationship with Stalin was a trading atmosphere, and Faymonville was doing exactly what they wanted, not only in terms of giving the Soviets anything that the Americans could deliver, but also in terms of short-circuiting the executive control that the embassy and Standley wanted. They did not comment on his direct attack on the aid policy. Instead, they focused on Standley's relationship with Faymonville, as if the whole problem were a clash of personalities. Standley told them that he got along fine with Faymonville, that it was the system that was wrong. The ambassador was correct. The problem between him and Faymonville was not one of jurisdiction or personality but of policy.

Roosevelt told Standley that he still had his full confidence and that he would see what could be done about Faymonville. He promised nothing else, although Standley thought the president "was in general agreement with my suggestions." That was the end of the meeting. Roosevelt, however, was not being candid with Standley and he tried to replace him with Joseph Davies. Davies again turned down the offer. Roosevelt decided to stay with Standley probably because there was no one else readily available, and even though the ambassador was obviously unhappy, he did not appear to have the impudence to challenge the president's policy.[4]

Standley's advice, needless to say, was not heeded. He was the second ambassador in a row to conclude, after being on the scene, that the policy of unilateral and uncritical deference was categorically in error. Henderson, Bohlen, and Kennan had reached the same conclusion. FDR's mind, however, was closed on the subject of Stalin. He knew Stalin was capable of a treacherous treaty with Hitler, but the president believed that sincere and generous aid would make Stalin less likely to try to embrace Hitler once again and might encourage him to cooperate with the United States in building a secure and perhaps democratic world. He did not think that a policy of reciprocity would be a better way of building a relationship and character. As for the paradox of trying to construct a partnership for peace and democracy with a treacherous dictator, FDR apparently resolved it by falling back on the notion that Stalin was an evolving democrat whom he could handle and bring along. Curiously, FDR assumed that Hitler would be receptive to a separate peace with Stalin despite the fact that Hitler had already proven by rejecting Stalin's pleas for peace before the June attack that he was not interested so much in territory as in utterly destroying Communism, enslaving the Slavs, and exterminating the Jews. Steinhardt had already reported that Stalin would have done anything to avert the Nazi attack, including conceding huge swaths of territory to Hitler. Part of the reason for Stalin's surprise at being attacked in June 1941 was his belief that Hitler would never attack because he could obtain territorial concessions without going to war.[5]

Standley, of course, was not always a critic of Roosevelt's policy, which should have lent more weight to his change of view. He was, in fact, a solid supporter of unconditional aid, which helps explain why he was named ambassador in the first place.

William H. Standley was born in 1872 on a ranch in Ukiah, California, a small, mainly Russian settlement not far from the former Russian base at Fort Ross near San Francisco. Standley made his career in the military. He entered the naval academy in 1891 and graduated four years later in the middle of his class. He was promoted to lieutenant in 1899 and then assigned to the Navy Yard at Mare Island, California. During World War I, he was placed in charge of buildings and grounds at the naval academy and thereby became an ex officio member of the Naval Academy Labor Board. In that capacity he met Woodrow Wilson's assistant secretary of the navy, Franklin D. Roosevelt. Standley knew that Roosevelt was destined for greater things. He described him as "a working politician, wise beyond his years, in all the little tricks of politics which bring in the votes on Election Day."

In 1919 Standley was promoted to captain. He thought that he had reached his top rank. Then, in July 1924, to his surprise, he was named assistant director of navy war plans in the Office of the Chief of Naval Operations in Washington, D.C. To his greater amazement, he was promoted to rear admiral and director of fleet training in 1927. The next year he was named assistant chief of naval operations, and then in 1933, with his friend in the White House, he was promoted to admiral and chief of naval operations. His career was meteoric, and although he was competent, he was also honest enough to admit that his promotions came about because of luck and friends who looked after him.

Standley was thrilled to be at the top, to be working for a president who was committed to building a strong navy, to be enthusiastically embraced by Roosevelt, and to be made a "full-fledged member of the New Deal Cabinet." For the next four years he worked closely with the new president to strengthen the navy. By the end of 1936, the navy had become respectable, and Standley retired, having achieved his goal of building a strong navy. FDR tried to persuade him to stay on, but he was tired and wanted to make some money before going back to his avocado farm in California. He was replaced as chief of naval operations by Admiral William D. Leahy on January 1, 1937.[6]

Standley now looked for a well-paying job, so that he and his wife, Evelyn, could settle down comfortably in southern California. He initially worked for the New York World's Fair as the director of foreign participation and then in early 1939 became a consultant for the Electric Boat Company in New London, Connecticut. He gave up hope of returning to California when the war broke out, and in February 1941 he agreed to rejoin the government as a member of the Planning Board of the Office of Production Management. He also took to the speakers' circuit, urging Americans to support the Allies and denouncing Germany, Italy, and the Soviet Union as enemies of democratic civilization.[7]

After the Nazi invasion of the Soviet Union, Standley changed his view about the USSR and, rather deftly, swung solidly behind FDR's policy of unconditional aid. Nonetheless, he was surprised when Roosevelt asked him to accompany the Beaverbrook-Harriman mission to Moscow as the American naval representative with the rank of minister. In many ways, however, he was a logical choice. He was a friend of Roosevelt. He was a retired admiral. And he had supported the policy of unconditional aid. He was a trusted professional who could help with the naval needs of the Soviet Union.

His experience as part of the Beaverbrook-Harriman mission was a turning point. It was the event which pushed his name to the forefront of those being considered as a possible replacement for Steinhardt. It was not that he did anything significant while on the mission but, rather, that he was philosophically in tune with the president's desire to do anything possible to help the Soviets against the Germans. He recorded that he endorsed Harriman's description of the purpose of the mission as an effort to "give and give and give, with no expectation of any return, with no thought of a quid pro quo." He later complained that he had nothing to do in Moscow, that his Soviet naval counterparts had very little information and referred all questions to Stalin, and that Harriman handled all the key discussions. But that was not unexpected, or at least it should not have been, given the imperious personalities of Stalin and Harriman.

Standley did have some memorable impressions of the trip. He remembered that the flight from Archangel to Moscow was a white-knuckled affair. The Russian pilots, he recorded, flew just "a few feet above the treetops," neglected "usual safety measures," and wandered on two occasions "into forbidden zones" where "ground antiaircraft guns opened up on us." He was also astonished, he said, when Harriman, after only a few days in Moscow, told him and the other members of the mission to "get busy and turn in your reports at once. You will have only three or four more days." There was really nothing to turn in, according to Standley. He further realized during this initial visit that all power centered on Stalin, whom he described as "a pleasant and simple man, short and slightly stooped" but with "a discerning and piercing eye." Standley was struck by the moods of Stalin, alternating between warm enthusiasm and cold anger. Eventually he decided that this was a technique which Stalin had cultivated to obtain concessions from friend and foe alike.

Standley took every opportunity to walk around Moscow to try to get to know the city and its people. He found it to be bleak, wretched, and fearsome. He was impressed by the work being done to build the subway and to widen the streets, but in the back streets of Moscow he found "all the filth and squalor of the slums of any great city." As he explored Moscow, his mind drifted back to his youth. His fond memories of his Russian neighbors warmed his disposition toward the Russians of the Soviet Union. He admired the Russians' sense of duty, basic warmth and friendliness, and tremendous capacity for pain and suffering, but he found reprehensible their lack of initiative and serflike submissiveness to what he felt was an arbitrary and whimsical order. Eventually he concluded that life in Soviet Russia probably had not changed much from the time of the czars, that there were still basically two classes: the privileged and the repressed. He saw Stalin as a modern czar who kept the people down. He consoled himself, however, with the thought that life would get better in the Soviet Union. A middle class would develop, he was convinced, although "it will take time—much time." In that sense, the admiral was in agreement with FDR's general belief about the Soviet Union's future.[8]

Standley met Steinhardt while in Moscow, and he recorded that he felt sorry for the ambassador and the other American representatives. In his opinion, they were very lonely and isolated. On this point Standley was correct. All wives, children, and female employees of the American embassy had left Moscow on the eve of the Nazi invasion after Steinhardt received advanced word of the attack from the German embassy. A thousand-pound bomb exploded just fifty yards from Spaso House in the summer of 1941 and blew out virtually all the windows in the ambassador's house. The residence itself was in poor repair, and it proved impossible to get building materials. The chancery building, filled with water from burst pipes, was boarded up and left to the scavenging rats. The embassy's skeleton staff worked out of the ambassador's house. The city itself was under siege, and there were periodic power and heating shortages. Fresh vegetables and fruits were impossible to obtain. In fact, matters got worse shortly after the Beaverbrook-Harriman mission departed. In mid-October, as the German siege of Moscow tightened, the Soviet government shifted the seat of government and the foreign embassies to Kuibyshev, a godforsaken provincial city some five hundred miles to the east on the Volga River. The diplomatic community considered wartime Moscow not simply a hardship but a living hell. Kennan compared it to imprisonment in a Nazi detention camp. Diplomats were isolated and treated as if they carried the plague. Bohlen remembered that departing from the Soviet Union "was like coming out into the fresh spring air from a room where the oxygen content was sufficient to sustain life but insufficient to produce any mental or spiritual orientation." General Marshall, too, thought that living conditions in Soviet Russia were unbearable for Americans.[9]

All in all Standley was happy to leave Moscow. He knew the winter of 1941 would be cold and frightening. Snow was already falling in Moscow in early October, and the ferocious German military machine was bearing down on the Soviet capital. He had had enough of Moscow after one week. It was too oppressive, too cold, too dismal, and too dangerous. When he finally left the Soviet Union, he recorded in his memoirs that he "felt an unaccountable lifting of spirits."

Although his role had not been major, Standley was pleased with the results of the Beaverbrook-Harriman mission. Glad to be part of the team that was building a "rude shock" for Hitler, he hoped the Soviets could hold out until American aid arrived. He also agreed with Harriman's optimistic conclusion about the future of American-Soviet relations on the eve of their departure from the Soviet Union: If the United States delivered the promised aid and if personal relations were retained with Stalin, "the suspicion that has existed between the Soviet Government and our two governments [American and British] might well be eradicated."[10]

Once back in the United States he made a series of speeches strongly supporting the policy of unconditional aid and praising the Red Army and the Soviet government. He slipped easily into the administration's effort to build up support for the Kremlin. The Soviet Union, he argued, was fighting the war for democracy, and accordingly the United States had an obligation to make good on Soviet material losses. There could not be the "old cry of 'too little and too late'" in the case of aid to Soviet Russia.[11] "The Russian people . . . are fighting bravely and with a common purpose that shines in the eyes of every one of them," he announced in a radio message at the end of October. "That common purpose is to hold the small gains which they have made in self-government. They know that their liberty is menaced by a slavery worse than that which their fathers endured under the czars, and they are facing the issue squarely. They are fighting calmly and stoically for privileges which we in this country take entirely too much for granted."[12]

Standley was flabbergasted when in January 1942 Harriman walked up to him and calmly asked, "Are you going to Russia?" Standley replied that he thought the Beaverbrook-Harrriman mission had completed its work. Harriman then explained that the president wanted him to return to Moscow as the ambassador. Harriman explained that the reason Roosevelt did not ask him directly was that he "decided to leave it up to Secretary Hull so that you can decline with honor, if you wish." Having just left the funereal air of Moscow, Standley was not enthusiastic about the idea. But eventually, after Secretary Hull offered it, he decided he could not "refuse duty, however onerous, in wartime." He guessed that he was not the first choice, but he did not mind and deep down he was flattered. The Soviet government gave an unusually quick assent to Standley's appointment, undoubtedly because it wanted the post filled to strengthen the alliance.[13]

It was the Lend-Lease group that first recommended Standley to Roosevelt after both Davies and Harriman turned the president down. General Burns had also been considered for the post, but he was deemed too critical to the Lend-Lease operation in Washington. The Lend-Lease leaders liked Standley because he was a military officer who they thought might appeal to Stalin and lead to a real friendship that would open doors. They also preferred him because he and FDR were naval men and got along quite well. They reasoned that Standley might be an ideal liaison between Stalin and FDR. He was accustomed to taking orders and there seemed little chance that he would challenge the policy of his commander in chief.[14]

In fact, Admiral Standley spoke out in favor of unconditional aid to the USSR. He quickly adopted FDR's faith that the Soviet Union was a country in transition, moving toward democracy, and desperately in need of sympathy. He knew that relations between the United States and the Soviet Union had not been warm, but he now believed that the Soviet Union was changing. However, a sour note did creep into his faith. He was not as optimistic about the pace of democratization as, say, Davies, who believed that the USSR was about sixty years behind the United States. Standley placed it about 165 years behind America. Nonetheless, he made it clear that the Russian people, like the Americans in the eighteenth century, "were fighting for independence, for liberty, and for the right to live their own lives free from oppression."[15]

Admiral Standley described himself as "an American of average intelligence." He had a sense of humor and he enjoyed swapping stories with his military attachés—his "boys"—and with the journalists on the Moscow beat. He also had a propensity for colorful speech. For example, he described the dining car on the train between Kuibyshev and Moscow as "a dingy, filthy old car, on which Ivan-the-Terrible might once have dined."[16]

Politically, Standley was well connected, having been close to Roosevelt and the power brokers of the Potomac for quite a few years. He had many friends in high places, particularly in the military bureaucracy. He counted among his confidants General George Marshall, Admiral William Leahy, and Admiral Ernie King, all powerful men in Washington. He was not, however, an intimate of Roosevelt, and beyond his military connections he had no real base of support. He knew Cordell Hull and Sumner Welles, but the State Department was not his bailiwick. He knew the top men in the new Lend-Lease Administration— Hopkins, Harriman, Stettinius, and General Burns—but he was not close to any of them. He had a good reputation, though, and he was known to be a friend of Roosevelt, which carried a great deal of weight. When FDR informed Stalin that Standley was his choice for ambassador, he called him "an old and trusted friend." Stalin quickly replied that he was happy to have Standley.[17]

Since the Americans had committed themselves in the wake of the Beaverbrook-Harriman mission to render massive aid to the Soviet Union, the Lend-Lease Administration loomed large in the life of the American ambassador in the Soviet Union as well as in the conduct of American foreign policy generally. "It was obvious," Robert Sherwood wrote, "that Lend-Lease should become the most vital element in the relations between the United States and all the Allied combatant nations and many neutrals as well." With Harry Hopkins in charge, it "became identified as 'Roosevelt's own personal Foreign Office.'"[18] Soon all other government activity was subordinated to the needs of the Lend-Lease Administration, and its main job now, aside from supplying the British, was to pour aid into the USSR.

"I feel very sure the Russians are going to hold this winter," FDR wrote Churchill, "and that we should proceed vigorously with our plans both to supply them and to set up an Air Force to fight with them."[19] In effect, Roosevelt simply decided to circumvent the State Department and the process of diplomacy in favor of a new, ad hoc institution, the Lend-Lease Administration, which was run by people whose principal credential was loyalty to Roosevelt and his policy.

General Faymonville was appointed Lend-Lease administrator in Moscow in October 1941 just as Steinhardt was recalled. Bullitt, Kennan, Bohlen, and Henderson, among others, considered him too trusting and too naive of Stalin and his intentions. He reported directly to the Lend-Lease Administration in Washington, going around the ambassador in Moscow and the State Department. Evidently, FDR assumed that Standley, a military man who was not a professional diplomat, would not mind that setup, would work with Faymonville, and would iron out the wrinkles so that the Soviets could obtain what they wanted. Standley, however, demanded before he left Washington and took up the appointment as ambassador that Faymonville report to him. Hopkins worked out a compromise in which Faymonville would retain his autonomy but apprise Standley of everything that he was doing.[20]

In the ways of intrigue and diplomacy, Admiral Standley was naive. He readily admitted that he was not a diplomat. "I had no illusions," he later recalled, "as to my qualifications to be a diplomat. I knew that I was just an ordinary, run-of-the-mill Naval officer as far as diplomatic experience went." His plan was "to approach Molotov and Stalin in a frank and open manner, lay the cards on the table, and, as it were, talk turkey in plain sailorman language. These men with whom I was to deal, I told myself, were only men, human beings born of woman. With my long experience in handling men from every walk of life, surely I would have no trouble with these."[21] Later, he had reason to question his assumption about the genesis of the Bolshevik leaders.

Admiral Standley prepared for his new assignment by meeting officials from the State Department and the Lend-Lease Administration over a three-week period. He wasn't surprised by what they told him. Working and living conditions in Moscow were primitive. The staff at the embassy had been cut to a minimum and, to make matters worse, it was divided between Moscow and Kuibyshev. The shattered windows in Spaso House, where the Moscow staff worked, were not fixed because of a glass shortage and were simply covered with plasterboard. Heating the building proved to be virtually impossible.

Standley's official residence would be typhus-ridden Kuibyshev, which lacked even the sparse conveniences of wartime Moscow. Over 500,000 refugees filled the town and strained the supply of potable water, food, and housing beyond capacity. Dust and mud, depending on weather conditions, caked the squalid buildings. A weather-beaten building called Sadovia housed the embassy, but snow and icy winds in the winter and legions of flies in the summer made it virtually unusable. Fresh vegetables were rare, except for the small garden that the staff carefully cultivated. Transportation between Kuibyshev and Moscow was erratic and slow, and transportation out of the Soviet Union was virtually impossible without Herculean efforts involving weeks of preparation. The only Soviet officials dealing with foreign affairs in Kuibyshev were Molotov's two assistants, Vyshinsky and Lozovsky, but they could never answer questions. They referred everything to Molotov and Stalin, who stayed in Moscow, and their replies were slow and often in need of further clarification, which started the whole process over again. At seventy years old, Standley knew he could not take too much hardship, but he was going to give it his best effort.[22]

Once his appointment was announced, he found himself, like Steinhardt, deluged with requests by citizens, especially Polish-Americans, whose loved ones were caught up in the war. Deeply sympathetic to their plight, he tried, while in the Soviet Union, to check on the whereabouts of specific individuals but without much success.

His main tutor on Soviet affairs was Loy Henderson, who was now chief of the Division of European Affairs at the State Department. Henderson held views of the Soviet Union rather close to those of Steinhardt and Bullitt. As a result, he was at odds with Roosevelt's policy and, of course, was ignored by the White House. Just before Standley's departure, Henderson complained to Sumner Welles that, despite the alliance, the Russians "do not in general desire the presence of American citizens in the Soviet Union" and continue to support international revolution, including "the eventual overthrow by force of this Government and for the establishment of a Communist dictatorship." Henderson was particularly critical of the American Communist Party, which he said only supported the war effort "to the extent that such an effort might be helpful to the Soviet Union."[23]

Henderson wanted a policy based on the attitude that Moscow had adopted toward the United States: cold, formal, cautious, and harsh. Like Steinhardt and Bullitt, he was convinced that the quid pro quo approach would put American-Soviet relations on firm ground. It is difficult to say how much influence he had on Standley, even though the new ambassador referred to him as his "immediate boss." Eventually, Standley did adopt the Henderson-Steinhardt-Bullitt view, but it was born directly out of his experience in Moscow. He was initially an enthusiastic backer of unconditional aid.

Before Standley left for the Soviet Union, FDR briefed him about his "duties in Moscow and the more pressing problems" in American-Soviet relations. The president wanted him to iron out the Lend-Lease supply problems, discuss with the Soviets the development of a supply route over Siberia from Alaska, check on the release of the Polish officers whom the Soviets had captured in 1939 when they invaded Poland, try to obtain the release of American pilots who had landed in Siberia when their planes had run out of gas after bombing Japan, talk about the coordination of military intelligence, the improvement of radio communication, and the exchange of technical information between the United States and the Soviet Union, and emphasize the need for a personal meeting between Stalin and Roosevelt, possibly off the coast of Alaska or Siberia.[24] Joseph Davies also met with Standley before he left and gave him a copy of his new book, *Mission to Moscow*.

The type of ambassador that FDR wanted in Moscow was someone who would help with the military assistance plans. He did not want a critic or an intellectual but a technician. Admiral Standley filled the bill. FDR's central concern now was to supply the Soviet armed forces with the wherewithal to stop the Nazi invasion. Military matters were the first priority. The embassy had been divided previously into roughly equal military and civilian branches, but now that military matters were supreme, the writ of the civilian diplomats was severely curtailed. Placing a military man in charge of the embassy made sense to FDR. He naturally assumed that Standley would carry out the military aid program without complications. After all, Standley had been chief of naval operations and understood the absolute necessity of keeping the military supply line full and flowing.

Standley finally arrived in the Soviet Union in April 1942. Steinhardt had departed Moscow in November 1941. In the six-month interlude much had happened. The British found themselves fully engaged with the Germans and Italians for control of North Africa and the Mediterranean Sea. Churchill agreed in early December to begin cooperating with the United States on the development of an atomic bomb.[25] The Japanese attacked Pearl Harbor on December 7, 1941. The next day the United States and Great Britain declared war on Japan. On December 11 Hitler and Mussolini declared war on the United States, and the United States reciprocated. The United States was now a full partner with the English, the Commonwealth nations, and the Soviets in the war against Germany and Italy, and the lead partner with England, the Commonwealth, and China in the war against Japan. The Soviet Union and Japan did not declare war on one another. The Soviets, however, chose not to provide any assistance to the American-British effort in Asia. On December 8, Roosevelt requested that American pilots, operating out of Manila, be allowed to use Vladivostok as a reloading base for bombing runs on Japan. Molotov rejected the request on the grounds that the Soviet Union had a nonaggression pact with Japan and was too involved with Germany to open a second front in the East. On December 11, the president and Hopkins asked that the Soviet government not publicize its official position of neutrality in the Asian war but, instead, keep the Japanese guessing, thus forcing them to divide their forces. Again, the Soviets refused. It was clear from the beginning that the American-Soviet alliance was Soviet-centered.[26]

In addition, the alliance with the Soviet Union undercut the Roosevelt administration's proclaimed goals in fighting the war. The Four Freedoms and the Atlantic Charter seemed to be empty words after the Soviet Union became an American ally. The Declaration of the twenty-six United Nations on January 1, 1942, which announced that the war was "for the protection of life, liberty, independence, and religious freedom and for the preservation of civil rights and justice," rang hollow because of what people knew of Stalinism. For American soldiers the real motivation was to punish the Japanese for their attack on Pearl Harbor. The Germans stood in the way of full punishment because they were allied to Tokyo, so they had to be fought first in order to get at Japan. The Americans could not see any connection between the perfidy of the Japanese and the anti-Jewish campaign of the Nazis, especially since the new Soviet ally did the same thing as the Nazis. And Stalin was not long in proving that they were right, which made Roosevelt's task of altering Stalin's image all the more difficult. Of course, the president knew that Soviet Russia was not an advocate of the goals set out in the various declarations, but he did believe that it would become a supporter in time. In the interim, he was quite willing to overlook evidence that the Soviet Union was not a backer of democracy and pluralism, which, of course, made him appear naive to his ambassadors and Russian experts and hypocritical to the Soviets. For example, when Litvinov asked if all twenty-six nations who signed the Declaration of January 1 had to be consulted, Roosevelt laughed and said decisions would be made by the major powers, that is, "the USSR, USA, Great Britain, and China." FDR also told Molotov that, although the American people considered Japan to be the principal opponent, he considered Hitler the main enemy.[27]

The direct involvement of the United States in the war undoubtedly brought mixed feelings to the Soviets. Of course, they were happy over the addition of such a strong ally whose industrial power, from a Marxist point of view, virtually guaranteed victory.[28] They were particularly hard pressed in December 1941 with the Nazis pushing up against both Moscow and Leningrad. The neutrality pact with Japan, backed up by excellent espionage in Tokyo that revealed that Japan would not likely attack the Soviet Union, and American pressure on Japan that culminated in Pearl Harbor, enabled Stalin to move his armies from Siberia and Outer Mongolia to meet the Nazi drive against Moscow. By mid-December the fresh Soviet troops had managed a counteroffensive that shocked the Germans, whose own offensive had stalled in the snow. The Russian offensive was soon stopped, but it was a deep psychological blow to the vaunted German troops who had heretofore run over all enemies. The situation was still critical, and the Soviets knew that the Germans would launch an all-out offensive in the spring. American assistance was vital. However, Stalin had to be apprehensive about the political goals of the United States and the possibility of a common front by the Anglo-Americans.

In the hope perhaps of achieving a fait accompli before the Americans weighed in, Stalin pushed Britain in December 1941 for political agreements. He demanded that Anthony Eden, the British foreign minister, who was in Moscow to gain Stalin's trust and to sign a treaty of alliance with the USSR (December 16-22, 1941), agree to a secret protocol attached to the treaty that guaranteed the Soviet Union its 1941 borders with Poland, Romania, and Finland and control of the Baltic States. The protocol also allowed the Soviet Union to set up bases in Finland and Romania. Stalin reminded Eden that England had an alliance with czarist Russia during World War I when the Russian empire included Finland, the Baltic States, Bessarabia, and half of Poland, and, he added, "To the best of my recollection no English statesman at that time raised any difficulties about this alliance on the grounds that these territories were included in czarist Russia." The Soviet dictator also stressed that Poland should be compensated for its loss of territory by taking German territory probably up to the Oder River. Stalin, moreover, wanted Germany to be partitioned and occupied by Great Britain, the Soviet Union, and the United States and forced to pay reparations. Thus, Stalin laid out in rough outline in 1941 what became the territorial divisions after the Teheran and Yalta Conferences in 1943 and 1945, respectively.

A territorial agreement seems to have been Stalin's priority in December 1941, even before a second front in Western Europe. He told Eden on December 16 that he understood the British were tied down in Africa and Asia and could not immediately assist the Red Army. He also reported, following the Soviet offensive, that "the German army is not so strong after all." But he stressed, "It is very important for us to know whether we shall have to fight at the Peace Conference in order to get our western frontiers." In return for recognition of his territorial claims, Stalin would support the creation of British military bases in Denmark and Norway. In addition, the Soviet Union would help against Japan. Stalin told Eden, "We can do nothing now [against Japan], but in the spring we shall be ready, and will then help." Stalin added that the differences between Russia and Japan could only be resolved by force.[29]

Eden, who was sympathetic to the Soviet Union, was taken by surprise. He did not want to agree—in fact, could not—to such territorial issues, but at the same time he wanted to do what was necessary to gain Stalin's trust. At first, he demurred, arguing that the Soviet demands violated the Atlantic Charter, which Stalin had accepted in general. Stalin replied that he thought the Charter was "directed against those people who were trying to establish world dominion. It now looks as if the Charter was directed against the U.S.S.R." Stalin also said that the Soviets should be rewarded for "bearing the brunt" of the conflict.[30] His refusal to allow the Red Army to retreat had squandered six million men so far, a cruel blow to the people of the Soviet Union and to the Allied cause, but certainly no reason to reward Stalin.

Eventually, Eden agreed that Soviet territorial ambitions might be construed in such a way as to appear not to violate the Charter, but he could not summarily accede to them because the British government had promised the United States that it would not sign any territorial agreement. However, he added, if given time for consultation with the United States and the British Dominions, it might be worked out, particularly if Poland were not included in the agreement. Sir Stafford Cripps, the British ambassador, a dedicated socialist, worked on Eden and convinced him that agreeing to Soviet demands at least regarding the Baltic States was the price that had to be paid to assure the suspicious Stalin that the British were sincere in seeking the alliance. Cripps maintained that it was an "acid test," although Stalin never used that term. In fact, Stalin was demanding from the British what he had demanded from the Nazis. He remained remarkably consistent in his territorial demands from the beginning of the war.[31]

Stalin told Eden that he was open to postponing a decision on Poland, but he refused to believe that Eden could not accept the territorial protocol without first consulting with the United States. He feared that he would be the odd man out, who would "have to come cap in hand" to beg the Anglo-Americans for territory. Molotov told Eden, "We are talking of common war aims, of what we are both fighting for. On one of these important aims, our western frontiers, we have no support from Great Britain." Seeing that Eden was not prepared to deal with the territorial issues, Stalin finally agreed to allow him time to gain approval, but in the meantime he refused to sign a treaty of alliance. There was no point, he told Eden, if there were no agreement on postwar territorial and political issues.[32]

Eden returned to London and immediately pushed for some compromise on Stalin's territorial demands. He wanted to concede the Baltic States but hold firm on Poland. He was supported by Cripps, who had convinced Eden of the necessity of recognizing Stalin's claims to gain his trust, and by Lord Halifax, now the British ambassador to the United States. Beaverbrook also lined up behind Eden, arguing that the Soviet Union was more essential to England than the United States and thus London had to please Stalin, not Roosevelt. Clement Attlee, the lord privy seal and the future prime minister of the Labour Party, and Sir Alexander Cadogan, the permanent undersecretary in the Foreign Office, opposed Eden, stating that recognition was a violation of the Atlantic Charter. Cadogan also made the point that cooperation with Stalin would be difficult and that, at any rate, England could not act without the United States. Churchill was shocked by Stalin's demand and rejected at first Eden's proposal because it seemed to be a reward for aggression. He wanted to maintain the spirit and letter of the Atlantic Charter. Eden was ready to accept the Soviet Union, in his biographer's phrase, as "a genuine ally of liberal democracy and an agent of 'progress,'" but Churchill had his doubts.[33]

However, by March 1942 with the Germans poised to mount a massive offensive in the east, Churchill altered his stand. He decided then that granting Stalin's territorial demands would boost Soviet morale, curb any desire on Stalin's part to sign a separate peace with the Nazis, and fill in for a second front in Western Europe and for supplies, which were not yet up to commitments. He told Roosevelt, "The increasing gravity of the war has led me to feel that the principles of the Atlantic Charter ought not to be constructed so as to deny Russia the frontiers she occupied when Germany attacked her. This was the basis on which Russia acceded to the Charter, and I expect that a severe process of liquidating hostile elements in the Baltic States, etc., was employed by the Russians when they took these regions at the beginning of the war. I hope therefore that you will be able to give us as free hand to sign the treaty which Stalin desires as soon as possible." The British willingness to compromise the Atlantic Charter in 1942 was a fact that Eden and Churchill preferred to forget in the last years of the war, but it certainly proved that they shared the same hope that FDR harbored in his breast, namely, that Stalin's trust and goodwill could be purchased through concessions.[34]

To the British request for support on Stalin's territorial demands, the American government, to its credit, responded with a categorical refusal. Eden thought that Stalin's position "was amoral," that the United States' position was "exaggeratedly moral," and that the United Kingdom was caught in the middle. Cripps, who hoped to use the promise of American help to entice Stalin out of his alliance with Hitler, thought that Roosevelt and Churchill were "stupid about the frontier question." The pro-Soviet British ambassador also did not like Steinhardt, whom he considered "a typical bumptious U.S.A. business-lawyer type."[35]

Roosevelt did not want to deal with territorial issues prematurely or to be faced with a British-Soviet fait accompli. He made it clear to the Soviets as early as December 8, 1941, that the United States was interested in Finland and hoped that the Soviet Union and Finland could come to terms.[36] He also showed concern about the Baltic States and requested information from Moscow on how it defined the boundaries of the Soviet Union.[37] He wanted to wait on territorial decisions, possibly until a peace conference where, like Woodrow Wilson at Versailles, he could play a dominant role. In addition, he hoped to avoid alienating Polish and Baltic voters in the United States by publicly agreeing to Stalin's demands. He was also certainly influenced by Undersecretary of State Sumner Welles, who took a firm stand on the Atlantic Charter and common sense. Welles noted in April 1942 that English willingness to accept the Soviet annexation of the Baltic States was "not only indefensible from every moral standpoint, but likewise extraordinarily stupid" because it would inevitably produce additional demands, for example, against eastern Poland.[38] That was solid advice to which FDR did not listen often enough, although in December 1942 he did take credit in a conversation with Vice president Wallace for blocking the British from recognizing Soviet control of the Baltic States.[39] At the same time, though, Roosevelt was willing to hint to the Soviets that they would probably get what they wanted. He implied to Litvinov that the difficulty was American public opinion. According to Litvinov, when the problem of the Baltic States, Bessarabia, and Bukovina came out, FDR smiled and said that "he will deal with these issues at the end of the war" and, further, that "he wishes to meet with Stalin with whom he would quickly come to an agreement, since they were both realists."[40]

FDR also felt that he was better able to handle Stalin than Churchill, the British Foreign Office, or the U.S. State Department. It was at this point that Roosevelt put Churchill on notice that he wanted an exclusive relationship with Stalin. On March 18, he informed Churchill, "I know you will not mind my being brutally frank when I tell you that I think I can personally handle Stalin better than either your Foreign Office or my State Department. Stalin hates the guts of all your top people. He thinks he likes me better, and I hope he will continue to do so."[41] A week earlier he had told Litvinov the same thing. On what basis Roosevelt came to this conclusion is a mystery. He had not met Stalin, and Bullitt and Steinhardt had informed him and soon Standley would inform him that Stalin was not trustworthy. Of course, Davies and Hopkins were telling him the opposite. Perhaps they, hubris, and the misguided belief in a shared destiny led Roosevelt to assume that he could "handle" Stalin.

Curiously, William Standley was not told of the territorial dispute or of a new plan that FDR was hatching to defuse the imbroglio over territory and Soviet security needs. He was being bypassed even before he arrived in the Soviet Union. Standley flew the South Atlantic route to the Soviet Union, which took him through South America, Africa, and Teheran. In Teheran he ran into an American military mission, under the command of Major General John N. Greely, which had been sent to the Soviet Union to visit and to expedite "delivery of supplies and materials from the United States to the Soviet Union through the Near East, but the Soviets refused to grant the soldiers visas."[42] Standley thought the Soviet refusal to grant visas to an American military mission was bizarre, given the alliance, but he decided, despite the pleas of General Greely, not to allow the mission to fly with him since he "felt it would be most unwise to enter upon [his] duties by introducing into the Soviet Union a mission to which they object[ed]."[43]

General Greely waited for over a year for visas and never did get them. In October 1943 General John R. Deane replaced him and with the influence and support of W. Averell Harriman, who became ambassador in October 1943, visas were finally issued. General Deane later recounted his experience in a book entitled *The Strange Alliance*.[44]

The new ambassador arrived at Kuibyshev on April 7. His staff, who divided their time between Moscow and Kuibyshev, included Walter Thurston, Llewellyn Thompson, Charles Dickerson, G. Frederick Reinhardt, his personal secretary, Edward Page, who was an astute observer of the Russian scene and a product of Robert Kelley's training program, his personal physician, Commander Frederick Lang, and a bevy of military attachés, of whom the most prominent were Captain Jack Duncan and Major Joseph Michella. In Moscow there was, of course, General Faymonville, who ran the Lend-Lease program out of the partially reopened Mokhovaia building, which had housed the offices of the embassy. His Lend-Lease staff now numbered almost twenty-five persons, and in the opinion of the British ambassador it was an unofficial second embassy.[45] Needless to say, its function and scope frustrated Standley and confused the State Department.[46] The Soviets, however, thought the arrangement was ideal. They came to rely on Faymonville for military information and supplies, and Lozovksy praised Roosevelt for his great leadership and insight in appointing Faymonville to the Moscow Lend-Lease post.[47]

Standley had his first meeting with Stalin and Molotov in Moscow on April 23, 1942, twelve days after he arrived in the capital. Stalin kept him waiting to show his disdain for the new ambassador—a gratuitous insult that was typical of Stalin but hard for Standley and the embassy to understand. Nonetheless, Standley approached Stalin respectfully. He took the initiative and directed the meeting to the issues that FDR had outlined for him before he left Washington. He told Stalin that the president wanted a personal meeting, perhaps in Alaska as early as the summer, because he "was sure that if the two of you could sit down together and talk matters over, there would never be any lack of understanding between our two countries." A meeting was critical to FDR. It would allow him to use his trump—engaging charm—to reassure Stalin that he did not have to worry about Soviet security. Standley also informed Stalin about the American plan for a new Lend-Lease route across Siberia from Alaska, the so-called Alsib route, which would supplement the Persian Gulf-Iran route along which some 70 percent of the supplies passed, and the North Sea route. He added that the United States would be pleased if the Soviets would release the American aviators who had been forced to land in Siberia after bombing Japan, that there was a need for better and more frequent flights, consultation, and communication between Moscow and Washington, and that he was there to confirm America's Lend-Lease commitment to the Soviet Union and to solve any problems related to Lend-Lease. Standley also gave Stalin details on the bombing campaign against Japan.

To Standley's surprise, Stalin and Molotov were not friendly. Obviously, there was to be no honeymoon period. They complained that Lend-Lease supplies were not being received quickly enough and that "Russian orders" were not agreeably accepted by American firms. They also criticized the way the United States convoyed its ships, which seemed to be a complaint conjured up especially for an old sailor like Admiral Standley. Molotov gruffly told Standley that the American pilots would remain in internment "in order not to have trouble with our Japanese friends" and that the United States had "to prevent any such landings in the future." Stalin was not enthusiastic about the Alsib route, but later, when he was assured that only Russian pilots would fly over Siberia, he agreed to arrange it, and the route went into operation in October 1942. Stalin also informed Standley that the subject of a meeting with Roosevelt had been the topic of "messages" and that possibly it could be worked out. Standley took that to mean that it was being negotiated over his head and that, at any rate, Stalin was not going to reveal his plans to him. All in all, the ambassador was shocked by the rudeness, suspicion, and churlishness of the leaders of America's new ally.[48]

In his day-to-day relations with the Soviet representatives in Kuibyshev, Standley found the same attitude. They never answered questions or shared information. All of his complaints, whether they related to the fact that the Soviets were allowing the Japanese to fish in Soviet waters or were refusing to issue visas for the Soviet wives of American diplomats, were referred to Moscow and usually went unresolved. When he tried to arrange inspection tours of nearby factories, he was rebuffed. When he asked about broadcasting the "Voice of America" in the German language for Germany from Moscow, he was turned down. When Thurston requested information about Japanese gasoline production, no information was forthcoming.[49] For Standley, this was not how allies behaved.

When Standley returned to Kuibyshev from his meeting with Stalin and Molotov, he learned from Sir Archibald Clark-Kerr, the new British ambassador, that Molotov had just left the Soviet Union for England and the United States.

Standley was disturbed that he had not been informed of the trip either by Washington or Moscow, but it was more than a straw in the wind. It was further evidence that he was going to be marginalized right from the beginning.[50] His sole purpose was to keep the Soviets happy by resolving Lend-Lease problems.

President Roosevelt, as it turned out, had asked Stalin to send Molotov to Washington to discuss a "very important military proposal involving the utilization of our armed forces in a manner to relieve your critical western front."[51] Obviously, Roosevelt was referring to a second front in Europe and, in fact, the Americans were ready to try it. As early as January the president had recommended to Litvinov that American forces replace and thus free Soviet troops in Iran to fight on the eastern front. He also thought some assistance could be rendered in Murmansk and that the Soviets should occupy part of Norway to guarantee ice-free passage of supplies into Murmansk. Stalin did not like the idea of pulling back Soviet troops from Iran, which he had occupied with England in August 1941, and he was in no position to occupy part of Norway, even with Roosevelt's blessing. Molotov told Litvinov to inform Roosevelt that there was "no immediate danger" in the Caucasus and Murmansk region, so there was no need to substitute troops and, furthermore, the Soviet Union had no territorial or other ambitions against Norway, so it must not accept any proposal of occupation.[52] Molotov suggested a second front in Europe, but FDR told Litvinov that a second front might instead be launched in North Africa.[53] On April 11, however, the president informed Litvinov that he now favored a second front in Europe in the summer of 1942 but that the British were not convinced that it could be done. At any rate, Roosevelt decided on April 12 to invite Molotov to come to Washington. Stalin now thought that a second front in Europe was a real possibility, and on April 25 he dispatched Molotov to the West. The Soviet foreign minister's purpose was to obtain a firm commitment for a second front from the Allies and approval for the 1941 borders of the Soviet Union. The latter concession was to be included in a formal treaty establishing a British-Soviet alliance. The Soviets wanted to obtain a concrete agreement on spheres of influence before the Americans and British got together and simply dictated a new order to the Soviets. Molotov was also certainly planning to gauge the nature and strength of the Anglo-American relationship and the personalities of Roosevelt and Churchill.[54]

The Soviets, as it turned out, did not have to worry about an Anglo-American common stand. The British hoped to produce such a position, but Roosevelt wanted to keep the relationship loose and the goals general, to the exasperation of the British. "It is absolutely necessary," Churchill pleaded with Roosevelt, "for us to have a plan which we can put to him [Stalin] fairly and squarely. It is bound to be a joint plan, and we can do nothing until I hear from you."[55] FDR, however, turned a deaf ear. He had it in mind that one of the major causes of the war was the suppressed nationalism of various, colonial peoples, and that to prevent war from erupting again, the colonial empires, including the British empire, would have to be dismantled.

Furthermore, Roosevelt was under the false impression that the Soviet Union was an anti-imperialist state, too. On the common ground of anti-imperialism, FDR perhaps thought that he could find a bond with the suspicious Soviets. At any rate, Roosevelt was sensitive to the Soviet fear of being ganged up on by the Anglo-Americans, so he wanted to avoid any appearance of predetermination by Washington and London. Actually, he was apprehensive that the British and the Soviets might try to dictate political conditions to the newest member of the alliance. It was that fear which led Roosevelt to request that Molotov come to the United States before he visited England. By the same token, it was Stalin's hope that a fait accompli could be delivered to the Americans that led him to deny FDR's request and send Molotov to London first.

It soon became clear in London that the Soviets wanted both territorial commitments and a second front, but if they could only have one now, they wanted the second front. The German offensive had started on the eastern front, and Stalin's priority now was a western front. The British were open to acquiescing in the territorial demands, but not the second front, and they told Molotov that there was even a problem regarding the territory, namely, that the Americans were dead set against it to the point that they would denounce the Anglo-Soviet alliance.[56]

Roosevelt also made this position clear to Litvinov, who had replaced Oumansky as the Soviet ambassador in the United States in November 1941.[57] Molotov told Litvinov to temporize despite FDR's insistence that he be informed of the Soviet Union's view of its boundaries.[58] Given the American stand and the Soviet Union's first priority, Molotov went ahead and signed the treaty setting up the military alliance between England and the Soviet Union without any understanding about Soviet territorial demands.[59] He left London empty-handed for Washington. His goal was to draw the Americans into a commitment for a second front.

Molotov's visit with Roosevelt was an eye-opener. Although FDR hoped to postpone territorial decisions, he was simultaneously sensitive to Stalin's security needs and the danger of pushing Stalin to work out a separate peace with Nazi Germany by failing to meet his territorial demands. The likelihood of a separate peace, however, was far-fetched because it was Hitler, not Stalin, who controlled the issue, and he made it abundantly clear when he started the invasion that it was a war to the death against the Communists. Nonetheless, FDR thought Stalin was capable of a separate peace, which he was and tried to do, but that was reason to distrust him, not try to win him over, and to try to get Hitler removed, not solidify his position with an eventual declaration of unconditional surrender. For the moment, FDR's hope was that he could meet Stalin and persuade him at that meeting that his security needs would be guaranteed, so that he would not need a prior agreement on territory that could publicly undermine the Atlantic Charter and the confidence of the American voters, especially those of East European extraction, in the democratic principles for which the United States, however muted, maintained that it was fighting.

The president proposed four policies to appeal directly to Stalin. In contrast to the British, who wished to trade territory for the Soviet effort on the eastern front, Roosevelt wanted to postpone territorial decisions and initiate a second front in Europe to take the pressure off the Red Army now. The commitment for a second front was not absolute and categorical, but it was encouraging to Molotov. Roosevelt, in front of Molotov, asked General George Marshall if Stalin could be told that a second front was being readied. Marshall, caught between the dour Molotov and the beaming Roosevelt, could only respond, "Yes." The general tried to qualify his answer by informing the Soviet foreign minister that the major problem with starting a second front in 1942 was the shortage of transport ships, that most American transport ships were busy bringing Lend-Lease supplies to the Soviet Union, and that Lend-Lease shipments would inevitably be disrupted if the United States shifted its transport fleet to a second front effort. Molotov, however, remained unconvinced that both could not be done, and in the end Roosevelt, based on Marshall's evaluation, allowed Molotov to draft a statement indicating that Stalin could "expect a second front this year."[60]

Second, Roosevelt proposed to Molotov that all countries be disarmed except the United States, the Soviet Union, England, and China, and that these four "united nations" serve "as the policemen of the world." If the United States and the Soviet Union insisted on this approach, Roosevelt continued, all other countries would have to accept it, including the British whom he implied might not go along. Roosevelt stressed that he did not want too many "policemen" because then they might start fighting with one another. The concept eventually became the root of the UN Security Council.

Molotov specifically asked if France, Poland, and Turkey were to be disarmed and if this approach represented Roosevelt's "final and considered judgment." When FDR answered affirmatively to both questions and added that forced disarmament must replace the traditional balance of power as the new basis of international peace, Molotov could hardly hide his glee and surprise. He told FDR that his proposal was very important, very realistic, and would find support in Moscow.[61]

Molotov could not but conclude that Roosevelt was, after all, a hypocritical imperialist, that the Atlantic Charter was, as Stalin thought, so much propaganda, for certainly the American president was not so naive as to think that a disarmed Turkey, Poland, France, and Germany would operate independently of the interests of an armed neighbor who happened to be a "policeman."

Third, Roosevelt informed Molotov that the European empires, including the British, had to be disbanded. For FDR, colonialism was a major cause of the war and he was determined to bring down the empires. For a Marxist-Leninist like Molotov, this was a textbook example of the classic conflict between a young capitalist state and a declining, ossified capitalist empire. It was also obvious that the United States and England were not as close as the Soviets might have feared and there was no immediate danger of a common Anglo-American position.

Finally, the president tried to reassure Molotov about Soviet security needs. FDR guaranteed that Stalin's security needs would be met. He had already told Litvinov that the United States would guarantee Soviet interests at the end of the war. The key for Roosevelt was a personal meeting with Stalin that would exorcise forever what he thought was the Soviet leader's inordinate fear of betrayal and insecurity. He suggested a meeting in Alaska.[62]

FDR apparently was oblivious to the contradiction between the third and fourth parts of his approach. He could roil against colonialism and simultaneously guarantee the territorial integrity and possible expansion of the Soviet empire only by misclassifying the Soviet Union, either through ignorance or ideology, as something other than an empire.

Beyond the measures geared to appeal to Moscow, the president also registered American interest in the fate of Finland, asked about Soviet aid against Japan, stressed the need for postwar cooperation between the United States and the Soviet Union, and informed Molotov that, although Japan was the main enemy in the popular mind, Germany was the focus of his attention. The American government did ask, however, for permission to bomb Japan from Soviet territory, which Stalin refused. It also assured Moscow that it would assist the Soviet Union if Japan should join Germany by attacking the USSR.[63]

The most immediate significance of the Molotov-Roosevelt meeting was, in Molotov's mind, the promise of a second front in 1942. The Soviet foreign minister certainly wanted a more precise commitment on a second front, but when it was not forthcoming, he returned to London with what he had: a commitment of sorts. Before he left Washington, though, he had lunch with Davies at the Soviet embassy and urged him to use his influence at the White House to support the need for a second front. He also visited with Secretary of State Hull and told him, as he had informed Roosevelt, that the Soviet Union could offer no help against Japan. In London, the British were surprised by the American position, but eventually they also gave Molotov halfhearted approval of the idea of a second front in 1942. They did think, though, that Marshall's plan for an invasion of France in 1942 was unrealistic and simplistic.[64]

After Molotov returned to Moscow, the Soviets turned up the pressure to firm up the western commitment. The Soviet press announced that a second front would take place in 1942, a strategy that put pressure on both the Allies and the Germans. At the same time, Molotov met with Standley and Clark-Kerr and told them that a second front was an absolute certainty. He added that the Soviet people would be cruelly disappointed if it did not materialize. He rejected

Clark-Kerr's clarification that no hard-fast promise had in fact been given by saying that the test of the British-Soviet alliance lay in a second front and that the British and the Americans must understand this. Typically, Standley had not been informed by Washington that a second front was a viable option. He learned of it from a broadcast of the British Broadcasting Corporation. Molotov confirmed it in a separate meeting on June 19 when he told Standley about his meetings in Washington and asserted that Roosevelt was very realistic and had put forward the idea of a second front in Europe in 1942.[65]

Molotov's interview and the Soviet publicity about a second front shocked Standley. He had not been told that his government had committed itself to a second front, and he realized that a major problem was developing. "If such a front does not materialize quickly and on a large scale," he informed Secretary of State Hull on June 22, 1942, "these people will be so deluded in their belief in our sincerity of purpose and will for concerted action that inestimable harm will be done to the cause of the United Nations."[66]

On July 4, Clark-Kerr, with Standley's concurrence, informed Molotov that the difficulties of organizing a second front in 1942 had been explained to him in London and Washington and "that he might be overestimating the probability of the early establishment of a second front in Western Europe this year." He reported to London that Molotov understood the British government's position.[67] Standley hoped that Clark-Kerr's meeting would end the Soviet demand and hope for a second front in 1942, but Standley had to telegraph Washington on July 22 that Stalin and Molotov continued to act as if a second front were a certainty. He told Secretary Hull that Molotov had not given him any indication that he understood the position outlined in Clark-Kerr's report and that if a second front were not planned, Molotov and Stalin had better be told "directly and privately."[68] Standley understood that the Soviet government was using the publicity of an expected second front to create pressure on the West to fulfill its expectation, to pep up the morale of the Soviet soldiers, and to undermine the morale of the Germans. Nonetheless, he felt the West had better make its position absolutely clear. On July 23 FDR told Litvinov that the United States was committed both to convoying aid to the Soviet Union and to organizing a second front in Europe but that Churchill believed a campaign in North Africa was more realistic. He wanted to know Stalin's opinion. Litvinov informed him that only pressure on Hitler in Belgium, Holland, or France would directly benefit the USSR. Nonetheless, FDR confirmed to Litvinov on July 30 that North Africa would be the main target in 1942.[69]

In early August Churchill and Harriman arrived in Moscow for what Churchill called "a raw job." The British leader had to inform Stalin that there would be no second front in Europe in 1942 but that instead there would be an invasion of North Africa. At first, Stalin seemed to approve the change of plan, but then he complained bitterly, accusing the British of a lack of courage. Churchill and

Stalin argued vehemently, and at one point the British prime minister was on the verge of departing Moscow in a huff. Eventually, Stalin smoothed over relations and accepted the inevitable.[70]

There was another problem with the second front that was apparent from the very first time that Moscow requested it in July 1941. Stalin's government refused to provide any significant and useful information on the eastern front, thus preventing the West from establishing priorities in supplies in the multifront war that it was waging around the world. The western delegations and ambassadors could not even obtain weather information. Standley and his military attachés were kept in the dark despite pleas for basic information and coordination. Roosevelt also found the Soviets taciturn and introverted. When he asked Stalin to increase contacts between the naval, air force, and army leaders, Stalin replied that "these contacts can take place in Moscow" where, of course, there was only one-way communication with General Faymonville. In the words of historian Steven Miner, when it came to opening the second front, "the Soviets were frequently their own worst enemies."[71]

Harriman was not a party to the critical meetings between Churchill and Stalin. Roosevelt sent him along with Churchill to watch his two allies, but he did not empower him to negotiate, so he had to sit out the important meetings. He puzzled over Stalin's hot-cold behavior and eventually came up with an explanation. He told Standley, who had not been included in any of the discussions, that Stalin was affable and agreeable, but "whenever he gets tough with us, it's the Politburo attitude he's expressing, not his own views on the major subject at issue." Standley politely disagreed, arguing that he thought it was a tactic that Stalin used to soften up opponents for concessions.[72]

Harriman's view won wide acceptance in the Roosevelt administration. It helped explain the odd behavior of the Soviets, why they were more brusque at times than at other times, never mind that it directly contradicted another perception of Harriman, Roosevelt, and Hopkins, namely, that Stalin was supreme in the Soviet Union. Harriman also cabled the president that Stalin wanted special "binding ties" with the United States and Great Britain and that he was the kind of leader who could exchange views with "you and the Prime Minister . . . in the frankest manner without fear of breaking the personal relationship." Stalin also told him that the Soviets could not participate in the war against Japan, but wanted the United States to keep pressure on Japan with naval operations in the Pacific Ocean and by bombing Tokyo in order to prevent Japan from opening a Soviet front.[73]

Standley resented the fact that he had not been included in the Stalin-Churchill-Harriman talks, particularly since the British ambassador had participated. He also did not like the fact that he was always the last one to find out what was going on. He complained periodically, to no avail, to Secretary Hull that he was not being kept informed.[74] He had been at the Moscow post for five months, and virtually everything that went on during that time had proceeded without him.

No sooner did Harriman and Churchill leave Moscow than FDR sent Wendell Willkie, his Republican opponent in the 1940 election, to the Soviet Union in September with a threefold message. Willkie emphasized the theory of convergence, maintaining that the United States and the Soviet Union were becoming increasingly alike and that they represented mankind's best hope for the future. He also asked Stalin to treat the Poles decently, and he made headlines by criticizing the lack of a second front in 1942.[75] He pointedly avoided Standley, did not include him in a meeting with Stalin, and, when he could not escape him, made fun of the ambassador in front of the Russians. Standley deeply resented Willkie's performance and eventually reminded him "that there is only one United States representative in the Soviet Union, and I, the American Ambassador, am that representative."[76] There was no need for such outrageous behavior, which embarrassed Standley, undercut the prestige and influence of the embassy, and underlined the puerility of American foreign policy leadership. Standley was completely capable of performing the tasks that Roosevelt had assigned both Harriman and Willkie. On October 6, in a discussion with Stalin, he had to admit that he did not know what Willkie and Stalin had discussed because Willkie did not brief him. The special representatives were simply bringing confusion and misdirection to a tense and complicated relationship. In fact, Vyshinsky thought Willkie was a "typical American delegate: a businessman making a big, unrestrained pretense about democracy."[77]

Standley was obviously becoming increasingly vexed over being disregarded and kept in the dark about developments. He also disliked the policy of unconditional aid. After personally seeing the policy at work for almost six months, he decided that it was a mistake. He particularly objected to the independence of General Faymonville, who answered directly to the Lend-Lease Administration in Washington. He wanted a better grip on Faymonville. The Soviets rarely asked the embassy for anything because, according to Standley, they got everything they wanted, including highly sensitive military information, from Faymonville. He contemptuously referred to Faymonville as one of "Harry Hopkins's Lend-Lease boys." Standley had been trying to build bridges with the Soviets through the exchange of intelligence and by screening Walt Disney films, but he found himself and his staff totally isolated.[78]

On July 10 he approached the Soviet government with the Faymonville problem. In Vyshinsky's words, "Acting rather shyly, Standley started talking about a rather difficult mission he has been instructed to fulfill by the United States government: the heart of the matter was that Soviet military agencies tended to discuss with Moscow Lend-Lease mission head, Brig. Gen. Faymonville, various military issues which were outside his competence." According to Vyshinsky, Standley declared that the American government wanted "to inform the Soviet authorities that Soviet military agencies, when they wished to discuss any military issues save for the Lend-Lease program, should approach the ambassador, military attaché, or various military representatives accredited with the embassy." Vyshinsky replied that he would pass this request on to his government. Standley's disingenuous attempt to persuade the Kremlin to alter its policy of working with Faymonville by claiming that it was the wish of the United States government was futile. If Washington did not want Faymonville giving information, then Washington would have recalled or otherwise curtailed Faymonville. Standley was simply underlining his own lack of power and influence, which was the Soviet conclusion. When Henderson visited the embassy in December 1942, Vyshinsky decided that the presence of such "an experienced and intelligent representative" was an attempt to strengthen Standley's weak position.[79]

Needless to say, the Soviets did not change their modus operandi with Faymonville. In fact, judging by a number of documents in the Russian archives, the Soviet military used Faymonville as a kind of super military agent.[80] Once it became clear to Standley that the Faymonville problem was not going to be resolved except through Roosevelt's intervention, Standley asked to return to Washington in October for important consultations and, to the exasperation of Roosevelt and Hopkins, he delivered a ringing critique of unconditional aid.

After his meeting with Roosevelt and Hopkins, Standley decided that he would not go back to Moscow until he at least had definite orders placing Faymonville under his authority. He stayed in the United States through November and into December. Finally, Harry Hopkins asked him on December 10 when he was going back. He replied that he would return as soon as he saw the orders placing Faymonville under his jurisdiction. Irritated, Hopkins had Edward Stettinius issue the order the next day. On December 12 a cable to Faymonville informed him that he was "subject to overall coordination and supervision by the Chief of the Diplomatic Mission." Standley was satisfied and left for the Soviet Union on December 19. However, unbeknownst to the ambassador, other messages were sent to Faymonville that qualified the new order and allowed him to maintain "his own relations with any Soviet authorities who approached him" and "to give the Soviets any information that Washington officials considered necessary."[81]

11

The News Conference

While Standley was gone, the great Battle of Stalingrad unfolded. It and the ensuing Battle of Kursk in July 1943 were the proverbial turning points in the war. When Standley finally reached Kuybyshev in January, the Battle of Stalingrad was still raging, but it was clear by then that the Soviets had turned the tide against the German invasion. The embassy was moved from Kuibyshev back to Moscow in January 1943. In February the German Sixth Army, led by Field Marshal Friedrich Paulus, surrendered to the Red Army. In that same month the British cornered Rommel and his army in Tunisia and the Japanese gave up Guadalcanal to the Americans. In the summer of 1943, following the stalling of the German offensive in the spring and the German defeat at the great tank battle at Kursk in July, the Red Army launched a massive offensive that forced the Germans to retreat on all fronts. The Red Army was now driving toward the west. It recaptured Kharkov on August 23 and Smolensk on September 28.

Standley soon had reason to question the effectiveness of his meeting with Hopkins and Roosevelt. He discovered that, even though he had just returned from the United States, FDR had not seen fit to tell him that he had invited Stalin to join him and Churchill for the Casablanca Conference in January. Stalin turned down the invitation on the grounds that the war was so critical on the eastern front that he could not be absent from the Soviet Union for even a single day.[1]

His absence at the Casablanca Conference, as Ivan Maisky argued, pretty well precluded the possibility of a second front in France in 1943. It was an important meeting where the Americans and British planned future strategy against Germany and its allies, and the failure of Stalin to be present or to send Molotov meant that the British argument to continue a Mediterranean campaign aimed at knocking Italy out of the war met with no substantive objections. Roosevelt, although willing to contemplate an invasion of France, realized, too, that the supply of transport ships and landing craft was not sufficient to carry out a Mediterranean thrust, an already planned American advance in the Pacific, and yet a third campaign in France. Stalin, as it turned out, was not yet ready to meet his allies together or to associate himself or Molotov prematurely with a political conference dealing with Germany. In fact, he was attempting to reach a separate treaty with Germany precisely at the time of Casablanca. With the German defeat at Stalingrad becoming clearer with each passing day, Stalin wanted to know if German leaders were willing to end the war in the east on the basis of the territorial agreements of 1939, something which his two western allies had heretofore been unwilling to accept. As historian Keith Eubanks noted, "Any meeting with Roosevelt and Churchill would only have wrecked the negotiations" with Germany.[2] The Germans, however, spurned Stalin's overtures. For Hitler, it was war to the end.

Nonetheless, Stalin's refusal to attend the Casablanca Conference worked in his favor. Roosevelt desperately wanted to please Stalin and, according to his son, came up with the idea of unconditional surrender from Germany after he recalled U. S. Grant's moniker during the Civil War. At a news conference in Casablanca, FDR declared that the West would accept nothing less than unconditional surrender from Germany and Japan. Roosevelt's purpose was to reassure the Soviets that the West would not sign a separate treaty with Germany and to relieve his own uneasiness about postponing a second front in France. He was also venting his hatred of Germany and his determination to demilitarize and denazify the German people. Harriman, who was at Casablanca, thought FDR issued the declaration to dampen Soviet suspicion of the West and to avoid Woodrow Wilson's mistake of promulgating peace terms before the enemy surrender and thus opening the door to "bargaining over terms, or cries of deception from the Germans after the war." It also was clearly calculated to shape and appeal to American public opinion, although in the popular mind the main enemy was Japan, not Germany.[3]

Churchill, who indicated after the war that he was surprised by FDR's announcement, eventually remembered, after he checked the record, that he had once fully endorsed the policy of unconditional surrender.[4] Kennan, on the other hand, saw unconditional surrender as an absolutely fundamental error and "as the source of all other ills" affecting American wartime diplomacy. He later denounced "the unshakeable American commitment to the principle of unconditional surrender; the tendency to view any war in which we might be involved not as a means of achieving limited objectives in the way of changes in a given *status quo* but as a struggle to the death between total virtue and total evil, with the result that the war had absolutely to be fought to the complete destruction of the enemy's power, no matter what disadvantages or complications this might involve for the more distant future. From this flowed, of course, the congenital reluctance of American statesmen and military leaders to entertain the suggestion that there could be considerations of a political nature that could conceivably take precedence over those of military efficiency and advantage."[5]

If Roosevelt did not please Kennan with the policy of unconditional surrender, he thought that he had at least won Stalin's favor. Stalin, however, was not exhilarated by the declaration of unconditional surrender, either, and he refused to embrace it himself. He made his opposition clear at the Teheran Conference, and his argument against it was that it might extend the war and reduce flexibility. Curiously, Roosevelt did not recall Stalin's opposition. Churchill had to gently remind him of it in a subsequent letter.[6] In a letter to Roosevelt and Churchill after the Casablanca Conference, Stalin did not even mention unconditional surrender, but simply reiterated that the main task was to open a second front in Europe in 1943. However, Stalin was shrewd enough to keep the West committed to the policy once it was promulgated. Molotov told Standley on April 5, 1943, that "the harmony of the allied nations" depends on refusing to negotiate "a separate peace treaty with Germany or its allies unless it is mutually agreed to."[7]

After the Casablanca meeting Roosevelt offered to send General George Marshall, chairman of the Combined Chiefs of Staff, to Moscow to brief Stalin. The Soviet leader, however, rejected the proposal. Churchill and Roosevelt also offered to send air squadrons to the Soviet Union to help battle the Germans on the eastern front. Stalin turned down that proposal, too. Back in London, Harriman asked the Soviet ambassador, Ivan Maisky, to explain Stalin's unfriendly attitude. Maisky responded that Stalin was suspicious of the western leaders and believed that they secretly hoped to drag the USSR into the war against Japan.[8]

Roosevelt, of course, was interested in having the Soviets commit themselves against Japan, and he attempted on several occasions to get talks going about a Soviet role in the Far East. Stalin, however, totally absorbed with the war in Europe and finding his allies unwilling to reward him with territorial commitments or to help him with a second front in France, spurned all American requests even to begin negotiations about a Soviet campaign against Japan. He also refused to break his nonaggression pact with Japan, even though Japan was a principal enemy of the United States, his ally and benefactor. Indeed, the Soviets were still holding the American pilots who had landed on Soviet territory after bombing Japan in order to give Japan no pretext for hostilities against the Soviet Union, which, in light of Japanese defeats, was a highly unlikely prospect. To be sure, Stalin planned to enter the war against Japan once the German threat was defeated, and he made this position clear at the foreign ministers' conference in Moscow in 1943 and at the Teheran Conference, but, as Bullitt explained to FDR in January and again in May 1943, Stalin saw no reason to assist the Americans in ending the war in Asia before he was in a position to take full advantage of the Japanese defeat or to distract the Americans from the war against Germany by opening to them the option of a quick victory over Japan through a modicum of Soviet assistance.[9]

Further, as Maisky declared, Stalin was highly suspicious of his allies. His suspicion increased dramatically when the Casablanca Conference failed to call for a front in France in 1943. It was further reinforced in the spring of 1943 when the Arctic convoys to the USSR had to be temporarily suspended because of huge losses suffered at the hands of German submarines. This problem was soon rectified, however, once the Allies gained access to German military and naval plans through the Enigma/Ultra intelligence system, developed an effective convoy escort plan, and invented the ten-centimeter radar that was so effective against U-boats.

Of course, Stalin was not entirely disappointed by the Casablanca Conference's decision to focus on a Mediterranean strategy. Concentrating on Italy was better than concentrating on Japan. The last thing that Stalin wanted was to have the war against Japan end prematurely. If he allowed the United States to use Soviet bases in Asia, the Americans might be tempted to focus on Japan and not Germany. He wished the Americans to stay fully committed on the European front and half-committed on the Asian front. Maisky made it clear to the British that the Americans would never be allowed to use Soviet airfields against Japan. He said the reason was that the Americans were anti-Russian, which, of course, in light of Lend-Lease was absurd.[10] The real reason was perhaps closer to Bullitt's assertion that Stalin believed that Soviet help would lead the United States to focus on Japan and defeat it before the Soviet Union could get fully involved. And, of course, the massive bombing of Germany by England and the United States and the campaign to knock Italy out of the war directly assisted the Soviet Union.

Standley was disturbed that he had not been informed about the Casablanca meeting, but he consoled himself with the thought that his trip home was not totally futile, for at least he thought that he had some control over General Faymonville. However, he quickly learned that he had been deceived by Roosevelt and Hopkins. Faymonville continued on as he had before, refusing to submit to the ambassador's authority. Standley retaliated by accusing Faymonville of being a traitor and a "pink." Public clashes soon ensued between Faymonville and Standley's military attaché, Joseph Michela, whom the ambassador had had promoted to the rank of brigadier general. Michella did not want Faymonville handling military information, and Standley backed him up, but to no avail. Standley also complained to Molotov about the lack of contact and information between the American military attachés and their Soviet counterparts who dealt only with Faymonville, but that was like talking to a stone. Soon Faymonville became persona non grata at the embassy, which made the Americans the talk of the Moscow diplomatic circuit. When General Burns, the executive director of the Lend-Lease Administration, arrived in Moscow in April, he threw his support behind Faymonville. "General Burns is of the same belief as Faymonville," Standley wrote his wife. "Russian interests come first, last and all the time; it's hopeless."[11]

Although Standley lost the battle to control Faymonville, the public clashes between Michella and Faymonville soon caught the attention of General Marshall in Washington. In early 1943, in response to charges that Faymonville "was so pro-Soviet as to raise the question in some persons' minds as to whether he was being 'blackmailed' by the Soviet Government," Marshall ordered an investigation into his background and loyalty. The investigation produced a thirty-five-page, single-spaced typewritten report, written by an associate of General Michella, that outlined "the old gossip" of the Moscow embassy and presented details regarding Faymonville that "were malicious and often inaccurate," but also made the telling point that the Lend-Lease official was sabotaging the embassy and giving intelligence information to the Soviets pro bono. In the late summer of 1943 the report finally made its way through the corridors of power in Washington.[12]

In the meantime, Standley soon realized that not only had he been duped on Faymonville but that his advice on the policy of unconditional aid was being totally ignored. He renewed his attack on the unconditional aid policy in private communications to Washington. He was incensed by the total lack of gratitude for the aid extended, by the Soviet unwillingness to share military information, especially regarding the Germans, and by the fact that American pilots were still interned in the Soviet Union. Of course, there were also the old problems that Steinhardt had faced, including the refusal of the Soviets to help locate Polish refugees, visa delays for official American personnel, persistent problems with currency exchange, severe difficulties with transportation, atrocious living quarters, the rigidly centralized Soviet bureaucracy, and the intrusive, ubiquitous presence of the Soviet secret police. Standley was especially upset over the Kremlin's refusal to provide information on the Polish army officers whom the Russians had captured in 1939 and its continuing internment of American pilots who landed in the Soviet Union after running out of gas following bombing runs on Japan. He and some of his staff members were eventually permitted to visit the imprisoned pilots after months of bureaucratic delays.[13]

While Standley seethed in Moscow, Roosevelt underwent a stressful meeting with former ambassador Bullitt at the White House. FDR had asked Bullitt in late 1942 for his thoughts on the machinery of preparation for civil administration in occupied territories. With the tide of battle turning against the Axis powers, the president wanted to start planning for the occupation of Europe and the postwar order. On January 29, Bullitt delivered his report to the president. It was a detailed criticism of the pro-Stalin policy.

Bullitt outlined, with amazing perspicacity and accuracy, the dynamics of Stalin's geopolitical thinking, the fate of Central and Eastern Europe if the policy of unconditional and uncritical aid and alliance continued, and an alternative policy to control and prevent Stalin from doing in Europe and Asia what Hitler was attempting to do in Europe. His ideas to produce a cooperative or, failing that, checkmated Stalin included restoration of the balance of power, a battle plan that made Japan rather than Germany the main focus of American military attention during 1943, American cooperation with England against Stalin, an invasion strategy that targeted the Black Sea and Balkans rather than France, the movement of western armies into Eastern and Central Europe before the arrival of the Red Army, immediate involvement of the Soviet Union against Japan, concrete and detailed plans to build democratic governments in the postwar era, curtailment of wartime aid to Moscow, and the use of postwar reconstruction aid as an inducement for Stalin to cooperate. Bullitt basically reiterated, as he himself said, the same formula, changed to fit the new circumstances of the war, that he had prescribed for FDR in 1934: "By using the old technique of the donkey, the carrot and the club you might be able to make Stalin move in the direction in which we want him to move."

Roosevelt's tête-à-tête with Bullitt was tense and heated. Bullitt stressed that the Soviet Union was an aggressive, expansionist power that aimed to place Communist regimes throughout Europe and that there was "only one guarantee that the Red Army will not cross into Europe—the prior arrival of American and British armies in the eastern frontiers of Europe. To win the peace at the close of this war," he concluded, "will be at least as difficult as to win the war." The former ambassador followed up his meeting with two letters in May and August that recapitulated the same argument. FDR was unmoved. He told Bullitt that his facts were accurate and his reasoning sound, but that Stalin was not an imperialist but a friend and ally who would work with FDR "for a world of democracy and peace."[14]

Years later, Kennan vouchsafed that Bullitt's advice "had no counterpart . . . as a warning of that date to the American president of the effective division of Europe which would ensue if the war continued to be pursued on the basis of the concepts then prevailing." Not only did Bullitt predict "with startling accuracy the situation to which the war would lead if existing policies continued to be pursued," but "he warned against placing any reliance on Russian good will."[15] Bullitt actually did not sound the earliest warning to Roosevelt. The Vatican in 1942 emphasized to Roosevelt's envoy, Myron Taylor, that the Communists could not be trusted and had to be stopped. Rome urged a separate treaty with a denazified Germany, a policy suggestion that was rejected by Roosevelt but not by Stalin.[16]

Although FDR was firm in his dismissal of Bullitt's analysis of Stalin, he decided to seek another opinion. He explained to Eden in March 1943 in Washington that Bullitt thought the Soviets intended to establish Communist governments throughout Europe, if given half a chance to do so, and he wondered what Eden's view was. The British foreign minister replied that it was really impossible to say if Bullitt were right or wrong, but that even if Bullitt were right, "we should make the position no worse by trying to work with Russia and by assuming that Stalin meant what he said." Roosevelt, according to Eden, agreed with him.[17] How Eden and Roosevelt could conclude that the situation would be no worse if Bullitt were right is a conundrum. If Bullitt were right, as indeed he was, the position would be made much worse, as indeed it was, by trusting Stalin. FDR probably never seriously entertained the notion that Bullitt could be right.

Eden and Churchill eventually agreed with Bullitt. As the tide turned in favor of the Allies, Eden wanted a more forceful policy toward Stalin, and Churchill soon began to advocate an Anglo-American war strategy identical with that which was being pleaded for by Bullitt—"an attack, that is," according to Kennan, "on the 'soft underbelly of the Axis' and an advance up through central Europe with a view both to cutting the Germans off from their access to the Balkans and to saving the peoples of that area from being taken under Russian political control."[18]

Roosevelt, however, wanted nothing to do with Bullitt and his approach implying a distrust and animosity toward Stalin. The president basically cut Bullitt off from the White House. But no sooner did he dismiss Bullitt than Standley let loose in Moscow with a Bullitt-like attack on the president's policy.

Standley's anger and frustration had been growing once he returned from the United States in January 1943 and discovered that his trip home and critique of unconditional aid had not altered Roosevelt's policy one iota. In late February 1943 Stalin made an address to the Soviet armed forces in which he claimed that the Red Army was virtually fighting the war alone against Germany, failing to mention any aid by the United States and Britain.[19] The president decided to overlook the slight because of the necessity of maintaining a strong alliance. Eleanor Roosevelt revealed what was undoubtedly on FDR's mind when she wrote their daughter, Anna, on February 28, 1943, that "Stalin's speech seemed to me arrogant and unwise, but I suppose it was for home effect and I confess" that the anti-Soviet attitude in some quarters "seems to me to justify Stalin's attitude. We can't take it for granted that we are the only trustworthy people in the world and we must believe in other people's intelligence and good intentions if we expect them to believe in us."[20] Standley, however, decided to take off on the issue of Soviet ingratitude. He thought it was high time that the principle of reciprocity was introduced.

"You know, boys, ever since I've been here," he announced to a small group of American journalists in the library of Spaso House on March 8, 1943, "I've been looking for recognition in the Russian press of the fact that they are getting material help not only through Lend-Lease but through Red Cross and Russian-American Relief, but I've yet to find any acknowledgment of that."

Edward Page, the ambassador's secretary and a Russian expert himself, swallowed hard and looked positively ill.

"Is that off the record, Mr. Ambassador, or may we use it?" inquired Henry Shapiro of United Press.

"Use it," answered Standley. The reporters grabbed their notepads and pencils to copy down Standley's remarks. He informed them that the American people knew huge amounts of aid and relief were being sent to the USSR but that the Russian people were ignorant of this fact. It was not right to misinform

William C. Bullitt

All photos were reproduced from the collections of the Library of Congress.

Joseph E. Davies, receiving a bronze plaque on August 7, 1946, from Senator Claude Pepper (D., Fla.) for his efforts in furthering good relations between the United States and the Soviet Union. Andrei Gromyko, Soviet delegate to the United Nations Security Council, looks on.

Loy Henderson and Andrei Gromyko

Laurence Steinhardt with his wife and daughter

Charles Bohlen (left) with Mikhail A. Menshikov

William Standley (right rear) with Molotov, Harriman, and Churchill in Moscow in August 1942

World War II poster advertising the democratic nature of the alliance between the United States, Soviet Russia, and Great Britain

Churchill, Harriman, Stalin, and Molotov in Moscow in August 1942

Casablanca Conference, January 1943. Left front: General George C. Marshall, President Franklin D. Roosevelt, and Admiral E. J. King. Left rear: Harry Hopkins, Lt. General H. H. Arnold, Lt. General Brehon Samervell, and W. Averell Harriman.

George F. Kennan, appearing before Congress

Churchill, Roosevelt, and Stalin at the 1943 Teheran Conference

the people of America who were donating so much aid and who thought they were helping the Russian people. By the same token the Russian citizens did not know that the aid was coming from the American people who were giving it out of friendship.

There was a break. A newsman inquired why the Kremlin had not publicized the assistance from the United States.

"The Soviet authorities," the ambassador responded, "seem to be endeavoring to create the impression at home as well as abroad that they are fighting the war alone and with their own resources rather than to acknowledge aid from anyone else."

A query about the state of the Lend-Lease legislation then followed. Standley believed the foreign relations committee had passed it but that it was not yet approved by Congress. "Congress is rather sensitive," he declared. "It is generous and big-hearted so long as it feels that it is helping someone. But give it the idea that it is not—there might be an entirely different story."

Another question had to do with the exchange of military information. "There is no obvious change," Standley answered, "in the Russian attitude regarding the exchange of information on the conduct of the war."[21] The news conference now ended.

The newsmen listening to Standley knew they had a major story. They rushed from Spaso House to the office of the Soviet censors in the Foreign Ministry where they turned over their notes for approval. Irritated and perplexed, the censors contacted higher officials about the stories. After a five-hour delay, approval finally came to let the news go. The chief censor, whose mother had died of starvation in Leningrad, was white with rage because he considered the American complaint to be a trifle compared with the Soviet Union's sacrifices on the eastern front.[22]

Sumner Welles, who got wind of the report before it was published in American papers on March 9, contacted Standley for verification and a copy of his remarks, if he had indeed made them. At a news conference on March 9, Welles announced that Standley did not consult with the State Department before he made his comments. He also stated that the alliance was based on trust and understanding, which the ambassador, whatever he said, would never call into question.

That evening, Moscow radio broadcast a report by Edward Stettinius, the head of the Lend-Lease Administration, on the fulfillment of the Lend-Lease legislation. On March 15, *Pravda* provided additional coverage of Stettinius's report.[23]

Molotov called Standley in on March 10, upbraided him for his tactlessness, and then explained the lack of publicity regarding Lend-Lease. "The Soviet Government did not consider it wise," he told Standley, "to emphasize in the Press the great extent of the assistance coming from America as that would be apt to come to the attention of the Axis powers and result in a greater effort to destroy the convoys." He also argued that the Soviet press published whatever the American and British press published regarding military aid to the Soviet Union. He further claimed that there was no need to publicize the aid. "The Russian people are aware of the receipt of Lend-Lease aid. The man in the street knows by heart the number of tanks and planes we have received from America." The Russians also resented the pressure in the face of their losses and of the disparity between western sacrifices and Russians sacrifices. One Russian grumbled, "We've lost millions of people, and they want us to crawl on our knees because they send us Spam. And has the 'warmhearted' Congress ever done anything that wasn't in its interests? Don't tell me that Lend-Lease is charity."[24]

Standley, however, stood his ground. He told Molotov that he found no substantive evidence of Moscow's gratitude for Lend-Lease. Furthermore, he drew a distinction between Lend-Lease aid, which he said was a business arrangement between governments, and relief, which he argued came from the generosity of the American people and deserved to be separately appreciated. He ended by stating his hope that there was no damage done to American-Soviet relations. Molotov did not think there was any damage, but clearly the Kremlin was not taking any chances, either. Not knowing whether Standley had orders to hold the press conference and worried about congressional action, the Soviets published, according to Standley, "a veritable rash of statements" thanking the United States for its Lend-Lease aid.[25] The ambassador was pleased. He had finally stirred the Soviets to acknowledge American assistance.

The victory, however, was small and not repeated. Generally, the Soviet government depreciated western aid and maintained that the Red Army won the war on its own in both Europe and Asia. The reason for the lack of publicity was that the aid was used by Stalin to bolster his own power. Roosevelt and Churchill were aware of this fact. Since the war, however, Russian scholars have stressed that the Soviet Union could not have waged successful warfare without western aid.[26]

Standley followed up his meeting with Molotov with an explanation to Hull. "We can only deal with them on a bargaining basis," he told Hull, "for our continuing to accede freely to their requests while agreeing to pay an additional price for every small request we make seems to arouse suspicion of our motives in the Oriental Russian mind rather than to build confidence."[27]

Standley also took the initiative on the interned American pilots. In early April he met with Molotov and suggested that the pilots "escape." He told Molotov, "It is indeed unfortunate for our great countries to be fighting a common enemy and yet have one of our fine bomber crews held prisoner by an ally and kept from fighting that enemy." Molotov responded, "To escape from the Soviet Union is impossible." Nonetheless, in May the pilots escaped to Iran, although they had to use nearly all their money to bribe a Soviet official.[28] Clearly, Standley's hard-nosed approach could pay off. In addition, Stalin wanted to curry favor with the West in the wake of the hard news about Soviet involvement in the Katyn Forest massacre that broke in April 1943.

The ambassador also defended Finland to the Soviet government. He was unrelenting in asking for information about Finnish-Soviet relations and in stressing to the Kremlin that the United States had a significant interest in Finland.[29] When Harriman replaced Standley, he, too, made Finland a special case. The diplomatic persistence eventually led a frustrated Stalin to tell Harriman that "if the Finns want peace, the Soviet government is ready" and that he "did not know that he had to advise Roosevelt" about the status of Finnish-Soviet relations.[30] The unrelenting, tough stand on Finland certainly helped produce a surprising development: an independent Finland. Soviet equivocation and solicitousness in the face of a constant diplomatic siege of the Kremlin on behalf of Finland should have served as an object lesson in how to deal with Stalin and how to preserve the freedom of the Baltic States and Poland.

The Roosevelt administration, however, did not like Standley's actions or attitude. Of course, it supported Finland, but it did not favor Standley's blunt approach. On the other hand, Harriman, who was in London, reported that British and American friends supported Standley's approach. He wired Hopkins, "The feeling is growing here that we will build trouble for the future if we allow ourselves to be kicked around by the Russians." To Stettinius, he wrote, "My experience is that the Russians are brutally and bluntly frank with us and we can well afford to be equally so." Clark-Kerr, the British ambassador, also heartily endorsed Standley's remarks.[31]

Roosevelt and Hopkins, however, now wanted Standley out. FDR informed Eden when he visited Washington in March 1943 that the United States did not have good diplomatic representation in Moscow. Welles went further and implied that Standley would soon be replaced. In July Hopkins told Soviet chargé d'affaires Andrei Gromyko in Washington that Standley was not "the kind of person who is up to the mark with the requirements of the time."[32] Before a replacement could be found for Standley, Roosevelt and Hopkins decided that the damage to American-Soviet relations had to be repaired. Someone whom Stalin trusted had to go to Moscow and reassure him. For that job there was no one better than Joseph Davies.

Roosevelt thought the keys to unlocking the democratic Stalin were a meeting between him and Stalin (preferably without Churchill),[33] unconditional aid to indicate American sincerity and generosity, and a concrete plan and timetable for a second front in France. Furthermore, by March 1943, with Standley complicating the relationship and Bullitt wanting to complicate it, he was willing to abandon his reluctance to make territorial agreements with Stalin. If that was the only way he could reach Stalin and convince him of the United States' desire to cooperate and befriend the Soviet Union, then it might not be a bad approach. He now thought, he told Eden in March 1943, that the Curzon Line was workable and that the Baltic States would be taken by the Red Army, although he hoped that the Russians would not absorb them without a plebiscite. He also believed that the Allies would "decide what Poland should have" from Germany.[34] He did not reveal to Moscow his new flexibility on the territorial issue, but he did hint at it by stressing to Litvinov and then Gromyko the need for a meeting between him and Stalin where the territorial question could be discussed.[35] Characteristically, he refused to be tied down to a written agreement about territory because he probably did not want American voters to know of his betrayal of the principles of the Atlantic Charter, but at the same time he wanted Stalin to know that the territorial issues could be worked out.

The decision to send Joseph Davies to Moscow in May 1943 clearly reveals Roosevelt and Hopkins's plan. They were concerned that the alliance with the Soviet Union was drifting. Hard-liners like Bullitt and Standley could influence opinion in the United States or the Soviet Union. Then where would the alliance be? Where would be the chance for cooperation and a new world order based on democracy? The end of the war was in sight. This was no time for a weakening of the alliance through criticism, suspicion, or realpolitik. The emphasis should be on unity. Something had to be done to reassure Stalin, to let him know that Standley was not speaking for the president and that now territorial issues might be worked out. Above all, Roosevelt wanted to meet Stalin. It pained FDR that Stalin did not seem to know the clouds of suspicion and mistrust that engulfed the alliance could be blown away with one quick meeting. Secretary of State Hull expressed Roosevelt's anxiety to Churchill in May 1943: "It's extremely important that our two countries should proceed systematically through carefully selected persons to talk Mr. Stalin out of his shell, so to speak, away from his aloofness, secretiveness, and suspiciousness until he broadens his views, visualizes a more practical international cooperation in the future, and indicates Russia's intention in the East and in the West." Hopkins was irritated that the British seemed closer to the Soviets than the Americans. He thought the situation was "haywire" because the United States and Soviet Russia were the superpowers that would have the responsibility for keeping the peace after the war.[36]

Joseph Davies epitomized the pro-Stalin camp in the West. In the view of Roosevelt and Hopkins, he could repair the damage that Standley had done, arrange a private meeting between Roosevelt and Stalin, help Stalin with his image in the West, and let Stalin know that the territorial issue could be settled on his terms and that there was no secret relationship or agreement between the United States and England.

12

Joseph Davies to the Rescue

When Ambassador Standley was informed in April 1943 that Joseph Davies would be arriving in Moscow in May as a special representative of the president with a rank higher than the ambassador and that he should make an appointment for him with Stalin, he did not have to be hit over the head with a hammer to get the message. He had tried his best. He was totally disillusioned by Roosevelt's policy of "speak no evil, hear no evil" in Moscow. Like Bullitt and Steinhardt, he had essayed on his own a policy of quid pro quo, and it seemed to work. When he pressed the Soviets at his now famous news conference, they responded with public expressions of gratitude for American aid, and when he strongly suggested to Molotov that Moscow arrange for the escape of the interned American pilots, the flyers soon were free in Iran. Pressure on behalf of Finland made the Soviets cautious. However, like Bullitt and Steinhardt, he and his initiatives were not appreciated. Standley considered Davies to be a clown, and if that was who the president wanted to represent him, he would not stand in the way. On May 3 he offered his resignation. Harriman shared Standley's view of Davies. He considered him totally incompetent and likely to botch the mission that the president had in mind. He thought Davies's views on Stalin and the Soviet Union were "utter nonsense" and that the former ambassador "never understood what was going on."[1]

The main purpose of the Davies mission was to carry a personal letter from Roosevelt to Stalin that had at its core an invitation to meet privately with the president. Churchill was not to be included because FDR and Davies both felt that Churchill and Stalin were rivals and that FDR was the referee. Roosevelt already had a personal tie to Churchill, so now he had to develop a special nexus with Stalin. A meeting was crucial to Roosevelt.

Roosevelt had consistently deferred political and territorial considerations, but now the end of the war was in sight. He had to act, and he had to act somewhat desperately because he had no plan or preparation other than the desire to carry on with the Soviet Union after the war in some kind of international organization. When Eden visited Roosevelt in March 1943, he found him preoccupied with American-Soviet relations and with the fact that he, unlike Churchill, had not yet met with Stalin.

Beyond delivering the letter and trying to arrange a meeting between Roosevelt and Stalin, Davies also had the job of correcting the damage done by Standley at his news conference. Davies was used to pulling chestnuts out of the fire. In 1936 he believed that he stepped in and redressed the damage that Bullitt had done to American-Soviet relations. Now both Roosevelt and Hopkins were convinced that he was the only man who, because Stalin trusted and liked him, could persuade Stalin that American policy had not changed and that Standley was talking on his own. Roosevelt actually wanted Davies to replace Standley as ambassador, but Davies's health was not good, and he was lucky to get approval from his physician just to visit Moscow. The president was concerned enough about Davies's health that he authorized a large contingent to accompany Davies, including his personal physician, nephew, valet, and a nine-man crew to fly his private plane. Davies was an expensive mailman, but the president felt the goals justified the cost.[2]

Davies's mission was made even more difficult by a horrifying discovery that unfolded as he prepared to depart Washington. In mid-April, retreating German troops uncovered a mass grave in the Katyn Forest, near Smolensk, containing thousands of Polish army officers. The Poles had been brutally executed. The Germans immediately blamed the Soviets for the massacre, and the Soviets responded by blaming the Germans. The Polish government-in-exile, led then by General Wladyslaw Sikorski, asked for an independent investigation by the International Red Cross. This never took place, but because the Poles refused to exonerate the Soviets from responsibility, the Soviets broke off diplomatic relations with the Poles, something that they had been wanting to do for some time. The Soviets then quickly pushed ahead and took the Katyn Forest.

In 1990 Mikhail Gorbachev admitted that Stalin had committed the crime, and he officially apologized to the Polish people, but in 1943 it was difficult to say conclusively who was responsible. Nonetheless, most leaders then had a sinking feeling that the crime was the work of the Soviet secret police, and it became official American policy not to discuss the "unpleasant subject" of Katyn. And, as Churchill told the Poles at the time, what could be achieved by breaking with the Soviets over the issue? Germany's defeat was still the first priority, and no tragedy, no matter how painful, could upset the alliance. "If they are dead," Churchill told Sikorski, "nothing you can do will bring them back."[3]

The British and American governments chose to ignore the possibility of a Soviet role in the Katyn Forest massacre. Before he left Washington for Moscow, Joseph Davies blamed the Germans for the murders. He maintained that Roosevelt agreed with him.[4] Harry Hopkins shamelessly denounced the Poles as troublemakers under the spell of "large Polish landlords" who simply wanted to prevent their large estates from slipping into Russian hands.[5]

Secretary Hull told Litvinov that Roosevelt wanted to make sure that the break with Poland did not lead to a break in Finnish-Soviet negotiations, implying to the Russians a possible trade of Poland for Finland. The Soviets used the tragedy to break ties with the official Polish government and set up their own Polish group, the Union of Polish Patriots, which they could manipulate. Standley saw this as an ominous development. "Might not the Kremlin," he cabled Hull on April 28, "envisage the formation of a belt of pro-Soviet states to protect it from the influence of the West?"

The Katyn Forest massacre and Standley's blast in the newspapers over Lend-Lease made the Soviets somewhat nervous about their position with the western states. Even though they were now on the offensive against the Germans, they did not want to compromise the goodwill that they enjoyed in the West. Accordingly, they received Joseph Davies very warmly and listened to him carefully.[6]

Davies arrived in Moscow on May 19. The next day Standley took him to the Kremlin to pay his respects to Molotov and to find out when Davies could see Stalin. To Standley's surprise, Molotov told them that Stalin would see them at nine o'clock that evening. Davies irritated Standley because he would not tell him the contents of the letter and had informed him that the president did not want him at the meeting with Stalin. Standley accompanied Davies to the Kremlin at the appointed hour and, after meeting with Stalin, explained the purpose of Davies's visit, namely, the delivery of a special letter from Roosevelt. "Our President," announced Standley, "has intimated that he does not want me to be present when his letter is delivered. With your permission, Mr. Stalin, I will withdraw." Perplexed, Stalin answered, "As you please."

Once Standley had departed, Davies informed Stalin and Molotov through their interpreter that he had a letter from Roosevelt to Stalin, which he then read. The letter explained that the president was vexed over the declining relationship of the Allies and wanted it improved or else he feared that a catastrophe could result. The stress in the alliance had worsened because of Standley's news conference. Roosevelt desired Stalin to know that U.S. policy had not changed. He also wanted a private meeting with Stalin without Churchill, someplace halfway between Moscow and Washington—possibly Alaska, Siberia, or the Bering Sea. Roosevelt wanted the meeting to be simple, without a large number of staff people. In that situation they could discuss matters informally and reach "what we call 'a meeting of minds.'"

Stalin, who doodled throughout Davies's presentation, asked why Churchill would not be included. Davies answered that Churchill and Roosevelt trusted each other, and the president would inform the prime minister about the meeting. Nonetheless, Roosevelt and Churchill had different ideas about colonialism and imperialism. If Stalin and Roosevelt were to meet, Davies opined, they would certainly come to an understanding.

"I am not sure," commented Stalin.

"Well, from what I know of what you both have done, I am sure," said Davies.

"But understanding alone is not enough," Stalin warned. "There must be reciprocity and respect." The ambassador replied that he would receive and was now receiving exactly that.

Davies then attempted to inform Stalin about Roosevelt's positions on international events. Stalin cut him off, though, and outlined his own plans. Germany's ability to make war had to be negated and Germany had to pay to rebuild the Soviet Union. The governments of Finland, Poland, and Bulgaria were to be independent and awarded territory as compensation for the damage inflicted on them by the Axis powers. England might need military bases in the Mediterranean and Europe, and America might require them in the Pacific region and elsewhere for reasons of security. The Soviet Union, according to Stalin, "wanted all European peoples to have the kind of government they themselves chose, free from coercion." Moscow needed warm water access and on its western border friendly regimes that, unlike past governments, were not secretly inimical. Stalin leveled a brutal attack on the Polish government-in-exile, which he maintained had betrayed Russia.

Stalin carried on with his doodling. Abruptly looking at Davies, he proclaimed: "I think your President is right. I think he represents America, as I understand it. He is a great man. I believe in him. You may tell your President I agree with him and it is necessary that we meet, as he suggests."

The Soviet dictator called for a map and then measured the distance between Moscow and Washington. He knew Roosevelt was paralyzed and had difficulty traveling. He told Davies that he could meet Roosevelt in Nome or Fairbanks, probably in July or August.[7]

Stalin then demanded more military assistance. He pressed Davies to inform the president that the Red Army required pursuit aircraft and high octane fuel. He claimed that only 700,000 troops, on both sides, were waging war in Africa. "How many, on the other hand, are fighting on our 2,000-mile front? Approximately, altogether over 4,000,000 Germans, Spaniards, Italians, Rumanians, Finns, and Russians. The Red Army is fighting on their front alone, and suffering under the occupation of a large part of our territory by a cruel enemy." He chided Davies, "We are waiting for a real offensive in the west to take some of the load off our backs. We need more fighting planes, more locomotives, more equipment, more rails, more food, more grain. Advise the President that our resolution remains indomitable."[8]

Before he took his leave of Stalin and Molotov, Davies told them that the Soviet image in the West would be greatly improved if they disbanded the Comintern and provided some evidence of religious freedom.[9] Cynically, he explained to Molotov that "a few statements about religious freedom in the USSR would be a very useful development among American citizens." He knew that such a policy was "not simply done, but if allowed to take place at the propitious moment, it would have great impact." Before Davies left Moscow on May 29, the Kremlin announced the dissolution of the Comintern and the appointment of a new patriarch for the Russian Orthodox Church. Whether or not Davies was the catalyst in these two developments is difficult to prove, but circumstantial evidence indicates that he played a role at least in the timing of the developments. Voroshilov also visited with Davies and told him the Soviets appreciated his friendship and that now even the "bourgeois class . . . is on the side of the socialist revolution, on the side of the Bolsheviks."[10]

Davies provided Stalin with a copy of an article that he had written for *Life* magazine in 1943 in which he argued that the Soviet Union was not a "predatory power," that it had been forced to join Hitler in 1939 by the West, that it had set aside the idea of world revolution, that it allowed religious toleration, and that at the end of the war the USSR would need for its security the Baltic States, the Curzon Line, part of Finland, and access to warm water ports, of which the Soviets had a traditional interest in Port Arthur, Dairen, and the Dardanelles. Davies reported to Harry Hopkins that Stalin liked the ideas in the article very much.[11] Davies also told Stalin that President Roosevelt wanted the Soviet Union to have its security needs satisfied and to join a "united nations" organization and work closely with the United States. Davies stressed the difficulty in the Anglo-American relationship. He said Roosevelt did not want the British playing the role of broker between the United States and the Soviet Union. He also reported that the United States would not cooperate with London against Moscow and implied that it did not want to confront a London-Moscow combination. Finally, he informed Stalin that there was a deep division between the American embassy and the Lend-Lease personnel, that the latter was playing it straight but that the embassy was "peddling stories" to the press.[12]

Stalin knew that Standley would soon be replaced. Davies failed to probe Stalin's postwar plans, including the curious lumping together of Finland, Poland, and Bulgaria with the demand that they have independent governments and be compensated for destruction caused by the Axis. Finland was fighting with the Axis against the Soviet Union because of the Soviet attack on and annexation of Finnish territory in 1939-40. Poland was now occupied and partitioned by the Germans, but it had been occupied and partitioned by the Germans and the Russians between 1939 and 1941. Bulgaria was an ally of Germany, although not at war with the Soviet Union.

Davies needed to boost Stalin's confidence that he would receive Roosevelt's support for an expansion of the Soviet empire in Eastern Europe and, possibly, East Asia, but still there was no firm agreement. With the Red Army's victory at Stalingrad, though, Stalin knew that he had strengthened his hand. If the West did not initiate its second front soon or if it left territorial issues in abeyance, armies would determine territorial divisions, and the Red Army was poised to reap a rich harvest. The willingness of Davies and Roosevelt to manipulate public opinion was also clear. Roosevelt was a skilled propagandist. It was a trait that Stalin held in high esteem. Davies had also confirmed the continuing anti-British bias of the American leadership, but now Stalin was being invited to exploit American-British differences and cooperate with the United States against England.

The next day Davies lied to Standley by telling him that he did not know the contents of the letter that he carried from Roosevelt to Stalin. He said it was written in Russian. He also refused to reveal the substance of his conversation with Stalin. The ambassador clearly counted for nothing. The Soviets were quick to discern the tension between Standley and Davies. Oumansky, who was temporarily back in the Foreign Ministry in Moscow before he took on the assignment of Soviet ambassador to Mexico, took Standley and Davies to the circus on May 21. In his report he wrote, "It seemed obvious that despite the outward friendly relations between them . . . , Standley was not delighted by the Davies visit and attention and hospitality rendered to it, while Davies in his turn was burdened by Standley's presence and preferred not to touch any political topics while the latter was around."[13]

Earlier that day Davies held a news conference with three American reporters, Eddy Gilmore, Quentin Reynolds, and Bill Downes. He discussed the meeting at the Kremlin, but refused to divulge the nature of Roosevelt's missive. "It was a secret letter, boys. I can't tell you its content," he declared.

Gilmore hit Davies with the hard question: "Did you discuss with Mr. Stalin the apparent lack of Russian cooperation, particularly with regard to giving us information about German military and naval matters, which might help to save the lives of many American soldiers and sailors?"

Davies turned red. "No, I did not discuss any such thing with Mr. Stalin. I'm here to deliver a personal letter from President Roosevelt to Premier Stalin, not to air a lot of opinions." He proceeded to state that the American-Soviet relationship was excellent, cooperative, and flourishing. He chided the newsmen for hurting the interests of the United States by openly criticizing the Soviet government. Davies was patronizing and critical to the point where, according to the British ambassador, the correspondents became angry, and soon the press conference became a shouting match that only stopped when Standley stepped in and escorted the reporters to the door. Davies apologized to the reporters the next day for his angry outburst, but really refused to back off his criticism. Reynolds, for his part, said that he went after Davies in order "to puncture the inflated ego of this pompous ass," whom he believed to be "a very bad American and a very dangerous one." The newsmen were uncertain why Standley could not deliver Roosevelt's letter to Stalin. They eventually guessed that it was an invitation for a meeting of the Big Three. They never thought that Roosevelt had cut Churchill out.[14]

On the evening of May 23 Stalin hosted a dinner for Davies and Standley.

The food was impressive for wartime Moscow, but as usual the dinner was constantly interrupted by a stream of toasts. Molotov hailed American-Russian collaboration and saluted Davies "as a real friend" who had enhanced friendship between Russia and the United States. Davies went off on a long peroration on the "horrors of war, the glories of Stalingrad and the greatness of the Soviet armies, peoples and leaders." He did not want Stalingrad to be rebuilt but to stay as a monument to German brutality. He cried when he spoke of the Russian sacrifice at Stalingrad, but Soviet eyes remained dry. For them, Stalingrad was history.

Standley and Clark-Kerr followed with toasts. Then Stalin gave a short toast to the Allied military forces. Molotov began a long list of toasts, but Stalin cut him off by announcing, "We will adjourn immediately to the projection room where we will see our guest of honor's motion picture, *Mission to Moscow*." Clark-Kerr noted that instead of wasting "the traditional two hours of boozing around those green and gold tables in the anteroom, we were hurried cold sober to the movie theater to see Mr. Davies's film about himself."

The movie celebrated the purge trials, projected Stalin as a national god and a genuine democrat, and lauded Davies's critical part in developing American-Soviet friendship during his time as ambassador. The film was filled with historical inaccuracies, gratuitous propaganda, and bad acting. The American and British representatives who knew their history were mortified. Litvinov called it "silly." But Stalin just grunted now and then. When the movie was over, he did not comment on it. He simply said, "One more drink, boys, and then home." The British ambassador thought the early hour indicated something was awry, but Stalin simply wanted time to compose a response to Roosevelt's invitation for a meeting. Andrei Gromyko later wrote that the movie "helped to strengthen American sympathy for the USSR."[15]

The next day Stalin again met with Davies. He gave him a letter for Roosevelt stating that he would meet with him in Fairbanks around July 15, but that the final date and the meeting itself would depend on the military situation. Stalin would contact Roosevelt by secret code regarding the final details. Before Davies left, Stalin reiterated his position on the postwar situation. He thought three or four Great Powers would have to maintain peace and security, that a united nations organization would be unwieldy and unworkable, that Russia would depend on its own army and outposts for security, and that Russia had to be certain that a united nations grouping would not be used against it. He also emphasized that the Soviet Union needed friendly governments on its borders with Poland, Finland, and Romania. Stalin again lashed out at the Polish government-in-exile, stating that it was anti-Russian.[16]

Davies finally left Moscow on May 29. Standley was relieved to see him go. He was angry that he had been circumvented and marginalized. His anger grew when, after escorting Davies to the airport, he saw the name of Davies's book and film, *Mission to Moscow*, emblazoned in large yellow letters on the nose of his plane in Russian and English. To him, the entire visit was a noisome publicity stunt. Standley wrote his wife that Davies "is just a plain *ass*."[17]

When Davies returned to Washington, Roosevelt and Hopkins immediately met with him to find out what was on Stalin's mind. Davies stressed to them that they must trust the Soviets. Stalin was no longer a Communist, Davies explained. He had rejected international revolution, restored the profit motive in the USSR, and now evolved to the point where he was a socialist. Davies reported to FDR that Stalin was ready for a meeting, but was unenthusiastic about a united nations organization, although he had no real objection if the Soviet Union, the United States, and Great Britain got the bases they needed. Davies added that Stalin was primarily interested in a second front in Europe. Davies's report about Stalin's willingness to meet privately with Roosevelt in Alaska was wonderful news. Davies had managed to pull off what no one else, including Standley, had been able to do. Roosevelt now looked forward to finalizing the details.[18]

Davies was still firm in his belief that Stalin was an evolving democratic capitalist. The real problem in Moscow, Davies emphasized, was Standley. In his private journal Davies wrote that the trouble with Standley was that he refused to give the Soviets "the benefit of any doubt." To his wife, Marjorie, he complained on May 28, 1943, that Standley thought relations should be a "two-way street."[19]

While Davies was en route to Moscow, the Trident Conference in Washington took place. Roosevelt and Churchill and their staffs hammered out the next phase of Anglo-American war strategy. The British wanted to pursue the Mediterranean policy aimed at knocking Italy out of the war and then develop strategy in accordance with what opportunities presented themselves in the wake of Italy's defeat. Roosevelt, however, wanted to focus on an invasion of France. The British were willing to consider an invasion of southern France, but Roosevelt wanted a cross-Channel invasion. He thought only that policy would convince Stalin of western goodwill. A southern strategy, although it would obviously help the Red Army in terms of draining off some German troops from the eastern front, would also put the Anglo-American forces closer to Eastern Europe, probably cause Turkey to join the Allies, and might imply suspicion of Stalin's intentions in Eastern Europe and the Balkans. Roosevelt preferred not to pursue the Italian campaign, but he could not counter the British argument that an Italian defeat, as well as increased bombing of Germany, were the quickest and most efficient ways to assist the Russians. The Americans, however, checkmated the British hope of taking advantage of Italy's defeat by forcing agreement that Allied troops and weapons would be transferred out of the Mediterranean to England after the Italian defeat in preparation for a cross-Channel invasion probably in May 1944. The Americans also decided that if the British tried to pursue the southern strategy, then the Americans would abandon the British in the Mediterranean and concentrate on the Pacific theater. "We will just pick up our toys," Hopkins stressed, "and leave the British alone and fight the war in the Southwest Pacific."[20]

Stalin knew, after talking with *New York Times* correspondent C. L. Sulzberger on July 5, 1943, that Roosevelt was bucking American public opinion by focusing primarily on any part of the European theater rather than on the Pacific front, and he definitely did not want the United States to emphasize Asia over Europe.[21] Perhaps the British should have insisted on the southern strategy, even if it led the Americans to focus on Japan. At least, then, the Soviets would not have been given the advantage of a second front in France. Although Roosevelt and Churchill were together for the duration of the conference, the president was too embarrassed to tell Churchill to his face that he was trying to arrange a secret meeting with Stalin without him.

One other significant development at the Trident Conference was that Roosevelt agreed to share fully with Churchill the atomic bomb secrets, and they decided not to share the information with Stalin or any other person. The view of some historians that this decision might have undermined all of FDR's other efforts to win Stalin's confidence seems far-fetched. The bomb was an unknown. Stalin was suspicious of Roosevelt, and every effort to date by Roosevelt to temper his suspicion was met by more demands and increased suspicion. As late as summer 1943 Stalin was still attempting to arrange a cease-fire with the Nazis and might well have bargained with western technological secrets, if he had had access to them, to convince the Germans to come to terms. And the world might very well have been much worse off if Stalin had exploded an atomic bomb in 1945 instead of in 1949. If one can count on Litvinov's evaluation rendered in 1945 where he lamented that the West did not confront Stalin earlier, Roosevelt's decision not to share the atomic secret with Stalin in 1943 might have been one of the few restraining pressures on Stalin.[22]

At any rate, Standley delivered the news to Stalin on June 4 that the West was not going to invade northern France in 1943 but instead would knock Italy out of the war. Stalin responded with characteristic anger. He wrote Churchill that an attack in the West had been promised for 1943. He complained that the Soviets were bearing the brunt of the fighting, losing morale because of western broken promises, and not being involved in the critical decisions. Churchill responded that it would do no good for the Russian war effort if the West lost 100,000 soldiers trying to invade northern France before it was prepared to do so. Stalin shot back on June 23 with an attack on British courage and pointed out that he assumed Churchill and Roosevelt knew when they promised a cross-Channel invasion that it would lead to casualties. Churchill was now offended and believed that all correspondence was at an end. Roosevelt stayed on the sidelines, concurring reluctantly with Churchill's arguments, but unwilling to get involved because of his fear that his secret meeting with Stalin might be jeopardized.[23]

Roosevelt finally decided to tell Churchill of the secret arrangement. He had Harriman brief the prime minister in London on June 24, and he had Harriman lie to Churchill, saying that Stalin, not he, had requested the meeting. Churchill was aghast. He immediately objected that a private meeting between Roosevelt and Stalin would hurt British morale. It was also an unpleasant indication of the shifting balance of power. When he could not get FDR to abandon the idea, he soon accommodated himself to it. What helped to persuade him was the rude communication from Stalin charging that the British were pusillanimous. He decided that perhaps a private meeting between Roosevelt and Stalin might produce some good. In addition, he feared that Stalin might negotiate a separate peace treaty with the Nazis. Rumors were rife in summer 1943 of Soviet attempts to work out a cease-fire on the eastern front. Roosevelt shared Churchill's concern and was in constant fear that Stalin might sign a separate peace treaty with Nazi Germany. On June 29 Churchill agreed that the meeting should go forward.[24]

Roosevelt waited anxiously throughout June for word from Stalin on the precise date of the meeting. But no word came. On July 4 the great Battle of Kursk started. On July 12 over 160,000 Allied troops landed in Italy. Western forces were finally on the continent of Europe. On July 13 Hitler called off the Kursk offensive because of the fear of the loss of Italy with its possible exposure of his southern flank and, of course, the formidable Soviet resistance at Kursk. The Germans were now fighting directly on two fronts. Gromyko reported to Moscow in mid-July that Hopkins told him of the importance of a meeting between Roosevelt and Stalin and said, "Roosevelt would surprise Stalin by how far he, Roosevelt, is ready to acknowledge our rights, in particular, on territorial issues." At the end of the month Hopkins again stressed the need for a meeting and for some concrete steps to improve the Soviet image in the United States.[25]

Stalin was now ready to meet with his western allies. He had tried again to work out a separate peace with the Germans on the basis of the Russo-German borders of 1941, but was again rebuffed.[26] Stalin no doubt saw the possibility of another Rapallo Treaty and the chance to have the capitalist states continue the war and so weaken themselves that Soviet Russia could later dictate a new Communist order in Europe. Now with western armies on the continent, the end was in sight. Although Stalin knew that the European war was not the main interest of the American people, he also could now conclude that the West would not likely disengage and leave the Soviets alone.[27] A meeting to find out western plans was essential, but Stalin did not want to meet with Roosevelt alone. He did not want to travel to Alaska because his security forces could not guarantee his security absolutely. He would be partly dependent on the Americans, and he did not trust them. Then he did not want to go too far from Moscow because he did not trust his own generals and fellow Communists. The purges, which he started in the 1930s, were still going on. He also feared traveling by airplane and, of course, that ruled out quick, long-distance travel. He also undoubtedly worried about the implication of a Communist leader going to a capitalist enclave. It would appear as if he were inferior and in a solicitous position. It would be better to have Roosevelt come to Soviet Russia or at least to a site that the Red Army controlled. Of course, he did not want to divulge his fears and calculations, so he told his western allies that he could not be gone from or out of secure communication with the eastern front. This meant that he could only travel to a place where Soviet forces controlled the communication and transportation lines between it and Moscow. When he informed Davies in May that he would meet with Roosevelt in the late summer, Stalin was probably lying. It is doubtful that he ever intended to meet with Roosevelt in Alaska or any place where he had to separate himself from Soviet security forces.[28]

Stalin finally informed Roosevelt on August 8 that a meeting in Alaska was impossible. He did say he could meet in Astrakhan or Archangel, cities not far from Moscow but to which Roosevelt could not possibly go. At the time of Stalin's message Roosevelt and Churchill were meeting in Quebec. With his plan for a private meeting with Stalin in disarray, Roosevelt decided to join with Churchill and urge Stalin to meet both western leaders at Fairbanks, Alaska, and, failing that, to agree to a meeting of the foreign ministers. Stalin replied on September 8 that the foreign ministers could meet in Moscow in October and that he could meet with Roosevelt and Churchill sometime between November 15 and December 15 in Teheran. Churchill immediately accepted. Roosevelt was pleased that Stalin had finally agreed to a meeting, but he was displeased by the location. He tried to get Stalin to change the site to a position closer to the eastern Mediterranean or to the Persian Gulf. Stalin, however, was adamant. It was Teheran or nothing.[29]

Roosevelt was being whiplashed. He wanted a meeting desperately with Stalin. He was convinced that the Soviet Union was a state with which the United States could work. The evidence of compatibility beyond an expedient alliance against a common enemy was hard to find. Standley's experience, isolated though he was, was no encouragement. The unwillingness of Stalin to meet with FDR, despite the president's most earnest entreaties, was also strange. The Katyn Forest tragedy, the interned American fliers, and the generally unfriendly relationship were all worrisome. Roosevelt was doing all that he could to cultivate Stalin from afar. He set up a Lend-Lease program in Moscow under General Faymonville that undercut the leverage of the ambassador, the embassy, the State Department, and the War Department to obtain important military and intelligence information that would have assisted the war effort against Germany and Japan. He demanded unconditional surrender from Germany. He closed his eyes to Soviet behavior at Katyn and uncivil behavior toward the Americans in the Soviet Union. He refused to defend the Polish government-in-exile, except for superficial publicity stunts. He indicated through Davies and in his talks with Litvinov that Stalin's security needs, even if they entailed Soviet control of part of Poland and the Baltic States, could be met. He kept the defeat of Japan as a secondary rather than primary goal of

America's war effort. He decided to launch a second front in northern France even to the point of passing up opportunities in southern Europe because he knew that was what Stalin wanted. He ran roughshod over his ambassadors if they criticized Stalin or advised that the American government adopt a policy that required Stalin to prove his democratic credentials. Obviously all of these policies directly benefited the Soviet Union.

Of course, German atrocities had to be stopped, but encouraging the German military to exterminate the Nazis might have achieved that goal, and holding back on the second front in France might have given the United States more leverage. Kennan explained in September 1944 that "as long as no second front existed, expediency suggested that the idea of collaboration be kept rather to the fore, the idea of spheres of interest rather in the background. But when the second front became reality, there was no longer any need for excessive delicacy" by Moscow.[30] Although it seems preposterous to say, it is possible, too, that the second front in Europe increased pressure on the fanatical Nazis to accelerate their extermination campaign, and the worse of the Holocaust came in 1943-45.[31]

Roosevelt could not figure out why Stalin was not reacting to his all-out pro-Soviet policies. Again Davies was called in. On September 25 Davies met with Hopkins. Two days later he met with Roosevelt. The former ambassador stressed that Stalin doubted American sincerity. He pointed out that the United States still had not recognized the Soviet border with Poland and still maintained diplomatic relations with Finland (an enemy of the Soviet Union). Davies also stated that the Soviets felt that the State Department and War Department hampered Lend-Lease aid to Soviet Russia, that the State Department had unfairly criticized Moscow over Katyn, that Roosevelt and Churchill were too close, and that Stalin wanted to be sure FDR would agree to the Soviet Union's western border at any summit meeting. Davies said Stalin might sign a separate treaty with Germany if the West pushed him into it as it had in 1939.

Davies outlined Stalin's position clearly and precisely. Like a good lawyer, he even cornered Roosevelt. He demanded to know the president's position on the Soviet Union's western border. Roosevelt responded that Stalin could have Poland and the Baltic States, but he hoped that there would be a plebiscite for the sake of public opinion.

Davies was immediately sent to Mexico City in early October to tell Ambassador Constantine Oumansky, whom Roosevelt, Hopkins, and Davies thought was very close to Stalin. Roosevelt had made a major concession. He was conceding at least eastern Poland and the Baltic States, but he was getting nothing in return from Stalin, not even a different place than Teheran for a meeting, to say nothing of the moral bankruptcy of his position. Historian Keith Eubanks concludes that Roosevelt "had given away a major bargaining point before being certain that Stalin would concede." If the president gave in so easily on the territorial issues, why should Stalin give him anything, including a friendly disposition or a meeting place more acceptable to Roosevelt?[32]

Roosevelt ultimately decided that Stalin had to be trusted to do the right thing, but even if Stalin behaved badly, the president believed that the occupation of Eastern and Central Europe might induce Stalin and the Soviet Union to become democratic. On September 3 he informed Francis Cardinal Spellman of New York, the putative leader of the Catholic Church in the United States and the vicar of the U.S. armed forces, that the European people would simply have to "endure domination in the hope that—in ten or twenty years—the European influence would bring the Russians to become less barbarous." In FDR's opinion Germany and Austria might become Communist, and Austria, Croatia, and Hungary might fall directly under Russian control. It was not that Roosevelt was being hypocritical in terms of his willingness to sacrifice some territories to Stalinism. He genuinely believed in the inevitable development of democracy worldwide. Historian Warren Kimball explained Roosevelt's thinking in reference to the Baltic States: "To argue in the short-term for democracy in the Baltic states would jeopardize the longer-term hopes he had for bringing the Soviet Union into the community of responsible leadership—the 'family circle.'"[33]

The mistake that Roosevelt made in informing Stalin of his willingness to concede Poland and the Baltic States was paralleled by another error of equal importance. Mussolini fell on July 25, Allied troops landed in Italy on September 3, and Italy capitulated on September 8. With the surrender of Italy, all of southeastern and southwestern Europe was suddenly exposed and in the balance. The Germans did not recover from the Italian defeat until some six weeks later when they poured troops into northern Italy to hold the line. But for almost six weeks Italy was a void waiting to be filled. Hungary and Bulgaria, both weak links in the Axis system, were on the verge of bolting the Tripartite Pact in 1943, so much so that the Nazis occupied Hungary in 1944 and forced Bulgaria to adopt a pro-Nazi government in the winter of 1943 to prevent a Nazi occupation. Bulgaria then switched sides and declared war on the Germans in 1944. The pro-Allied partisan forces of Tito grabbed control of Yugoslavia's Adriatic islands, Dalmatia, Montenegro, and most of Croatia and Bosnia-Hercegovina. A British-American invasion from the Adriatic and/or the Black Sea in 1943/44 after the Italian surrender would have found popular support across southeast Europe and would have forced the Nazis to pull out of the Serbian part of Yugoslavia to close their lines and protect their exposed flank. Romania was also toying with abandoning the Axis in 1943 and eventually, on August 23, 1944, declared war on the Axis and joined with the Red Army in a westward advance. Historian Joseph Rothschild concluded that if the West had moved quickly to exploit the Italian surrender, "the governments of several smaller Axis partners in East Central Europe would probably also have been emboldened to risk breaking with Nazi Germany at that time, when the Soviet armies were still engaged far to the east, deep inside the Soviet Union."[34]

Bullitt and Churchill favored a Balkan strategy. It would have complicated military planning and logistics, but the situation for pluralist governments in

East Central Europe would have been much better. Stalinism might have been contained, and possibly with no extension of the Stalinist empire into East Europe as a justification for its legitimacy and as a reward for the sacrifices of the Russian people, it would have collapsed in the Soviet Union much earlier than when it finally did in the 1990s.

Roosevelt, though, did not want to continue the southern European campaign after Italy surrendered. He was against it because he did not think that Stalin wanted it. He felt that Stalin preferred a second front in France, which, of course, Stalin did. When the Nazis were charging into the Soviet Union, Stalin wanted a front anywhere, including the Caucasus or Ukraine. By 1943, with his armies driving westward, he no longer wanted British-American troops in the east. He desired them to be far removed in Western Europe. With Bullitt and Churchill pushing for a southern strategy and Roosevelt arguing for a western attack, the Anglo-American war machine stalled on the European continent. Troops and weapons were withdrawn to England in the wake of the Italian surrender for an eventual invasion across the Channel in 1944 rather than deployed to exploit the golden opportunity to influence the fate of Eastern and Central Europe. It is paradoxical that the Americans were insisting on a withdrawal from the Continent in order to reinvade the Continent from another angle. Moreover, Roosevelt insisted that the Soviets be given a strong hand in Allied-controlled Italy. In the opinion of U.S. diplomat Robert Murphy, FDR's approach led to a vital Communist Party in Italy, including the return from Moscow of Party head Palmiro Togliatti, and to Soviet opportunities to build a Communist infrastructure in parts of Eastern Europe.[35]

The surrender of Italy and the weakness of the Central European members of the Tripartite Pact kept open the issue of where to invade in the late fall of 1943. It was still being hotly debated at the Cairo Conference in November 1943 where Roosevelt demanded that Stalin be allowed to decide at the upcoming Teheran Conference where the West should invade. Clearly, Roosevelt was not thinking ahead to the impact of the Italian defeat on Eastern Europe, although Churchill and Bullitt had pointed out its potential to him. Roosevelt wanted Stalin to decide whether the West should concentrate on Western Europe or the Balkans, and the issue was submitted to him at the Teheran Conference, where he predictably voted for an invasion of Western Europe.

Wedded to his idea of a democratic Stalin and having little background in military planning or operations, FDR was unwilling or unable to see American and British force in its true proportions and was unwilling or unable to understand war as an extension of politics. Although far from the conflict he did not view the war as a whole, in terms of the relations of the powers, and through omission or commission he effectively subordinated the political significance of the western armies to Stalin's will. He also did not concern himself about Eastern Europe's possible place in European strategy or Italy's or Turkey's place in

Mediterranean strategy. After the war Sumner Welles pointed out that, in light of recent history, the U.S. leadership should have anticipated the relationship between armies and politics and the need for concrete territorial agreements. He added ruefully that "knowledge of modern history has not been a forte of our most recent Secretaries of State" or, he might have added, of President Roosevelt.[36]

Ambassador Standley left Moscow on September 18. Problems in American-Soviet relations were everywhere, from Poland to Germany to Japan to the way the American embassy personnel were treated in Moscow. The more the problems mounted, the more the policy of concessions was asserted. Superficial concessions by Stalin, such as the dissolution of the Comintern, were hailed as major breakthroughs. Davies's counsel was sought, and he managed to explain away all inconsistencies in Soviet policy. Herbert Feis recalled that Davies "was disposed to explain every Russian demand, no matter how forward, on the ground that capitalist countries had caused the Soviet Union to feel a need for ample security; he regarded Stalin as a person of goodwill and fair intentions, who would respond fairly to generous treatment."[37]

General Faymonville did not long survive after Standley's departure. The report on his alleged disloyalty and the publicity surrounding his arguments with Standley and Michella in Moscow convinced enough people in Washington, including General Burns, that it was time to withdraw him. Davies tried to save him again and asked Hopkins to support him. Hopkins replied that he would like to help but that it was beyond him. Roosevelt had decided to replace Faymonville and the two military attachés with a "coordinated" military operation under General John R. Deane. It would operate under the command of the new ambassador, W. Averell Harriman. To the press, Roosevelt suggested that Faymonville had shown himself to be too friendly with the Russians. Of course, Faymonville was simply following orders. He was now being sacrificed, but the president was not changing the policy in any substantive way. The so-called Red General was gone, to be sure, but now the whole Moscow operation—the embassy and the Lend-Lease mission—was put under the control of one of the leaders of the "Hopkins Shop," Harriman.[38] In addition, the hard-nosed military attachés were removed and Roosevelt also cashiered the strongest critics of unconditional aid at the State Department. Conveniently, Undersecretary of State Sumner Welles, who wanted more reciprocity in the American-Soviet relationship, resigned at the same time because of personal problems. He was replaced by Edward Stettinius, whose appointment now gave the "Hopkins Shop" a compliant voice at the senior levels of the State Department.[39]

When Standley reached Washington, he was debriefed by Hopkins, Roosevelt, and Harriman. His impressions differed markedly with those of Davies. He told his superiors that Stalin could not be trusted and that the Soviets would try to set up satellites in Eastern Europe. He confessed that Stalin and Molotov were both still enigmas to him. He advised Harriman that Moscow was "a tough assignment." Harriman replied, "I know it will be difficult, but they're only human, those Russians. Stalin can be handled."[40] Harriman later confessed, "A large number of people in the West had the idea that they knew how to get along with Stalin. I confess that I was not entirely immune to that infectious idea."[41]

Part 5

W. Averell Harriman
1943-1946

13

"Uncle Joe"

"I am the president's loyal lieutenant," W. Averell Harriman told Winston Churchill on September 14, 1942. With those words, Harriman summarized his position and relationship to Roosevelt. Next to Harry Hopkins and Joseph Davies he was one of a handful of key advisers to Roosevelt during the war. In asking Harriman to accept the ambassadorship to Soviet Russia, FDR came as close as possible, given the fact that Hopkins and Davies were not available, to placing himself in Moscow. Harriman agreed generally with FDR's policy of concessions and friendship for the Soviet Union, although he preferred mutually advantageous rather than unilateral relationships.

Harriman considered himself a man of action, a doer, rather than a thinker or a bureaucrat. He rarely read books either for enjoyment or information. He wanted to be where the action was and to deal directly with the makers of history. Needless to say, he was not a great intellect, and some of his close friends found him "intellectually dull." Bohlen doubted that he ever really understood the Soviet system and put it kindly when he said, "Reading ideological books was not his forte." By all accounts, he was "short-tempered, parsimonious, ambitious, and superstitious." His wife Marie called him a "cheapskate." In the opinion of some, he was dilettantish. Lord Beaverbrook, who was jealous of him, said he never knew anyone who went so far with so little. Dwight Eisenhower called him a "nincompoop."[1] Although somewhat supercilious and superficial, he nonetheless would never allow minor problems or difficult personalities to get in the way of the all-important goal of wartime and especially postwar cooperation between the United States and the Soviet Union. He was dedicated wholeheartedly to the president's policy. He was eager to please both Roosevelt and Stalin, a quality that Stalin particularly was wont to exploit.

Harriman was born in 1891 not far from where Roosevelt was born and reared. He knew Franklin and Eleanor as youngsters and went to Groton School with Eleanor's younger brother. He believed that Franklin was a pleasant fellow but never presidential material. He thought of him as a wealthy patrician, like himself, who would be ideal for president of the Greater New York Boy Scouts'

Council, which was a position FDR held after the war. "He did not impress me," Harriman conceded in his memoirs, "as a man of great force or depth." FDR's struggle with polio, however, changed Harriman's opinion. The experience transformed FDR, according to Harriman, into a person of tremendous courage and strength. Harriman became an ardent admirer of his fellow New Yorker.[2]

Harriman was a true blueblood. He was the son of Edward Henry Harriman, described by a French journalist as the "Napoleon of railroad men," and of Mary Williamson Averell, the daughter of a New York banker and a railroad owner. His father built up a vast fortune based on his investment in the Union Pacific and Illinois Central Railroads and some shady dealings. When he died in 1909 he left an estate estimated at nearly $70 million to his wife, who in turn settled generous portions of the estate on each of her five children, making them all millionaires.

Averell, the next to last of the children and the older of two boys, lived a life of privilege and ease. Polo, skiing, and rowing filled most of his waking hours. After Groton School he went on to Yale University where his major interest seemed to be rowing boats and chasing women. In his senior year he was elected to the board of the Union Pacific Railroad, and after graduation he was named vice president for purchasing. His mother supervised his career and gently pushed him "forward as the titular head of the Harriman family."[3] Young Averell was anxious to make his mark, but he really did not show much business acumen. He made investments and negotiated deals, but many of his arrangements seemed poorly planned and ill-timed. Part of the problem was that he simply did not devote adequate time to his projects. He much preferred the playful drama of polo and the bedroom to the intense pressure of Wall Street and the boardroom. Mary Harriman, though, kept the family fortune growing with shrewd investments and advice from a family friend, Judge Robert S. Lovett, who supervised the Harriman railroad interests.

Harriman's personal life reflected a frivolity similar to his business endeavors. After graduation from Yale he married Kitty Lawrence and fathered two daughters. The marriage was not a happy one, however, and was punctuated with a scandalous affair between Harriman and a cabaret singer named Teddy Gerard. The couple divorced in 1928. While he was still married, Harriman also had an affair with Marie Whitney, the estranged wife of Cornelius Vanderbilt, and a member of his country club. Once she obtained a Reno-style divorce from Vanderbilt, who was also a notorious playboy, she and Harriman married in February 1929. The marriage lasted until her death in 1970, but Harriman found fidelity to be an insurmountable challenge. His most notorious affair was with Pamela Churchill, Winston Churchill's daughter-in-law, whom he met in war-ravaged London in 1941 when she was barely twenty-one. He married her in 1971 after Marie's death and after the death of Pamela's second husband, Leland Heyward.[4]

While Harriman was still married to his first wife, he tried to follow in his father's path and strike out on his own. Thinking he saw an opportunity to make money by providing transport ships to the United States government after it entered World War I in 1917, he resigned as vice president of the Union Pacific Railroad and entered the shipbuilding business. He won a lucrative contract from the government in 1917 by promising to build ships quickly using an assembly line, but when the war ended the next year, part of the contract was canceled and the market for transport ships dried up.

Harriman attempted to find a new use for his ships by forming a partnership with a German transatlantic passenger ship firm, the Hamburg-American Line. The Germans had lost their ships to wartime destruction or confiscation, and they wanted to use Harriman's ships to continue passenger service on their established routes while they built a new fleet. Harriman lost money on the venture because passenger traffic declined as a result of Prohibition and restrictive immigration laws. His mother came to his rescue and made good on his losses.[5]

Harriman then tried his hand at investing in a manganese mine in Soviet Georgia. He was enticed by the thought that he might control a good part of the world's supply of manganese, a mineral in high demand because of its use in making steel. By the mid-1920s the United States was already importing 100,000 tons of Georgian manganese worth $10 million. He went to the Soviet Union in 1926, met with Trotsky and other Soviet officials, and eventually signed a contract to modernize and develop the manganese mine. The Soviet bureaucracy, the changing investment climate associated with the end of the New Economic Policy and the power struggle following Lenin's death, and friction between the Georgians and Russians soon ruined the investment and led once again to Mary Harriman's intervention. Although Averell never criticized the Soviet government publicly, he privately concluded that business was impossible because the Soviet Union represented "the grandest aggregation of corruption, incompetence, and utter brutality that the world has seen for centuries." It was a rare insight into Soviet society that did not stay with him.[6]

Harriman had better luck with another company that he organized, W. A. Harriman & Company, an international investment firm. He set it up to take advantage of the fact that "the United States had become an international creditor nation and that Wall Street was likely to become increasingly the postwar financial center of the world." He and his brother also founded an international banking firm, Harriman Brothers and Company, which merged in 1931 with Brown Brothers to form one of the largest private banks in the United States. Behind both W. A. Harriman & Company and Harriman Brothers & Company, however, was his mother's money. When the Great Depression shook the bank and investment firm, she came to the rescue with massive infusions of money to keep Averell and his brother afloat. Once over the crisis of the Depression, the bank provided him with a nice income for the rest of his life, but he had little to do with its management.[7]

In 1930, at Judge Lovett's instigation, Harriman was elected chairman of the executive committee of the Illinois Central Railroad. Two years later, with Lovett's death, he was named chairman of the board of the Union Pacific Railroad. During his tenure, the railroads streamlined service and developed Sun Valley, Idaho, into a major ski resort. He showed himself at last to be hard-driving and competent at management, and both traits served him well in future business and diplomacy.

A Republican aristocrat through and through, he was nonetheless drawn to the progressive and reform-minded wing of the Democratic Party. Ironically, what attracted him was that he thought the regulatory agencies of a stronger federal government could eliminate useless competition. Like any businessman sitting atop a monopoly, he found the idea of more centralized government attractive. But it was not solely for business reasons that he preferred the Democrats. He liked their internationalist outlook, their desire, in contrast to the isolationist Republicans, to forge a new relationship with the community of nations and to reduce tariffs. In addition, he had a pragmatic commitment to social reform in the best tradition of noblesse oblige. He always remembered his father's sage advice: "In our democracy if men of wealth did not use their money for the public welfare it would be taken from them." The major influence in leading him to the Democratic Party was his sister Mary, who was a committed reformer and supporter of Franklin and Eleanor Roosevelt.[8]

In 1928, exasperated with the Republican Party because of "its isolationist tendencies and its reckless domestic politics," especially its support of tariffs and Prohibition, he supported Al Smith for president. He also sensed in the wake of the Depression the shift of power toward the Democrats, and he increasingly found political power to be an irresistible elixir. Soon he broke with the Republicans and joined the Democratic camp.[9]

With FDR's election in 1932, Harriman found himself spending a great deal of time in Washington defending railroad interests. The financial barons in New York had clearly lost their power to the centurions of the New Deal. Harriman found Washington political society to be absolutely intoxicating, and he wanted to be part of it. He had never demonstrated great skill or foresight at business or investment, and now he found something he really enjoyed—the company of politicians and the exercise of political power. He soon offered his services to his boyhood friend. Knowing full well that the New Deal had few supporters on Wall Street, FDR took up Harriman's offer for assistance and soon appointed him to the Business Advisory Council, which had the job of drumming up support for FDR's recovery programs. He also named him chairman of the National Recovery Administration for New York. On the Business Advisory Council Harriman met and befriended Edward R. Stettinius of U.S. Steel, an important contact who eventually became a Lend-Lease official and then secretary of state when Cordell Hull resigned in late 1944.

Ambitious, opportunistic, pragmatic, and wealthy, Harriman soon emerged as a leading force in the business community for New Deal programs. He quickly analyzed the power structure in Washington and decided that Harry Hopkins, "the Cardinal Woolsey of the Roosevelt administration," was the key to the president. He knew that "if the Business Advisory Board could sell Hopkins on some new idea, that would mean Roosevelt, too, was about three-quarters sold."[10]

Harriman cultivated Hopkins, patently flattering him and offering to do him favors. Hopkins was in many ways the direct opposite of Harriman. He was not wealthy, entrepreneurial, or cosmopolitan. Born and raised in Iowa, he came to FDR's attention as a social worker in New York. What FDR liked about him, above all, was his simplicity and his absolute loyalty. Loyalty was what Harriman and Hopkins had in common—loyalty to FDR. In addition, they both wanted to pull the United States out of the Depression, they held the Washington bureaucracy in contempt for its inefficiency, and eventually they shared an abject hatred of Hitler and Nazism. Harriman liked Hopkins's iconoclastic approach and his "irreverent attitude toward the high and mighty," and Hopkins was pleased by Harriman's attention and, to a certain extent, his deference.

When Roosevelt nominated Hopkins to be his secretary of commerce, a key position for the business community, Harriman threw his support and resources behind Hopkins. Throughout the 1930s the tie between Hopkins and Harriman grew fast and strong, and soon Harriman became known as "Hopkins's man."[11] His stature simultaneously rose with Roosevelt, and by the end of the 1930s, particularly after the death of Louis Howe, he emerged as one of FDR's closest advisers and friends. There were other key personalities around Roosevelt, to be sure, people like Henry Morgenthau Jr. and Frances Perkins, but Harriman was in the intimate inner circle.

When World War II broke out in 1939, Roosevelt and his chief advisers, including Hopkins and Harriman, were not inclined to have the United States become involved. Americans were firmly opposed to a more active role in either Europe or Asia. Nonetheless, Roosevelt, Hopkins, and Harriman agreed that Hitler was a direct threat to America and western civilization and they hoped that he would be destroyed. They also wanted to see Japanese aggression checked in Asia. As the war increasingly turned against the French and the British in 1940, the American government carefully but consistently expanded its support of these beleaguered countries, maneuvered public opinion to the point where there was growing support for intervention, and increased the economic and military-political pressure on Japan and Germany.

With the fall of France, the Roosevelt team agreed to allow the British to use American destroyers in exchange for American use of British bases, increased naval activity in the North Atlantic in support of Great Britain, warned Japan to stay out of Indochina, and increased its already existing effort to reduce the global supply of oil and raw materials going to Japan. That Roosevelt was maneuvering to involve the United States in a two-front war was at best problematical. The need for the Soviet alliance and the splitting of resources would have been much reduced if FDR had, as the British wanted, eased up on Japan, concentrated on Germany, and then, after Germany's defeat, turned on Japan. Nonetheless, Kennan's retrospective view that Roosevelt's pressure on Japan left Tokyo with no other option than to attack Pearl Harbor and thus involve the United States in the war in the "worst possible way" fails to appreciate the barbarism of Japanese aggression in Asia, the capriciousness of Hitler, and the power of American public opinion.[12]

Hopkins was sent to London in 1940 to tell Churchill that Roosevelt would back him, no matter what happened.[13] The Lend-Lease bill, providing extensive credit and aid to Britain and her allies, soon passed Congress, and in February 1941 Roosevelt asked Harriman to go to London to "recommend everything we can do, short of war, to keep the British Isles afloat."[14] He was to report directly to Roosevelt and Hopkins, not to Secretary of State Hull or to the State Department.

In London, Harriman found the situation critical, but with unusual aplomb he soon began cutting through, over, and around the bureaucracy to rush aid to the British. As the Lend-Lease Administration was built, he was given the position of Lend-Lease expediter in London and he virtually cut out the highly competent American ambassador, John Winant. With a direct line to Hopkins and Roosevelt, his power soon became obvious to Churchill and the British government. A close friendship soon developed between Churchill and Harriman, which allowed for frank and open discussions.

With the Nazi invasion of the Soviet Union in June 1941, Harriman reported that the British were greatly relieved. Churchill immediately extended the hand of alliance to the USSR, which Stalin eventually accepted. In July Harry Hopkins flew to Moscow to offer American assistance to the besieged Soviet government. He returned to Washington full of enthusiasm for Stalin and the eastern front. FDR responded with his unconditional aid program.

To Harriman's surprise and delight, Roosevelt asked him to go to Moscow in late September 1941 with Lord Beaverbrook, Churchill's representative, and work out a precise agreement for Lend-Lease aid. Harriman referred to Beaverbrook and himself as "greenhorns from London," but he was being facetious. Harriman had been to the Soviet Union in December 1926, when he went to check on his manganese concession. Although Harriman sold his concession, he continued to be interested in the Soviet Union. His knowledge of Soviet Russia and his business experience appealed to FDR.

Beaverbrook, the publisher of the *Daily Express*, was a close friend of Churchill. He knew the USSR had to stay in the war, and he also wanted to make sure that American aid to Moscow would be sufficient, even if it came at England's expense. Harriman and Beaverbrook were basically compatible and, most important for the Americans, Beaverbrook agreed with Harriman's determination to carry forward Roosevelt's policy of unconditional aid to the Soviet Union. In fact, Beaverbrook emphasized that the policy was "to make clear beyond a doubt the British and American intention to satisfy Russian needs to the utmost in their power, whether the Russians gave anything or not. It was to be a Christmas Tree Party."[15] Steinhardt, the American ambassador in Moscow, objected to the unconditional nature of the policy, but he was soon removed.

The Beaverbrook-Harriman mission was a resounding success from Harriman's point of view. He got on quite well with Stalin, and he committed the United States to providing the Soviet Union with the basic resources to fight the war. FDR praised him for a job well done and soon set in motion the Lend-Lease aid program for the USSR. Harriman was no believer in the theory of convergence, which was an article of faith with FDR, but he was a firm supporter of the policy of aid, friendship, and concessions.[16]

After the mission ended, Harriman returned to London to carry on as Lend-Lease expediter. He was happy to see Admiral Standley replace Steinhardt in Moscow, and he was greatly relieved when the United States entered the war after the Japanese attack on Pearl Harbor.[17] The United States was now an ally of the Soviet Union. With an alliance and a new ambassador in Moscow, he hoped now that American-Soviet relations would blossom.

Admiral Standley, however, did not do the job adequately from Harriman and Roosevelt's point of view. He criticized the policy of unconditional aid and failed to persuade Stalin to meet with Roosevelt. Harriman, under the influence of Churchill, had come to accept Standley's view that a more balanced relationship had to be developed with the Soviets, but he also thought that Standley lacked the charisma to fashion a personal relationship with Stalin. He thought that he had what it would take.[18]

With the Soviet victory at Stalingrad, the American success at Midway and Guadalcanal, and the British triumph at El Alamein, American-Soviet relations entered a new and delicate stage. It was fairly clear by the spring of 1943 that the Soviet Union, the United States, and England would be victorious over Germany and Japan. It was also obvious that there would be a change in the balance of power in Europe and Asia. American power was and would be unrivaled and unparalleled everywhere. Soviet strength was formidable, but it depended on western aid and would be curtailed by the visible need to reallocate resources from the military to the war-shattered Soviet economy and polity. Germany, Italy, and France were flattened or about to be flattened. England was already a second-level power dependent upon the United States to carry on. Japan was on the verge of being leveled in Asia, and China was enmeshed in turmoil. The United States could have used its power to dictate the postwar world order. Bullitt stressed that point with FDR in January 1943. He wrote, "Men at some times are masters of their fate. You have your power now—and while you have it you must use it. You will lose it the day Germany collapses." That Stalin ended up obtaining what he wanted instead of Roosevelt obtaining what he aimed for is a consequence not of Stalin's power but of Kennan's assertion in 1944 "that not only our policy toward Russia, but our plans and commitments generally for the shaping of the postwar world, were based on a dangerous misreading of the personality, the intentions, and the political situation of the Soviet leadership."[19]

By late spring 1943 it was critical for Roosevelt to have someone in the Moscow post upon whom he could rely as military concerns gave way to political discussions. Admiral Standley, the military ambassador, and Brigadier General Faymonville, the Lend-Lease military official, were not suitable political negotiators. Standley did not agree with the president's policy and had complicated the president's plans with his famous news conference. Faymonville, although he personified the policy, had attracted so much controversy because of that very fact that his ability to function had been impaired. The president wanted an alter ego in Moscow. He found him in W. Averell Harriman. Stalin also replaced his ambassadors in Washington and London, Maxim Litvinov and Ivan Maisky respectively, two men whom the western leaders liked because they were fairly cosmopolitan and had the reputation of favoring the western alliance. Their replacements, Andrei Gromyko in Washington and Fedor Gousev in London, were unknowns who fitted the Stalinist mold and lacked the independent flair of their predecessors. A premonition of Litvinov's removal came in January 1943 when Stalin asked Standley if American "ruling circles" were pleased with Litvinov. When Standley said that they were, he may very well have sealed Litvinov's fate.[20]

Roosevelt believed that Harriman could lay the foundation for a personal relationship between himself and Stalin. Harriman thought that he could, too, and he accepted the job. "As you know," he wrote the president on July 5, 1943, "I am a confirmed optimist in our relations with Russia because of my conviction that Stalin wants, if obtainable, a firm understanding with you and America more than anything else—after the destruction of Hitler. He sees Russia's reconstruction and security more soundly based on it than on any alternative. He is a man of simple purposes and, although he may use devious means in attempting to accomplish them, he does not deviate from his long-run objectives."

Churchill did not share Harriman's and Roosevelt's optimism about Stalin. He was opposed to a private meeting between Roosevelt and Stalin and further stressed that he feared there would be major problems with the Soviets. At the Quebec Conference in August 1943, he told Harriman, "Stalin is an unnatural man. There will be grave troubles."[21]

Harriman, however, was convinced that Churchill was wrong. In fact, the Americans were unquestionably more suspicious of Churchill and what they believed was his hope to use American power to maintain the British empire than they were of Stalin and his alleged desire to expand the Soviet empire. Hopkins told the earl of Halifax in 1943 that the United States was not and could not appear to be in England's pocket. And Eleanor Roosevelt certainly revealed something of FDR's thinking when she wrote, after meeting Churchill, that he was lovable, emotional, and very human, "but I don't want him to write the peace or carry it out."[22]

After the Quebec Conference Harriman put his affairs in order and prepared to depart for Moscow. In August and September he gathered the team that he wanted in Moscow. He planned to keep many of the same people who had worked for Standley except, of course, Faymonville, who was replaced by General John R. Deane, the secretary of the Joint Chiefs of Staff.[23] He also decided that Charles Bohlen or George Kennan, both experienced hands in Moscow, should join him as chief counselor. Roosevelt and Hopkins wanted Bohlen in Washington because he did not seem to be part of the "anti-Soviet" clique at the State Department, but they agreed to send Kennan as soon as he could be freed from a recent assignment in Portugal.[24] They allowed Bohlen to be temporarily assigned to Moscow for two months following Teheran. Because his wife Marie had severe problems with her eyes, Harriman took along his daughter, Kathleen, to help him with social activities.[25]

The new ambassador made it clear when he arrived that he was the only representative of the United States. He told Molotov, "The president has determined to put his trust in the person of the United States ambassador to the USSR." His staff, according to Kennan, knew that he was the chief. "No detail was too small to escape his attention. He wanted to know everything about everything." He worked eighteen to twenty hours a day, Kennan recalled, and he expected everyone to pull his own weight. He also made it clear to Stettinius that he did not want any special envoys coming to Moscow—he would handle all negotiations. Much like Roosevelt and Hopkins, he did not have a great deal of confidence in his foreign service advisers. He knew Stalin controlled politics in the Soviet Union, and he felt that he could learn more from a brief conversation with Stalin than the embassy staff could discover in months of study. Kennan thought that he was probably correct in that assumption because "power was so highly personalized" in the Soviet Union.[26]

Harriman was not impressed with Spaso House. It was in the same dilapidated condition that prevailed when Standley arrived in 1942. The windows were shattered, the shrubbery was dead, the heating and plumbing systems were faltering, and vents from oil-burning stoves were poking through bedroom windows. Plasterboard still covered the broken windows, and tattered drapes and wall coverings fell over walls in need of paint and plaster. Frescoes, cornices, and moldings were crumbling. Dirt from a dug-out bomb shelter was piled high in the backyard.[27] Even the Soviet bugging system was probably frayed. Harriman put up with Spaso House, though, and made it the center of American operations in Moscow. The chancery building was still not in full use for embassy staff, so Spaso House served as the embassy as well as the ambassador's residence. To make life more bearable, Harriman refurbished the American dacha outside Moscow and often retreated there with the staff for picnics and relaxation. The dacha had a small vegetable garden, too, that provided some relief from Spam and Lend-Lease rations.

Harriman found that being an ambassador, rather than a special representative, was more mundane and difficult. Like other foreign diplomats, he was kept isolated, and he was followed everywhere by four NKVD agents—two more than any other ambassador, which was some measure of his importance. Social life with the Soviets, when it did occur, consisted of drinking vodka to excess or watching Hollywood movies at Spaso House. In the hope of making quick escapes from Moscow, he eventually obtained permission from the Soviet government to have his own plane, a B-24 that he named *Becky*. Escapes, though, would not be easy because the Kremlin refused to give Harriman's pilot the location of Moscow's radio-navigation transmitters or weather information. And, of course, the plane was guarded by Soviet soldiers, who prevented any unauthorized departures. From the Soviet point of view, the plane was to be used only to transport Harriman back and forth between Moscow and Washington. When Bohlen asked if it could be used to carry an American military officer between Cairo and Moscow, he was turned down.[28]

Harriman's first winter in Moscow was utterly miserable. He was constantly sick, cold, and lonely. He knew that an ambassador could not expect privileged access to the Kremlin. But given his connection to Roosevelt and Hopkins, he could not understand why Stalin failed to pay more attention to him. He was rarely called upon, and when he was, it was invariably at night and usually well past midnight. Stalin's routine was absolutely grueling.[29]

Roosevelt gave his new ambassador a list of immediate concerns, which he was to explore with Stalin. First, he was to excite Stalin about meeting Roosevelt by stating that existing problems could be solved through a tête-à-tête. Second, he was to emphasize that the Soviets should not act unilaterally in taking territory, that the president personally wished to negotiate territorial issues with Stalin, and that a plebiscite should be held in the Baltic States. Of course, the president had already informed Stalin through Davies that there would be no fight over the Polish-Soviet border or Soviet control of the Baltic States. Third, he was to explore Soviet intentions against Japan, probe their willingness to coordinate military aspects of the war against Germany, and generally discuss Soviet security needs. Roosevelt thought the latter might include internationalizing access to the Baltic Sea and the Persian Gulf. Finally, Harriman was to inform Stalin that the United States wanted to break up and strip Germany of its air power to the point where "no German should be allowed to learn to fly."[30]

Harriman made his debut in Moscow in the company of Secretary Hull. Roosevelt was somewhat worried about Hull acting as a spokesman for the United States at the foreign ministers' meeting, since he was not part of the inner circle.

The president wanted Harriman there to keep an eye on the secretary of state. Hull, however, carried forward FDR's plan. He stressed cooperation with the Soviets and expressed joy that the Soviets had taken steps recently to address two of the major problems in American-Soviet relations, namely, the dissolution of the Comintern and the ending of religious repression. He also wanted to tie the Soviets to the vague and grandiloquent phrases of the Declaration of the Four Powers, a new document that FDR had approved and that represented his hope for democratic government in postwar Europe.

Molotov must have been suspicious and incredulous as he sat there and heard the soaring language tumble from Hull's lips, but once the Soviet foreign minister got the Allies' agreement to a second front in Europe and to the resumption of supply convoys to Soviet ports, he had no problem accepting the declaration. Molotov, however, only showed enthusiasm when Hull suggested, in contrast to the high-sounding phrases of the declaration, that all of the Axis leaders be executed after the war. The secretary of state remembered that Molotov and his entire delegation applauded wildly.[31]

Harriman reported to FDR that Hull did a good job. "His dignity and determination and sincerity in presenting our attitude toward the preservation of world peace . . . profoundly impressed the Soviet officials. I cannot overemphasize the important contribution his presence made toward the favorable outcome of the conference."[32]

Harriman also reported the Soviet attitude on a number of crucial questions. He told FDR that the Soviets expected their 1941 borders to be accepted by the West, that the London Polish government was "completely unacceptable" and so the "problem of Poland is even tougher than we believed," that Germany had to have a lower standard of living than the Soviet Union, that "Anglo-American decisions already taken" would be rejected, and finally that "the old 'cordon sanitaire' concept in Eastern Europe" was now an anachronism. Harriman stressed that Molotov seemed to grow friendly once he discovered that Eden and Hull had not made a priori decisions. The ambassador was also struck by Molotov and Litvinov's brutal attack on the London Poles, but neither he nor Hull nor Eden made any attempt to protest. His report to FDR was thorough, and it certainly contained the basic outline of the Soviet plan for Eastern Europe.[33]

The foreign ministers reached agreement on a second front in Europe in 1944, a United Nations organization, eventual Soviet involvement against Japan, treatment of Austria as a victim rather than as an ally of Germany, and a host of minor issues, including the possibility of sharing some of the surrendered Italian fleet with the Soviet Union.[34] Hull and Harriman were extremely pleased with the results and with the cordial atmosphere, and Harriman was convinced more than ever that the president's policy was correct. Gromyko reported that the Moscow Conference received positive news coverage in the United States.[35]

There was one sour note, however, immediately after the meeting. Molotov complained to Harriman that the Germans were transferring troops from Italy to the eastern front, that by their delay in taking Rome the Allies were not putting pressure on the Germans, and that the Allies greatly exaggerated the number of German troops in Italy. According to Archibald Clark-Kerr, Harriman was shocked by the charges and determined to show Molotov the secret cables of General Eisenhower to prove that he was wrong. Only with the greatest effort, Clark-Kerr reported, was he able to persuade Harriman not to take that step. Clearly, Harriman was disposed to going to great lengths to convince the Soviets that the Americans were being above board in the alliance. He did tell Molotov that the West was divided between a Mediterranean emphasis and another front in Europe and that Roosevelt and Stalin could decide the issue at Teheran.[36]

After the foreign ministers' meeting, Harriman left Moscow to join Roosevelt, Churchill, and Chiang Kai-shek at the Cairo Conference, which was held just before the Teheran Conference. The Cairo Conference dealt mainly with the war against Japan. Here China, the United States, and Britain reconfirmed the unconditional surrender demand from Japan, which had already been mentioned but not stressed at the Casablanca Conference. Once again the Soviet Union was not represented by a major official. Obviously Stalin wanted to avoid any premature and public commitment about the Soviet position against Japan.

Churchill wanted to use the opportunity of the Cairo Conference to meet privately with Roosevelt to work out a joint strategy for when they would face Stalin at Teheran. Roosevelt, however, spurned Churchill's attempts for a private meeting so that they would not appear to be "ganging up" on Stalin. He wanted to deal with Stalin individually and without the leverage of an Anglo-American agreement. He was deliberately giving up a major bargaining position in hopes of winning Stalin's appreciation and confidence. Churchill was absolutely shocked by FDR's approach. It made no sense whatsoever to him to go to Teheran without plans and strategies. He was soon to learn, however, that he, not Stalin, was the odd man out. At the conclusion of the Cairo Conference Roosevelt, Harriman, and Churchill pushed on to Teheran to meet Stalin. For FDR, the continuous travel was grueling. Volkogonov noticed at Teheran that he "had the mark of fatigue and illness on him."[37]

The Teheran Conference was crucial. It set the direction, as most of the leaders understood it would, for the alliance and for postwar political settlements. Either Hopkins or Harriman were at Roosevelt's side throughout the meeting. Bohlen was also there at every meeting between Roosevelt and Stalin to serve as FDR's translator and to take notes. Molotov told the Americans that the streets of Teheran were crawling with Axis sympathizers and that it would be helpful if Roosevelt would stay in the Soviet compound, so that none of the "Big Three" would have to travel back and forth between embassies. The British embassy was virtually next door to the Soviet embassy, whereas the American compound was about half a mile away. Churchill thought initially that it was a good idea because it would mean the leaders would not have to travel for meetings.[38] He changed his mind after Roosevelt used the arrangement as a way to isolate Churchill and organize private meetings with Stalin.

Harriman did not believe Molotov's assertion about Axis sympathizers, but he encouraged FDR to accept the Soviet offer for reasons of security and convenience. Roosevelt actually wanted to stay in the Soviet embassy anyway because it was a concrete sign that the Americans had nothing to hide from the Soviets and that FDR implicitly trusted Stalin. It would also mean that Roosevelt and Stalin could meet privately, and the president could begin the process of reassuring the suspicious and secretive Soviet dictator of America's good intentions.[39]

Each of the leaders at Teheran had already indicated his general position on the postwar order. Of course, that is not to say that each leader understood the others' goals or that any one of them had closely studied the others' statements for nuances that might shed light on fuzzily phrased generalizations. Stalin had indicated that he wanted control of Poland, the Baltic States, Bessarabia, and Bukovina and at least influence over other states in Eastern Europe. He wanted a sphere of influence in Eastern Europe, but one in which the Soviets controlled foreign and domestic policies. He also wanted Germany severely punished, and he demanded that it bear the brunt of the cost of the Soviet Union's postwar reconstruction. Beyond that, he had not indicated any goals. He certainly had hopes, particularly in light of the destruction of the balance of power in Europe and Asia, but he was too cautious to voice them in the face of American power.

Churchill hoped to save the British empire. He also wanted to punish Germany. He was quite willing to concede to Stalin the Baltic States and a sphere of influence in Poland. He thought it was obvious, given the geographical position of Poland and the disparity between Polish and Soviet power, that Poland would have to subordinate its foreign policy to Moscow's interests. He apparently did not conceive of a Soviet sphere of influence in Poland as meaning Soviet control of Polish domestic policy. Semantics were a problem with all three leaders. They often used the same words but meant something different, although Stalin clearly knew that his use of any words related to "democrat" or "freedom" were not only different than his allies' use but geared to take advantage of their wishful thinking.

Roosevelt wanted to punish Germany harshly. On that point, he would get no fundamental disagreement from Stalin. He also hoped for a firm commitment from Stalin about Soviet involvement in the war against Japan. Above all, he wanted to build an international organization that would help eliminate future wars, protect the rights of all nations, and promote democratic principles. His position was concrete in the sense that he had a specific goal, namely, a united nations institution, but also abstract in that the goals of the institution were general and the methods for achieving the goals were not clear-cut. He was adamant on one point, though, and that was the necessity of Soviet participation in the organization. He believed that the League of Nations failed because some of the major powers, including the United States, had refused to join. Now in a world where the Soviet Union and the United States were the major powers, it was crucial that they both belong to the new League of Nations. Together they could transform the globe, improving life everywhere.

Given the dispositions of the three leaders, there was ample room for disagreement. However, the discussions were placid and friendly because of two dynamics: the Allies still faced common enemies in Germany and Japan, and Roosevelt and Churchill wanted to reward and please Stalin. Churchill was naturally grateful to Stalin because the Red Army was keeping the Germans tied down in the East. Roosevelt, for his part, wanted Stalin to become a friend, to buy into the American plan of postwar collaboration, and to provide a specific timetable for entering the war against Japan. In addition, Stalin showed great skill at diplomacy. He allowed himself to be cultivated and, when opportune, he forcefully but tactfully pushed the interests of the Soviet Union. According to historian Adam Ulam, "What Stalingrad was to Stalin militarily, Teheran was diplomatically."[40]

At Teheran Stalin listened much more than he talked. Roosevelt, on the other hand, spoke frequently. He hoped to ingratiate himself with Stalin. He tried to charm the wily Georgian by taking him into his confidence, treating him as a fellow democratic politician, and telling him about his domestic political problems. He also confided to Stalin that he had difficulties with Churchill and British imperialism, that he thought the Soviet system was better suited to India than the parliamentary system, and that American troops would not be able to stay in Europe after the war—statements which undoubtedly surprised but pleased the Soviet leader, and Stalin was up to the opportunity. He readily agreed that Churchill will "never be satisfied" and that India would "follow the path of revolution," if change came "from below." He was probably not too shocked at FDR's words about the removal of U.S. troops. Maisky told the British before the Teheran Conference that the Soviets believed that the United States, given its tradition of isolation, would pull out of Europe shortly after the war, especially once the Americans experienced a few "unpleasant surprises," and that the fate of Europe would be left to England and the Soviet Union.[41]

On the issue of Polish-Soviet borders, Roosevelt told Stalin that he wanted the USSR to keep its 1941 borders and to shift Poland's borders to the Oder River, but that it was impossible for him to "publicly take part in any such arrangement at the present time" because there were six to seven million Polish voters in the United States, and 1944 was an election year. Stalin commented that he now clearly understood the president's position on Poland.

Roosevelt also said that when the Soviet Union reoccupied the Baltic States, it was important for Stalin to satisfy public opinion in the West by allowing a plebiscite, although "he personally was confident that the people would vote to join the Soviet Union." Stalin protested that the issue of public opinion was not raised when czarist Russia held the Baltic States as an ally of England and the United States during World War I. Roosevelt apologetically explained that the public neither knew nor understood that point of view. Undeterred, Stalin replied that some propaganda work had to be done to educate public opinion in the West. The president then explained that a declaration on elections in the Baltic States would help him in the next election. He appealed to Stalin as a fellow democrat. He asked if some form of a unifying election could be held at some convenient moment. Stalin replied that it could be done, but this did not mean a plebiscite under "some form of international control." Roosevelt agreed. Stalin then asked: If this election were held, "would the result settle the question once and for all?" The president agreed that it would. No one could accuse Stalin of dissimulation on Soviet plans for the Baltic States.[42]

Roosevelt, who was frantic to break the ice with Stalin, decided after three days of negotiations to try the tactic of using Churchill as the butt of jokes and ridicule. Stalin guffawed loudly whenever FDR picked on Churchill, and the president concluded that Stalin and he were now friends. As Roosevelt recounted the episode to Secretary of Labor Perkins, he said that henceforth "we talked like men and brothers" and for the first time "I called him 'Uncle Joe.'" However, in the opinion of one historian, FDR "insulted Churchill who admired him and demeaned himself before Stalin who trusted neither man." Charles Bohlen, who was translating FDR's comments into Russian, also disapproved of FDR's attack on Churchill.[43]

Nonetheless, Roosevelt decided that he had found common ground with the Soviet dictator. In private meetings with Stalin, the president continued to criticize Churchill and made it clear that he was not at all sympathetic to the continuation of the British empire. Stalin quickly exploited the opening. He informed Roosevelt that the Soviets were more comfortable with the Americans and agreed with their assessment of the British imperialists. The British were now blamed for the problems of the alliance, including the lack of a second front. Roosevelt had conveniently provided Stalin with an excuse for the difficulties in American-Soviet relations. As late as 1945 Stalin was still using the "British Conservatives" as the whipping boy to explain why the alliance was awry.[44]

Even Harriman, who had developed good rapport with Churchill, saw merit in blaming the British for the failure of the policy of cooperation.[45] Clark-Kerr complained to Eden that "Averell is a bit of a weather-cock," always tilting toward Moscow when the British and the Soviets disagreed.[46] Clark-Kerr's comment was a specific reference to Stalin's refusal to have General Burrows, the British military liaison, represent England on the Anglo-Soviet-American military commission. Stalin claimed Burrows was anti-Soviet, and Harriman weighed in with the suggestion that "a fresh appointment" would be good.[47] Clark-Kerr was not one of Harriman's admirers. When Harriman visited Moscow in 1942 in the company of Churchill, Clark-Kerr called him "a champion bum sucker."[48]

Stalin also played on FDR's anticolonialist tendencies in dealing with France. He stressed that Allied forces should not shed any blood attempting to reestablish French control in Indochina, which, in retrospect, was good advice. He did not, however, reveal what he had in mind for the vacuum that would follow in Southeast Asia once the Japanese were defeated and the French were proscribed from regaining their colonies. Both Stalin and Roosevelt agreed that General Charles DeGaulle, the leader of the Free French forces, was imperious and difficult to deal with. Stalin did not like him, perhaps because DeGaulle had refused to recognize the 1941 borders of the Soviet Union when he visited Moscow in 1943.

Once Roosevelt had revealed his disposition about Britain, Stalin felt secure enough to taunt Churchill openly under the guise of his particular brand of heavy humor. He "jokingly" accused the British of being soft on the Germans and of having a "secret liking for the Germans." He told Churchill that the German General Staff had to be destroyed and that the best way to do this was to shoot 50,000 German officers. At this point, Churchill, taking Stalin seriously, protested vehemently and declared that Britain would never be a party to such an atrocity. Roosevelt loved it. It tickled him to see his allies quarreling, for it gave him a chance to step in and show Stalin that he understood him, that he was not one with Churchill, that he and Stalin could work together. With Churchill quite upset over Stalin's professed desire to kill 50,000 German officers, Roosevelt offered a compromise: kill 49,000 rather than 50,000.

Churchill stormed out of the room, only to have Stalin and Molotov catch him and tell him it was a big joke. Churchill returned, but he never did believe that it was entirely a joke, and he had to know that he was, in effect, the odd man out.[49]

To Churchill's chagrin, Roosevelt refused to have any private meetings with him at Teheran. This hurt the British leader, made him feel the president was not being evenhanded, and ultimately led him, to Stalin's delight certainly, to seek private meetings with Stalin, so that he could be sure the Soviet dictator understood the British position on various key issues, especially the second front in France. He feared rightly that Roosevelt might not fully understand or appreciate the British stand.[50]

Curiously, Roosevelt has always been portrayed as the mediator between Churchill and Stalin at Teheran. He did, of course, try to assume that role when particularly controversial issues polarized Churchill and Stalin, but most of these issues called for a firm moral stance, not equivocation, and he invariably came down on the Soviet side. Part of the problem, of course, was that FDR wanted to win Stalin's confidence, to bedazzle Americans with his ability to get on with "Uncle Joe" on the eve of the 1944 presidential election, and to show that he was not Churchill's lackey.[51]

Stalin was the key player at Teheran. He was the only one who had private meetings with the other two and knew their positions and fears. And despite his tactical criticism of British imperialism, Stalin actually favored imperialism as the logical way to reorganize the globe following the defeat of Germany and Japan. He would support, he revealed, the annexation by Britain and America of any territory they required, provided they backed Soviet annexations and did not take the same regions that the Soviets wanted.[52]

Stalin's approach was nicely reflected in the case of Finland. Like the Baltic States, Finland had been part of the Russian empire before 1917, and it presently was fighting on the side of Germany. It would seem that the Soviet interest in annexing Finland would be almost as great as it was in taking the Baltic States, yet the Soviets did not demand Finland in the wartime conferences, and after the war they made no attempt to acquire it. The reason for this happy circumstance might very well have been the fact that FDR expressed interest in Finland as early as December 8, 1941, when he met with Litvinov following the United States' entrance into World War II, and then again at Teheran, the United States did not break relations with Finland even after the Soviets complained about the tie, and the American ambassadors consistently showed support for Finland at the Kremlin. The American stand probably convinced Stalin that the United States considered Finland's independence vital to its interests. Poland's history might have been different if someone had resolutely defended it before, during, and after Teheran. Characteristically, Roosevelt continued to believe after Teheran that the United States and the Soviet Union could cooperate on the basis of anti-imperialism.

On the all-important issue of Germany, both Churchill and Roosevelt made clear their intention to punish Germany severely. There would be an occupation, possibly even a breakup, reparations, territorial losses, and a massive resettlement of Germans living in the eastern borderlands to the western parts of Germany. Churchill did not wish to go as far as Roosevelt in breaking up Germany, but he was in a vengeful mood. The leaders did not get down to specifics on Germany at Teheran, but they all agreed Germany would be flattened out. The most direct and lasting consequence of this decision was the expansion of Soviet influence into Poland and Eastern Europe. That was obvious at Teheran. Churchill certainly knew that a weak Germany meant that Soviet influence would be predominant in Eastern Europe. What he did not apparently appreciate, however, was that Soviet influence would affect more than simply the foreign policy of otherwise independent states. It meant the creation of Communist satellite governments. It seems, in retrospect, that Churchill's hatred of Germany blinded him to the danger of destroying the balance of power in Europe, which had guided British statesmen for centuries. Bullitt had taken note of this attitude in January 1943 and vainly tried to persuade Roosevelt to work with Churchill to restore the balance of power in Europe as one step necessary to prevent Soviet domination of Central and Eastern Europe.[53]

As for Roosevelt, he evidently did not comprehend the implications of obliterating Germany, either. As late as the fall of 1944 he was pushing the so-called Morgenthau Plan, which would have reduced Germany to a pastoral state. He abhorred spheres of influence and balance of power and thought these principles no longer had a role to play in keeping the peace. He also thought that Stalin was a crypto-democrat, so strengthening his hand in Eastern and Central Europe through the destruction of the balance of power would paradoxically help democracy blossom in Germany. Basically, he had two objectives on the German issue: to level Germany and to accommodate Stalin.

Stalin had to be pleased with the general discussions regarding Germany. Roosevelt staked out a position that was so extreme that Stalin was able to come forward and say that he thought Roosevelt's plan was too draconian. However, at the same time, he did not like Churchill's less than draconian but still fairly stringent plan. He preferred something in between. He said, in a concessionary tone, that if he had to choose, he would side with Roosevelt. This plan would give him Eastern Europe, open up Central Europe and the Balkans to Soviet encroachment, and allow him to assume the role of a moderate. Stalin added one other item about Germany. The Soviets, he stipulated, needed part of Prussia along the Baltic Sea, including the port of Königsberg. No one objected.

The decision to flatten out Germany at Teheran sealed Poland's fate. It could not escape the Soviet Union's sphere of influence. That much was obvious and acquiesced in at Teheran. Churchill and Roosevelt, however, apparently did not believe at Teheran that this meant Poland would be controlled internally. The disposition of Poland, of course, was extremely sensitive for them. Great Britain had gone to war to protect the territorial integrity of Poland, and the United States was likewise committed to a free, if reduced, Poland. Poland had an unassailable moral right to its 1939 borders, and large numbers of Polish-American voters were intensely interested in the destiny of their native land.

Yet overriding all of these moral and political factors was the burning desire to please Stalin. Roosevelt's solution to this dilemma was to distance himself from the Polish issue. He was not prepared to discuss it intelligently at Teheran. He had no Polish experts in the American delegation, and he was not familiar with Poland's history, resources, or geography. He allowed Churchill to take the lead on compromising Poland's territory, explaining to Stalin that the election in 1944 kept him from openly endorsing the adjustments. Churchill knew what Stalin wanted, and so, with Roosevelt's quiet approval, he decided to give it to him without Stalin even having to ask for it. The leader of the government that went to war to protect Poland suggested to Stalin that the Soviet Union keep its 1941 border with Poland and that Poland be compensated by moving its western border into Germany up to the Oder River. When Stalin piously asked if the Poles should be consulted, Churchill stressed that it would be better for the Allies to agree and then present the Poles with a fait accompli.[54] And so it was.

Stalin knew that the Polish government-in-exile would never freely accept Soviet territorial demands and, of course, satellite status. He planned to replace it with a Communist government grown in a Moscow greenhouse. But he had to be concerned about British and American support for the London Poles. After Teheran, he had less to worry about. He launched a vicious attack on the Polish government-in-exile, calling its leaders Fascists and allies of the Germans. Sadly, neither FDR nor Churchill sprung to the defense of the Poles, and Stalin probably concluded that the Poles really had no strong supporter in the West. Once he sensed that the Poles were vulnerable, he could anticipate that not only was he going to get part of eastern Poland but that he would also be able to stipulate the type of government that Poland would have in the postwar period. In addition, of course, he could not miss the cynicism and hypocrisy of Roosevelt and Churchill. They waved the banner of the Atlantic Charter and waxed eloquent about human rights and freedom, but when it came to Poland they were quite Machiavellian.

Furthermore, the Polish issue was critical because it was the key state in Eastern Europe by virtue of its size, geography, and population. As a result, it was the likely model for the rest of the smaller Eastern European countries. The Soviets understood this, and so did the other Eastern European governments. Immediately after the Teheran Conference, Eduard Beneš, the leader of the Czech government-in-exile in London, flew to Moscow because it was now clear that the Soviet Union was going to dominate Eastern Europe. He wanted to finalize arrangements for setting up a coalition government with the Communists in Czechoslovakia. His apparent success persuaded Harriman to push in 1944 for a similar solution for Poland, that is, one where the Polish government would be reorganized to include both London Poles and Moscow Poles.[55]

On the war in Asia, Roosevelt took the lead from Churchill. His plan here was to bribe the Soviets to come into the war against Japan. The president kept prodding Stalin to disclose the price for his involvement. He suggested that the port of Dairen be internationalized. Stalin was suspicious of Roosevelt, but he also must have been amazed. He knew that Roosevelt was trying to get the Soviet Union committed against Japan, but he would not fall into that trap. He was, to be sure, planning to declare war on Japan to gather in the rich territories of northeast Asia, but not while his armies were still fighting the Germans. He commented that Dairen was Chinese territory.[56]

What undoubtedly surprised Stalin was that Roosevelt, whose soldiers were shedding blood in the Pacific, whose pilots would be imprisoned if they landed on Soviet territory, and whose ships and planes were denied all support at Soviet bases in the Far East, was essaying to bribe him to come into a war that he could not be kept out of. The question was not if the Soviet Union would enter the war, but when. There was no need to procure Soviet involvement. Stalin affirmed at Teheran that the Soviet Union would strike Japan after Germany was defeated. Khrushchev revealed, as Bullitt had predicted, that Stalin was afraid that Japan might surrender before the Soviet Union could declare war on it.[57]

Roosevelt, nonetheless, pushed Stalin for the terms of Soviet involvement, inviting him to write up his own bill. Stalin was only too happy to begin spelling out the Soviet requirements. At minimum, the Treaty of Portsmouth would have to be repealed, which meant restoring to the Soviet Union those privileges which czarist Russia had enjoyed at the height of Russian imperialism against China before the Russo-Japanese War (1904-5).[58] Astoundingly, Roosevelt did not balk at this. So much for the Atlantic Charter.

The president also outlined at Teheran some of his plans for the postwar period. He had long been seeking a way to guarantee postwar peace and stability, and the idea of the "four policemen"—the United States, Great Britain, the Soviet Union, and China—had occurred to him early in the war, but he had been reluctant to expand it into a concept of a new League of Nations. Eventually he came around to putting the "policemen" in a new organization, the United Nations, which would have one body, the General Assembly, open for membership to the nations of the world, and a separate command group, the Security Council, which would include only the "policemen" as permanent members. The major powers, especially the United States and the Soviet Union, would cooperate on the principles of liberalism *eventually*, and they would keep the small powers in their regions under control without actually occupying them. The idea was vague, but it represented a new world order that did not smack of colonialism, balance of power, and spheres of influence.[59]

Roosevelt also stressed that there had to be only one global organization, rather than a series of regional blocs, in order to concentrate the effort of overcoming traditional American isolationism. He showed the problem to Stalin by stating that if Japan had not attacked the United States, he would never have obtained congressional approval to send the American military to Europe.

Stalin at first opposed the new organization, but eventually he agreed to set up a commission to talk about it because the Americans wanted it so desperately. Stalin was no doubt surprised by Roosevelt's desire for another League of Nations, since the last one had proved that no state would subordinate its national sovereignty to some international body. However, if it in no way impinged on Soviet sovereignty, he was not above trying to use the plan to extract concessions from the Americans, since it was that important *to them*. He did emphasize to Roosevelt that the body would need power to stop German and Japanese aggression in the future.[60]

The second front, of course, preoccupied the leaders at Teheran. Churchill, along with Bullitt, had wanted a second front in the Balkans. By the time of Teheran Churchill was willing to settle for two invasions: one in France and the other in the Balkans. FDR wanted only one invasion, and he asked Stalin which target he preferred. Stalin quickly endorsed the invasion of France over any effort in the Balkans, and Roosevelt sided with him. Churchill's plan for a second invasion of the Balkans was shelved on the grounds that the western armies could not initiate two attacks. Churchill, however, thought that it could be done despite the Balkans' rough topography. An important element, of course, was the assistance of partisan forces in the Balkans and the willingness of some Axis allies to turn against Germany if they saw a chance for western help. The lack of Anglo-American action when Italy surrendered in 1943, however, was a difficult lesson to overcome. The Bulgarian regent, Professor Bogdan Filov, recorded in his diary on March 13, 1944, "We have to remain loyal to Germany to the end. . . . The Italians not only did not gain anything but now are even held in contempt by the Anglo-Americans."[61]

With Churchill blocked on the Balkans plan, Stalin demanded concrete details about the invasion of France. Specifically, he wanted to know the date and the commander. Churchill and Roosevelt promised that it would come off in May, possibly June 1944, and that General Marshall would probably be the commander. Later, Eisenhower was named instead. Stalin naturally was pleased by the commitment.

Before the conference broke up, two other concessions were made to Stalin. Churchill suggested that the Soviet Union deserved to have warm water ports, the implication being that the Soviets were to get a base in the Dardanelles. The Soviets pressured Turkey after the war for just such a base, citing Churchill's remarks at Teheran as justification. The final concession was a reiteration of the earlier proposal to give Moscow part of the Italian fleet. Stalin was promised one battleship, one cruiser, eight destroyers, and four submarines for northern Russia, and 40,000 tons displacement of merchant shipping for the Black Sea.[62]

Roosevelt was deeply impressed by Stalin. He found him to be witty, quick, and humorous. To his friend and assistant press secretary, William Hassett, he described him as "a man hewn out of granite." Churchill told Stalin at Teheran that although he and FDR were not red, they were now quite pinkish. Stalin replied, "Mr. Prime Minister, rosy cheeks are a sign of health."[63]

Roosevelt, Harriman, and Hopkins were convinced that at Teheran Stalin had been dazzled by American largess and was now firmly behind the American-Soviet partnership. FDR confided to Hopkins that Stalin was much tougher than he had expected, but that in the end he was "gettable." Stalin, according to Roosevelt, was, like Churchill, a brilliant actor. He was tough, cynical, and ruthless on the outside, but "when Russia could be convinced," to quote Sherwood's account, "that her legitimate claims and requirements—such as the right to access to warm water ports—were to be given full recognition, she would prove tractable and cooperative in maintaining the peace of the postwar period."[64]

Whether this assumption was true or not, FDR failed to establish any basis whereby the United States and Britain could play a role in defining Soviet Russia's legitimate claims and requirements. FDR did nothing to give the West any leverage on Stalin. Bullitt had provided the president in January 1943 with a long list of potential counterpoints to Soviet contrariness, but FDR would have none of it.

Roosevelt knew that the Soviets had been given a strong hand at Teheran, but he thought it was essential to keep them happy and committed to cooperation and eventual participation in the United Nations. As Harriman summarized, the Teheran Conference should have laid to rest "the feeling that existed among the Russians that we were not doing enough, and the doubts that existed as to our real intentions."[65]

In line with his belief in political convergence, Roosevelt did not go home thinking that he had doomed democracy in Poland and the Baltic States. He genuinely seemed to believe that Stalin would eventually do the right thing, which in FDR's mind meant the development of democracy in occupied territories, possibly using his own Good Neighbor Policy in Latin America as a paradigm for Soviet rule in Eastern Europe and Asia.[66] He valued Teheran as a basis for American-Russian friendship and cooperation for future action. He was convinced that Stalin was reasonable. He wanted to keep his commitments to Stalin, whatever they were, because Stalin was an evolving democrat. He told Churchill on January 13, 1944, "It is of importance that we shall acquire and maintain the confidence of our Ally," and "I think you will agree that we must not go back on what we told Uncle J."[67] Roosevelt did not envision the concessions at Teheran as a de facto extension of the Soviet empire. He thought democracy was on the march with the Red Army. General Alan Brooke, the chief of the Imperial General Staff, thought that FDR was in Stalin's pocket at Teheran, but Roosevelt hoped that he had outwitted Stalin, creating conditions for his metamorphosis from dictator to democrat.[68] Forrest Davis, a writer for the *Saturday Evening Post* who had his stories approved by the White House, reported after Teheran that Roosevelt's plan of cooperation for the postwar world hinged on Stalin and that Stalin had bought into his "great design."[69]

From the Soviet point of view, the decisions of Teheran imposed no obligation on Moscow regarding the growth of democracy or the holding of elections in the Baltic States or Poland, and the decisions were final and not open to renegotiation. There could be no new negotiations on Poland or the Baltic States. These were now internal matters for the Soviet Union to settle, although Stalin understood that Roosevelt could not publicly endorse Soviet actions because of his domestic problems. Stalin was looking forward to what other territories he might obtain. The opportunity for expansion was unprecedented in Russian history. He was not going to miss this chance. He knew, too, that the Soviet Union had been accorded a formidable hand at Teheran, but he firmly believed that it was a just reward for the Red Army's sacrifice and the result mainly of the skill of his diplomacy rather than the incompetence of Roosevelt and Churchill.[70]

14

"The Russian Bear is Biting"

Harriman returned to Moscow immediately after the Teheran Conference. He was confident about the future. His spirits were buoyed when Stalin met with him on December 18 and told him that he now felt he knew President Roosevelt very well and that he was comfortable with him. The ambassador was thrilled that his intuition had been borne out. Roosevelt's charm seemed to have worked its magic once more. Harriman even had his daughter Kathleen and a newly assigned foreign service officer, John Melby, join a Soviet-led research team into the Katyn Forest massacre. Kathleen and Melby both concluded that the Germans had committed the atrocity, and Harriman quickly endorsed their conclusion and so informed Roosevelt and Hopkins.[1]

Problems soon developed, and the new ambassador found it difficult to remain optimistic and in good spirits. There were, of course, the usual problems of visas, food shortages, insensitive Soviet bureaucrats, obtrusive NKVD agents, and social isolation. Being a good soldier, Harriman was prepared to accept these realities of life in Moscow. What really bothered him was that on the central issue of the well-being of the alliance, the Soviets were uncooperative, unfriendly, brusque, and at times downright hostile. They continued to intern American pilots who landed in Siberia after bombing Japan. Harriman tried to remain calm when asking Molotov to release them by explaining that it was not good for the morale of the American soldiers, and the pilots found it "somewhat difficult . . . to understand why they should be kept in the Soviet Union which they regarded as an ally of the United States."[2] Puzzled by the Soviet actions and attitude, Harriman told Churchill in early 1944, "The Russian bear is demanding much and yet biting the hands that are feeding him."[3]

The Soviets also refused to allow the United States to use airfields in Ukraine to shuttle-bomb Germany or to use airfields in Siberia and the maritime provinces to bomb Japan. Additionally, they would not share weather information, increase air transportation with the West, or justify their huge Lend-Lease requests in terms of need. Harriman reported to the State Department that the Kremlin was making demands for equipment that could not possibly be delivered within two years and thus could have no bearing on the war. He also wrote that the Soviets were making many unilateral decisions: they treated the Curzon Line as if it were the accepted border; they announced that the Pruth River was the border with Romania, which meant that Bessarabia and northern Bukovina were part of the Soviet Union; and they acted as if the Baltic States were Soviet territory. Most disturbingly, they refused to deal with the London Poles, whom they accused of being tainted with Fascism and hostile to the USSR.[4] Harriman, however, contributed to Soviet obduracy regarding Poland when, in a meeting with Molotov on January 16, he invited the Soviet foreign minister to outline Stalin's demands for a reconstituted Polish government. He wanted to settle the Polish issue because its successful resolution, with Polish and Soviet leaders in public agreement, would strengthen the alliance and boost American public opinion in favor of Roosevelt's leadership and reelection.[5] On February 2 Harriman informed Stalin "that the settlement of the Polish issue was primarily of course a matter for Marshal Stalin to deal with." He said that he would not defend the Poles and that the president had only "a superficial interest in Poland." Stalin replied that "the President does not need to be anxious" and that "American-Polish voters should not be concerned."[6] In March he stressed to Stalin that the Soviet Union could have its way in Poland but that it should be sensitive to American public opinion.[7] Harriman's approach, whether he realized it or not, was tantamount to encouraging Stalin to push hard for a Communist government in Poland rather than a negotiated settlement with the Polish government-in-exile.

Back in Washington, the State Department, which had become a backwater during the ascendancy of the military relationship, was increasingly disturbed by Soviet behavior. Hull cabled Harriman on February 9 that the Soviet government must choose between cooperation and its "unilateral and arbitrary methods of dealing with problems."[8] In addition, the Division of European Affairs within the State Department produced a number of studies in February and March which pointed out that Comintern activity, despite the dissolution of that body, was continuing in Europe and elsewhere and that the Soviet Union persisted in maintaining that there was "an irreconcilable chasm between 'socialism' and 'capitalism.'"[9]

On February 1 Stalin criticized Roosevelt and Churchill for not yet delivering the Italian ships promised at Teheran or some suitable substitute of American and English ships. The criticism was importunate, particularly since the Russians were doing no fighting at sea against the Germans, and the English and Americans, who bore the brunt of the sea war against Germany and Japan and supplied the Soviet war machine by sea, were trying to use the Italian ships to expedite the second front in northern France, which the Soviets wanted more than the Italian ships. Churchill thought it best not to answer Stalin's criticism and demands immediately, but Roosevelt announced at a press conference on

March 3 that Stalin was going to get one-third of the captured Italian fleet. Harriman, Churchill, and his military advisers, however, persuaded him to reconsider the offer, and soon Roosevelt simply acted as if he never said it.[10] The Kremlin, however, continued to press the issue, and in April the United States delivered the cruiser *Milwaukee* to the port of Murmansk as a substitute for the Italian ships.[11]

In late April Harriman left Moscow to brief Roosevelt on his impressions to date. He stopped in London to see Churchill on May 2 and found the British leader quite distressed over Soviet-Polish relations. Churchill argued that Stalin was unreasonable on Poland, but Harriman did not agree. The real problem, he explained to Churchill, was the anti-Soviet disposition of the London Poles. Churchill demurred, but Harriman persisted and urged the prime minister not only to recognize Soviet territorial demands against Poland but to accept a reconstituted government in Poland that would be shorn of anti-Soviet Poles and would pursue policies similar to Beneš's exiled Czech government.[12] Churchill, however, was not yet ready to accept a reorganization and still did not really think that the Soviets were going to colonize Poland. On April 1 he had cabled Roosevelt that, although the Soviets are "determined to find fault and pick a quarrel on every point, I have a feeling that the Soviet bark may be worse than its bite and that they have a great desire not to separate themselves from the British and American Allies." Wistfully, he concluded, "It may be that, while unwilling to say anything of a reassuring nature to us about Poland, they will in fact watch their step very carefully. This may be of great benefit to Poles in Poland."[13]

In Washington Harriman found FDR and Hopkins still firmly committed to the grand alliance with the Soviet Union. The president, according to Harriman, did not want to discuss problems with Moscow, and Poland was a taboo subject, at least until after the November election. FDR, though, wanted Harriman to tell Stalin that he would appreciate it if Stalin would give the Poles "a break." His immediate recommendation to Harriman was that he try to arrange another meeting between himself and Stalin, possibly in Alaska. His faith in the efficacy of face-to-face meetings was unshaken. He also shocked Harriman when he reiterated to him basically what he had told Cardinal Spellman in 1943, namely, that he "didn't care whether the countries bordering Russia became communized." Harriman did not want to go that far. He thought the best solution would be a Polish government that followed the Soviet lead on foreign policy but retained its domestic freedom, a model that he saw in the Beneš Czech government, which had already made its pact with Stalin in December 1943. He believed that the Polish government was unreasonable and informed Gromyko in Washington that the Polish issue "will probably be resolved only after the Red Army liberates Poland."[14]

One of the major reasons that Harriman returned to Washington was to obtain a seasoned expert as his second-in-command in Moscow. As the problems mounted with the Soviet Union, he felt more than ever the need for expert analysis. Kennan had been promised to him, but Hopkins forgot to inform the State Department after he became seriously ill with cancer. Harriman and Bohlen now took matters into their own hands. They invited Kennan, who was in Washington awaiting a new assignment, to dine in Harriman's room at the Mayflower Hotel. There they offered him the job, which Kennan quickly accepted. Kennan made it clear, however, that he was opposed to the administration's policy. Harriman responded that his opposition was no problem and that he himself, after a few months in Moscow, was no longer completely in line.[15]

Kennan's opposition, though, was more profound than Harriman's disenchantment. He returned to Moscow in late June 1944 and within weeks concluded that the nature and course of American policy toward Russia was fundamentally flawed and headed for disaster. He found Soviet suspicion of the West to be unchanged since the days of Bullitt. In fact, he determined that the relationship was more strained than ever. He reported that the secret police treated the U.S. representatives, despite the alliance, as spies and "dangerous enemies, to be viewed with suspicion and held at arm's length from Soviet citizens—lest we corrupt them." He also noted that the Russians did not mind "the resentment and sense of grievance" that their policy of suspicion and isolation engendered in foreigners. "We are being very successful these days," he was told by a Soviet acquaintance. "The more successful we are, the less we care about foreign opinion. This is something you should bear in mind about the Russian. The better things go for him, the more arrogant he is. That applies to all of us, in the government and out of it. It is only when we are having hard sledding that we are meek and mild and conciliatory. When we are successful, keep out of our way."[16]

Kennan was even more concerned that there was no plan to check Soviet expansion in Europe. In September 1944 he wrote Harriman, "The Kremlin finds itself committed by its own inclination to the concrete task of becoming the dominant power of Eastern and Central Europe. At the same time, it also finds itself committed by past promises and by world opinion to a vague program which western statesmen—always so fond of quaint terms agreeable to their electorates—call collaboration." The problem, Kennan continued, was that "the first of these programs implies taking. The second implies giving. No one can stop Russia from doing the taking, if she is determined to go through with it. No one can force Russia to do the giving, if she is determined not to go through with it."[17]

Harriman, who returned to Moscow on June 1, appreciated Kennan's sharp analysis, but he was hardly ready to act on it. He remained firmly committed to FDR's policy. He was boosted in his faith by the fact that on his way to Moscow he stopped in London and was told by Eduard Beneš that the Poles and the Soviets were secretly meeting in London and that a compromise Polish government was possible.[18] When he reached Moscow he was further encouraged by the fact that the Soviets allowed the Americans on June 2 to start shuttle-bombing Germany from three bases (Poltava, Piryatin, and Mirgorod) in Ukraine where American bombers could land, refuel, and rearm. Harriman considered this to be a major concession. His enthusiasm was not dampened by the simultaneous refusal of the Soviets to allow the Americans to use Soviet airfields to bomb Japan.[19]

The Allied invasion of France took place on June 6, 1944. The Soviets were delighted because it not only reduced German resistance on the eastern front, but it also meant that there would be no western armies competing with the Red Army for positions in Eastern Europe, and it took away the American option of being able to concentrate on Japan. Churchill, who had futilely pushed for an invasion of the Balkans, ruefully informed Eden on the eve of the D day invasion that the Soviets, once the West was committed in France, "will take every conceivable advantage they can of their position" and "will have the means of blackmail, which they have not at present, by refusing to advance beyond a certain point, or even tipping the wink to the Germans that they can move more troops into the West." He sighed, "Although I have tried in every way to put myself in sympathy with these Communist leaders, I cannot feel the slightest trust or confidence in them. Force and facts are their only realities."[20] Churchill saw some hope in involving the Turks in some way on the Allied side, even if it were short of war, but Stalin undercut him. On June 28 Molotov complained to Harriman that the American ambassador in Ankara, none other than Laurence Steinhardt, was supporting a British proposal to involve Turkey. He objected again on July 10 about Steinhardt's backing of the British. Finally, the American government agreed on July 22 not to treat Turkey as an ally as long as Turkey refused to declare war on Germany.[21]

In the afterglow of the invasion, Harriman found the Soviet leaders to be warm and friendly, but soon, to his chagrin, the smiles and warmth vanished over the wrenching problem of Poland. By the spring of 1944 Stalin had mounted a multifaceted campaign against the Poles. He attacked the Polish government-in-exile by claiming that it was pro-Fascist and imperialistic (he complained to Harriman that the Poles not only refused to recognize the Curzon Line but wanted to annex Vilnius, the capital of Lithuania). He also tried to address the fears of the Catholic Church, both in the United States and in Vatican City, that the advance of Communism in Poland meant religious persecution. In April he met in the Kremlin with the Reverend Stanislaus Orlemanski, a naive Polish-American priest, who announced to the world that there was no religious persecution under the Communists. Stalin also thought that the Orlemanski meeting would help FDR with Polish-American voters. He reinforced this aspect of his campaign by inviting another American Pole to the Kremlin in April, a certain Professor Oscar Lange, who was a respected economist at the University of Chicago but who also supported the Soviet line on Poland. Finally, he made an all-out effort to improve the image of the Moscow Poles as something more than puppets of the Kremlin. He described them as democrats who were fighting for Poland, unlike the London Poles. Harriman made little attempt to rebut any part of Stalin's campaign. He told Molotov that the Orlemanski-Lange trips would eventually have a favorable impact on American public opinion and he himself asked to meet with the Moscow Poles, thus conferring legitimacy on them.[22] The Polish government in London was up against a steamroller, and it had virtually no friends or advocates in Washington or London.

Even before the D day invasion Harriman informed Molotov that FDR was under an obligation to see the leader of the exiled Polish government, Stanislaus Mikolajczyk. Harriman was apologetic in tone, making it clear to the Soviets that FDR's meeting with Mikolajczyk was forced by the pressure of the upcoming election. Molotov replied that the Soviet government understood Roosevelt's position, that he had made it clear at Teheran. The Soviet foreign minister then pointedly asked, "Is there something new on this issue?" Harriman assured him that there was absolutely nothing new.[23]

FDR followed up with a letter to Stalin on June 17, explaining that he did not want to interfere in Polish-Soviet relations but that it would be helpful if Stalin could meet with the Polish leader, too. Harriman again used a concessionary tone on the Polish matter in a meeting with Molotov at the end of June.[24] He also told FDR that secret negotiations were under way between the Poles and Soviets for a compromise similar to the Beneš government, which was an additional reason, besides trust in Stalin's democratic evolution and the upcoming election, for the president's unwillingness to support Mikolajczyk or to become involved in the Polish issue.[25]

In any event, American demureness made it easy for Stalin to increase his demands on the Poles. He told FDR that he would be happy to see Mikolajczyk, but before he could recognize the Polish government, it would have to be reorganized to include "Polish politicians in the U.S.A. and the U.S.S.R. and especially Polish democratic leaders who are in Poland."[26] No longer was Stalin simply requiring Polish recognition of the Curzon Line. Now their government had to be recognized in such a way as to give pro-Moscow Poles the dominant positions. Roosevelt and Harriman did not balk at this new twist.[27] Hull informed Harriman that the president told the Polish prime minister that "Stalin did not wish to 'Sovietize' Poland and urged Mikolajczyk to have faith in the good intentions of Stalin."[28] Molotov, meanwhile, complained to Harriman that Mikolajczyk's trip to Washington appeared to be official. Harriman denied it.[29]

On July 27, while Mikolajczyk was en route to Moscow, the Soviets announced that they had signed an agreement with the Polish-Communist Committee of National Liberation, now set up in Lublin, to keep order in the "liberated" parts of Poland. Clearly, Stalin was not going to turn liberated Poland over to the London Poles, and when Mikolajczyk arrived in Moscow, Stalin told him that he would have to deal with the Lublin Poles. Harriman was nonplussed over this turn of events, but Kennan told him that the Russians were riding high and "will be confident they can arrange the affairs of eastern Europe to their own liking without any great difficulty, and they will not be inclined to go far out of their way either for the Poles or us." After Harriman talked with Mikolajczyk in Moscow, he informed Molotov that the Polish leader stood behind the Polish Constitution of 1935. Molotov shot back that Mikolajczyk was simply trying to appeal to the democratic tendencies of the American government, but in any event the Polish Constitution of 1935 was not democratic and was clearly Fascist. Harriman had no response.[30]

Kennan had another thought on Poland, but he didn't share it with the ambassador. He believed that the Soviets wanted total control in Poland in order to hide the crime of the Katyn Forest massacre. In the end he believed the London Poles were the leaders of a doomed government.[31]

August 1944 brought further disillusionment for Harriman on the Polish issue. On August 1, the people of Warsaw, led by the guerrilla army of the exiled government, the Home Army, rose up against the Nazis. They were motivated by the nearby presence of the Red Army, just across the Vistula River within sight of Warsaw. They were also motivated by the Polish-language radio broadcasts—originating from the Soviet camp—urging them to rebel and by the desire to show the world that the Polish people were willing to fight and die for their freedom and their homeland. The Poles, encouraged by the British, thought that they could count on assistance from the Red Army.[32] To the bewilderment and shock of the Poles, Americans, and British, the Red Army did not lift a finger to help the outgunned and outmanned citizens of Warsaw. It also prevented the few Polish divisions accompanying it from going to the rescue of the beleaguered city. When General Zygmunt Berling, the commander of a Polish division, tried to cross the river on his own, he was repulsed. For his impudence, he was given a low-level position in what became Communist Poland.[33]

Stalin also refused landing rights on Soviet-controlled airfields for American and British planes attempting to ferry supplies to the besieged Poles, and Soviet planes that controlled the skies over Warsaw suddenly disappeared for the duration of the uprising. Stalin denounced the Polish rebels to Roosevelt and Churchill as a "group of criminals."[34] By the beginning of September Warsaw was devastated and the Polish Home Army was broken. The Soviets then allowed western planes to use their airfields to drop supplies to the Poles, and Stalin called the situation "unsatisfactory."[35] But Polish resistance by then was virtually nil, and most of the supplies fell into German hands. The Red Army remained immobile for the next three months, allowing the Germans ample time to mop up the remnants of the Home Army. This guerrilla force, which had so effectively hampered the Nazi occupation of Poland, would not be a factor in the Soviet occupation, which possibly explained the Soviet actions. Over 250,000 Polish lives were lost in the uprising and its suppression.[36] The Soviets, however, defended their position by stating that the revolt was a "reckless adventure," that the Red Army had outrun its supply lines and could not move forward, and that crossing the Vistula River was more of an obstacle than the Soviets had anticipated. Even if the Soviet arguments were true, there was still, as historian Adam Ulam pointed out, much that the Red Army could have done to help the Poles *without* crossing the Vistula. Molotov also put the Americans on warning by informing Harriman on August 11 that the Polish business was distracting the Soviet Union from potential action against Japan.[37]

Kennan reported that the Embassy was in shock over the Soviet position. He said there was no doubt in Harriman's, General Deane's, or his own mind "as to the implications of the position the Soviet leaders had taken." Kennan stated, "This was a gauntlet thrown down, in a spirit of malicious glee, before the Western powers." In effect, Kennan went on, the Soviets were implying: "We intend to have Poland, lock, stock, and barrel. We don't care a fig for those Polish underground fighters who have not accepted Communist authority. To us, they are no better than the Germans; and if they and the Germans slaughter each other off, so much the better." As for American opinion, Kennan stated that it was clear to everyone in the Embassy that "it was a matter of indifference" to the Soviets what the Americans thought of their policy toward Poland. Kennan urged a full showdown with Soviet Russia. He felt that Stalin's policy in Warsaw showed the Kremlin's true colors and that the West had to make a stand. He wanted the United States to consider cutting off its military aid and support to the Russians. Kennan believed that Soviet Russia had lost its right, if it ever had any, to western aid because of its diabolical policy toward the Poles.[38]

Harriman did not follow Kennan's advice, but he did lash out at the Soviets for their brutal policy toward Poland. He demanded to see Molotov, but instead he was received by Vyshinsky to whom he bitterly complained about Warsaw. He also wrote Roosevelt, "I am for the first time since coming to Moscow gravely concerned by the attitude of the Soviet Government." It appears, he went on, Soviet actions are "based on ruthless political considerations." He also expressed his outrage over Soviet behavior to Hopkins.[39]

But the Soviets were not cowed by Harriman's representations, and Roosevelt was not moved by his premonitions. Molotov told him that if the American attitude did not improve, the Soviet Union would withdraw its permission for the American shuttle-bombers to use the three bases in Ukraine. When Harriman reported this threat, the State Department ordered him to curb his criticism because of "the importance of the continuance and smooth functioning of the shuttle bombing arrangements which should not in any way be allowed to be imperiled by this [Warsaw] question." Clearly no outrage, no tragedy could budge the "Hopkins Shop" or FDR from their tie to Stalin. In the words of one historian, "No episode in World War II is uglier in the light cast on Stalin's viciousness and Roosevelt's deference, if not actual cravenness, to Stalin than the Warsaw Uprising." Ironically, the American bombers at the main base in Poltava were virtually destroyed on the ground on June 22 when the Germans launched a retaliatory bomber raid. The Americans wanted to resupply Poltava after the Warsaw Uprising or, preferably, move the bases to Poland or Romania, but Moscow temporized and the shuttle-bombing ended in September 1944.[40]

In September 1944 Kennan offered Harriman a lengthy analysis of the Soviet Union, which Harriman passed on to Hopkins. Bohlen also received a copy from Harriman's personal assistant, Robert Meiklejohn.[41] The analysis was important because it examined the weaknesses and strengths of the Soviet Union and it provided insight into the present and future objectives of Soviet foreign policy, not only in relation to Poland but to Europe, the United States, and beyond. It followed closely upon his recommendation that now was the time to stand up to Soviet Russia.

Kennan stressed that the Soviet Union was a closed dictatorship. Many leaders, both Communists and non-Communists, had been purged in the 1930s. The group that remained revolved around Stalin. They were, like him, isolated, xenophobic, patient, and dissembling. Unlike him, they had no independent judgment. They were his virtual clones. None of them was identified with the western alliance. Most put "the preservation of a rigid police regime in Russia far ahead of the happy development of Russia's foreign relations." This left the West in a precarious position, according to Kennan, because it had no advocates within the Kremlin, and now that the second front was under way, it had lost leverage with Moscow.

Second, Kennan believed that the Soviet dictatorship had support from the people because of the victorious direction of the war but that there was a wall between the people and the government. The people tolerated the overbearing paternalism of the government, with its brutality, insensitive bureaucracy, and inordinate preoccupation with security, but they would not allow the government to shape or touch their souls and they hoped for a better day. This explained, according to Kennan, why the regime erected a wall between foreigners and its citizens and why there was always a feeling of tension beneath the enigmatic but seemingly unchanging face of Russia.

Third, Kennan stated that Soviet Russia was greatly weakened by the war but that its government would not be dependent on western economic assistance for reconstruction, national defense, or raising the standard of living. The Soviet government had absolute control over the economic wealth and labor of the country and would tighten the belts of its citizens and export gold, oil, timber, and other resources to keep its independence. Of course, Kennan pointed out that the Soviets would take aid that did not lead to a relationship of dependency. Kennan estimated that, without western aid, it would take Soviet Russia many years to rebuild its economy but that it would be done. Of course, he pointed out that some industry had been moved to the east and was not damaged by the war.

Fourth, Kennan said that American minds found Soviet Russia puzzling because Russia was a land where contradiction was the essence of life and where morality and reality had no basis in fact but only in the ever-changing will of those in power. Accordingly to Kennan, the Kremlin had no problem with the contradiction of allying with the United States, which was vocally opposed to imperialism and spheres of influence, and of pursuing a policy of expansion. It also had no problem with dissimulation or with the exploitation of weaknesses, confusion, and contradictions in the camps of its allies or enemies.

Fifth, Moscow believed that America's major war objective—collective security and international cooperation through a united nations organization—was naive and unrealistic. Moscow was carving out its own security in Eastern and Central Europe with its army as Germany collapsed. It would join such an organization for purposes of keeping western aid coming and preserving its new empire, but it would rely on its own power, not the United Nations, for protection.

Finally, Moscow was interested solely in expansion and power, not in cooperation with the United States and not in sharing power with other groups in Central and Eastern Europe. According to Kennan, Moscow was aiming for unilateral control throughout Eastern and Central Europe and planned to occupy Poland and as much of Europe as the Allies would allow. Kennan thought that the Kremlin wanted to set up Communist regimes, but the essential matter was the willingness of any government to follow the will of Moscow.[42]

The Kennan analysis and early recommendation that the United States should now challenge Soviet Russia flew in the face of the administration's policy. Hopkins, if he read the reports, did not act on them. Harriman, for his part, was influenced by them, but still could not bring himself to endorse policies that, if followed to their logical end, advised sobering up Moscow by taking a stand against it and possibly by attacking its weaknesses. He reported that when he wrote out cables urging a tougher policy, he ended up throwing them into the fireplace.[43]

Harriman instead found consolation in the theory of the divided Kremlin. The heart of the problem, he concluded, was that the Party and NKVD zealots were unhappy over Stalin's concessions at Teheran and were now pressuring Stalin to take a hard line. The Kremlin, according to Harriman, was divided into two camps: the hard-liners led by Molotov and Beria, and the soft-liners headed by Stalin. Stalin encouraged this view and explained to Harriman in September that he had misjudged the Warsaw Uprising.[44]

Nonetheless, Harriman had too much respect for Kennan's mind and was himself too much of a horse trader to change his ways. He cabled Hopkins that "to get a trading atmosphere into our negotiations over mutual assistance in the war is, as you know, most distasteful to me; but trading seems to be the language the

Soviets understand, and once commitments have been made in Washington we don't find them at all impressed by an obligation on their part to reciprocate."[45]

The ambassador thought that there was still one significant source of leverage that the Americans controlled, and this was the Soviet need for postwar reconstruction loans, credits, and equipment. Harriman stressed to Hopkins that this lever should be handled very carefully but that it could be used to influence Soviet behavior.[46] He cabled Hull that a loan was "one of the most effective weapons at our disposal to influence European political events in the direction we desire and to avoid the development of a sphere of influence of the Soviet Union over Eastern Europe and the Balkans."[47]

Of course, the United States was also counting on the United Nations to moderate Soviet behavior. Meetings had been going on at Dumbarton Oaks since the end of the Teheran Conference to hammer out the structure of the future United Nations, and the Americans were insisting that all major powers belong and, more important, that all members, including the permanent members of the Security Council, forego their vote, and thus veto, on issues in which they were involved. The Soviets, however, demanded that they retain the right to veto. Some American leaders thought that they might get the Soviets to alter their opposition if Washington appealed to them on the grounds that their opposition would fuel domestic criticism of FDR and his policies. In the middle of the Warsaw Uprising, FDR beseeched Stalin to tell his negotiating team at Dumbarton Oaks to be more reasonable.[48] Ultimately, the issue was left to further negotiation.

Kennan informed Harriman that the two major levers that the United States was counting on to influence the Soviet Union were unworkable or unenforceable. He told the ambassador that the Soviet Union would not be dependent on American reconstruction aid. They would take it, but they would not be influenced. Second, in regard to the United Nations, Kennan believed that the Soviet Union would only endorse a United Nations if it guaranteed U.S./U.K./Soviet hegemony, in other words, the end-of-the-war status quo. They saw "trickery" in the American idea that the permanent members of the United Nations Security Council should not have a veto on matters in which they were involved. The Soviet Union, he reiterated, wanted a sphere of influence where it could do what it wanted and with its allies' support, and then it would give similar backing to its allies' actions in their spheres.[49]

Kennan was struck by the naïveté of the American position. It failed to take into account Soviet determination to be an independent world power, Soviet belief that security was synonymous with control, and Soviet willingness to use revealed weaknesses as a way to extract additional advantages. Kennan said that he was particularly opposed to pleading "domestic political pressures, or the pressures of public opinion" to try to move the Kremlin. He recounted in his memoirs that he "had been shocked on being told . . . that FDR had once sent a private request to Stalin to use his influence with the American Communist Party to prevent it from supporting him, FDR, in a presidential election, lest this support prove embarrassing to him."[50]

Harriman was undoubtedly confused. He desperately wanted to implement FDR's policy of unconditional aid, cooperation, and friendship, but the Kremlin was unfriendly, uncooperative, and ungrateful. Its behavior during the Warsaw Uprising was reprehensible, but it soon became apparent to Harriman that it was not exceptional but, rather, part of a continuing pattern.

On September 10, the ambassador cabled Hopkins that during the past two months, the hard-liners in the Kremlin had gained power and American-Soviet relations had taken a startling turn. "The Soviets now appeared completely indifferent" to American interests and efforts to cooperate. "I have evidence that they had misinterpreted our generous attitude toward them as a sign of weakness, and acceptance of their policies." He warned Hopkins that "unless we take issue with the present policy there is every indication the Soviet Union will become a world bully wherever their interests are involved." Harriman was especially disturbed over Soviet policy toward Poland, but there was plenty of other evidence to indicate that the American policy of uncritical friendship and aid was not producing reciprocal policies in Moscow. The Kremlin continued to intern American pilots, refused in fall 1944 to allow an American convoy of five hundred trucks to cross the Soviet Union from Iran to China in order to support American bomber squadrons operating out of China against Japan, and vetoed all requests for American reconnaissance flights over Soviet-held territory. Nonetheless, Harriman remained optimistic. "I am disappointed but not discouraged," he said. "The job of getting the Soviet Government to play a decent role in international affairs is however going to be more difficult than we had hoped."[51]

General Burrows, the British military attaché, agreed with Harriman. He reported that the Soviet government was bounding with confidence and arrogance, that it was maintaining that the Red Army had defeated the Germans alone, that the Russians were the new "chosen race," and that westerners were portrayed as enemies. "Our policy of giving everything without return," he went on, "has played into the hands of those who advocate and are spreading" these ideas.[52]

On September 18 Harriman received an inquiry from Secretary of State Hull. He informed Harriman that Gromyko had suddenly become quite unreasonable, and Hull was wondering "whether Stalin and the Kremlin have determined to reverse their policy of cooperation with their Western Allies."[53]

In his reply to Hull, Harriman enlarged on his earlier explanation to Hopkins. He emphasized that he did not believe the Soviets had changed their policy of cooperation with the West, but that the West and the Soviet Union had different interpretations of what had been agreed on at the Moscow Foreign Ministers' Conference and the Teheran Conference. For example, Harriman wrote, the Soviet concept of a "friendly government" amounted to Soviet control of the government, which the West certainly never intended. In addition, the Soviet government thought that the United States agreed or acquiesced in everything it said or did at the conferences or elsewhere if the Americans did not immediately object.

What was needed now, the ambassador urged, was a strong but friendly quid pro quo policy. They should feel "our displeasure" when they were unreasonable. There was a strong antiwestern element in the Kremlin, he reported, that was determined "to protect the Russian people from almost all contact with and influence of western civilization and ideas." But Stalin and "the principal men in the Government" wanted good relations with the West, and the United States should encourage this group. The Soviet Union was a "strange country," Harriman reflected, but if the United States were patient, friendly, and, where necessary, forceful, it would evolve into a responsible power.[54] Harriman's position still reflected the influence of Roosevelt's "converging" philosophy, except that he now thought reciprocal actions rather than unconditional concessions were the key to the metamorphosis of Stalin's Russian empire.

Harriman was clearly beginning to listen to Kennan. Kennan had told him that the Soviets were essentially empire builders, seeking to seize as much territory as possible to guarantee their security. They had never changed, according to Kennan. They quite easily balanced the contradictory policies of expanding their empire and collaborating with the West. "As long as no second front existed, expediency suggested that the idea of collaboration be kept to the fore, the idea of spheres of influence rather in the background. But when the second front became reality, there was no longer any need for excessive delicacy. The resultant bluntness of Soviet policy has caused some surprise and questioning in the West."[55]

Litvinov, who had been removed as Soviet ambassador to the United States in 1943, shared some of Kennan's views. He informed Secretary Hull on May 7, 1943, before he left Washington, that the Soviet system was inflexible and that Stalin had a skewed perspective on western public opinion. On October 6, 1944, in an interview in Moscow, he told left-wing reporter Edgar Snow that Stalin was attempting to build an empire in Eastern Europe, even though this was leading to a rift in the alliance. "Diplomacy might have been able to do something to avoid [a split]," Litvinov told Snow, "if we had made clear the limits of our needs, but now it is too late, suspicions are rife on both sides." Litvinov was suggesting that Stalin was greedy and attempting to go beyond the legitimate security needs of the Soviet Union in expanding into Eastern Europe. Litvinov apparently was spared Stalin's revenge because Stalin "undoubtedly valued Litvinov's contacts in the West, and he may have thought the foul publicity abroad was not worth the execution."[56] Besides, the West did not act on his admonition.

Harriman was inching toward a change of policy, but Roosevelt and Hopkins were not. "There was little disposition in Washington," he later wrote, "to pick quarrels with the Russians." On his own authority, however, he and General Deane decided to experiment with the quid pro quo approach, much as Bullitt, Steinhardt, and Standley had, on a few minor matters. He reported his experiments were quite successful, and on September 29 he again pressed the policy on FDR.[57]

Roosevelt and Hopkins, however, remained unchanged. In fact, the desire to please Stalin stretched even to individuals. Victor Kravchenko, a member of a visiting Soviet purchasing mission, defected to the United States in 1944. Stalin complained, and Hopkins and Davies recommended that he be forcibly returned to the Soviet Union. Roosevelt had reservations, though, because he thought Stalin would shoot Kravchenko—an indication that FDR knew something about Stalin. Hopkins argued that once he was in Stalin's hands no one would know what would happen to him—an indication that he, too, knew something about Stalin. As it turned out, Attorney General Francis Biddle refused to extradite him partly because there was no legal basis to do so and partly because he was providing information to the Federal Bureau of Investigation. In 1946 Kravchenko published his autobiography, *I Chose Freedom*, a withering attack on Stalin's government.[58]

By the fall of 1944 it was quite clear that political, not military, considerations were dictating the movement of the Red Army. While Marshal Zhukov's army sat on the banks of the Vistula outside Warsaw, other armies drove into Romania and Hungary. Finland surrendered to the Soviet Union on September 19. If Moscow were primarily interested in the rapid defeat of Germany, military logic dictated a drive on Berlin. Instead, the Red Army carved out a huge zone of occupation throughout Eastern Europe. Churchill saw what was happening.

Following the Second Quebec Conference in September 1944, Churchill, with Roosevelt's blessing, flew to Moscow in October to try to arrive at some understanding with Stalin. Hopkins, however, whom Churchill mistakenly considered an avid Anglophile, persuaded the president that he should not allow Churchill to negotiate with Stalin on behalf of the United States. Harriman, on Roosevelt's instructions, immediately informed Stalin that the United States would not be bound by any agreements between London and Moscow. Stalin expressed surprise, since he assumed Churchill, after just seeing Roosevelt at Quebec, was coming to speak on behalf of the West.[59] Thus undercut, Churchill produced for Stalin his famous formula, which divided Eastern Europe into zones of influence: 50 percent influence each for the USSR and Great Britain in Yugoslavia and Hungary, 90 percent influence for the USSR and 10 percent for Britain in Romania and just the opposite in Greece, and, finally, 75 percent influence for the USSR and 25 percent for Britain in Bulgaria.[60] Harriman was invited to the formal meetings but not to the private ones where the division of Eastern Europe was proposed, but he did know in rough outline about the spheres of influence agreement and he described it to FDR before Churchill left Moscow.[61]

On Poland, Churchill hoped that the Soviets would be satisfied with the

Curzon Line as their border. He requested that Stanislaus Mikolajcyzk, the president of the Polish government-in-exile, come to Moscow. When he arrived, Churchill demanded that he accept the Curzon Line as Poland's border. Molotov told him in front of Harriman, Churchill, and Stalin that Roosevelt had accepted the Curzon Line at Teheran. Mikolajcyzk was shocked because FDR had told him in Washington that no decision had been made. When Harriman did not object, the Polish leader knew he had been betrayed.

Faced with such pressure, Mikolajcyzk equivocated in Moscow, but once back in London, he pleaded with his fellow Poles to accept Churchill's demand. When they turned him down unless Stalin first agreed to turn over Lwow and its oilfields to Poland, Mikolajcyzk resigned—another tragic blow for Poland. Of course, Stalin was already moving to set up his own Polish government, and Churchill was, at best, trying to save some role for the London Poles.

Harriman told Churchill in Moscow that he had no recollection of FDR unequivocally agreeing to the Curzon Line, and although he knew the president was leaning toward accepting it, he believed that FDR was hoping that Stalin would turn Lwow and its rich oilfields (which were east of the Curzon Line) over to Poland. Churchill stated that he, too, did not recall FDR's assent. When they brought this discrepancy up to Stalin at the next meeting, he dismissed it with the claim that Roosevelt agreed to it in a private meeting with him. A search of Bohlen's notes from Teheran did indeed produce evidence that FDR had agreed in a private talk with Stalin to the movement of the Polish-Soviet border, although without a specific reference to the Curzon Line.[62] Of course, Roosevelt had already told Stalin through the Davies-Oumansky connection in October 1943 that he would not stand in the way of Stalin's plans for the Polish-Soviet border or the Baltic States. Indeed, when Harriman outlined the spheres of influence agreement that Churchill and Stalin had worked out, FDR wired his general approval to Stalin and Churchill, although, as always, he remained uncommitted and reserved the right to disagree on specifics. But he definitely appeared to be backing off his initial reluctance to have Churchill negotiate on behalf of the West. Hopkins, too, relented. He met with Gromyko on October 10 and, while he said that the United States did not want to be presented with faits accomplis regarding the Baltic States, he also stressed "that the USA was not interested in the territorial situation in the Balkans," that this was an issue of interest, first, to the Soviets and, second, to the British, but that the president nonetheless wanted to participate in such territorial discussions.[63] As for Churchill, he was not being candid with Harriman. In his private discussions with Stalin, the main topic was not Poland but Soviet recognition of British preeminence in Greece and the Mediterranean. In the end, Churchill agreed to trade Poland for Greece, and Roosevelt appeared to sanction the arrangement.[64]

In light of Churchill's visit and FDR's tacit acquiescence, Stalin undoubtedly concluded that he had an agreement on Poland. He knew Roosevelt had a public relations problem with Polish-American voters, but the issue was settled before Yalta where it was effectively confirmed and made more palatable to western public opinion by dressing it up with phrases like *democratic politicians* and *elections.* Churchill's percentage formula, of course, could only be carried out by armies, and since England did not have an army in Eastern Europe, except in Greece as of October 1944, it could never claim its sphere of influence in Bulgaria, Romania, or Hungary. When the English complained to Stalin about their lack of influence in Yugoslavia, Stalin unctuously retorted that he, too, was dismayed because Tito, the leader of the Communist guerrilla forces, had cut him out and taken everything for himself.[65] Because England did not have an army in Eastern Europe and because FDR was unwilling to use force to support political ends, Churchill's percentage gambit was mainly histrionic except for two results: Stalin thought he had an agreement on Poland, and any backsliding was evidence that his western allies could not be trusted. Second, it helped to keep the Red Army out of Greece.

Of course, when Churchill went to Moscow in October 1944, the British and the Americans were in a weak bargaining position not only because they could not or would not use military power to support political ends, but also because they had already acquiesced in Stalin's annexation of all or part of independent states, the British as early as 1942, the Americans in late 1943. Eden summed up the problem in 1944: "Our powers of leverage are, I am afraid, much weakened by the fact that we have either in public or in private, already acquiesced in the strength of [Soviet] claims to the Baltic States and Bessarabia."[66]

When Bohlen saw Harriman's cable describing the deal between Churchill and Stalin, he flew into a rage. He later said that the arrangement was cynical and unrealistic. The Soviets could not be trusted, he asserted, and it was fantasy to believe that the Communists would share power according to some percentage formula. "A non-Communist Premier with Communist ministers would be like a woman trying to stay half pregnant," he claimed.[67] He was right, but the formula was an effort to try to save something in Eastern Europe.

Kennan outlined his view for Harriman in late 1944. He thought that the idea of spheres of influence was now the only realistic approach and that it had always been the Soviet objective. "Our people, for reasons which we do not need to go into, have not been aware of this quality of Soviet thought, and have been allowed to hope that the Soviet government would be prepared to enter into an international security organization with truly universal power to prevent aggression." The fact of the matter was, though, Kennan went on, the Soviets were carving out a sphere of influence in Eastern and parts of Central Europe, and "we are now faced with the prospect of having our people disabused of this illusion."[68]

In one of the meetings between Churchill, Stalin, and Harriman, Stalin wanted to know from Harriman what the USSR would receive for joining in the war against Japan. With that question in mind and with the disturbing pattern of Soviet behavior unfolding in Eastern Europe, Harriman returned to the United States for consultation in October. He found Roosevelt tired and weak, suffering from an enlarged heart and congestive heart failure as well as the rigors of the election campaign. To Harriman's dismay, FDR refused to deal with the problems in Eastern Europe. He "consistently shows," Harriman noted, "very little interest in Eastern European matters except as they affect sentiment in America."[69]

Roosevelt told Harriman that he found European matters difficult and he preferred to leave them to Churchill and Stalin while he concentrated on the Pacific arena. He was willing to recognize the Curzon Line if the British, Poles, and Soviets also agreed, but he told Harriman to tell Stalin that it would be a nice gesture if the USSR would give up Lwow. Harriman was struck by the naïveté of FDR's remarks. He was still convinced that he could "persuade Stalin to alter his point of view on many matters that, I am satisfied, Stalin will never agree to." Harriman jotted down in his notes, "I do not believe that I have convinced the president of the importance of a vigilant, firm policy in dealing with the political aspects in various Eastern European countries when the problems arise."[70]

As for the Far East, FDR was willing to give the Soviets something for their involvement against Japan, but he did not know what. He told Harriman to find out what Stalin wanted. He readily agreed to a Soviet request for a stockpile of two to three months' supply of military equipment to be used against Japan. Before Harriman left, FDR expressed his desire for another meeting with Stalin. The Soviet dictator informed Roosevelt on October 9 that he could meet with him and Churchill in the Black Sea area. The president asked that the location be switched to a Mediterranean site—Cyprus, Malta, or Athens.[71]

Back in Moscow Harriman informed FDR that Stalin wanted to meet him in the Black Sea region. Roosevelt again asked for a meeting in the Mediterranean, suggesting now Alexandria, Jerusalem, or Athens. He was hoping for a location with a warm climate because of his poor health. Also, a trip by Stalin to the Mediterranean would have balanced his earlier trip to Teheran. Stalin, however, was adamant, even to the point of informing Roosevelt that his physicians advised him against travel to the Mediterranean. Faced with such obduracy and anxious to impress Stalin once more, Roosevelt agreed in December to meet the Soviet leader at Yalta. Harriman also reported Stalin's demands in the Far East. He wanted Sakhalin, the Kurile Islands, the lease of Dairen and Port Arthur, and the lease of the Chinese Eastern Railroad in Manchuria. As Stalin had indicated at Teheran, the Soviets wanted control of Manchuria and the repeal of the Treaty of Portsmouth. Since Stalin was putting forth such huge demands, Harriman thought it opportune to elicit from him an agreement to allow American bombers to shuttle-bomb Japan from bases in the Soviet Far East. Stalin agreed that some program could be worked out, but he never acted on it—a recurring pattern that Harriman and General Deane found exasperating.[72] General Deane summarized the problem in the relationship in a letter to General Marshall:

> The truth is they want to have as little to do with foreigners, Americans included, as possible. We never make a request or proposal to the Soviets that is not viewed with suspicion. They simply cannot understand giving without taking, and as a result even our giving is viewed with suspicion. Gratitude cannot be banked in the Soviet Union. Each transaction is complete in itself without regard to past favors. The party of the second part is either a shrewd trader to be admired or a sucker to be despised.
>
> Our files are bulging with letters to the Soviets and devoid of letters from them. This situation may be reversed in Washington, but I doubt it. In short, we are in the position of being at the same time givers and supplicants. This is neither dignified nor healthy for U.S. prestige.[73]

Harriman also cabled the State Department in January 1945 that Molotov had told him that the Soviet Union would be willing to accept a $6 billion loan at 2.25 percent interest over thirty years from the United States. Oddly, Harriman noted, the Soviet foreign minister acted as if he were doing the United States a favor.[74] To Harriman's surprise, Treasury Secretary Henry Morgenthau Jr. and his assistant, Henry Dexter White (later shown to be a Soviet agent),[75] wanted to improve the Soviet terms and give the USSR a credit line of $10 billion at 2 percent for thirty-five years. Obviously, the president's policy was to be continued into the postwar period. Roosevelt himself set the tone in a message to his new secretary of state, Edward Stettinius, on January 5, 1945: "It is my desire that every effort be made to continue a full and uninterrupted flow of supplies to the U.S.S.R."[76] The British considered Stettinius to be "Stalin's biggest (if unconscious) asset in the Allied camp."[77] He was pro-Soviet, but he took his marching orders from Hopkins and Roosevelt.

With victory on the horizon, Harriman spent part of his time before the Yalta Conference trying to interest Prince Janusz Radziwill, a Polish aristocrat who was in Moscow secretly working as a Soviet agent, to join him in business deals in Eastern Europe and the Soviet Union, especially in mining and railroads. Harriman's willingness to countenance plans of self-aggrandizement rather than focus on the political future of Eastern Europe fit the Marxist profile of a capitalist. Pavel Sudoplatov, who hosted a luncheon for Harriman on the eve of Yalta for the purpose of discussing Soviet policies in occupied Eastern Europe, including a willingness to allow religious toleration, was amazed that Harriman was mainly interested in business deals and in making sure that there would be enough vodka and caviar at Yalta.[78]

Just before the Yalta Conference, Kennan penned a note to Secretary Stettinius that argued forcefully against the president's preoccupation with personal ties to Stalin. The behavior of Soviet officials, he wrote, "is not influenced by games of golf or invitations to dinner. Their egos have usually taken a pretty thorough subduing before the individuals themselves even appear on the international scene. Persons abroad who have to deal with them will do better to study carefully the ideological conceptions in which they have been trained rather than to bother about their individual propensities. There has been no more common nor more fateful mistake in the judging of Russian matters by our people . . . than the efforts to explain all Soviet phenomena in the light of reactions to the personality of the individual."[79]

Roosevelt's faith in personal ties as a way to influence Stalin was known to the Soviet dictator. The president had written Stalin on March 18, 1944, that they could meet "as old friends." According to Sudoplatov, who prepared the psychological reports for Stalin on the American delegation at Yalta, Stalin knew that personal friendship was the key to manipulating the president. He knew Roosevelt had no concrete plans for Eastern Europe other than friendship with Stalin. Even more telling was Hopkins's testimony to Gromyko in October 1944 that there would be "no differing opinions" between Roosevelt and Stalin when they met. Harriman also reinforced to the Soviet government the vital importance of the personal tie between Roosevelt and Stalin.[80]

15

"The Russians Have Given So Much"

Yalta looms large in the history of American-Soviet relations. It represents the climax of Roosevelt's policy of attempting to cooperate with the Soviet Union. Roosevelt was sick, and within two months of Yalta he was dead. Hopkins was also sick, and during the Yalta Conference he had to drag himself out of bed to attend sessions. But sickness and weariness do not explain what happened at Yalta. It was, rather, the logical end of Roosevelt's policy of uncritical friendship and unshakable belief that Stalin was developing, *mutatis mutandis*, into a liberal democrat rather than being and remaining an ideological opponent competing for power and advantage. Yalta was a natural consequence of Churchill's visit to Moscow in October 1944, of Teheran in 1943, and of FDR's long-term desire to trust and gain the confidence of Stalin. It was also, of course, as Kennan stressed, a result of the American tendency to view war as a way to eradicate evil rather than to achieve limited and realistic objectives.[1]

By February 1945 it was clear that the wartime alliance, always strained and cold, was entering perilous waters. Roosevelt, increasingly depressed and perplexed by the failure of his policy to transform the alliance into friendship, had settled on a simple formula at Yalta to change matters: he would try to accommodate the Soviets in what they argued were their legitimate security needs. He would also charm Stalin to the point where Stalin would implicitly trust him. Then he would involve the Soviet Union in the United Nations and through that institution help it to cope with its traditional suspicion and to grow and accept a position of leadership in a world moving toward democratic socialism.

He wrote Churchill a short but revealing note on September 27, 1944, that the Soviet Union must belong to the United Nations and that "it should be possible to accomplish this by adjusting our differences through compromise by all the parties involved. And this ought to tide things over for a few years until the child learns how to toddle." Reluctant to deal with the nitty-gritty details of how to protect and to implement his dreams and his hopes, how to guarantee freedom and independence for the peoples of Europe and Asia, he decided that the United Nations could solve the welter of confusing demands and aspirations welling up in 1945. The key to making it effective, he was convinced, was to persuade the Soviet Union to join what would be the successor to the League of Nations. The president, in historian Warren F. Kimball's view, "never changed this approach." In fact, Kimball argues that "the child" that FDR referred to, rather than being the United Nations, "could just as well have meant the new, more reasonable, more liberal Soviet Union that FDR hoped would emerge from the war."[2]

Roosevelt attempted to impress Stalin at Yalta by using the same tactics that he had demonstrated at Teheran. He again confided his political problems to Stalin. He stressed that American troops could not remain in Europe for more than two years, a revision from his earlier statement at Teheran that they would leave Europe immediately after the war, but still a position that surely pleased Stalin. Once again he attacked the British and Churchill, so that Stalin would know that the Anglo-Americans were not "ganging up" on him. He urged Stalin to propose a toast to the execution of 50,000 German officers, knowing it would antagonize Churchill. He told Stalin that Germany must be ruthlessly punished and that he "was more bloodthirsty now."[3]

Inscrutable and passive, Stalin listened. Roosevelt twisted this way and that as he tried to find some common ground with the dictator of the Kremlin, but he never really understood him. Stalin needed Roosevelt and American industry to defeat Hitler, and he would have made some accommodations to guarantee that assistance. However, he was not pressured to make any changes, except for some loose talk about future collaboration. He received massive amounts of aid with no strings attached. He had to assume, as Kennan told Harriman, that the aid was given to benefit the giver as much as the receiver.[4] There was absolutely no reason to alter his suspicion of the United States or to hold back on the expansion of the Soviet empire.

The alliance was clearly one of convenience established to deal with the common problem of Hitler. Now that the reason for its coming into being was gone, there was really nothing to sustain it. Stalin was more interested in the expansion and consolidation of the Communist system in Europe and Asia. He did not care if Roosevelt understood him or if he understood Roosevelt. His goal was power. He would agree with such sonorous documents as the Declaration of Liberated Europe, which promised elections, self-determination of peoples, and human rights because it was good propaganda and made his western allies happy, but certainly not because he believed in them or planned to implement their ideals in his sphere of influence.

Stalin knew that the real key was the disposition of the armies, and at Teheran he had obtained a guarantee that the western armies would start at the opposite end of Europe, as indeed they did in June 1944. By the time of Yalta the Red Army appeared to be on the verge of occupying most of Eastern Europe itself. Romania switched sides and joined the Red Army's offensive against Hungary on August 23, 1944. Bulgaria had a confusing endgame. It declared war against the Axis, tried to sign a cease-fire with the United States and England, but ended up at war with the Soviet Union. Bulgaria had the distinction of being the only country simultaneously at war with the Axis and the Allies. On September 8, 1944, it officially surrendered to the Red Army and joined it in a western offensive against Austria and Hungary. Germany pulled out of Serbia in August 1944 after Romania and Bulgaria turned against it because its flank was now exposed. Tito's partisan forces, unable up to then to force the Germans out of Serbia, soon filled the Serbian vacuum. Hungary and Austria were still available for possible western occupation, but the Red Army was bearing down on them, and Stalin wanted demarcation lines separating the two converging forces that would essentially exclude the West from Hungary and Austria as well as from the rest of Eastern Europe.

Kennan decided by February 1945 that it was too late to do anything meaningful about Soviet expansion in East Europe. He was concerned about Western Europe and more convinced than ever that the only solution was now spheres of influence. He asked Bohlen, who was at Yalta, "Why could we not make a decent and definitive compromise with it—divide Europe frankly into spheres of influence—keep ourselves out of the Russian sphere and keep the Russians out of ours?" Containment of the Soviet Union was necessary, he emphasized, but first it was necessary to define a "limit for Russian expansion and Russian responsibilities." Given the vast differences in goals and traditions between the United States and Russia, he even thought privately that a "compromise peace" with Germany was preferable to a postwar alliance with Soviet Russia.

Bohlen's reply reflected the administration's continued faith in Stalin and its public abhorrence of spheres of influence. He told Kennan that Soviet Russia had to be watched. But given the exigencies of the war and America's democratic traditions, there was not much the United States could do to control the Soviets if they should prove to be expansionist and uncooperative. "Either our pals intend to limit themselves or they don't," Bohlen told Kennan. "I submit, as the British say, that the answer is not yet clear. But what is clear is that the Soyuz [Soviet Union] is here to stay, as one of the major factors in the world. Quarreling with them would be so easy, but we could always come to that."[5]

Roosevelt still thought that he could control events by cultivating a friendship with Stalin. He still believed that he could change Stalin into a follower of Woodrow Wilson by pouring aid into the USSR. He was disinclined, even fearful, to make demands on Stalin, which, according to Kennan, simply convinced Stalin that Roosevelt needed him more than he needed Roosevelt.[6] From the very beginning of the American-Russian relationship, when Stalin was weakest and most vulnerable, when the Germans were storming across the plains of Ukraine, Belorussia, and Russia, he made demands of Roosevelt, and Roosevelt complied. FDR did everything in his power to make Stalin a permanent friend and ally.

Stalin, however, did not befriend Roosevelt, because Roosevelt was dangerous. Roosevelt presided over the most powerful country in the world. Stalin was leading a country which, to be sure, had a huge military force but which also had been devastated by war and torn apart by dissension and outright political opposition. The Germans had ravaged the industrial and agricultural base of Ukraine, and many millions of Soviet citizens, to say nothing of the citizens of the Baltic States, had initially welcomed the Germans as liberators. Tens of thousands of Red Army soldiers had been captured by the Germans, and Stalin could not be sure if they had surrendered voluntarily or involuntarily. He knew that his totalitarian government had been shaken, and he also knew that the people had not fought for him and Marxism-Leninism but for their homeland and against Nazi excesses. He was also aware that citizens expected better conditions and a better life than had existed under collectivization in the 1930s. He knew that contacts with the West had inevitably grown during the war, despite his best efforts to curb them. He could not tell Roosevelt of his fears. He could not inform Roosevelt that friendly ties with the West would destroy his dictatorship. He could not detail the weakness of the Soviet economy. He could not even admit publicly that the USSR would not have defeated the Germans without American Lend-Lease equipment and the military assistance of the western allies.[7]

In 1941 Stalin told Hopkins that Hitler's "greatest weakness was found in the vast numbers of oppressed people who hated Hitler and the immoral way of his Government."[8] It was certainly true of Hitler, but it was even more descriptive of Stalin.

Stalin's goals were fairly clear. He wanted to restore his dictatorial power throughout the Soviet Union and to hide the weakness and vulnerabilities of his empire. Second, he wanted to extend his system to the new territories where his armies were. Finally, he wished to be poised to take advantage of whatever opportunities were available to spread the Soviet system in the wake of the political collapse of Germany and Japan. Stalin decided to keep the Soviet Union on a war footing and take a hostile attitude toward the United States.[9] Hostility was the only policy that opened up the possibility that Washington would be impressed with Soviet strength, as opposed to concentrating on Soviet internal weakness, would adopt a defensive policy, and ultimately would allow Stalin to hold the initiative in both his empire and the international arena. Stalin had to be encouraged by the ignorance and naïveté that the American leaders had demonstrated heretofore. He knew from espionage sources that the American government did not have a solid plan for Eastern Europe. He also had a spy, Alger Hiss, who worked for the State Department, in the American delegation at Yalta. Undoubtedly Hiss simply confirmed what Roosevelt and Hopkins were already trying to do publicly: please the Soviet Union. In fact, Roosevelt and Hopkins, one Soviet official believed, included Hiss in their coterie of advisers precisely because he had excellent contacts with the Soviet government and was pro-Soviet.[10]

Roosevelt could afford to talk about his fears and problems. He was frank and openly invited Stalin to exploit his candidness, which Stalin did, but the United States was so strong that it could overcome FDR's mistakes by applying its power if it chose. The Soviet Union, though, was genuinely weak. Stalin could exploit the differences between Roosevelt and Churchill, carefully use the image of Soviet strength to cajole, and take advantage of Roosevelt's apparent dupability. But he could not bring real force to bear because the United States could lash out and destroy him. At Yalta it was much better for Stalin to remain silent about Soviet weaknesses and problems and let the western leaders continue to be impressed by the might of the Red Army. An image of strength would guarantee that Stalin's voice would be heard and that Roosevelt's desire to impress him would continue.

The Soviet demands were explicit. Stalin wanted Poland to be placed under Soviet authority. He was determined to snuff out Polish independence, although he couched his plan in terms of Soviet security. The western leaders did not seriously oppose his design. In fact, they had assented to it before Yalta. At the conference it was now formally agreed that the USSR's border would be the Curzon Line and that Poland's western border would be the Oder-Neisse Rivers, although the statesmen could not reach agreement on whether it would be the Western Neisse or the Eastern Neisse. The Soviets preferred the former because it would give the "Communist" government of Poland more territory—part of Silesia—and dump millions of German refugees into the western occupation zones of Germany. The Soviets, in addition, demanded that the western leaders abandon the London Poles and recognize the Lublin Communist government as Poland's legitimate government. They promised to hold free elections and to include democratic leaders in the Lublin government, but they also made it clear that they would define what a "democrat" was and that the Red Army would remain in occupation. It was eventually agreed that the Lublin government would be "reorganized" and that Molotov, Harriman, and Clark-Kerr would undertake the reorganization in consultation with the Lublin government and "other democratic leaders from Poland and from abroad." Harriman realized that such negotiations would be difficult. He told Bohlen at Yalta that in dealing with the Russians, "You always have to buy the horse twice."[11]

Stalin also laid claim to the Baltic States, and at Yalta the western leaders did not even bother to discuss these lands. They were swallowed without an obituary. Romania, moreover, was to be harnessed to expand the Stalinist system south and to guarantee Stalin's control over part of the traditional route connecting Turkey and the Balkans to Russia. The Soviets had simply announced earlier that Bessarabia and Bukovina were part of the USSR, and no one objected at Yalta. They did agree to hold an election in Romania, as in other occupied countries, but what kind of election could be held with the Red Army in occupation? From Stalin's point of view, there was no doubt that a Communist government would sit in Bucharest.

Beyond those issues, Stalin took what he could get. The opportunities were truly dazzling. There was no other power on the continents of Europe or Asia to stand in the way of Soviet expansion. The Americans were stronger, but their homeland was far away, their soldiers would be leaving Europe within two years, and they were rather gullible. The Soviet Union, despite its own weaknesses, was the dominant power in Europe and Asia and logically could dictate to both continents.

Stalin agreed with the American desire to reduce Germany to impotence. The division of Germany and Berlin into zones of occupation was confirmed at Yalta, although the previously agreed upon division was altered, at British insistence, to allow the French to carve a fourth zone out of the American and British zones. Germany was to pay reparations, and the formula worked out was that the total amount due would be $20 billion with half of that going to the USSR and the other half split among the other Allies. The Soviet Union also annexed part of eastern Prussia, including the warm water port of Königsberg. The Soviets, moreover, wanted two to three million German workers to help rebuild the Soviet economy.

Austria and Vienna were similarly divided into four occupation zones, although Austria was considered a victim rather than an ally of Germany. Chances were also excellent that the Soviets could grab Bulgaria, Hungary, and Czechoslovakia. The Red Army was occupying those countries, and thus it would be difficult for the West to block Soviet power there. The Soviets agreed to free elections, but they undoubtedly assumed that everyone knew that soldiers and voters do not mix. The point was proved in Hungary where the Communists did eventually allow a genuine free election after the war. The Communists lost the election, but it made no difference. The Communists remained firmly in power and thereafter avoided the embarrassment of free elections.

As for the Far East, Stalin could not expect much, for the Soviets were not even in the war against Japan. They still rigidly abided by the nonaggression treaty that they had signed with Tokyo in April 1941. Nonetheless, Stalin floated out far-reaching demands: Sakhalin Island, the entire archipelago of the Kurile Islands, Outer Mongolia, and virtual control of Manchuria by Soviet use of Manchuria's two great ports, Port Arthur and Dairen, and its railroads.[12] Roosevelt did not balk at the Soviet stipulations. In fact, he thought it was the price that had to be paid to involve the Soviets against Japan. Accordingly, he agreed to convince Chiang Kai-shek to accept these incredible terms which, in effect, amounted to restoring the Russian position in the Far East between 1900 and 1904 to the Soviet government. Needless to say, there was no chance that Chiang Kai-shek could resist the American leader. Indeed, the Nationalist Chinese wanted an agreement with Soviet Russia to help check the Communist Chinese.

What did the United States obtain for its efforts in the war? The Soviets agreed to join the United Nations, but only after they had neutralized it. After Teheran they soon came to realize that the United States seriously sought as its major objective in the war the creation of the United Nations. Just before Yalta it was agreed that the permanent members of the Security Council would have the right to veto decisions. Churchill confided to Stalin in October 1944 that he also wanted the veto. With that concession, the organization became virtually harmless from the Soviet perspective, so the Soviets shrewdly began to object to the way the Americans were proposing that the body function in order to ply meaningful concessions from the United States.

Andrei Gromyko, the Soviet ambassador in Washington, also served as the Soviet delegate to the Dumbarton Oaks Conference in 1944, which was working on the structure of the United Nations. He demanded that the veto be extended to procedural questions and that the Soviet Union be granted sixteen seats in the General Assembly to cover all of its republics. The Americans could not understand his unreasonableness and brusque manner. The answer was revealed at the Yalta Conference. Here the Soviets suddenly agreed to accept the American proposals on voting procedure and reduced their demand from sixteen seats to three seats, one each for Ukraine, Belorussia, and Lithuania. The Americans were so elated by the Soviet concessions that they readily accepted them before the Soviets had a chance to reduce their demands further to only two seats, which is what they eventually did anyway, since it would have been rather embarrassing to have the newly digested state of Lithuania represented in the United Nations.

Stalin made one other demand at Yalta. He wanted all Soviet citizens repatriated to the Soviet Union whether they desired to return or not. The western leaders quickly assented, and when the time came, they complied completely, even though they were puzzled as to why they literally had to force Soviet citizens to go back to the USSR.

Roosevelt, Hopkins, and Harriman all thought that much progress was made at Yalta. They came away convinced that the Soviets had made concessions. Hopkins told Roosevelt at the end of the conference, "Mr. President, the Russians have given in so much at this conference that I don't think we should let them down." Hopkins's specific comment was in reference to the debate over reparations, but it was indicative of the tenor of the American approach at Yalta and was exactly the response the Soviets were hoping to elicit by their tough bargaining on unessential issues like the number of Soviet seats in the General Assembly. The president was convinced that a foundation had been laid for future cooperation and friendship with the Soviet Union. An exultant Hopkins told his friend Robert Sherwood, "The Russians had proved that they could be reasonable and farseeing and there wasn't any doubt in the minds of the President or any of us that we could live with them and get along with them peacefully for as far into the future as any of us could imagine."[13]

Harriman, however, was not quite as optimistic, and his lack of enthusiasm became more pronounced when he returned to Moscow. Kennan, of course, was likewise pessimistic. He thought that the Yalta Conference's references to the reconstitution of the present Polish-Communist regime "on a broader democratic basis" and the organizing "of free and unfettered elections . . . on the basis of universal suffrage and secret ballot" smacked of "the shabbiest sort of equivocation, certainly not calculated to pull the wool over the eyes of the western public but bound to have this effect." He further emphasized to the ambassador that the extension of Poland's border into Germany would so turn the Germans against the Poles that Poland "must become, by the unalterable logic of events, the military, economic, and political responsibility of the Soviet Union."

In the weeks following Yalta a chill wind blew across the West from Moscow, confirming the pessimism of Harriman and Kennan. In March the Kremlin consolidated the power of the Communist provisional government in Poland. There was no evidence that "free elections" were in the offing or that the Allies would have a formative role in constructing the new government. Harriman and Clark-Kerr met on a continuing basis with Molotov after the Yalta Conference to build the new Polish government, but they got absolutely nowhere. Molotov refused to bring in the London Poles for advice and counsel and argued that the Lublin government, now called the Warsaw government, was to be the core of Poland's government and that it had veto power over any proposals. Kennan, who served as Harriman's translator "through the many hours of unreal, repetitious wrangling with Molotov," had no doubt "that it was all a lost cause."[14]

The Soviets also demonstrated unbearable crassness toward American prisoners of war whom the Red Army had liberated. When Roosevelt complained that the Soviets were not releasing or properly caring for these POWS or allowing them visitors, Stalin replied that the glorious Red Army could not be bothered with "odd officers."[15] Stalin also informed FDR on March 27 that Molotov had to attend a session of the Supreme Soviet of the USSR and thus would not be able to go to the inaugural meeting of the United Nations in San Francisco. It was a cruel blow to Roosevelt, who had based his war aims on Soviet participation in the United Nations. The Soviets also arrested sixteen Polish guerrilla leaders from the Home Army whom, with American assistance, they had identified and to whom they had promised safe conduct. Harriman reported that Allied POWs were being robbed by Russian soldiers and that the Red Army was engaging in wholesale atrocities against the citizens of Eastern Europe, especially women. He reported that the Czech leader Beneš, who was collaborating with Stalin, urged the Czechoslovakian people to tolerate the brutality because the Red Army troops "have gone through hard times."[16]

Stalin's harshness and defiance were undoubtedly tied to ideology and to the arrogance of being the dominant military power in Eastern Europe. But he was probably also upset that his two allies were essaying, through their support of the London Poles and their insistence on an election, to go back on their earlier accord or acquiescence on Poland. Indeed, FDR was retreating. He was not doing so because he was dropping his emollient approach toward Stalin. Rather, in the opinion of Warren F. Kimball, he did not want the embarrassment of Poland, specifically his endorsement of a Soviet sphere of influence there, which Stalin refused to sugarcoat with even a specious election, to turn American public opinion against him, the United Nations, and an international activist role for the United States. And Churchill, in Kimball's opinion, was equivocating, because he had already cashed in on his part of the bargain when the British army instead of the Red Army occupied Greece, and now he was hoping to frustrate Stalin's plan in Poland by goading the United States into action to protect Poland, because he knew it would play well with both Conservative and Labour constituencies in the election that would have to be called after Germany's imminent surrender. He did not want to confront Stalin directly himself because of the deal that he had cut with the Soviet dictator in Moscow. He simply deluged the White House in March with missives demanding that Roosevelt stop Stalin.[17]

This sense of betrayal over Poland could perhaps partially explain Stalin's sudden attack on Roosevelt in early April. The catalyst was a report, which Harriman perfunctorily passed on to Molotov, that a German military officer wanted to meet with western military officers in Berne, Switzerland, to arrange a surrender of German forces on the Italian front. The Soviets demanded to be present at the meeting, but the Americans, including Harriman, thought it was unnecessary since it was preliminary and concerned only the German forces in Italy. Harriman also thought it was good to give the Soviets some of their own medicine by refusing to be cooperative or solicitous. Harriman told General Marshall that the Soviets were demonstrating "a domineering attitude toward the United States which we have before only suspected. It has been my feeling that sooner or later this attitude would create a situation which would be intolerable to us." On April 3 Stalin accused Roosevelt of treachery, or lying, or being the dupe of his advisers. Stalin suspected that the British and Americans were working out a separate treaty with the Germans that would have ended fighting on the Italian front but continued it on the eastern front.[18]

The president, shocked and angry, replied with restraint on April 5, "It would be one of the great tragedies of history if at the very moment of victory, now within our grasp, such distrust, such lack of faith, should prejudice the entire undertaking after the colossal losses of life, material, and treasure involved."[19] On April 4 Harriman again urged the adoption of a mild quid pro quo approach. On April 6 he reported that the Soviet government was acting unilaterally in setting up governments in the territories under its control and could not care less about the United Nations.[20]

In the face of FDR's stern reply, Stalin now retreated and tempered his tone. Roosevelt accepted Stalin's apology and on April 13, the very day that he died, he dismissed the blowup in a cable to Stalin as a "minor misunderstanding" that was over and done with. Harriman was flabbergasted. He wanted a stronger protest. He asked FDR if he could not delete the word *minor*, but the president shot back that he wanted the word *minor* retained and that he considered the incident minor. In the end, FDR refused to alter course. He never abandoned his conciliatory approach toward Stalin, and because he did not, Churchill soon came around and accepted the other side of his bargain with Stalin, namely, Soviet control of Poland's government.[21] Word of Roosevelt's death reached the embassy on the night of April 13.

That Roosevelt's policy of collaboration and friendship now needed some modification seemed obvious to Harriman. He was thinking of a friendly quid pro quo, which was not precisely defined in his mind, but still he began pushing for some change as he became disillusioned in the weeks following Yalta. In late March, reflecting Kennan's growing influence, he began thinking that the United States should rebuild Western Europe to protect it from Soviet influence. This was the first indication of what would later become the Marshall Plan. On April 2 Harriman telegraphed Roosevelt that unless the United States adopted a policy of cordial reciprocity, "the Soviet Government will become convinced that they can force us to accept any of their decisions on all matters and it will be increasingly difficult to stop their aggressive policy. We may get some temporary repercussions, but if we stand firm, I am satisfied it is the only way we can hope to come to a reasonable basis of give and take with these people."[22]

However, Harriman did not want anything forceful done. He would not even allow Kennan to write critical reports about Soviet behavior because he thought it would damage the alliance. Kennan was kept under wraps, in fact, until Harriman finally resigned from the Moscow post in January 1946. Then Kennan let loose with the so-called Long Telegram, which criticized American policy and urged a policy of defensive expansion, later misleadingly called containment. Harriman thought the real problem lay with Molotov and his ilk in the Kremlin, and not with Stalin. He hoped that a slight change from unconditional aid might lend support to the Stalin team, which wanted good relations with the United States.[23]

Roosevelt's death was a shock to Harriman. He did not know Truman very well, and he was afraid that Truman might damage the American-Russian relationship. He now decided that he had to rush home to meet and provide advice to the new president. Secretary of State Stettinius, however, who had taken over for Hull, saw no reason for Harriman to be in Washington. The ambassador managed to force Stettinius to invite him by convincing Stalin to send Molotov to the United States as a way of showing sympathy over the death of FDR. Molotov's official purpose was to meet the new president and to attend the opening session of the United Nations in San Francisco. Harriman was now needed to provide information on Molotov. He left Moscow on April 17 in his private plane and reached Washington by the southern route in just over forty-nine hours, a new record. The Soviet foreign minister decided to go on his own by way of Siberia and Alaska.

Once in Washington, Harriman pushed the idea that FDR's policy had to be modified. He referred to the Soviet presence in Europe as a new "barbarian invasion of Europe," a phrase which he borrowed from an article that Bullitt had just published in *Life* magazine. On April 23 he met with Truman and some of his key advisers at the White House, including Stettinius, Bohlen, Secretary of War Henry Stimson, Army Chief of Staff General George Marshall, and Secretary of the Navy James Forrestal. Harriman talked mainly about Poland. He said that the Kremlin was opposed to free elections because it feared the Communist Poles would lose. The question before the United States now was whether it "should be a party to a program of Soviet domination in Poland."[24] The ambassador was moving toward a hard line.

Truman was inclined to listen to hard-line advice. Harriman was surprised to learn that Truman was actually reading and understanding the cables from the embassy in Moscow.[25] The new president wanted to follow generally FDR's plan for a grand alliance with Moscow. However, the world had changed dramatically in the month following Roosevelt's death. The Soviets seemed to be following a unilateral policy of setting up Communist regimes in the territories that they controlled in Eastern and Central Europe. Scientists in the United States had successfully split the atom and had transferred twenty-two pounds of enriched uranium from Oak Ridge, Tennessee, to Los Alamos, New Mexico, in late April to prepare for a test of the atomic bomb. This seemed to open up the whole question of whether or not the United States still needed the Soviet Union in the war against Japan. Harriman wasn't sure, but when he was briefed on the new weapon in late April, he thought it reduced the need for Soviet involvement. After he witnessed what the Soviets were doing in Eastern Europe, he was reluctant to allot them additional territory in Asia. He wanted Stimson to explore the issue. Stimson, however, did not take up the question. He was more concerned about the deteriorating American-Soviet relationship. He thought that the atomic bomb should be shared with the Soviet Union in order to entice it to abandon its insecurity and hostility and open up to the global community.[26]

Truman did not directly face the stark choice of selecting the bomb over Soviet participation against Japan or vice versa. The bomb was so secret that policy options were never fully discussed by the American leadership. Both Truman and Stimson saw the bomb as a military weapon that would be used to shorten the war and save lives, both American and Japanese. And there was uncertainty over its effectiveness and consequences. The Americans would only have fissionable material left for two or three bombs after they exploded a test bomb, and even if they were as powerful as the scientists said, there was no guarantee that the bombs would explode when dropped or that the Japanese would surrender. The Japanese had a proven reputation for fighting to the death. In June 1945 the United States lost 48,000 soldiers taking Okinawa. The real choice that Truman and Stimson felt was before them was to see if they could get the Japanese to surrender by threatening them with the bomb and Soviet involvement.[27]

When Molotov arrived in late April in Washington, Truman did not mince words. He told the Soviet foreign minister that "Stalin has to keep his word" and that Washington was getting off "the one-way street." He stressed that the United States wanted good relations with the Soviets, but he also demanded that the Soviets live up to their agreements at Yalta, including free elections in Eastern Europe. He pointed out that Poland was a symbol of the possibility of future American-Soviet collaboration. Molotov was insulted and said no one had ever talked to him that way. He obviously was excluding Stalin, who would put his wife in prison in 1948.[28]

Harriman was taken aback at Truman's bluntness. In fact, he later pinpointed it as the beginning of the cold war, but he didn't disagree with the central message. He flew out to San Francisco and there sounded the warning that the Soviet Union was building an empire in Eastern Europe and that the United States had to act to prevent the possibility of a domino effect. Kennan, who was now running the embassy in Harriman's absence, released a barrage of telegrams describing the Soviet threat. Truman found the cables convincing.[29] When the war officially ended on May 8, he approved an order to discontinue Lend-Lease aid to the USSR, because the Soviets had not yet entered the war against Japan.[30] Harriman had been urging that aid be used as leverage, but he was not expecting the cut to be so rigid and legalistic. Truman, to be sure, had signed and understood the order, but he, too, did not anticipate the effect of its immediate application. When the Soviets and many American commentators bitterly complained about this unfriendly act, he was shocked. He now decided that following the advice of the hard-liners had landed him in trouble. He immediately reinstated the aid, and he and Harriman blamed the problem on overzealous subordinates.[31]

By May Harriman began to worry that there might be too dramatic a swing against the Soviet partnership. Polls showed that in February 1945 the American public believed that England was the major problem in the alliance, but by May it held that the Soviet Union was the major problem.[32] Polls were fickle, but Harriman did not like the direction. He decided with Bohlen that a summit meeting between Truman and Stalin might improve the relationship.

Harriman immediately informed Truman that "Stalin was not getting accurate reports from Molotov or any of his people and as a result had grown deeply and unjustifiably suspicious as to our motives which he probably thought were designed to deprive him of the fruits of victory." In other words, Stalin was not the problem but the solution. Truman must go and meet Stalin face to face, Harriman argued, and resolve these difficulties. Harriman was backed up by Joseph Davies and Charles Bohlen. Truman bowed to their experience.[33]

Truman actually had been thinking along the same lines after the disturbance set off by the discontinuation of Lend-Lease aid to the Soviet Union. In fact, he told Molotov that he wanted to meet Stalin in Moscow.[34] A tripartite summit was needed in the wake of Germany's defeat, and it made sense to Truman that he should meet informally with Stalin and Churchill before the summit to get to know them both, but he did not want to leave the country just then because he wanted to know the results of the atomic bomb test, although his official reason was that the budget was before Congress. He had called in Joseph Davies for advice. Davies condemned the emerging hard-line approach and said that Stalin was a reasonable man. Truman then asked Davies to go to Moscow to see what had to be done to improve the relationship, but Davies begged off. When Harriman and Bohlen heard that Truman could not leave immediately for a meeting with Stalin, they recommended that Truman send Harry Hopkins.

Truman decided to send Hopkins, even though he was very ill and near death. At the same time, he sent Davies to London to tell Churchill that he wanted to meet Stalin alone before the meeting of the "Big Three" at Potsdam and that he would not first stop in London to avoid the appearance of "ganging up" on the Soviets.[35] Truman was now following the Roosevelt line.

Churchill balked at a separate meeting between Truman and Stalin. From his point of view, it was "an affront, however unintentional, to our country after its faithful service in the cause of freedom from the first day of the war." He also disagreed with the implication "that the new disputes now opening with the Soviets lay between Britain and Russia." Churchill also did not like the phrase "ganging up" as characterizing any meeting between him and Truman. From his point of view, "Britain and the United States were united by bonds of principle and by agreement upon policy in many directions," and they "were both at profound difference with the Soviets on many of the greatest issues." Churchill undoubtedly was also astonished at the emissary that Truman sent to him. The British prime minister had a very low opinion of Davies and considered him to be "most sympathetic" to the Soviet regime.[36]

Before Hopkins and Harriman left for Moscow, it was decided that Soviet violations of Yalta to date would be overlooked, such as the establishment without elections of Communist governments in Romania and Bulgaria. Bohlen, who also went to Moscow with Hopkins and Harriman, summarized the approach on April 19, 1945, in a memorandum to the secretary of state. Under the Yalta agreement, he wrote, the USSR "is hardly fulfilling its obligations. We are, however, more interested in getting Soviet agreement to apply in the future the principles of the Yalta Declaration than in insisting on a review of Soviet action."[37]

In Moscow, Hopkins and Harriman did a lot of talking about friendship and American public opinion and groped for some explanation for the decline in American-Russian relations. Harriman pointed out that Truman wanted to continue Roosevelt's policy of friendship, and Hopkins's presence in Moscow, a man who was "one of the leading proponents of the policy of cooperation with the Soviet Union," was proof of that desire. Harriman also explained that the British were not included because "the United States and the Soviet Union should talk alone on matters of special interest to them," which was to say that London would simply be presented with faits accomplis. Stalin readily agreed to exclude the British. In fact, he blamed the deterioration of the American-Soviet relationship on England.

Stalin spelled out the immediate problem in American-Russian relations rather simply: the United States had to recognize the Communist government of Poland, and it had to agree that the Soviet Union had the right to have "friendly" governments on its borders. Hopkins and Harriman declared that the United States wanted the Soviet Union to have "friendly countries all along the Soviet borders," and as for Poland, they said that the United States "had no special interest in Poland and no special desire to see any particular kind of government." Harriman fully realized that "friendly" governments meant Communist governments.[38] The difficulty, they explained to Stalin, was that Poland was "a symbol of our ability to work out problems with the Soviet Union." In effect, they informed Stalin, the nub of the dilemma was American public opinion. They then invited Stalin to come up with the "diplomatic methods" necessary "to settle this question, keeping in mind the feeling of the American people."

Stalin replied that if that were the American position on Poland and the other countries along the borders of the Soviet Union, then there were no problems. And he had a solution for the Polish issue. The Soviets would give four minor posts to Polish leaders not identified with the Warsaw government, maybe even one to a pro-Soviet American-Pole, such as Oscar Lange from the University of Chicago. Hopkins and Harriman thought that solution would work and that the United States would then accept the government in Warsaw.[39]

Hopkins and Harriman also raised the question of the sixteen Polish leaders who had been arrested by the Soviets after they had been promised safe conduct. Stalin turned aside the query by informing the Americans that the Soviet government had information about crimes that these men had committed that was not available to the West. But he guaranteed that they would be given fair trials. The Americans were satisfied with this response. "The business went, I think, very well," Hopkins told Beaverbrook, "and I am sure those Polish prisoners got off easier than they otherwise would have."[40] Two of the Polish leaders died in prison before the year was out.

The final issue was the war against Japan. The Soviets found it hard to understand why the United States kept trying to involve them in a war which the Americans had virtually won. When Molotov visited the United States in April 1945 to attend the first session of the United Nations, he diffidently asked Truman "whether the agreements in regard to the Far Eastern situation made at Yalta still stood."[41] Even though Truman assured him that they did and that "he intended to carry out all of the agreements made by President Roosevelt," the Soviets were still suspicious. Stalin informed Hopkins and Harriman that the Soviet Union would be in position to enter the war by August 8, 1945, but that the "actual date of operation would depend on the execution of the agreement made at Yalta concerning Soviet desires." Otherwise, he explained, it would be difficult "to justify entry into the Pacific War in the eyes of the Soviet people." Harriman assured him that "the Soviet Union would re-assume Russia's historic position in the Far East."[42]

Stalin wanted Chiang Kai-shek to agree to the loss of territory that the Americans had promised at Yalta. He was not interested in having the Chinese Communist Party replace Chiang Kai-shek's government because then the Soviets could not take part of China's territory and would be faced with a united Communist state not dependent on the Red Army for its continuation in power. It would be much easier to manipulate and control the Chinese—both Nationalist and Communist—if a weak Chiang Kai-shek, propped up by the Americans, stayed on.[43] Stalin was simply waiting for a formal agreement ratifying the Yalta concessions. However, he would not stay out of the war and promised territory if it appeared that Japan would surrender. He must have been puzzled by the American insistence that the Soviet Union become involved because the United States controlled the water and air space around Japan. The Americans also had a secret weapon that Stalin knew about.[44]

American leaders, though, believed that the United States would still have to invade Japan with significant casualties, and they didn't know the impact of the bomb. They also believed that the Japanese would not surrender. From that perspective Soviet involvement, despite the Soviet actions in Eastern Europe, seemed to offer the hope of ending the war early and reducing the number of casualties.

Hopkins took advantage of the trip to Moscow to consult with Kennan, whose reputation in Washington was growing. He asked him if the United States could improve on its deal with Stalin over Poland. Kennan replied that it was the best that could be achieved but that the United States should not endorse the Soviet action in Poland.

"Then you think it's just sin," Hopkins queried, "and we should be agin it."

"That's just about right," answered Kennan.

"I respect your opinion," said Hopkins, "but I am not at liberty to accept it."[45]

At the beginning of July, Washington extended diplomatic recognition to the Communist government of Poland. The British soon followed suit.

Kennan wanted the United States to accept the reality of divided spheres of influence and get on with the job of rebuilding Germany. Harriman, Churchill, Stimson, and McCloy all agreed. In fact, Churchill had described the reality of Europe with his "Iron Curtain" metaphor in a memo to Truman in May 1945. After the Hopkins visit to Stalin seemed to produce a solution for Poland, Germany emerged as the new source of American-Soviet friction.

When Edwin Pauley, a businessman and Democratic fund-raiser from Oklahoma, arrived in Moscow in June to begin discussing the implementation of the reparation clauses of the Yalta agreement, both Harriman and Kennan were against setting a precise amount for the Soviets. Kennan believed that the Russians would loot whatever they wanted from their zones without an accounting, and Harriman saw firsthand on his way to Potsdam in July that Kennan was absolutely correct. As it turned out, no agreement on reparations was reached during the Pauley negotiations, so the matter was put on the Potsdam agenda. A major problem was that the Soviets had shifted Poland's border to the Western Neisse in Germany unilaterally, and this move complicated the whole question of reparations.

Harriman was weary of the Soviets, but he hoped that the Hopkins agreement on Poland and the impending meeting between Truman and Stalin would halt the deteriorating partnership. He saw no reason, though, to weaken the western zones of occupied Germany to rebuild an uncooperative Soviet Union. He was also skeptical of Stimson's idea that a nuclear partnership between the Soviet Union and the United States would make Moscow amenable to working with Washington.[46]

The American delegation at the Potsdam Conference included Truman, Harriman, Stimson, Davies, Bohlen, Marshall, McCloy, Pauley, and the new secretary of state, James Byrnes. James Forrestal also showed up before the conference ended. Churchill represented the British at first, but he was replaced by Clement Attlee after losing an election to the Labour Party during the conference, an unforeseen consequence of Truman's decision to delay the summit meeting. Stalin was there with Molotov and the Red Army.

The warriors justifiably congratulated themselves on their victory over Germany. Then they got down to work. The occupation of Germany that had been worked out at Yalta was confirmed. France was given a zone in both Berlin and western Germany that was carved out of the American-British zones. The Soviets did not object to including France, providing they did not have to share any of their occupied territory with the French. Reparations remained a problem because of accountability, and although a new formula was hammered out at Potsdam, it was soon abandoned. The Americans and British agreed to accept temporarily, until a formal peace conference was held, the Western Neisse River as Poland's border with Germany. They also agreed to accept Soviet annexation of the Königsberg (soon to be renamed Kaliningrad) region of eastern Prussia. Davies had a direct hand in formulating the concessions to the Soviets on the Western Neisse border and the new reparations formula.[47]

Truman's main goal at Potsdam was to obtain Moscow's involvement in the war against Japan. Stalin confirmed that the Soviets would enter the war around mid-August, and Truman looked forward to what would be, in his mind, the crushing blow that would force the Japanese to surrender.[48]

There was another blow that the Americans were preparing. The world entered the atomic age when the United States and its British and Canadian allies successfully tested the atomic bomb on the second day of the conference. The bomb was now a military option against Japan. Truman informed Stalin of the new weapon and was relieved when Stalin did not ask for details. Truman and the other Americans assumed that the Soviets were basically ignorant of atomic technology. In fact, the Soviets had been working on their own bomb since 1942 and had a spy by the name of Klaus Fuchs at the heart of the American-British research team that developed the bomb. After Truman informed Stalin of the successful test, Stalin ordered the Soviet research team to accelerate its efforts.[49]

On July 25 Stimson gave the order to prepare to drop the atomic bomb on Japan. A vaguely worded warning was issued at Potsdam to Japan to surrender or face "prompt and utter destruction." Moderate Japanese members of the cabinet were sending out peace feelers that sought to modify the unconditional surrender demand to include Japan's right to retain the institution of the emperor. The Americans, however, believed that the Japanese militarists would fight to the end and that unconditional surrender was the only option.[50]

With the conclusion of the Potsdam Conference, Harriman thought that the American-Russian alliance was back on track. He wondered about the prudence of allying with Moscow again in a second war, but the die was cast. On August 6 an atomic bomb was dropped on Hiroshima. On August 9 a second bomb was let loose on Nagasaki. Stalin decided not to wait now. He called Harriman and told him that the Soviet Union had declared war on Japan on August 8. Japan offered to surrender on August 10. It wanted to retain the emperor. Stalin, whose troops were pouring into Manchuria, wanted unconditional surrender, but Harriman said the United States would accept Tokyo's offer. Stalin agreed, but he wanted to negotiate on who should be in charge of the occupation. Harriman was outraged that the Soviets, who had been fighting for less than two days, would challenge the right of General Douglas MacArthur to preside over the Japanese surrender. On his own authority, he told Stalin and Molotov that there was nothing to negotiate, that MacArthur was the supreme commander. The Soviets quickly accepted Harriman's verdict.[51]

With the end of the war, Harriman decided that his usefulness in Moscow was at an end. Besides, he and Secretary of State Byrnes did not get along. In October at the foreign ministers' meeting in London he showed up to discuss his resignation after Byrnes refused to invite him. Byrnes, however, talked him out of it. He enticed Harriman by the thought that he might be able to persuade Stalin that cooperation with the United States, rather than unilateral action, was the better approach for Moscow, the United States, and the world. Byrnes told him that Truman would write a letter to Stalin outlining the choice and that this communication would provide Harriman with a reason to meet with Stalin and determine whether there was a chance to save the wartime alliance.

Following his meeting with Byrnes, Harriman toured Europe and returned to Moscow convinced that it would be a travesty to turn Eastern Europe over to Moscow. Armed with his letter from Truman, Harriman visited Stalin at his favorite Black Sea resort in Gagra. He laid out the choice before Stalin: cooperation or unilateral action. By the second day, Harriman realized that Moscow had decided that a postwar alliance with the United States was not to its advantage. Back in Moscow he soon began gathering evidence that the Soviets were acting unilaterally and pursuing a policy of expansion. In a cable to the State Department in November he reported that the Kremlin had tightened its control in Romania and Bulgaria, introduced Chinese Communist troops into Manchuria, stirred revolution in northern Iran, and pressured the Turks to grant Moscow bases at the Dardanelle Straits. He groped for an explanation and ultimately decided that Soviet policy was the result of Moscow's insecurity over the atomic bomb.[52] Litvinov, Maisky, and Gromyko evidently believed or hoped that the relationship between the Soviet Union and the West established during the war would persist into the postwar period, but Stalin had a different idea.[53]

Harriman's analysis reached Washington just before Secretary Byrnes was to depart for Moscow for another foreign ministers' meeting in December. The agenda included problems in Eastern Europe, Japan, Iran, and elsewhere and a discussion of policies to control the atomic bomb. Byrnes was fully prepared to discuss sharing nuclear secrets with Moscow in return for safeguards against the development of nuclear weapons by other nations.

Byrnes was joined by Harriman, Bohlen, and Kennan at the Moscow meeting. Once the meeting got under way, the Soviets did not seem to be interested in the bomb. They quickly accepted an American proposal to set up an atomic control commission under the auspices of the United Nations if the commission reported to the Security Council, where they had a veto, rather than to the General Assembly. The Americans agreed to the Soviet stipulation. However, the whole agreement was rather vague and open-ended.

What the Soviets were really interested in was western recognition of the governments of Romania and Bulgaria. Stalin promised to include a few non-Communists in the governments in exchange for recognition. Byrnes decided to accept the Soviet offer. Harriman, Kennan, and Bohlen were dismayed. Kennan warned that the agreements being negotiated over Eastern Europe were "fig leaves of democratic procedure to hide the nakedness of Stalinist dictatorship." Harriman recalled later that Stalin's concessions "did not alter the brute facts or in any way loosen his grip on Eastern Europe." When Stalin was informed that his unwillingness to evacuate northern Iran would be brought up at the United Nations, he nonchalantly replied, "This will not cause us to blush."[54]

Harriman was now at wit's end. He felt that he had done everything possible to further the American-Soviet alliance. He could not now explain Moscow's actions. He felt his usefulness in Moscow was at an end, and he formally departed in January 1946. He turned the embassy over to Kennan, who remained in Moscow until late summer. In the months immediately following Harriman's departure, Kennan outlined in a series of cables, including the famous "Long Telegram," a new policy, eventually called containment, to explain Soviet behavior and to guide American diplomacy in the postwar world. An inquiry from the Treasury Department asking why the Soviet Union was not participating in the International Monetary Fund and the World Bank, and a speech by Stalin on February 9, in which he declared that the world war was caused by the inherent contradictions of capitalism, that the world was divided into Communist and capitalist camps, and that war was a possibility between the camps, were the immediate causes of the Long Telegram. In effect, Kennan explained that insecurity was the root cause of Soviet expansion and that the Americans should respond with reciprocity, dynamic leadership in those parts of the world where there were political vacuums, and efforts to restore their own economic and spiritual strength. He also favored the establishment of spheres of influence and the protection of those spheres where the United States had a vital interest.[55]

Kennan's emphasis on Russian insecurity was supported by Litvinov who in June 1945, still serving as assistant foreign commissar in Moscow, complained to Edgar Snow that the United States should have opposed Soviet expansion in the Balkans and Eastern Europe three years earlier. "Now," he lamented, "it's too late and your complaints only arouse suspicion here." In June 1946 Litvinov told CBS correspondent Richard C. Hottelet that the "root cause" of the cold war was Soviet Russia's antiquated belief that security was synonymous with expansion and control of territory: "The more you've got the safer you are." "Suppose the West were suddenly to give in and grant all of Moscow's demands?" Hottelet asked. "Would that lead to goodwill and easing of the present tension?" Litvinov quickly responded, "It would lead to the West's being faced after a more or less short time with the next series of demands."[56] Roosevelt's policy of appeasement, in other words, never had a chance of working.

Of course, at the heart of the security concerns for Stalin was the Communist system. Kennan thought ideology was only a "fig leaf" for traditional inferiority and insecurity, but the fact remained that Stalin's world outlook was framed by Marxism-Leninism. It was not simply a case of protection but of expansion of the system, because ultimate security would only come when the world or the centers of global power were ruled by Communist governments led by Moscow. Traditional Russian xenophobia played a role, but ideology was the shoal that held up Stalinism, accounted largely for Stalin's suspicion of the West, and sunk Roosevelt's policy of friendship and accommodation. Ideology was the main reason why all western efforts—British and American—to befriend Stalin were doomed. Ideology alone explained the profound cynicism in Ivan Maisky's remark that he always added Allied and Nazi losses in the same column.[57] "Stalin, like other Soviet leaders," Harriman recalled in 1981, "believed in the ultimate inevitability of a confrontation between the Soviet system and 'capitalist imperialism.' He did not trust us, and he could not believe that we would deal with him fairly."[58] Of course, Stalin did not have a master plan for setting up Communist governments in Europe and Asia.[59] He had no idea what he could get away with in the face of American power. He certainly hoped for the expansion of his system, but he backed down when faced with the prudent application of American power.

Truman found Kennan's analysis and conclusions persuasive and compelling, and he was inclined to listen to Kennan. He did not like what the Soviets were doing in Eastern Europe, Iran, Turkey, or Greece. When Byrnes returned from the foreign ministers' meeting with the tentative agreement to recognize the Communist governments of Bulgaria and Romania, Truman rejected it out of hand, saying that he wanted free elections in Eastern Europe and that he was "tired of babying the Soviets." He also demanded that the Soviets live up to their 1941 agreement and withdraw from Iran. The United States introduced the Iranian issue at the United Nations and implied a connection between recognition of the Soviet satellites and Soviet withdrawal from Iran. On March 5 Churchill made his famous "Iron Curtain" speech in Fulton, Missouri.

The Soviets announced in March that they would be departing from Iran in May, and they did. Perhaps they withdrew because of the line drawn between Eastern Europe, where events were still fluid, and Iran. Perhaps they saw a growing coordinated effort by the United States and Britain to work against the Soviet Union and they decided that withdrawal from an area of less vital interest might nip the concert in the bud. For Truman, however, the picture now seemed to be clarified. Firmness in the face of Soviet expansion or aggression produced results.[60]

Ultimately, the United States, following Kennan's advice, began to fashion the policy of containment. It was a short-term measure to halt the hemorrhage from Roosevelt's policy of appeasement. Under Truman and Eisenhower, it became a desperate but successful effort to expand pluralism in Western Europe, Japan, South Korea, and Taiwan. Under Kennedy, Johnson, Nixon, Ford, and Carter, it became a desperate and unsuccessful effort to defend the status quo in Asia, Africa, and Latin America. The weakness of containment was twofold: it did virtually nothing to help the beleaguered people of Poland, Hungary, Romania, Bulgaria, Czechoslovakia, Yugoslavia, China, Korea, the Baltic States, Bessarabia, Bukovina, Ukraine, Belorussia, Georgia, Armenia, Azerbaizhan, Kazakhstan, Uzbekistan, Tadzikistan, Turkmenistan, Kirghizia, and Russia itself—all of whom were suffering under Stalinism. It also left the initiative in international affairs in the hands of the Soviet Union, a closed, authoritarian state that paraded as a modern, progressive model for world development, and thus exposed the United States to the risk of nearly draining itself as it furiously raced, like the proverbial fireman, from one corner of the world to the next, to put out Communist conflagrations, failing with general consistency to distinguish between vital and peripheral interests and between ideological conflicts and indigenous social-economic-political problems.

The American ambassadors in Moscow, with the exception of Joseph Davies, and their chief advisers had, at one time or another, recommended a different solution: a policy, based on principled behavior, leadership, tradition, and the prudent use of power that sought to expand pluralism globally. Not only did they provide ample warning and advice on how to avoid or at least reduce the whole tragedy of Stalinist expansionism, but they outlined a way to promote pluralism. Alas, their premonition was discounted and their advice was rejected.

Epilogue

When FDR told Bullitt in 1943 that Stalin was not the rapacious dictator whom Bullitt had described but a security-conscious ally who wanted to work with the United States on establishing democratic governments in Europe and elsewhere, he was speaking from the point of view of a Wilsonian idealist who had adopted the theory of convergence. He and his key aides believed that democratic internationalism was spreading everywhere and that collective security in international institutions was the best way to achieve peace in the new global order. They thought that Soviet Russia was a country evolving toward democratic socialism. It had some rough edges due to its history and mistreatment by the Western Powers, including the United States, and so it had to be treated tenderly and much of its pathological behavior had to be overlooked or tolerated. The best and most logical policy for the United States to follow was patience, accommodation, friendship, and unilateral aid and appeasement during the war, until democracy took root in the Soviet Union and Stalin's suspicion of the West dissipated. Roosevelt, Hopkins, Davies, and Faymonville played leading roles in the development and implementation of this policy.

Bullitt, on the other hand, was reflecting the view of experience. Before going to the Soviet Union, he and FDR's other ambassadors to Stalin's Russia had agreed with Roosevelt's optimism. Some were more enthusiastic than others, but all hoped for a productive relationship with the USSR. After being posted in Moscow and actually experiencing the Soviet Union firsthand, all the ambassadors and advisers, except Davies and Faymonville, disagreed vehemently with FDR's approach and orientation. They determined that Stalin was not a democrat or even an evolving democrat. They believed that Stalin's regime was an abomination that had to be checked and ultimately changed. They recommended that the United States adopt a policy that responded to that reality, a policy of reciprocity and consistent, principled behavior, including the prudent use of force, on issues or practical problems where the United States and the Soviet Union shared interests and where the self-interest of the United States could be promoted. They also counseled against any long-term relationship with Stalin since he was, in their view, fundamentally at odds with the principles undergirding American society. They advised the use of forceful action and balance of power to check or change the Kremlin's behavior in order to bring it up to the minimum standards of civilized nations, to protect or promote American vital interests, and to produce a more compatible government in Moscow.

Bullitt, Steinhardt, Standley, Harriman, Henderson, Kennan, and Bohlen turned out to be right. Stalin's government did not hide its nature from the American representatives at the Moscow embassy or, for that matter, from Roosevelt. In day-to-day relations with the United States, it showed itself to be paranoid, secretive, arrogant, aggressive, unfriendly, xenophobic, and ruthless. Russia had traditionally kept its distance from foreigners, especially from the West, for reasons of external security and internal control, but Stalin's regime additionally harbored a suspicion of capitalist/imperialist governments that could organize in coalition against it and of democracy as a form of government. Stalin was a power-hungry revolutionary who found it difficult to cooperate with Roosevelt in even minimal matters, like releasing from prison captured American aviators or providing weather and logistical information on the eastern front, even though such help would have supported FDR's portrait of him as an ally and friend during World War II. Stalin believed that Communism was the way by which Russia was to guarantee its security and remain a world power. The importance of the alliance with the United States, aside from whatever technical and economic benefit he could obtain, was its value in controlling the external threats, Japan and Germany. That was the principal reason why the Soviet Union wanted a relationship to begin with and why it formed the alliance with the United States once Hitler attacked it. After these threats were gone or reduced, Stalin had very little use for the alliance with the United States. It was then a menace to him, and he wanted to reduce it by moving away from the United States, thus precipitating the so-called cold war. Of course, the Soviet Union paraded some of the shibboleths of democratic liberalism, since these were absolutely essential to maintaining popular support in the twentieth century even in such a highly centralized society as Stalin's Russia, but it remained essentially a totalitarian country.

The cold war, or the ending of the postwar alliance and the subsequent global rivalry between the United States and the Soviet Union, is actually a misleading concept. American-Soviet relations did not suddenly go awry in 1945 after a successful alliance against Germany, Italy, Japan, and their allies. Relations were never warm, easy, and trusting. Before World War II Roosevelt tried to build a friendly relationship of cooperation within the parameters of American isolationism and domestic opponents who viewed Stalinism as a threat to the United States and western values. He thought Soviet Russia and the United States were converging toward similar social democracies. Bullitt and Davies worked hard and followed a policy of accommodating Moscow when and where they could. The Soviets, however, did not respond. Bullitt gave up and soon saw Stalin's regime as an inherently dangerous government but nonetheless one that could be controlled with the proper application of "the carrot and the club." Davies, like Roosevelt, never gave up the illusion, and eventually he explained Stalin's offensive behavior, both domestically and internationally, as forced on him by internal or external pressures, including American callousness to the Soviet Union's needs as it essayed to transform itself into a modern socialist state.

During the war Roosevelt did everything in his power to turn Stalin's regime toward friendship with the United States. Steinhardt, Standley, and Harriman all labored to break down barriers between the United States and the Soviet Union. Steinhardt and Standley quickly tired of the unilateral nature of the policy and demanded reciprocity. Harriman held out longer for unilateralism, but he, too, concluded that FDR's one-way approach was not eliciting any change of behavior in Moscow. After the war, when the Nazi and Japanese threats were gone, Stalin no longer wanted the alliance if it meant internal openness. Of course, he would take American aid and money, but not if it translated into American strings and interference and demanded some reciprocity and verifiable accountability from him. He was not necessarily dedicated to setting up Communist governments in every country that the Red Army occupied if the United States should take a strong position against him, but he was for it if he could get away with it.

The United States was a danger because it was a democratic, capitalist state that had proved itself to be an awesome military force, many times more powerful than the Soviet Union. Stalin feared an open comparison of technological and military strength with the United States. Such a test would reveal to Soviet citizens and foreigners alike the hollowness of the propaganda that claimed that the Soviet Union was the leading state of the world. It would diminish and make futile many of the incredible sacrifices and sufferings that the Soviet people were enduring. It would also open Soviet Russia up to military challenges by foreign states. From Stalin's point of view, it was better to trumpet Soviet Russia's power, keep the people isolated from external information, and keep the foreigners ignorant about Russia's condition than to warmly embrace the United States as an ally. It was better to seek security through the expansion of power into regions bordering the Soviet Union in Europe and Asia and, beyond the neighboring countries, through defined spheres of influence and an accepted balance of power than to seek security through membership in a supranational organization that impinged on national sovereignty and exposed vital interests to democratic compromise and major power scrutiny.

Stalin's experience during the war with Roosevelt, Hopkins, and Davies certainly gave him reason to believe that he could outwit and outmaneuver the American leadership, despite his weakness and cowardice. Although he undoubtedly believed that his political and diplomatic strength against the United States was due to the superiority of his ideology, he also knew that his position directly benefited from the philosophical orientation of the American leadership—men who publicly spoke of ideals, morality, and partnership, but who were quite willing to appease him when he complained, demanded no quid pro quo in the relationship, and disregarded their ambassadors and specialists. Their supine approach opened the door for the growth of Stalinism and inversely weakened the opportunity for the expansion of democracy. Stalin saw that importunate demands and irascible behavior were consistently rewarded and that Roosevelt invariably catered to his whim and proved to be a diffident and expedient democrat.

Roosevelt told Secretary of Labor Frances Perkins during the war that he wished someone could inform him about Russia, that he did not know "a good Russian from a bad Russian."[1] He actually had a bevy of first-rate advisers daily informing him about Russia and explaining how to distinguish a good Russian from a bad Russian. But he cared nothing for the solid information coming from his experts. Instead, he relied on people who did not know Russia to confirm a priori beliefs that Stalinist Russia was evolving into a modernized, pluralist democracy. He sacrificed concrete advantage, vital interest, and the freedom of the citizens of other countries in vain pursuit of these beliefs. By their strange light Stalin was viewed as an evolving democrat, a righteous figure doing his best for his people, and Churchill was seen as an ossified imperialist, a leader of an empire in decline, albeit also as a dear friend who shared a common culture.

The representatives in Moscow and the experts on the Soviet Union in Washington, Joseph Davies aside, provided excellent information and analysis on Soviet behavior and on how to control that behavior. They offered solid recommendations for American policy, and even Davies can partially be excused for his distortions and fatuousness on the grounds that he was simply giving Roosevelt what he demanded.

Kennan stated that "the central function of the diplomat" was "to serve as a sensitive, accurate, and intelligent channel of communication between one's own government and another one."[2] The American ambassadors and the embassy staff generally fulfilled that charge. Some were better than others, but all except Davies showed themselves to be careful, intelligent, competent, and objective.

The best representatives, William Bullitt and Laurence Steinhardt, were close to career diplomats. They were intelligent, well informed about international affairs, and familiar with American and Russian history. They were excellent observers and reporters. Steinhardt was more detached than Bullitt and thus more objective in his evaluation of Stalinism, but neither Bullitt's emotionalism nor Steinhardt's detachment moved FDR to change course. Both men had common sense and the ability to see the big picture without getting caught up in the twists and turns of daily events. They worked hard on behalf of their government, had integrity and honesty in abundance, and demonstrated excellent communication and management skills. They also showed a penchant for analyzing information and eliciting the best work from subordinates and technically trained assistants. Bullitt was more visceral than Steinhardt, but only out of a desire to protect the president and alert him to the raw wickedness of Stalinism. Steinhardt and Bullitt showed that there is a great advantage in having American ambassadors in critical posts who are intelligent, self-confident, observant, and communicative. Both provided sound advice to Roosevelt about the Soviet Union.

William Standley and W. Averell Harriman shared many of Bullitt's and Steinhardt's abilities and talents. They refused to sugarcoat or rationalize Stalinism, despite their clear desire to please Roosevelt. They were both pro-Soviet in the beginning, but once in Moscow they soon informed Roosevelt that his policy of appeasing Stalin was in error and that Stalin was a dissimulating, duplicitous enemy. Standley lacked the rhetorical and analytical gifts of Bullitt and Steinhardt, but he was blunt, honest, and fair.

Harriman did his best to excuse Stalin and the Stalinist system precisely because that was what Roosevelt wanted. Reality often intruded, however, and he found himself deviating from the Roosevelt line and demanding that Washington take a more forceful stand against Stalin's arrogance and premeditated violence. He found it difficult to throw off the belief that the Soviet Union was evolving into something better, but eventually he agreed with Bullitt, Steinhardt, and Standley that strength and reciprocity, rather than appeasement, were the best policies for the United States to adopt toward the Soviet Union. He kept Kennan on a leash throughout most of 1944 and 1945, but he clearly shared many of Kennan's views and eventually urged them on Roosevelt and Truman. Harriman would have reflected and pushed for a more forceful policy toward Stalinism earlier if Roosevelt and Hopkins had shown the least bit of interest in wanting to curb Stalin's insatiable appetite for power and control. By 1945 he was agreeing with Bullitt that the Soviet Union had to be stopped. However, he did show a tendency to placate and excuse Stalin and to put business interests above the political rights of the peoples of Eastern Europe.

The least successful and most destructive representative from the viewpoint of America's interest was businessman and lawyer Joseph Davies. He made egregious errors in judgment and observation. He greatly exaggerated the industrial development of Stalinist Russia and totally misrepresented the purge trials, Communism, and Stalinism. He sustained Roosevelt's high opinion of Stalin and the Stalinist system. He was a parvenu who isolated and dismissed competent people to prevent any criticism of Stalin or of Roosevelt's policy of aiding and befriending Stalin. He had no knowledge of the history, culture, and language of the Russian people or others who lived under Stalin's domination. Furthermore, he fabricated facts and offered fanciful and preposterous interpretations of Stalin's crimes. He did recognize the prevalence of terror in Soviet society, but he dismissed it as a necessary consequence of rapid modernization. Davies, though, was the ultimate sycophant. If Roosevelt had been more realistic, Davies would have been less superficial. Davies's biographer, Elizabeth Kimball MacLean, offers a sympathetic although balanced picture of Davies and points out that he was, ironically, in basic agreement with Kennan's call "for a frank acceptance of power politics and recognition of spheres as a basis for postwar stability."[3] It seems, however, that there is a fundamental difference between Kennan's acceptance of a Soviet sphere of influence in Eastern Europe, in order to limit the extension of Stalinism that Roosevelt and Davies's policy abetted, and Davies's active support for the expansion of a Soviet sphere of influence in Eastern Europe, and not only Eastern Europe but also after the war in northern Iran and Turkey. MacLean does point out that Kennan would never negotiate areas of vital interest, whereas Davies was quite willing to put everything on the table.

The consequences of FDR's error in appeasing Stalin were costly and tragic. On the microlevel, it led to FDR's decision to bypass his ambassadors and State Department specialists who had a contrary view of Stalin. In effect, FDR cut himself off from people who knew Stalin and Soviet Russia. He operated in an ideological vacuum, relying on representatives who shared his belief in Stalin's democratic nature. His approach introduced confusion and conflicting lines of authority in U.S. foreign policy and held up the institutions of ambassador and embassy in Moscow for ridicule.

The president's policy also encouraged Stalin's gratuitous behavior toward the American representatives in Moscow, who were isolated, regularly scorned, and treated disrespectfully. When FDR put Faymonville in Moscow and then ran Hopkins, Harriman, Willkie, Burns, and Davies in and out of Moscow, and then ran Davies back and forth between the Soviet embassy in Washington and the White House, he undercut the prestige and the ability of the embassy, the ambassadors, and the State Department to negotiate. The Soviets simply refused to give the embassy or the State Department specialists concrete information on military plans, weather, logistics, and resources that could assist the western war effort in Europe and Asia. They also declined to provide a rationale and accountability for Lend-Lease equipment. They equivocated about releasing from prison the American pilots who landed in Siberia after bombing Japan. They published little news in the Soviet Union that was favorable to the United States.

FDR's approach also enabled Stalin to separate Roosevelt and Churchill and to adopt a demanding tone toward Roosevelt. Roosevelt wanted to please Stalin, and the Soviet dictator fully exploited this tendency, including the rather cavalier ultimatum that Roosevelt travel not only to Teheran but to Soviet Yalta despite his weak physical condition.

On the macrolevel, Roosevelt's policy contributed to the spread of Stalinism in Eastern and Central Europe and northeast Asia and strengthened Stalinism in the Soviet Union. The president overlooked Stalin's role in the Katyn Forest massacre in 1943, his attacks on the Polish government-in-exile, and his refusal to help the Poles in Warsaw in 1944. In addition, he sanctioned Soviet plans to annex the Baltic States and parts of Romania, Finland, and Poland, and sacrificed concrete military and political advantage in order to reduce Stalin's suspicion and to involve him in the collective security arrangement called the United Nations. The alliance with one of the most brutal dictators in the world also robbed the American war effort of inspiration and vision. It is possible, too, to argue that FDR's insistence on unconditional surrender, as a measure to reassure Stalin and assuage his suspicion, played a role in prolonging the war in Europe and in dropping the atomic bomb on Japan. Insisting that the Soviet Union become involved in the war against Japan also opened the door to Stalin's turning over to the Communist Chinese control of Manchuria and captured Japanese weapons which greatly assisted Mao in his civil war against Chiang Kai-shek.

Of course, great praise is due the Russians and other peoples of the Soviet Union in the war against the Nazis. They fought hard and heroically. Their casualties were astronomical. Even though poor leadership and military tactics that spent human lives frivolously contributed to the large number of war dead in Soviet Russia, the Soviet people did bear the brunt of the Nazi war machine between 1941 and 1945. Their effort played the major role in defeating the Nazi invasion. They were transformed into a formidable fighting machine by the heat of battle, the heat of Nazi atrocities, and the heat of Stalin's ruthlessness, brutality, and controlled violence. The people's sacrifice and heroic effort count for a lot. One does not need a warm, communicative, open, friendly ally in the fight to stop Hitler. However, Stalin's paranoia and perverse ideology in needlessly sacrificing the people of the Soviet Union, in wasting the talents of the men and women, especially the officers, of the Red Army during the first eighteen months or so of the war count heavily against him and dilute the sacrifice of the Soviet people because much of it was so utterly unnecessary and futile. Only now, with the opening of the Soviet archives, are the Russians themselves beginning to realize that their leadership failed them dismally at the beginning of the war and was responsible for the horrendous death toll in the Soviet Union as compared with every other country involved in the war, including Nazi Germany.[4]

The Soviet people were not fighting to protect Stalinism. It was, in many minds, as bad as or worse than Nazism. Stalinism survived not because of its superiority to Nazism, not because Stalin was a more brilliant military leader than Hitler, but mainly because of the critical role of the Red Army and the heroic struggle of the people of the Soviet Union and because of the poor judgment of the western leaders, like Eden and Churchill in 1942, but particularly Roosevelt, who wielded the power to modify or at least contain Stalinism during the war. As they have in the past, the Russians rose up against the invader and fought valiantly in defense of their homeland. They thought their struggle would bring new freedoms and end the oppression and fear that were such a part of the Stalinist creed. Stalin's position was enhanced by Roosevelt's coddling, which stemmed from his belief that Stalin was an evolving social democrat. Ironically, his role forced pluralism, which the United States was promoting, into a defensive posture internationally while Stalinism, which was absolutism in a fresh garb, ended up as a dynamic ideology, making awkward advances in Asia, Africa, and Latin America.

Roosevelt's approach made the Soviet-American relationship worse because it encouraged Stalin to act precipitously, arrogantly, and ruthlessly. Even though Stalin and his policies would have complicated American-Soviet relations in any circumstance, a mutually beneficial relationship between the United States and the Soviet Union was not impossible; nor was it ruled out that the United States could help precipitate a change in the Soviet Union, including a change that could see the collapse or diminution of Stalinism. The policy that would have achieved this serendipitous situation was the one recommended by most of the ambassadors and Russian specialists who wanted the president to take a forceful or realistic line. Even when the Nazis were an offensive threat, all of the ambassadors, except Davies, who had been in Moscow before and during the American-Soviet alliance up to late 1943, agreed that the president's policy of unilateral aid and uncritical friendship was counterproductive. They recommended even during the period of greatest peril to the Soviet Union that the policy of reciprocity and critical friendship would be better for the American-Soviet alliance and, needless to say, for American principles. In support of their belief they pointed out that in every instance where their approach was tried on a minor issue, such as the Kim affair, it succeeded in affecting Soviet behavior in a way that suited American interests. On a broader level, Finland's independence seems to be partly attributable to the ambassadors' persistent intercession in the Kremlin. And, of course, Stalin was most malleable and solicitous toward Germany and Japan when they adopted forceful policies toward him. The fact was that the Soviet Union was weak and the United States was strong, and a forceful policy would have produced a political-economic postwar picture that reflected this.

If Roosevelt had followed the advice of the Traditionalists, he would have adopted policies that viewed Stalin as an emerging threat as the Nazi danger waned. Specific policies would depend on Stalin's behavior and reaction and the wartime circumstances. Bullitt outlined a long list of actions in 1943 that could have been implemented to check Stalin or at least improve the opportunity for the growth of democratic internationalism in Europe and Asia. At minimum, FDR should have backed away from the policy of unconditional surrender of Germany in order to encourage the Germans to get rid of the Nazis, to shorten the war, and to provide more flexibility for wartime strategy. This was especially important because Stalin did not endorse unconditional surrender. Roosevelt also should have fully exploited the surrender of Italy in 1943, used Italy as a model to entice other countries to drop out of the Axis, and seriously explored the possibility of landing troops in Yugoslavia, Bulgaria, and Hungary and involving Turkey in the war. He should have developed a plan to build democratic governments and coalitions in Eastern Europe. He also should have insisted on a Soviet declaration of war against Japan in 1943—at least the use of Soviet air bases against Japan and support rather than imprisonment of American pilots who ran out of fuel and had to land in Siberia after bombing runs on Japan. He still had the second front in France with which to bargain. After the Warsaw Uprising in 1944 he should have backed the Polish government-in-exile and made sure that demarcation lines separating Soviet and western troops were far east of Berlin. He also should have pushed for a quick end of the Pacific war by canceling unconditional surrender and at least informing Stalin that the USSR was not needed in the war against Japan and would not receive any territory at China's expense to come into that war. He should have worked closely with Churchill to present Stalin with faits accomplis and used his military advantage to achieve political objectives. He also should have demanded decent treatment of the American representatives in Moscow. He should have told Stalin in no uncertain terms that Poland and the Baltic States would have a free government, that his huge empire was an ample security belt.

Of course, public opinion in the United States would have to back such a policy, but informing the American people of the reality of the alliance and of the nature of Stalin's Russia, instead of misleading them about the democratic nature of Stalin, would have been easy and logical, especially given FDR's skills at rhetoric and persuasion. In fact, one of the fundamental problems with FDR's approach was that the alliance with Stalin cheated the American war effort of a democratic vision. FDR found it difficult to convince anyone, although he tried, that the war was about freedom and democracy when he was allied with one of the most brutal dictators that the world had ever seen. He presented a distorted image of Stalin as a freedom-loving ally and democrat, but the American public, although willing to allot Stalin a measure of popularity as an ally, was not persuaded of his commitment to freedom and democracy in light of the Nazi-Soviet alliance, the Soviet attack on Finland, the Baltic States, and Poland, the Katyn Forest massacre, and Soviet behavior during the Warsaw Uprising in 1944. The war, from the American point of view, became primarily a desire to pay back Japan for attacking Pearl Harbor and to defeat Hitler because he was an ally of Japan and stood in the way of paying back Japan immediately and with full force. The contradiction between FDR's Wilsonian wartime and postwar goals and his alliance with one of the worst criminals in history prevented Roosevelt from truly inspiring the American public and soldiers. He would have been more successful if he had told the truth and declared that Stalinism would have to go the way of Nazism, that the war was about ridding the world of all undemocratic and inhuman ideologies. In July 1941, Bullitt advised the president to "develop our war production faster than Germany can develop war production in Soviet territory," and to make clear to the American people that, while the United

States will back "anyone (even a criminal) fighting Hitler," the Communists have not "become the friends of democracy."[5]

When it came to Stalin, Roosevelt can be faulted for putting ideology before common sense. In the face of Stalin's perverse behavior, utter confusion in American war goals and objectives, and the sage advice of the very people he put in place to provide him with expert advice on Stalin and the Soviet Union, FDR stayed with his plan to cooperate with Stalin.

In 1975 George Kennan gave a retrospective assessment of Roosevelt's foreign policy leadership: "The truth is—there is no avoiding it—that Franklin Roosevelt, for all his charm and for all his skill as a political leader, was, when it came to foreign policy, a very superficial man, ignorant, dilettantish, with a severely limited intellectual horizon."[6] This view is harsh and misses an important point. Roosevelt, as Warren Kimball has pointed out, had a worldview that wanted pluralism to spread into the Soviet Union and elsewhere around the world.[7] His mistake was in separating democracy from morality. It led him to misunderstand and prop up Stalinist Russia. If he had taken a leadership role in promoting the values for which the United States stood, if he had listened to the Traditionalists, Stalinism would have likely fallen before the 1990s, and instead of years of cold war, the world, including Soviet Russia, might have witnessed an unparalleled growth of pluralism.[8]

In the conduct of foreign policy, where the goal is to intelligently promote the security, economic well-being, and vision of the society, it is important to be guided by experience, not ideology. This means the traditional ways of checking aggression, maintaining the peace, and providing security—including the balance of power, intelligent diplomacy, and the need to balance long-term moral and political consequences against short-term moral and political interests—should be seen as having permanent merit. FDR's initial unwillingness to sanction Soviet control of the Baltic States in 1942 was the right course. But FDR did not adopt it out of conviction. He was a supporter of national self-determination, and this certainly played a role in his initial refusal to give in to Stalin's demands on the Baltic States. If a policy in support of democratic government and national self-determination were going to succeed in the Baltic States, it had to be supported, especially as the war turned more favorable to the Soviet-American-British alliance, by consistent, principled diplomacy and military planning, as Bullitt recommended, rather than wishful thinking about Stalin's evolution toward democracy.

Most of the ambassadors and embassy staff in Moscow provided valuable information and advice for the making of American foreign policy. They were intelligent, independent men who based their recommendations on experience, even though some of them were not trained in diplomacy. The president did not follow their advice. If a whole succession of representatives and experts are nearly unanimous in their view of a policy or issue, the president should have absolutely no qualms about implementing their recommendations, and if his own view is different, he should reconsider his policy. He should be extremely reluctant to circumvent the State Department and its expert opinion, particularly if he and his close advisers are not students of foreign affairs.

FDR is overwhelmingly praised by western scholars. British historian Hugh Thomas and Mexican writer Carlos Fuentes have nominated him for the most significant person of the twentieth century. Arthur Schlesinger Jr., Robert Dallek, Robert Divine, James McGregor Burns, William Leuchtenburg, and countless others have hailed him as a statesman and leader. He is lauded as a giant in the realm of domestic policy. He is celebrated as the man who led the United States out of the Depression and restored hope in democratic government. He is also praised as the leader who organized the victory over Nazism and Japanese militarism and initiated a popular Good Neighbor policy in Latin America. In his Soviet policy, he is likewise deemed the man who did what had to be done to forge the alliance that pummeled Hitler and to work at reducing Stalin's inordinate suspicion of the United States. His policy was cut short by Truman but survived in the détente effort that began in the late 1960s.

The image that comes out of his relationship with his ambassadors in Moscow is quite different. He was great in many respects, but on the critical issue of providing a vision for the American people, of promoting American interests abroad, of using the power at hand to reduce the expansion of Stalinism, he failed, and his failure clouds his other achievements. Historian Gerhard Weinberg claims that FDR realized that unconditional concessions were necessary because Stalin would not have tolerated conditions.[9] Roosevelt, of course, would never have known, because he did not attempt to stipulate conditions. The record shows that the only time that Stalin was moved was when pressure was applied— whether it was in relations with Germany, Japan, Finland, or the American ambassadors who experimented with a quid pro quo approach.

Although it is easy to sympathize with Roosevelt's view that a new liberal democratic order was about to descend on the world, the reality was that democracy and liberal political and economic institutions were not inevitable and did not develop in Stalin's Russia. Pluralism today has won out against Communism at the close of the twentieth century, but other ideologies, most notably the various ethnic and religious nationalisms that are using religion for narrow, nationalist political purposes, including so-called ethnic cleansing and genocide, are demolishing democratic internationalism's claim, with its hydra of conflicting nationalisms on display at the United Nations, to be the model of the new world order. In addition, variations on Communism and Nazism are again appearing as various societies, torn from their traditional cultural values and adrift in a world that values power and money, seek an escape from poverty and insecurity and equal access to the privileged life of the developed nations. Moreover, nativist cultures are surging and, as Samuel Huntington has emphasized, "The powerful currents of indigenization at work in the world make a mockery of western expectations that western culture will become the world's culture."[10]

The real cutting edge for American leaders should not be the inevitability of pluralism, but the degree to which societies play a positive role in promoting international peace, cooperation, and order. American foreign policy must aim, of course, at protecting American security and vital interests, and all the traditional tools of diplomacy have a part to play, including shrewd and careful use of perceived military advantage, astute ambassadors, and foreign policy expertise. An essential element of America's vital interest is, as FDR understood, to promote an international order based on principles of democracy. His mistake was in detaching support for a new international order from objective morality. A secular international order, one devoid of common values that truly unite people, has no staying power.

Notes

Abbreviations

Note: The standard way of referring to Russian documents is name of document and archive, then collection (*fond*), register (*opis'*), file (*delo*), and page (*list*).

AVP	Arkhiv vneshnei politiki [Archive of Foreign Affairs], Russian Federation, Moscow
BP	Charles E. Bohlen Papers File, National Archives
DP	Joseph E. Davies Papers, Library of Congress
DVP	Ministerstvo inostrannyk del Rossiiskoi federatsii, Dokumenty vneshnei politiki 1939 god [Foreign Ministry of the Russian Federation, Foreign Affairs Documents for 1939], vol. 1: 1 January-31 August 1939; vol. 2: 1 September-31 December 1939. Moscow: Mezhdunarodnye othnosheniia, 1992
FDR Library	Franklin Delano Roosevelt Library, Hyde Park, N.Y.
FO, PRO	Foreign Office, Public Records Office, Kew Green, London
FRUS	U.S. State Department, *Foreign Relations of the United States*
HHP	Harry Hopkins Papers, FDR Library, Hyde Park, N.Y.
KIVMV	*Komintern i Vtoraia Mirovaia voina* [Comintern and the Second World War]. Moscow: Pamiatniki istoricheskoi mysli, 1994.
NA	National Archives, Washington, D.C.
OF	Official File, FDR Library, Hyde Park, N.Y.
OGBSSSR	*Organy gosudarstvennoi bezopasnosti SSSR v Velikoi Otechestvennoi voine* [State Security Organs of the USSR in the Great Fatherland War]. Moscow: Kniga i Biznes, 1995.
PPF	President's Personal File, FDR Library, Hyde Park, N.Y.
PSF	President's Secretary's File, FDR Library, Hyde Park, N.Y.
RTsKhIDNI	Rossiiskii tsentr khraneniia i izucheniia dokumentov noveishei istorii (Russian Center for the Preservation and Study of Contemporary Historical Documents), Moscow
SAOVVOV	Ministerstvo inostrannyk del SSSR [Foreign Ministry of the USSR], *Sovetsko-Amerikanskie otnosheniia vo vremia velikoi otechestvennoi voiny 1941-1945* [Soviet-American Relations during the Period of the Great Fatherland War, 1941-1945], vol. 1 (1941-1943), vol. 2 (1944-1945). Moscow: Izdatel'stvo politicheskoi literatury, 1984.

SP   Laurence A. Steinhardt Papers, Library of Congress
WAHP   W. Averell Harriman Papers, Library of Congress
WSP   William H. Standley Papers, Library of Congress

Preface

1. Warren F. Kimball, *The Juggler: Franklin Roosevelt as Wartime Statesman* (Princeton: Princeton University Press, 1991), 7. For samples of the work by these scholars, see Robert Dallek, *Franklin D. Roosevelt and American Foreign Policy, 1932-1945* (New York: Oxford University Press, 1979); Daniel Yergin, *Shattered Peace: The Origins of the Cold War and the National Security State* (Boston: Houghton Mifflin, 1978); John Lewis Gaddis, *The United States and the Origins of the Cold War, 1941-1947* (New York: Columbia University Press, 1972); John Lewis Gaddis, *Russia, the Soviet Union, and the United States: An Interpretative History* (New York: John Wiley, 1978); Lloyd C. Gardner, *Architects of Illusion* (Chicago: Quadrangle Books, 1972); and Robert Divine, *Roosevelt and World War II* (Baltimore: Johns Hopkins University Press, 1969).

2. Kimball reviews many of the major historiographical views on Roosevelt in *Juggler*, 13-19. He discounts illness as a cause of FDR's concessions because the illness was not that debilitating and FDR's policy was consistent with his attitudes before his illness could arguably have affected him. Kimball does not state, however, that FDR had a concessionary policy toward Stalin from the beginning. For an earlier review of the literature on FDR's foreign policy leadership, see Robert Dallek, "Franklin Roosevelt as World Leader," *American Historical Review* 76 (Dec. 1971): 1503-13.

3. Yergin, *Shattered Peace*, 44-48, 72.

4. Lars T. Lih, introduction to *Stalin's Letters to Molotov*, edited by Lih, Oleg V. Naumov, and Oleg V. Khlevniuk (New Haven: Yale University Press, 1995), 62. Yergin's division of American foreign policy into the Riga School (personified by people like Kennan, Bohlen, and Henderson), which held the USSR to be revolutionary, and the Yalta School (personified by Roosevelt, Davies, and Hopkins), which believed the USSR to be traditional, is spurious because Stalin's Russia proved itself to be both revolutionary and traditional (heirs of Marx and of the czars), and members of the Riga School clearly saw that these characteristics coexisted and were not mutually exclusive. The Roosevelt group also believed the USSR was revolutionary in the sense of having evolved to a new state in human relations, although it also believed that Stalin's Russia was no longer a fire-breathing, revolutionary regime ready to overthrow capitalist governments if the opportunity arose. For a good review of Yergin's *Shattered Peace*, see Daniel Harrington, "Kennan, Bohlen, and the Riga Axioms," *Diplomatic History* 2 (winter 1978): 423-37. Stalin's mental outlook was formed fundamentally by Marxism-Leninism. His analysis of Roosevelt and of his policies are not understandable outside that context. The evidence, aside from his letters to Molotov and his own writings, is revealed in his foreign policy and Comintern directives, which are nicely reflected in newly published archival sources: Ministerstvo inostrannyk del Rossiiskoi federatsii, *Dokumenty vneshnei politiki 1939 god* (vol. 1: 1 Jan.-31 Aug. 1939; vol. 2: 1 Sept.-31 Dec. 1939) (Moscow: Mezhdunarodnye othnosheniia, 1992) hereafter cited as *DVP*, 1 or 2); Rossiiskaia akademiia nauk institut vseobshchei istorii, *Komintern i Vtoraia Mirovaia Voina (KIVMV)* (Moscow: Pamiatniki istoricheskoi mysli, 1994; Federal'naia sluzhba kontrrazvedki Rossiiskoi federatsii, *Organy gosudarstvennoi bezopasnosti SSSR v Velikoi Otechestvennoi voine (OGBSSSR)*, vol. 1, *Nakanune* (Nov. 1938-Dec. 1940) (Moscow: Kniga i Biznes, 1995).

5. Historian Steven Merritt Miner finds that the books based on the newly opened Soviet archives reveal that ideology was central to Stalin's outlook and policies. See his "Revelations, Secrets, Gossip, and Lies: Sifting Warily through the Soviet Archives," *New York Times Book Review*, 14 May 1995, 19-21. Stalin's dedication to revolution is revealed in his policy regarding the building of Communist governments in East Europe at the end of World War II. The rules for Communist parties in Bulgaria, Albania, and Romania and the procedures for agrarian reform in Poland, Hungary, and Romania were coordinated and drafted by the Communist Party of the Soviet Union. The model to be used in setting up the East European parties was the Soviet model. It was the basis for determining where a party was in the pursuit of socialism. See Anna Di Biagio, "The Establishment of the Cominform," in *The Cominform: Minutes of the Three Conferences, 1947/1948/1949*, edited by G. Procacci et al. (Milan: Feltrinelli, 1994), 17, 20. Historian Melvyn P. Leffler, however, believes that what the archival-based literature really shows is that, while ideology was important, Stalin was mainly a student of realpolitik. See his "Inside Enemy Archives: The Cold War Reopened," *Foreign Affairs* (July/Aug. 1996), 120-35. My own reading of the new material indicates that Stalin was committed to both ideology and realpolitik and that one or the other was primary, depending on circumstances, but that Stalin always returned to Marxism-Leninism to comprehend his world, analyze opportunities, and plan the future. He was a consummate chess player, but the board was red and the pieces were black and white within the ever-shifting morality of his personal interpretation of the direction of the international revolution. One measure of Stalin's commitment to revolution can be seen in his renewal of the antireligious campaign in the Soviet Union immediately after the war. The Russian Orthodox Church had played a major role in the defense of Russia and was fully behind the government, which was its traditional role. Nonetheless, once the Nazi threat was removed, Stalin persecuted this bulwark of Russian nationalism without remorse. Khrushchev even hit it harder, such that by the time the persecution stopped under Gorbachev and the subsequent breakup of the Soviet Union, 70 percent of the parishes and clergy were located outside the Russian Republic. For information, see the excellent book by Nathaniel Davis, *A Long Walk to Church: A History of Contemporary Russian Orthodoxy* (Boulder, Colo.: Westview Press, 1995). For information on the role of religion in the fall of Communism in the Soviet empire, see Dennis J. Dunn, "Religion, Revolution, and Order in Russia," in *Christianity after Communism: Social, Political, and Cultural Struggle in Russia*, edited by Niels C. Nielson Jr. (Boulder, Colo.: Westview Press, 1994), 15-28.

Vladimir Zubok and Constantine Pleshakov in *Inside the Kremlin's Cold War* (Cambridge: Harvard University Press, 1996) argue (p. 3) that Stalin was guided by both "imperial expansionism and ideological proselytism." In an interesting study, R.C. Raack finds growing evidence that Stalin viewed the German attack on Poland, France, and England as a war of attrition that would weaken the capitalist states and make them vulnerable to a Soviet attack on the West in 1941, a plan that was only derailed by Hitler's invasion of the USSR. His evidence is drawn from Viktor Suvorov's book *Icebreaker: Who Started the Second World War?* (London: Hamish Hamilton, 1990) and newly opened archival material. Raack's point is that Stalin never abandoned the strategy of revolutionary war as a means to bring down capitalism and bring on the Communist era. See R.C. Raack, *Stalin's Drive to the West, 1938-1941: The Origins of the Cold War* (Stanford: Stanford University Press, 1995); R. C. Raack, "Stalin's Role in the Coming of World War II," *World Affairs* 158 (spring 1996):

198-211; and R. C. Raack, "Stalin's Role in the Coming of World War II: The International Debate Goes on," *World Affairs* 159 (fall 1996): 47-54.

6. David Mayers, *The Ambassadors and America's Soviet Policy* (New York: Oxford University Press, 1995), 106.

7. George Kennan, "Comment," *Survey: A Journal of East and West Studies* 21 (winter/spring 1975): 31.

8. Kimball, *Juggler*, 183, 185-200.

9. The NKVD (Commissariat for Internal Affairs, predecessor of the KGB) archives are still not open, but this gap can be partially filled by using the NKVD documents in the Stalin and Molotov "Special Files" that are now part of the collections of the State Archive of Russian Federation (former Central State Archive of the October Revolution) and certain collections of the Russian Foreign Ministry Archive. Some documents considered sensitive are still in the Kremlin or the President of Russian Federation Archive, which remains closed. There is also valuable material in the Russian Center for Preservation and Study of Contemporary Historical Documents (the former Central Party Archive), which is open. American diplomatic historians have not yet waded into all of the new material. We are aware, however, that American-Soviet diplomatic historiography is about to be revised. See, for example, John Lewis Gaddis, *We Now Know: Rethinking Cold War History* (New York: Oxford University Press, 1997). The main schools of thought on this subject so far are the orthodox, revisionist, and postrevisionist. The orthodox scholars, led by Herbert Feis, Arthur M. Schlesinger Jr., and Joseph M. Jones, place responsibility for the cold war on the shoulders of Stalin and the Soviet Union. Revisionist scholars represented by William Appleman Williams, Gar Alperowitz, Lloyd Gardner, Walter LaFeber, and Joyce and Gabriel Kolko blame Truman or capitalism. The postrevisionist historians, including John Lewis Gaddis, George Herring, and Lynn Etheridge-Davis, blame both the Soviet Union and the United States. Among American scholars who specialize in Soviet studies, there is also polarization regarding Stalinism, the cold war, and the nature of Soviet society. For a good review see Miner, "Revelations, Secrets, Gossip, and Lies," 19-21. Vojtech Mastny in *The Cold War and Soviet Insecurity* (New York: Oxford University Press, 1996) argues that the cold war started because of Stalin's ideologically rooted insecurity (although as an ideologue he was not necessarily revolutionary), and it persisted into the 1990s because of the fundamental clash of values between the United States and Stalinist Russia.

10. David Mayers's *Ambassadors and America's Soviet Policy* does treat the ambassadors, but it is more general, stretching from czarist times to the present and focusing on bureaucratic history.

Prologue: Early 1943

1. William C. Bullitt, "How We Won the War and Lost the Peace," *Life*, 30 August 1948, 94.

2. Rexford G. Tugwell, *In Search of Roosevelt* (Cambridge: Harvard University Press, 1972), 308-9.

3. Paul Hollander, *Political Pilgrims: Travels of Western Intellectuals to the Soviet Union, China, and Cuba, 1928-1978* (New York: Oxford University Press, 1981), 110.

4. Louis Fischer, *Men and Politics: An Autobiography* (New York: Duell, Sloan,

and Pearce, 1941), 293. Robert A. Rosenstone, *Romantic Revolutionary: A Biography of John Reed* (New York: Vintage Books, 1975), 301.

5. S. J. Taylor, *Stalin's Apologist: Walter Duranty, the New York Times's Man in Moscow* (New York: Oxford University Press, 1990), 5, 352.

6. Harriman carefully explained Roosevelt's outlook to me in a personal interview in Washington, D.C., on 19 November 1981. He had made an earlier and brief reference to Roosevelt's advocacy of the theory of convergence in his memoirs. See W. Averell Harriman and Elie Abel, *Special Envoy to Churchill and Stalin, 1941-1946* (New York: Random House, 1976), 170. He also elaborated on it in an interview with George Urban from which the Roosevelt quote is taken. See George Urban, "Was Stalin (the Terrible) Really a Great Man? A Long Conversation with Averell Harriman," *Encounter* 57 (Nov. 1981): 23. Many authors have pointed out that Roosevelt believed Stalin was more of a Russian nationalist than a Marxist revolutionary. See Kimball, *Juggler*, 30; Thomas R. Maddux, "Watching Stalin Maneuver between Hitler and the West: American Diplomats and Soviet Diplomacy, 1934-1939," *Diplomatic History* 1 (spring 1977): 140-54; Eduard Mark, "October or Thermidor? Interpretations of Stalinism and the Perception of Soviet Foreign Policy in the United States, 1927-1947," *American Historical Review* 94 (Oct. 1989): 937-62; Edward M. Bennett, *Franklin D. Roosevelt and the Search for Security: American-Soviet Relations, 1933-1939* (Wilmington, Del.: Scholarly Resources, 1985).

7. Sumner Welles, *Where Are We Heading?* (New York: Harper, 1946), 37.

8. Oumansky to Molotov, telegram, 2 July 1939, *DVP,* 1:525.

9. Forrest Davis, "Roosevelt's World Blueprint," *Saturday Evening Post,* 10 April 1943.

10. Robert C. Tucker, foreword to *Stalin's Letters,* ed. Lih, Naumov, and Khlevniuk, xi.

11. Edward M. Bennett, *Recognition of Russia: An American Foreign Policy Dilemma* (Waltham, Mass.: Blaisdell, 1970), 104.

12. Most scholars agree that Stalin deliberately starved the peasants to force them to accept collectivization. See Robert Conquest, *Harvest of Sorrow: Soviet Collectivization and the Terror-Famine* (New York: Oxford University Press, 1986), and Robert C. Tucker, *Stalin in Power: The Revolution from Above, 1929-1941* (New York: W. W. Norton, 1990), 189-95. So far the material coming out of the Soviet archives supports Conquest and Tucker. See, for example, Stalin's letters to Molotov from the Rossiiskii tsentr khraneniia i izucheniia dokumentov noveishei istorii [Russian Center for the Preservation and Study of Contemporary Historical Documents] (RTsKhIDNI) as found in Lih et al., *Stalin's Letters,* 203, 207. Also see Edvard Radzinsky's fascinating new biography of Stalin, which is based extensively on archival sources and underscores that Stalin used terror and famine to break the peasantry: *Stalin,* trans. by H. T. Willetts (New York: Doubleday, 1996). A revisionist study by Robert W. Thurston, *Life and Terror in Stalin's Russia, 1934-1941* (New Haven: Yale University Press, 1996) argues that terror was not the key to Stalin's regime and that most people supported the government.

13. S. J. Taylor, *Stalin's Apologist,* 184, 222. Duranty's reports on Stalin's collectivization were not only incomplete but deliberately misleading. Taylor explains Duranty's fatuousness on grounds of personal ambition whereas an early study by Whitman Bassow attributes it to an inferiority complex related to an unattractive appearance and physical disability. See Bassow's *The Moscow Correspondents: Reporting*

on Russia from the Revolution to Glasnost (New York: William Morrow, 1988). Another possibility is Duranty's adoption of the theory of convergence with its attendant moral relativism. The term *terror-famine* comes from Robert Conquest's book, *Harvest of Sorrow*.

14. Mayers, *Ambassadors*, 105.

15. John Daniel Langer, "The 'Red General': Philip R. Faymonville and the Soviet Union, 1917-1952," *Prologue* 8 (winter 1976): 220.

1. Stalin's Kiss

1. Orville H. Bullitt, ed., *For the President: Personal and Secret*, introduction by George F. Kennan (Boston: Houghton Mifflin, 1972), 63-66; Bullitt to Phillips, 4 January 1934, U.S. State Department, *Foreign Relations of the United States: Diplomatic Papers: The Soviet Union, 1933-1939* (Washington: Government Printing Office, 1952), 57-60 (hereafter cited as *FRUS: Soviet Union*). For a recent general biography of William Bullitt, see Will Brownell and Richard N. Billings, *So Close to Greatness* (New York: Macmillan, 1987).

2. Stalin's own writings are clear on his opposition to bureaucrats and weak revolutionaries. His recently published letters to Molotov demonstrate the consistency of his determination to root out any compromise with nonrevolutionary forces which, in his mind, could be Communists who want to slow down the pace of the revolution because of its violence or capitalists who are irredeemable and irreversible enemies of the revolution, although they may appear reasonable and friendly. See, for example, I. V. Stalin, *Sochineniia* (Moscow, 1946-), 4:366-68, 5:197-222, 9:158-59, 13:159-233. Also see letters 4, 27, 30, 40, 42, 43, 44, 47, 49, 50, 51, 57, 60, 61, 63, 67, 69, 74, 76, 77, 78, and 79 in Lih et al., *Stalin's Letters*.

3. Lih et al., *Stalin's Letters*, p. 200.

4. The debate over whether Stalin was primarily a revolutionary or a practitioner of realpolitik seems to be tilting toward the former. See Miner, "Revelations, Secrets, Gossip, and Lies," 19-21.

5. Bullitt, *For the President*, 65.

6. In his memoirs Molotov speaks of Stalin as if he were a demigod. He sees him as superior in terms of his revolutionary faith and intuition to Sergei Kirov, Nikolai Bukharin, and the many other contenders for leadership. See Feliks Chuyev, *Sto sorok besed c Molotovym: Iz dnevnika F. Chuyeva* (Moscow: Terra, 1991), 171, 307-13, passim.

7. Nikita Khrushchev, *Khrushchev Remembers: The Glasnost Tapes*, ed. and trans. Jerrold L. Schechter and Vyacheslav Luchkov (Boston: Little, Brown, 1990), 87.

8. Bullitt to Phillips, 4 January 1934, *FRUS: Soviet Union*, 57.

9. See Lih et al., *Stalin's Letters*. For biographical information on Molotov, Voroshilov, Kaganovich, Malenkov, Mikoyan, and Suslov, see Roy Medvedev, *All Stalin's Men* (New York: Anchor/Doubleday, 1984).

10. Bullitt to Phillips, 4 January 1934, *FRUS: Soviet Union*, p. 56.

11. Stalin to Molotov, 29 August 1929, 1 September 1929, 7 October 1929, 5 December 1929, in Lih et al., *Stalin's Letters*, 174-76, 182-83. Stalin was particularly critical of Litvinov's failure to see the revolutionary aspect of foreign policy.

12. Bullitt, *For the President*, 65.

13. For details on these individuals, see Robert C. Tucker, *Stalin in Power*, and

Robert Conquest, *The Great Terror: Stalin's Purges of the Thirties*, new ed. (New York: Oxford University Press, 1990).

14. Bullitt, *For the President*, 65; Bullitt to Phillips, 4 January 1934, *FRUS: Soviet Union*, 59.

15. Tucker, *Stalin's Letters*, xi-xii.

16. Bullitt to Phillips, 4 January 1934, *FRUS: Soviet Union*, 59; Bullitt, *For the President*, 67.

17. In my interview with him, W. Averell Harriman, who served as both a confidant and ambassador in Moscow for Roosevelt, emphasized the importance of the theory of convergence in explaining Roosevelt's policies. I found his explanation convincing. For Burns's view and Roosevelt's words, see James MacGregor Burns, *Roosevelt: The Soldier of Freedom* (New York: Harcourt Brace Jovanovich, 1970), 609.

18. Michael R. Beschloss, *Kennedy and Roosevelt: The Uneasy Alliance* (New York: W. W. Norton, 1980), 48.

19. Rosenstone, *Romantic Revolutionary*, 301, 349; Hollander, *Political Pilgrims*, 122; M. Wayne Morris, *Stalin's Famine and Roosevelt's Recognition of Russia* (Lanham, Md.: University Press of America, 1994), 73-74; Fischer, *Men and Politics*, 293.

20. See Cordell Hull, *The Memoirs of Cordell Hull* (New York: Macmillan, 1948), 1:296-302; Morgenthau diaries, Farm Credit diary, Henry Morgenthau Jr. Papers, FDR Library; *FRUS: Soviet Union*, 21-23, 43-46; Robert P. Browder, *The Origins of Soviet-American Diplomacy* (Princeton: Princeton University Press, 1953), 31-38; Mayers, *Ambassadors*, 101-5. There are many good books on the Roosevelt-Litvinov agreement. See James K. Libbey, *Alexander Gumberg and Soviet-American Relations, 1917-1933* (Lexington: University Press of Kentucky, 1977); Thomas R. Maddux, *Years of Estrangement: American Relations with the Soviet Union, 1933-1941* (Tallahassee: University Presses of Florida, 1980); Donald G. Bishop, *The Roosevelt-Litvinov Agreement: The American View* (Syracuse, N.Y.: Syracuse University Press, 1965); Bennett, *Recognition of Russia*. The Reverend Walsh was the Catholic Church's official voice on Soviet matters. See Mark, "October or Thermidor?" 941n. 14.

21. Taylor, *Stalin's Apologist*, 184-85.

22. Bullitt to Phillips, 4 January 1934, *FRUS: Soviet Union*, 50.

23. Bullitt, *For the President*, 66-67.

24. Mayers, *Ambassadors*, 101. For information on America's "window" in Riga and its valuable files on Soviet Russia, see Natalie Grant, "The Russian Section: A Window on the Soviet Union," *Diplomatic History* 2 (spring 1978): 107-15. For a good survey of the history of the American foreign service, see Clare Boothe Luce, "The Ambassadorial Issue: Professional or Amateurs," *Foreign Affairs* (Oct. 1957), 105-21.

25. Bullitt, *For the President*, 65; Yergin, *Shattered Peace*, 27.

26. See Charles E. Bohlen, *Witness to History, 1929-1969* (New York: W. W. Norton, 1973), 4-13; Mayers, *Ambassadors*, 99-100, 110; Yergin, *Shattered Peace*, 26-29; Thomas Maddux, "American Diplomats and the Soviet Experiment: The View from the Moscow Embassy, 1934-1939," *South Atlantic Quarterly* (autumn 1975), 470-71. For a thorough survey of Henderson's career and outlook, see H. W. Brands, *Inside the Cold War: Loy Henderson and the Rise of the American Empire* (New York: Oxford University Press, 1991). On Bohlen, see Michael T. Ruddy, *The Cautious Diplomat: Charles E. Bohlen and the Soviet Union, 1929-1969* (Kent, Ohio: Kent State University Press, 1986).

27. Lih et al., *Stalin's Letters,* 178.

28. Bullitt to Phillips, 4 January 1934, *FRUS: Soviet Union,* 59-60; Bullitt, *For the President,* 67-69.

29. Bullitt to Phillips, 4 January 1934, *FRUS: Soviet Union,* 60

30. To ensure that France did not become too belligerent in 1935 and threaten Germany during rearmament, the Comintern instructed the French Communist Party to stymie the French government's efforts to extend military service. See Adam B. Ulam, *Expansion and Coexistence: The History of Soviet Foreign Policy, 1917-1973* (New York: Praeger, 1974), 228-29.

31. Tucker, *Stalin in Power,* 275.

32. Bullitt to Phillips, 4 January 1934, *FRUS: Soviet Union,* 60-61.

33. Bullitt, *For the President,* 71. Also see Bullitt to FDR, 24 December 1933, President's Secretary's File (PSF), FDR Library.

34. Soviet newspapers made it clear that Moscow hoped the United States would control the Japanese threat. See, for example, *Izvestiia,* 10 November and 29 December 1933, and *Trud,* 20 November 1933.

35. Lih et al., *Stalin's Letters,* 229.

36. Hitler discounted the United States because of its small army and virtually nonexistent air force. See Gerhard Weinberg, *A World at Arms: A Global History of World War II* (Cambridge: Cambridge University Press, 1994), 87.

37. Anne Bullitt, the ambassador's daughter, described Spaso House as the domain of a vodka merchant. Others have said it was the palace of a prerevolutionary sugar baron. Interview with Ambassador Thomas Pickering, 26 September 1993, Spaso House, Moscow. Also see Bullitt, *For the President,* 80, and Walter Isaacson and Evan Thomas, *The Wise Men: Six Friends and the World They Made* (New York: Simon and Schuster, 1986), 159, 162; Rebecca B. Matlock, "Backdrop to History: Spaso House," *Foreign Service Journal,* April 1989, 41-44.

2. Russia and the State of Grace

1. Bullitt, *For the President,* xiv.

2. Ibid., xxxvi-vii.

3. Personal interview, 10 November 1981, Washington, D.C.

4. Bullitt, *For the President,* xv.

5. Bohlen, *Witness,* 16-17.

6. Bullitt, *For the President,* 12.

7. Eugene Lyons, *Assignment in Utopia* (New York: Harcourt, Brace, 1937), 500.

8. Rosenstone, *Romantic Revolutionary,* 301, 349.

9. In a letter to Colonel Edward M. House, Bullitt admitted, "I wish I could see Russia with as single an eye as Reed. I am unable to wind through the welter of conflicting reports about the Bolsheviki to anything like solid conviction." See Bullitt to Colonel House, 20 May 1918, Bullitt Papers, Yale University.

10. Bullitt, *For the President,* xli.

11. Ibid., xv.

12. Ibid., xxxviii.

13. Ibid., xl.

14. Beatrice Farnsworth, *William C. Bullitt and the Soviet Union* (Bloomington: Indiana University Press, 1967), 13, 17.

15. Bullitt, *For the President,* xl.

16. Farnsworth, *Bullitt,* 30-31. Bullitt wanted Wilson to organize a committee of specialists to study Russia, chaired by someone who would report directly to the president. See Bullitt to Colonel House, 20 May and 20 September 1918, Bullitt Papers.

17. William C. Bullitt, *The Bullitt Mission to Russia* (New York: B. W. H. Huebsch, 1919), 63-64.

18. Bullitt, *For the President,* 64, 69.

19. Ibid., 6.

20. George F. Kennan, *Memoirs, 1925-1950* (Boston: Little, Brown, 1967), 80.

21. Louis B. Wehle, *Hidden Threads of History* (New York: Macmillan, 1953), 113.

22. Bullitt, *For the President,* xlii, 20. He told Colonel House that FDR could arouse the nation "by the old Jeffersonian appeal of liberty to the individual and service to the nation." See Bullitt to House, 3 September 1932, House Papers, as found in Gardner, *Architects of Illusion,* 11.

23. Wehle, *Hidden Threads,* 113; Bullitt, *For the President,* 21-24.

24. Wehle, *Hidden Threads,* 119.

25. Bullitt, *For the President,* 38-40; Mayers, *Ambassadors,* 101-5. See memorandum by Kelley, 27 July 1933; Packer to Bullitt, 31 August 1933; Hull to Roosevelt, 21 September 1933; Hull to Roosevelt, 5 October 1933; memorandum by Moore, 4 October 1933; and memorandum by Bullitt, 4 October 1933, all in *FRUS: Soviet Union,* 6-17.
Many books deal with the problems of recognizing the Soviet Union. See, for example, Peter Filene, *Americans and the Soviet Experiment, 1917-1933* (Cambridge: Harvard University Press, 1967); John Richman, *The United States and the Soviet Union: The Decision to Recognize* (Raleigh, N.C.: Camberleigh Hall, 1980); Maddux, *Years of Estrangement;* Bennett, *Recognition of Russia;* Joan Hoff-Wilson, *Ideology and Economics: U.S. Relations with the Soviet Union, 1918-1933* (Columbia: University of Missouri Press, 1974); Arthur M. Schlesinger Jr., *The Age of Roosevelt,* vol. 1: *The Crisis of the Old Order, 1919-1933* (Boston: Houghton Mifflin, 1957); Bennett, *Roosevelt and Security.*
Some scholars, notably John Richman, blame Robert Kelley for the strain in American-Soviet relations both before and after WWII. See Thomas Maddux, *Years of Estrangement,* 17-25; Hugh DeSantis, *The Diplomacy of Silence: The American Foreign Service, the Soviet Union, and the Cold War, 1933-1947* (Chicago: University of Chicago Press, 1980), 21-33; and Frederic L. Propas, "Creating a Hard Line toward Russia: The Training of State Department Soviet Experts, 1927-1937," *Diplomatic History* 8 (summer 1984): 209-26. Herbert Feis maintains that Kelley supported FDR's policy once recognition was given. See Herbert Feis, *Characters in Crisis* (Boston: Little, Brown, 1966), 308ff.

26. Mayers, *Ambassadors,* 102-5; Taylor, *Stalin's Apologist,* 6, 184, 188-89, 222; memorandum by Kelley, 27 July 1933, *FRUS: Soviet Union,* 6-11. The term *terror-famine* is taken from Conquest, *Harvest of Sorrow.*

27. Bennett, *Recognition of Russia,* 104; memorandum by R. Walton Moore, 3 October 1933, *FRUS: Soviet Union,* 14-17; Moore to secretary of state, 4 November 1933, box 18, Moore Papers, FDR Library.

28. Bennett, *Roosevelt and Security,* 10; Mayers, *Ambassadors,* 103.

29. Lih et al., *Stalin's Letters,* 232.

30. Frances Perkins, *The Roosevelt I Knew* (New York: Viking Press, 1946), 87.

31. The FDR Library contains a file of letters, telegrams, and other communiqués between Roosevelt and Bullitt that indicate a close, personal relationship between the two men. See President's Personal File, 1124 William C. Bullitt, 1933-1944, FDR Library.

32. The president was skeptical about the State Department's commitment to friendly relations with the Soviet Union. He felt that the department dragged its feet, and he was advised that the State Department bureaucrats, especially Robert Kelley, would not carry out his desire for harmonious relations with the Soviet Union. The minister of Latvia, Arthur Bliss Lane, actually urged FDR in 1936 to remove Kelley's influence from the State Department on the grounds that his anti-Soviet attitude could be a factor in leading Moscow to seek rapprochement with Nazi Germany. See Lane to FDR, 8 October 1936, PSF, FDR Library. Also see Richman, *United States and Soviet Union,* 68; Bennett, *Roosevelt and Security,* 78; and Propos, "Creating a Hard Line." Kelley's Eastern European Division was abolished in 1937, and Kelley was transferred to Turkey. See Yergin, *Shattered Peace,* 34ff. Roosevelt also felt that diplomats generally were "fossilized bureaucrats" and "frivolous dilettantes," and he much preferred to circumvent the professionals and use friends or trustworthy political allies on diplomatic initiatives. See DeSantis, *Diplomacy of Silence,* 79; William L. Langer and Everett S. Gleason, *The Challenge to Isolation: The World Crisis of 1937-1940 and American Foreign Policy* (New York: Harper, 1952), 2-10.

33. Stalin, *Sochineniia,* 7:167-90.

34. Arthur U. Pope, *Maxim Litvinoff* (New York: L. B. Fischer, 1943), 401-2; *Izvestiia,* 13 and 14 December 1933.

35. David Mayers sees "fragmentary evidence" that the Soviets were not enthusiastic about Bullitt's appointment: *Ambassadors,* 110.

36. Bohlen, *Witness,* 16-17; File I.F.3 Official American Personnel in USSR, Records of the Division of Eastern European Affairs, 1917-1941, Record Group 59, National Archives (hereafter cited as RG 59, NA).

37. Langer, "Red General," 209-11; James S. Herndon and Joseph O. Baylen, "Col. Philip R. Faymonville and the Red Army, 1934-43," *Slavic Review* 34 (Sept. 1975): 483-84.

3. "The Donkey, the Carrot, and the Club"

1. Nikolai N. Krestinsky, deputy foreign minister, USSR, to A. A. Troyanovsky, Soviet ambassador to the United States, 7 July 1934, Arkhiv vneshnei politiki (AVP), Russian Federation, Moscow, col. 0129, reg. 17, file 129, pp. 96-97.

2. Ivan A. Divilkovsky, "From Conversations with Bullitt," 12 March 1934, AVP, col. 0129, reg. 17, file 129, p. 28.

3. A. A. Troyanovsky to M. M. Litvinov, 3 March 1934, AVP, col. 0129, reg. 17, file 129, p. 127.

4. Memorandum by Hull, 26 March 1934; Bullitt to Hull, 28 March 1934; Bullitt to Hull, 2 April 1934, *FRUS: Soviet Union,* 71-76.

5. "On Services for Embassies" and "On America," 1-8 April 1934, RTsKhIDNI, col. 17, reg. 162, file 16, p. 31.

6. Hull, *Memoirs*, 1:303. Cf. Bullitt to Hull, 21 March 1934, *FRUS: Soviet Union*, 69. Also see Bullitt to Hull, 14 June 1934, and Bullitt to Hull, 15 June 1934, *FRUS: Soviet Union*, 106-7. Bullitt also informed Litvinov that the Johnson Bill, which would close U.S. credit markets to countries in default on their debts to the United States, would hurt the Soviet Union. Litvinov replied that it would not damage the Soviet Union because the Soviets could satisfy their needs elsewhere and, besides, there were many other countries in default, including England, France, and Italy. See Bullitt to Hull, 8 April 1934, *FRUS: Soviet Union*, 80. The United States finally obtained some suitable land for an embassy in 1972 and a building was eventually constructed. However, it apparently will never house the full embassy because of extensive Soviet bugging of the building. Now that the Soviet government has fallen, the Americans are thinking of building a new addition to the existing embassy and using the "bugged" building for routine matters.

7. Bullitt, *For the President*, 83. Cf. Bullitt to Hull, 16 June 1934, *FRUS: Soviet Union*, 110-11.

8. Troyanovsky to Litvinov, 3 March 1934.

9. Bullitt to Hull, 30 June 1934, *FRUS: Soviet Union*, 113.

10. Evgenii Vladimirovich Rubinin, "Conversation with Bullitt," 13 May 1934, AVP, col. 0129, reg. 17, file 1, pp. 71-73; Bullitt to Hull, 9 November 1935, *FRUS: Soviet Union*, 265.

11. Bullitt, *For the President*, 83.

12. Phillips to Bullitt, 23 April 1934, *FRUS: Soviet Union*, 85. FDR told Moore to try to settle the debt issue and to extend credits to the Soviet Union that would facilitate the process of settlement. FDR to Moore, 31 August 1934, ibid., 139.

13. Bullitt, *For the President*, 83.

14. Bullitt to Roosevelt, 14 July 1934, (PSF), FDR Library.

15. Bullitt, *For the President*, 91. Cf. Bullitt to Hull, 27 July 1934, *FRUS: Soviet Union*, 123-24.

16. Mayers, *Ambassadors*, 113.

17. Bullitt, *For the President*, 92.

18. Mayers, *Ambassadors*, 113.

19. Charles W. Thayer, *Bears in the Caviar* (Philadelphia: J. B. Lippincott, 1950), 115-29; Bohlen, *Witness*, 23-24; Bullitt, *For the President*, 93.

20. Bullitt to Roosevelt, 14 July 1934, August 5, 1934, PSF, FDR Library. Also see Thayer, *Bears in the Caviar*, 160; Edgar B. Nixon, ed., *Franklin D. Roosevelt and Foreign Affairs* (Cambridge: Harvard University Press, 1969), 2:171.

21. Bullitt, *For the President*, 97; Bullitt to Hull, 15 September 1934, *FRUS: Soviet Union*, 147.

22. Bullitt, *For the President*, 96-98. Also see Bullitt to Hull, 8 April 1934, *FRUS: Soviet Union*, 80; Bullitt to Hull, 16 June 1934, ibid., 109, 111; Bullitt to Hull, 9 July 1934, ibid., 115-16.

23. Roosevelt to Bullitt, 9 May 1934, 3 June 1935, PSF, FDR Library.

24. Krestinsky to Troyanovsky, 7 July 1934; F. V. Weinberg diary, memorandum of conversation with Loy Henderson, 5 November 1934, AVP, col. 0129, reg. 17, file 129, p. 39; E. V. Rubinin, chief, Third Western Department of Soviet Foreign Ministry, memorandum of conversation of Rubinin with Wiley, counselor of the U.S. Embassy, 16 October 1934, AVP, col. 0129, reg. 17, file 129, pp. 45, 48; Rubinin, "Conversation with Bullitt," 19 May 1934, pp. 71-73; Rubinin, "Conversations with Ameri-

cans," 25 July 1934, AVP, col. 0129, reg. 17, file 129, p. 66. Joseph Pilsudski was the military leader and eventual president of Poland who led the Polish forces against the Red Army in the Russo-Polish War of 1920-21. He was quite anti-Soviet.

25. "Conversation with Bullitt from the Diary of B. E. Skvirsky," 7 January 1935, col. AVP, 0129, reg. 18, file 1, pp. 164-66.

26. Bullitt, *For the President,* 104, 107.

27. N. N. Krestinsky, memorandum of meeting with Bullitt, 15 April 1935, col. AVP, 0129, reg. 18, file 1, p. 2.

28. Litvinov diary, memorandum of conversation with Bullitt, 4 May 1935, col. AVP, 0129, reg. 18, file 1, p. 3.

29. T. Arens, memorandum of conversation with Bullitt, 6 May 1935, AVP, col. 0129, reg. 19, file 1, pp. 176-78.

30. Bullitt, *For the President,* 116. For information on Kirov's murder, see Robert Conquest, *Stalin and the Kirov Murder* (New York: Oxford University Press, 1989).

31. Tucker, *Stalin in Power,* 277.

32. Bullitt, *For the President,* 118-21.

33. Ibid., 151.

34. Based on his letters to Molotov, Stalin actually believed in the guilt of these men. See Lih et al., *Stalin's Letters,* 44-62.

35. Pavel Sudoplatov et al., *Special Tasks: The Memoirs of an Unwanted Witness—A Soviet Spymaster* (Boston: Little, Brown, 1994), vii.

36. Bullitt, *For the President,* 155-57. Also see Bullitt to Hull, 20 April 1936, *FRUS: Soviet Union,* 291-95. For details on the Collective Security policy, see Jonathan Haslam, *The Soviet Union and the Search for Collective Security, 1933-1939* (New York: St. Martin's Press, 1984); Jiri Hochman, *The Soviet Union and the Failure of Collective Security, 1934-1938* (Ithaca, N.Y.: Cornell University Press, 1984); Maxim Litvinov, *Vneshniaia politika SSSR* (Moscow, 1937).

37. Litvinov to Troyanovsky, 14 July 1935, AVP, col. 0129, reg. 18, file 1, pp. 63-64.

38. Bullitt to Hull, 19 July 1935, *FRUS: Soviet Union,* 224-25.

39. Oleg V. Khlevniuk, *1937: Stalin, NKVD, i Sovetskoi obschestvo* (Moscow, 1992), 81-82. Historian Roy Medvedev estimated the total number of victims killed by Stalinism at about 35 million. See *Moskovskiye novosti,* 27 November 1988, 8-9. Aleksander Tsipko, in a brilliant analysis, explains Stalinism as a result of a moral vacuum where revolution and violence are laws unto themselves and Bolshevik leaders deliberately and fatally turned power over to Stalin. See *Nauka i zhizn,* no. 11 (Nov. 1988): 45-54; *Nauka i zhizn,* no. 12 (Dec. 1988): 40-48; *Nauka i zhizn,* no. 1 (Jan. 1989): 46-56; and *Nauka i zhizn,* no. 2 (Feb. 1989): 53-61.

40. Charles E. Bohlen, *The Transformation of American Foreign Policy* (New York: W. W. Norton, 1966), 57.

41. Bullitt, *For the President,* 130-31, 136-37. Also see Bullitt to FDR, 15 July 1935, PSF, FDR Library.

42. Bullitt to Hull, 21 August 1935, *FRUS: Soviet Union,* 245-46.

43. Bullitt to Hull, 29 August 1935, 711.61/541, RG 59, NA.

44. Memorandum by Kelley, attached to Bullitt to Hull, 1935, 761.00/260, RG 59, NA; Hull to Bullitt, 23 August 1935, Congress, Communist International VII 861.00/72, RG 59, NA.

45. Bullitt to Hull, 19 July 1935, *FRUS: Soviet Union,* 224-25.

46. Bullitt to the State Department, 9 November 1935, *FRUS: Soviet Union*, 264.

47. A. Neiman, memorandum of conversation with Bullitt, 13 November 1935, AVP, col. col. 0129, reg. 18, file 1, pp. 29-30; Neiman, memorandum of conversation with Henderson, 30 December 1935, ibid., p. 6.

48. Joseph Rothschild, *Return to Diversity: A Political History of East Central Europe since World War II* (New York: Oxford University Press, 1993), 5.

49. Bullitt, *For the President*, 104, 151-52.

50. Bullitt to Hull, 20 April 1936, *FRUS: Soviet Union*, 291.

51. Bullitt, *For the President*, 156.

52. Bullitt to Hull, 4 March 1936, *FRUS: Soviet Union*, 289-90.

53. Bullitt to Hull, 20 April 1936, *FRUS: Soviet Union*, 293.

54. Isaacson and Thomas, *Wise Men*, 166.

55. Bullitt, *For the President*, 156.

56. Farnsworth, *Bullitt*, 153-54.

57. Kennan, *Memoirs*, 80.

58. Litvinov to Troyanovsky, 14 July 1935, AVP, col. 0129, reg. 18, file 1, p. 63-64; Neiman, conversation with Bullitt, 13 November 1935, ibid., pp. 29-30; Litvinov diary, memorandum of conversation with Bullitt, 4 May 1935, ibid., p. 3.

59. A. Neiman, memorandum of conversation with Bullitt, 9 November 1935, AVP, col. 0129, reg. 18, file 1, pp. 25-26.

60. S. Stolyar, memorandum of conversation with Kennan, 7 December 1935, AVP, col. 0129, reg. 18, file 1, pp. 14-15.

61. A. A. Troyanovsky to N. N. Krestinsky, 28 September 1935, AVP, col. 0129, op 18, file 1., p. 67.

62. A. Neiman, memorandum of conversation with Bullitt, 13 November 1935, AVP, col. 0129, op 18, file 1., pp. 29-30.

63. Henderson to Hull, 16 November 1936, *FRUS: Soviet Union*, 310-11.

64. Langer, "Red General," 211-12.

65. Rubinin, "Conversations with Americans," 25 July 1934, p. 66; Krestinsky to Troyanovsky, 7 July 1935; E. V. Rubinin, "Conversation with Wiley," 16 October 1934, p. 48.

66. Bullitt, *For the President*, 181; memorandum by Moore, 3 December 1936, *FRUS: Soviet Union*, 319.

4. "His Brown Eye Is Exceedingly Kindly and Gentle"

1. Joseph E. Davies, *Mission to Moscow* (New York: Simon and Schuster, 1941), 358.

2. Davies to Hull, 6 June 1938, *FRUS: Soviet Union*, 572-73.

3. Ibid., 573-77; Stalin to Molotov, 19 June 1932, RTsKhIDNI, col. 558, reg. 1, file 5388, in Lih et al., *Stalin's Letters*, 229.

4. Davies, *Mission*, 358, 362.

5. Robert C. Williams, *Russian Art and American Money, 1900-1940* (Cambridge: Harvard University Press, 1980), 253.

6. Davies, *Mission*, 358.

7. Ibid., 359.

8. Ibid., 356.

9. Davies to Hull, 9 June 1938, *FRUS: Soviet Union*, 571. Also see memorandum by Bohlen, 2 February 1938, ibid., 511.

10. Memorandum by Davies, 5 June 1938, ibid., 571; Davies, *Mission*, 356-57.

11. Keith Eubanks, *Summit at Teheran* (New York: William Morrow, 1985), 71. For a sampling of Davies's critics, see Bohlen, *Witness*, 44, 56; Kennan, *Memoirs*, 82-84; Conquest, *Great Terror*, 188, 468; Tucker, *Stalin in Power*, 408, 503; Hollander, *Political Pilgrims*, 130; Farnsworth, *Bullitt*, 174-75; David Mayers, *George Kennan and the Dilemmas of U.S. Foreign Policy* (New York: Oxford University Press, 1988), 43-44.

12. Elizabeth Kimball MacLean, *Joseph E. Davies: Envoy to the Soviets* (Westport, Colo.: Praeger, 1992), 8; Nancy Rubin, *American Empress: The Life and Times of Marjorie Merriweather Post* (New York: Villard Books, 1995), 106.

13. Davies, *Mission*, 28, 367, 356, 359; MacLean, *Davies*, 18.

14. MacLean, *Davies*, xi, 16-18; Keith Eagles, *Ambassador Joseph E. Davies and American-Soviet Relations, 1937-1941* (New York: Garland, 1985), 20-23.

15. Rubin, *Empress*, 211-12.

16. Ibid., 216-17.

17. MacLean emphasizes that Davies's bias against and disdain of European and Old World values played "a crucial role in his approach to Soviet-American relations": *Davies*, 17.

18. Ibid., 217-28; Davies, *Mission*, xii.

19. Letter to Roosevelt, 25 January 1937, Davies Papers (DP), Library of Congress.

20. Farnsworth, *Bullitt*, 232n. 17.

21. Kennan, *Memoirs*, 82. Henderson stopped the resignation plan. See George M. Baer, ed., *A Question of Trust: The Origins of U.S.-Soviet Diplomatic Relations, the Memoirs of Loy W. Henderson* (Stanford, Calif.: Hoover Institution Press, 1986), 422-23.

22. Isaacson and Thomas, *Wise Men*, 168.

23. Farnsworth, *Bullitt*, 232n. 17; John Gunther, *Roosevelt in Retrospect: A Profile in History* (New York: Harper, 1950), 263.

24. Bennett, *Roosevelt and Security*, 78, 145, 103.

25. Davies, *Mission*, 4, 6. See also Davies diary, 2 January 1937, DP.

26. Rubin, *Empress*, 220.

27. Davies to Hull, 19 January 1937, *FRUS: Soviet Union*, 358-59; memorandum by Henderson, 16 January 1937, ibid., 440-41.

28. Maxim Litvinov, *Notes for a Journal* (New York: William Morrow, 1955), 243-44.

29. C. Oumansky, Soviet chargé in the USA, to M. M. Litvinov, people's commissar of foreign affairs, USSR, 19 January 1937, AVP, col. 0129, reg. 20, file 3, pp. 99, 97.

30. F. V. Weinberg diary, "Conversation with Henderson and Kirk," 10 May 1938, AVP, col. 0129, reg. 21, file 1, p. 45.

31. Kirk to Hull, 25 November 1938, *FRUS: Soviet Union*, 593-94. Also see Davies, *Mission*, 174-75; Propas, "Creating a Hard Line," 209-26.

32. Maddux, "American Diplomats," 472; Bennett, *Roosevelt and Security*, 141; Davies to FDR, 18 January 1939, Official File (OF) 3601; Langer, "Red General," 213-14. See also Donald B. Schewe, ed., *Franklin D. Roosevelt and Foreign Affairs* (New York: Clearwater, 1979), 13:125.

33. Isaacson and Thomas, *Wise Men*, 168. Also see Davies to Kelley, 10 February 1937, DP. Historian David Mayers views Davies's role in Kennan's removal as one of genuine concern for Kennan's health: *Ambassadors*, 121.

34. Memorandum by Assistant Secretary of State George Messersmith to Secretary of State, 3 January 1938, *FRUS: Soviet Union*, 504-5. FDR was certainly buttressed in his suspicion of the State Department professionals by Eleanor Roosevelt, Harry Hopkins, Felix Frankfurter, Harold Ickes, and Henry Morgenthau Jr. Messersmith even argued that the embassy staff in Moscow was ignorant of Soviet affairs. See Bennett, *Roosevelt and Security*, 142-43.

35. Kennan, *Memoirs*, 83-85.

36. Bennett, *Roosevelt and Security*, 102, 105; Robert Conquest, *Stalin: Breaker of Nations* (New York: Penguin Books, 1991), 244.

37. Bennett, *Roosevelt and Security*, 104.

38. William Phillips, *Ventures in Diplomacy* (Boston: Beacon Press, 1953), 203.

39. MacLean, *Davies*, 37-38. Historian Thomas Maddux points out that FDR needed the analysis of the embassy experts to balance Davies's erroneous view of Stalin's social and economic policies, the purge trials, and political control: "American Diplomats," 469-70, 485-87.

40. Kennan, *Memoirs*, 86; memorandum by Henderson, 2 July 1938, *FRUS: Soviet Union*, 586.

5. "The System Is Now a Type of Capitalistic State Socialism"

1. Davies, *Mission*, 15-16, 20-23.

2. Davies to Colonel House, 27 January 1937, DP; Davies, *Mission*, 12; Davies to Roy Van Bomel, 25 January 1937, DP.

3. *New York Times*, 19 December 1936. Andrei Gromyko reported that the cream debate was all in jest. He saluted Davies as a "colorful, positive figure" who was a major influence on Roosevelt and American ruling circles. See Gromyko, *Memories*, trans. Harold Shukman (London: Hutchinson, 1989), 27-28.

4. Davies diary, 25 January 1937, DP; Davies, *Mission*, 26, 368.

5. Memorandum to Henderson, 1 February 1937, DP; Davies, *Mission*, 29. Davies maintained an interest in the Soviet Union until his death in 1957. He kept a diary while in Moscow and later during World War II, and he produced a book in 1941 called *Mission to Moscow* based on his service as ambassador. Unfortunately, many of the records that he kept or produced are an exercise in self-promotion and are unreliable. Nonetheless, they are valuable as a general guide to the events of his ambassadorship and, if used carefully, do provide some insight into his approach and philosophy. Henderson reported that he respected Davies, even though he disagreed with him, and that they remained friends. See Baer, *Question of Trust*, 413-14, 422-23.

6. Davies, *Mission*, 275; Langer, "Red General," 214; Taylor, *Stalin's Apologist*, 266-67, 276.

7. Kennan, *Memoirs*, 82; Bohlen, *Witness*, 45, 51-52.

8. Davies to Hull, 19 January 1937, *FRUS: Soviet Union*, 359; Langer, "Red General," 211; Herndon and Baylen, "Faymonville," 495-96.

9. Davies, *Mission*, 44-45; Martin A. Weil, *A Pretty Good Club: The Founding Fathers of the U.S. Foreign Service* (New York: W. W. Norton, 1978), 92; personal

interview with Elbridge Durbrow, 10 November 1981, Washington, D.C. Durbrow maintained to this author that Davies's records are unreliable because he altered them to make himself look more astute than he was. If that is the case, Davies did not succeed. Also see Maddux, *Years of Estrangement*, 182n. 9. For sympathetic treatments of Davies, see MacLean, *Davies*; Yergin, *Shattered Peace*; Mayers, *Ambassadors*.

10. Davies diary, 28 June 1937, DP.

11. Davies to Hull, 1 April 1938, DP; Davies, *Mission*, 324. Also see Kenneth Bourne and D. C. Watt, eds., *British Documents on Foreign Affairs: Reports and Papers from the Foreign Office*, vol. 14, *The Soviet Union* (Frederick, Md.: University Publications of America, 1983), 367-68.

12. Memorandum by Kuniholm, 26 May 1937, *FRUS: Soviet Union*, 442-44.

13. Davies, *Mission*, 105.

14. Henderson to Hull, 14 May 1937, *FRUS: Soviet Union*, 374-76; Henderson to Hull, 13 June 1937, ibid., 380; Henderson to Hull, 20 August 1937, ibid., 389; Henderson to Hull, 20 September 1937, ibid., 391, 394; memorandum by Kennan, 24 November 1937, ibid., 399, 446-47; Henderson to Hull, 13 January 1938, ibid., 506-7; memorandum by Bohlen, 2 February 1938, ibid., 509-12.

15. Davies, *Mission*, 62, 65, 85-87.

16. Memorandum by Davies, 9 June 1938, DP.

17. Davies to Hull, 9 June 1938, *FRUS: Soviet Union*, 571.

18. Davies, *Mission*, 179; Langer, "Red General," 212-13.

19. Tucker, *Stalin in Power*, 191-92; see also James William Crowl, *Angels in Stalin's Paradise: Western Reporters in Soviet Russia, 1917-1937: A Study of Louis Fischer and Walter Duranty* (Washington, D.C.: University Press of America, 1982); Taylor, *Stalin's Apologist*; and Hollander, *Political Pilgrims*.

20. Davies, *Mission*, 117-18.

21. Ibid., 76, 334.

22. Ibid., 103.

23. Davies to Steve Early, 4 April 1938, DP.

24. Davies to Hull, 1 April 1938, *FRUS: Soviet Union*, 550-51; Davies to Hull, 6 June 1938, ibid., 555, 558; Davies, *Mission*, 308-9, 67-68, 120-21, 191-92.

25. Davies, *Mission*, 67, 112; Davies diary, 11 March 1937, DP.

26. Henderson to Hull, 22 December 1937, *FRUS: Soviet Union*, 401-3; memorandum by Bohlen, 2 February 1938, ibid., 510-11.

27. Davies, *Mission*, 272-73; Langer, "Red General," 212.

28. Davies, *Mission*, 43-44; Langer, "Red General," 212-13.

29. Memorandum by Kennan, 13 February 1937, *FRUS: Soviet Union*, 363.

30. Davies to R. Walton Moore, 25 January 1937, DP; Davies to Colonel House, 27 January 1937, DP.

31. Davies diary, 26 January 1937, DP; Davies, *Mission*, 150.

32. MacLean, *Davies*, 4, 17, 184.

33. Davies, *Mission*, 170; Davies diary, 9 July 1937, DP; Langer, "Red General," 212-13.

34. Davies, *Mission*, 160-61, 168; Davies to Roosevelt, 10 July 1937, DP.

35. Henderson to Hull, 11 June 1937, *FRUS: Soviet Union*, 378; Henderson to Hull, 18 February 1938, ibid., 517-19.

36. Langer, "Red General," 213; Herndon and Baylen, "Faymonville," 495.

37. Davies, *Mission*, 272. Davies's characterization of the purges as a way to destroy Hitler's fifth columns in USSR evidently was written in late 1941.

38. Isaacson and Thomas, *Wise Men*, 174.

39. Langer, "Red General," 212; Bohlen, *Witness*, 57; Rubin, *Empress*, 230.

40. Williams, *Russian Art*, 253.

41. The new material being released on the purges is overwhelming. Documents have been published in numerous journals and newspapers since 1988, including *Novy mir, Argumenty i fakty, Izvestiia, Pravda, Nedelya, Voprosy istorii, Vovaia i noveyshaia istoriia, Novoye vremia, Voyenno-istorichesky zhurnal, Literaturnaiya gazeta*, and *Moscow News*. In addition, new information is available in Walter Laqueur, *Stalin: The Glasnost Revelations* (New York: Scribner, 1990); Robert C. Tucker, *Stalin in Power;* Khrushchev, *Glasnost Tapes;* Arkady Vaksberg, *Stalin's Prosecutor: The Life of Andrei Vyshinsky* (New York: Grove Weidenfeld, 1991); Dmitri Volkogonov, *Stalin: Triumph and Tragedy*, ed. and trans. by Harold Shukman (New York: Grove Weidenfeld, 1991); Konstantin Simonov, *Glazami chelovek moevo pokoleniia: razmyshleniia o I. V. Staline* (Moscow: Pravda, 1990); Sudoplatov et al., *Special Tasks;* and Alan Bullock, *Hitler and Stalin: Parallel Lives* (New York: Vintage Books, 1993). Even Molotov admitted in a series of interviews between 1969 and 1986 that Stalin made some mistakes. See Chuyev, *Sto sorok besed c Molotovym*.

6. "Less Objective and More Friendly"

1. Davies, *Mission*, 79, 108; Davies to Hull, 10 July 1937, *FRUS: Soviet Union*, 386-87.

2. Oumansky to Litvinov, telegram, 21 January 1939, *DVP*, 1:66-67. Oumansky reported that the American government was divided over when to recognize Franco's regime. See Oumansky to Litvinov, telegram, 6 March 1939, *DVP*, 1:166-67.

3. Davies, *Mission*, 59-60, 78-79; Davies to Hull, 19 February 1937, *FRUS: Soviet Union*, 373.

4. Order of People's Commissar of Defense Kliment Voroshilov and People's Commissar of Internal Security Lavrenti Beria on aid to the Chinese government in Manchuria, no. 8, 15 April 1939, *OGBSSSR*, 36-37; memorandum of conversation between Molotov and Chinese ambassador Yan Tsze, 10 September 1939, *DVP*, 2:57-59.

5. Davies, *Mission*, 108-9.

6. Ibid., 171; Henderson to Hull, 20 August 1937, *FRUS: Soviet Union*, 388-89.

7. Soviet embassy to the State Department, 4 August 1937, *FRUS: Soviet Union*, 405.

8. Davies to Hull, 25 March 1937, *FRUS: Soviet Union*, 466.

9. Maddux, *Years of Estrangement*, 96; Schewe, *Roosevelt and Foreign Affairs*, 13:125; Davies to FDR, 18 January 1939, OF 3601.

10. Davies, *Mission*, 241-42, 247-48.

11. Ibid., 290-92.

12. Ibid., 304, 297-99, 301, 306; Henderson to Hull, 18 February 1938, *FRUS: Soviet Union*, 514-15.

13. Davies, *Mission*, 318, 321; Davies to FDR, 4 April 1938, PPF 1381, Davies Folder. Also see Davies to Hull, 18 April 1939, *FRUS: Soviet Union*, 756-57. In Brus-

sels he informed the Soviet ambassador, E. V. Rubinin, of his fear. See Rubinin to Litvinov, 25 February 1939, *DVP,* 1:154-55.

14. Davies, *Mission,* 264, 344-50.

15. Memorandum by Hull, 7 June 1938, *FRUS: Soviet Union,* 566-67.

16. Davies, *Mission,* 371; Davies diary, 24 June 1938, DP.

17. Faymonville shared Davies's opinion. See Langer, "Red General," 214.

18. Davies, *Mission,* 177.

19. Personal interview with Elbridge Durbrow, 10 November 1981, Washington, D.C.

20. FDR to McIntyre, 22 September 1937, and McIntyre to Davies, 22 September 1937, PPF 1381, Joseph E. Davies Folder; Rubin, *Empress,* 245.

21. Davies, *Mission,* 341, 368; F. V. Weinberg diary, "Conversation with Davis," 10 June 1938, AVP, col. 0129, reg. 21, file 1, p. 42.

22. Davies, *Mission,* 343, 365.

23. Davies to Hull, 1 April 1938, *FRUS: Soviet Union,* 549-50.

24. Rothschild, *Diversity,* 35-36.

25. The Soviet ambassador to England, Ivan Maisky, was encouraged by the British reaction to Hitler's pressure on Czechoslovakia. See Maisky to Litvinov, telegram, 14 March 1939, *DVP,* 1:183-84; Maisky to Litvinov, telegram, 17 March 1939, *DVP,* 1:198; Litvinov to Maisky, 19 March 1939, *DVP,* 1:206-8; Maisky to Litvinov, telegram, 1 April 1939, *DVP,* 1:243.

26. Robert Coulondre, *From Stalin to Hitler: Memoirs of Two Embassies, 1936-39* (Paris, 1950), 165.

27. Kirk to Hull, 11 March 1939, *FRUS: Soviet Union,* 739.

28. Litvinov to German ambassador F. Schulenburg, 18 March 1939, *DVP,* 1:202-4. On Skoda, the Soviets wanted to see if Germany would fill their orders for weapons. See A. F. Merekalov to Litvinov, 18 April 1939, *DVP,* 1:293-96; memorandum of conversation between Merekalov and German Secretary of State E. Weizsacker, 17 April 1939, *DVP,* 1:291-92.

29. Ulam, *Expansion and Coexistence,* 266-69.

30. *Documents on German Foreign Policy, 1918-1945,* series D (Washington: Government Printing Office, 1956), 6:139.

31. Churchill described to Maisky Hitler's reaction to the ultimatum. See Maisky to Litvinov, telegram, 1 May 1939, *DVP,* 1:325.

32. See, for example, Maisky to Litvinov, telegram, 14 April 1939, *DVP,* 1:273-74.

33. Maisky to Litvinov, telegram, 1 April 1939, *DVP,* 1:243.

34. Memorandum of conversation between A. F. Merekalov and German Secretary of State E. Weizsacker, 17 April 1939, *DVP,* 1:291-93.

35. Stalin [to list of Soviet ambassadors, including Oumansky, Maisky, and Merekalov], telegram, 3 May 1939, *DVP,* 1:327. The Germans immediately asked the Soviet embassy for biographical information on Molotov. See G. A. Astakhov to Molotov, 6 May 1939, *DVP,* 1:339-41.

36. Maisky to Molotov, telegram, 6 May 1939, *DVP,* 1:338-39. Churchill criticized the delay in a conversation with Maisky on October 6. See Maisky to Molotov, telegram, 7 October 1939, *DVP,* 2:168.

37. Ulam, *Expansion and Coexistence,* 272-73; Davies to Hull, 10 May 1939, *FRUS: Soviet Union,* 761.

38. Although the military mission from the West did not arrive until July, conversations about possible alliances and ties were carried on by the respective embassies as early as May. See memorandum of conversation between Molotov and F. Schulenburg, 20 May 1939, *DVP*, 1:386-87; memorandum of conversation between Molotov and British and French ambassadors (written by V. Potemkin), 27 May 1939, *DVP*, 1:401-4; G. A. Astakhov to Molotov, telegram, 30 May 1939, *DVP*, 1:405-6; G. A. Astakhov diary, 30 May, 2 June 1939, *DVP*, 1:409-12. Historian Thomas Maddux puts forth the curious notion that Stalin was making overtures to the United States and West in the face of Hitler's threats, but that the anti-Soviet bias of the Russian experts and State Department kept the United States from responding to these overtures and thus Stalin was forced to sign a nonaggression pact with Hitler. See Maddux, "Watching Stalin Maneuver."

39. Hull, *Memoirs*, 1:657-58.

40. Henderson to Dunn and Hickerson, 22 July 1939, *FRUS: Soviet Union*, 773-75.

41. Oumansky to Molotov, 6 June 1939, *DVP*, 1:424-25.

42. Bullitt to Phillips, 4 January 1934, *FRUS: Soviet Union*, 59.

43. Oumansky to Molotov, telegram, 1 July 1939, *DVP*, 1:517-19.

44. Oumansky to Litvinov, telegram, 21 March 1939, *DVP*, 1:214-15; Oumansky to Litvinov, telegram, 18 April 1939, *DVP*, 1:296-97; Oumansky to Molotov, telegram, 27 May 1939, *DVP*, 1:404; Oumansky to Molotov, 6 June 1939, *DVP*, 1:422-25; Oumansky to Molotov, telegram, 17 June 1939, *DVP*, 1:482-83; Oumansky to Molotov, telegram, 2 July 1939, *DVP*, 1:524; Oumansky diary, 9-26 June 1939, *DVP*, 1:445.

45. Oumansky diary, 6 June 1939, *DVP*, 1:430.

46. Oumansky to Molotov, telegram, 2 July 1939, *DVP*, 1:524-25.

47. Report on Soviet-American relations by Oumansky and Gromyko for Molotov, 9 August 1939, *DVP*, 1:589-93. Despite the litany of complaints, the Soviet embassy in Washington was treated with respect and consideration. The American embassy in Moscow, on the other hand, was barely tolerated, and the Soviet government usually looked for some advantage for itself in even minor matters. For example, when the embassy sought information about a counterfeit American passport in December 1938, the Soviet Foreign Ministry was slow to respond and then asked Lavrentia Beria, the head of the NKVD, to check to see whether counterfeit American passports would cause great damage to American interests. See M. Litvinov to L. Beria, 22 December 1938, AVP, col. 06, reg. 1, file 159, p. 2.

48. FDR to Weinberg, 5 July 1938, OF 220-A, Russian Miscellaneous; Davies to Hull, 17 January 1939, *FRUS: Soviet Union*, 598-99; Langer, "Red General," 214.

49. Bohlen, *Witness*, 56; Bennett, *Roosevelt and Security*, 180; Langer, "Red General," 214.

7. Old Testament Justice

1. Khrushchev, *Glasnost Tapes*, 46, 50-51, 53.

2. Oumansky to Molotov, telegram, 27 May 1939, *DVP*, 1:404; Oumansky to Molotov, 6 June 1939, *DVP*, 1:422-25; Oumansky to Molotov, telegram, 17 June 1939, *DVP*, 1:482-83; Oumansky to Molotov, telegram, 2 July 1939, *DVP*, 1:524; Oumansky diary, 9-26 June 1939, *DVP*, 1:445. For an account of Soviet talks with the

English and French, see "Short Account of Working Relations of Military Missions of USSR, England, and France," 12-22 August 1939, *DVP,* 1:663-70.

3. Welles to Steinhardt, 4 August 1939, no. 741.61/824a, RG 59, NA.

4. Steinhardt to Welles, 16 August 1939, no. 741.61/828 1/2, RG 59, NA.

5. Steinhardt to Hull, 16 August 1939, no. 761.62/538, RG 59, NA. Also see Steinhardt to Welles, 16 August 1939, no. 741.61/828 1/2, RG 59, NA; also Bohlen, *Witness,* 61-82. Herwarth and the German ambassador, Friedrich-Werner von Schulenburg, opposed the Nazis. Schulenburg was executed by the Nazis in 1944 after he was implicated in a nearly successful assassination of Hitler. Herwarth lived on to become the Federal Republic of Germany's representative to England. For details of his career, including his involvement with the American embassy in Moscow, see Hans Herwarth, *Against Two Evils: Memoirs of a Diplomat-Soldier during the Third Reich* (New York: Rawson, 1981).

6. Bohlen, *Witness,* 81-82; Isaacson and Thomas, *Wise Men,* 276. Although the United States informed London, the British did not receive the information because of incompetence or Soviet penetration of the Foreign Office Communications Department and were surprised by the Nazi-Soviet Pact. See Weinberg, *World at Arms,* 41.

7. I. M. Maisky outlined Hitler's plans to Eduard Beneš, the Czech leader, and explained them as essentially defensive. See Maisky diary, 23 August 1939, *DVP,* 1:645-46.

8. Steinhardt to Hull, 24 August 1939, no. 761.6211/93, RG 59, NA. The best book on the Nazi-Soviet alliance is Anthony Read and David Fisher, *Deadly Embrace: Hitler, Stalin, and the Nazi-Soviet Pact, 1939-1941* (New York: W. W. Norton, 1989).

9. Secret Political Protocol, 23 August 1939, *DVP,* 1:632.

10. Steinhardt to Rudolph E. Schoenfeld, 9 December 1939, Steinhardt Papers (SP), Library of Congress.

11. German-Soviet Agreement on Friendship and Boundaries between USSR and Germany, 28 September 1939, *DVP,* 2:134-35; Secret Political Protocol, 28 September 1939, *DVP,* 2:135-36. Lithuania was traded by Germany as punishment for refusing to join the Nazi-Soviet attack on Poland. See Weinberg, *World at Arms,* 53.

12. Memorandum of conversation between Molotov and Chinese ambassador Yan Tsze, 10 September 1939, *DVP,* 2:57-59; memorandum of conversations between Molotov and Japanese ambassador S. Togo, 9 September 1939, *DVP,* 2:554-57, and 14 September 1939, *DVP,* 2:75-77; Joint Protocol Reached between Commander of Soviet-Mongolian Forces and Japanese Army on Cease-fire, *DVP,* 2:90; memorandum of conversation between Molotov and Japanese ambassador S. Togo, 11 November 1939, *DVP,* 2:276-78; answer of USSR government on mutual relations with Japan, 16 November 1939, *DVP,* 2:309; agreement between Soviet and Japanese governments, 19 November 1939, *DVP,* 2:317-18; N. I. Generalov diary, 7-18 September 1939, *DVP,* 2:39-43.

13. Steinhardt to Hinkie, 4 June 1940, SP.

14. After Sweden, Steinhardt served in Peru, Soviet Russia, Turkey, Czechoslovakia, and Canada. The best study of Steinhardt is J. E. O'Connor, "Laurence A. Steinhardt and American Policy toward the Soviet Union, 1939-1941" (Ph.D. diss., University of Virginia, 1968). The ambassador's correspondence from Moscow between September 1940 and November 1941, when he was withdrawn, has been lost. See his

papers at the Library of Congress for additional information. For details on his life, see Constantine Oumansky, "Profile of USA Representative to USSR Laurence Steinhardt," 7 August 1939, AVP, col. 06, reg. 1, file 159, pp. 28-33, 38-39; and "Laurence A. Steinhardt," *Current Biography 1941* (New York: H. W. Wilson, 1941), 822.

15. Hull, *Memoirs,* 1:603.

16. Joseph Davies entertained Untermeyer in Moscow in August 1937 and reported that he was a great admirer of the Soviet system: *Mission,* 210-11.

17. Michael Aronson challenges the assumption that the czarist regime of Alexander III was one of the great persecutors of the Jews. See his *Troubled Waters: The Origins of the 1881 Anti-Jewish Pogroms in Russia* (Pittsburgh: University of Pittsburgh Press, 1990); see also Mayers, *Ambassadors,* 125.

18. V. N. Barkov dairy, 5 March 1940, AVP, col. 0129, reg. 24, file 4, p. 14.

19. Steinhardt to Edward Page Jr., 21 June 1939, SP.

20. Messersmith to Hull, 16 December 1939, *FRUS: Soviet Union,* 867.

21. Roosevelt to Hull and Welles, 22 December 1939, *FRUS: Soviet Union,* 868-69; Bennett, *Roosevelt and Security,* 182.

22. Oumansky to Molotov, 6 June 1939, *DVP,* 1:424.

23. Oumansky to Molotov, telegram, 1 July 1939, *DVP,* 1:517-19; Oumansky diary, 6 June 1939, *DVP,* 1:430.

24. Baer, ed., *Question of Trust,* 520-22. On Steinhardt's view of his staff, see Steinhardt to Henderson, 23 December 1939; Steinhardt to M. A. Thompson, 1 December 1941; Steinhardt to Henderson, undated; Steinhardt to Henderson, 11 August 1939, SP. Bohlen, however, thought Steinhardt was too aggressive and egotistical. See Bohlen, *Witness,* 88-89.

25. Oumansky to Molotov, 6 June 1939, *DVP,* 1:424; Henry C. Cassidy, *Moscow Dateline* (Boston: Houghton Mifflin, 1943), 76; Steinhardt to Alvin Untermeyer, 5 March 1940, SP.

26. Steinhardt also used publicists to extol his importance, and he demanded attention from the State Department and from Roosevelt. See Mayers, *Ambassadors,* 125.

27. Steinhardt to Morris Schindler, Seeman Brothers, 7 June 1939; Steinhardt to Charles Dickerson, 6 June 1939, SP.

28. Steinhardt to Henderson, 11 August and 20 October 1939, SP.

29. Steinhardt to John Browning, 26 December 1939, SP.

30. Steinhardt to Hull, 23 December 1940, U.S. State Department, *Foreign Relations of the United States 1940, vol. 3, The British Commonwealth, the Soviet Union, the Near East, and Africa* (Washington: Government Printing Office, 1958), 436-37; Cassidy, *Moscow Dateline,* 76.

31. Steinhardt to Nathaniel P. Davis, 13 March 1940; Steinhardt to Henderson, 29 January 1940; and Steinhardt to John C. Wiley, 2 February 1940, SP.

32. Steinhardt to Colvin Brown, 1 February 1940, SP.

33. V. N. Barkov diary, 16 April 1940, AVP, col. 0129, reg. 24, file 4, pp. 21-23.

34. Steinhardt to Anthony J. D. Biddle, 23 February 1940; Steinhardt to Henderson, 29 January 1940, SP.

35. Steinhardt to Carl Trygger, 26 March 1940, and Steinhardt to Alvin Untermeyer, 5 March 1940, SP; memorandum by Henderson, 29 [30] August 1939, *FRUS: Soviet Union,* 847-54.

36. Steinhardt to Hull, 2 September 1939, *FRUS: Soviet Union,* 854; A. Gromyko to V. Molotov, 1 September 1939, AVP, col. 06, reg. 1, file 159, p. 38.

37. Profile of USA Representative to USSR Laurence Steinhardt compiled by Constantine Oumansky, 7 August 1939, AVP, col. 06, reg. 1, file 159, pp. 28-33, 38-39.

8. "A Silent Partner to Germany"

1. Memorandum of conversation between Molotov and Polish ambassador, 8 September 1939, *DVP*, 2:26; Steinhardt to Hull, 9 September 1939, *FRUS: Soviet Union*, 779-80; Ulam, *Expansion and Coexistence*, 282-83; Steinhardt to Hull, 16 August 1939, *FRUS: Soviet Union*, 778.

2. Steinhardt to Hull, 17 September 1939, *FRUS: Soviet Union*, 782-83. Molotov stunned the Polish ambassador with the news of the invasion. See memorandum of conversation between V. P. Potemkin and Polish ambassador, 17 September 1939, *DVP*, 2:94-97. Potemkin presented the ambassador with two notes from Molotov.

3. NKVD directive for western oblasts of Ukraine and Byelorussia by Lavrenti Beria, 15 September 1939, *OGBSSSR*, 79-81; management of frontiers by NKVD troops in Kiev District and orders for the Red Army crossing into Poland, 17 September 1939, *OGBSSSR*, 85-86; written notes on border administration and border government relations with Germany, 3 June 1940, *OGBSSSR*, 208-9.

4. The Soviet delegation in Washington informed Molotov that the press asked Hull if the embargo would be extended to the USSR and he answered that the question was not yet settled and that the United States was in no hurry to act until a clear picture emerged in Europe. See D. S. Chuvakhin to Molotov, telegram, 23 September 1939, *DVP*, 2:127. For a solid treatment of the Soviet move into Poland, see Jan T. Gross, *Revolution from Abroad: The Soviet Conquest of Poland's Western Ukraine and Western Byelorussia* (Princeton: Princeton University Press, 1987), and Keith Sword, ed., *The Soviet Takeover of the Polish Eastern Provinces, 1939-41* (New York: St. Martin's Press, 1991).

5. Steinhardt to Hull, 26 September 1939, no. 740.0011 European War 1939/554; Steinhardt to Hull, 29 September 1939, no. 740.0011 European War 1939/624; Steinhardt to Hull, 23 October 1939, no. 761.6211/268; Steinhardt to Hull, 29 October 1939, no. 300.115(39) City of Flint/60, RG 59, NA. Steinhardt's analysis is supported by the economic relationship between the USSR and Germany. See Molotov to Ribbentrop, 28 September 1939, *DVP*, 2:138.

6. Steinhardt to Hull, 15 November 1940, no. 761.62/804, RG 59, NA.

7. Quote is from the copy of Stalin's speech that T. S. Bushuevaia found in the "Secret Booty Funds of the Special USSR Archive," first published in *Novy mir* in 1995 and cited in Raack, "International Debate Goes On," 51. Also see Raack, "Stalin's Role," 198-99.

8. Letter from G. Dimitrov to E. Browder on the Tasks of Communists in the Condition of the Imperial War, end of September/beginning of October 1939, *KIVMV*, 135.

9. Directive of Executive Committee of Comintern Secretariat with Respect to the Beginning of the War, 8 September 1939, *KIVMV*, 88-89; Position of Communist Parties in Connection with the Conclusion of the Soviet-German Nonaggression Pact (no date), *KIVMV*, 73-83; Information on Thinking in Germany from the Conclusion of the Soviet-German Pact and War to 3 January 1940, *KIVMV*, 231-36.

10. War and Tasks of Communists, end of September 1939, *KIVMV*, 109. On

Stalin's control of the Comintern, see Niels Erik Rosenfeldt, *Stalin's Secret Chancellery and the Comintern* (Copenhagen: C. A. Reitzels, 1991).

11. Directive of Executive Committee of Comintern Secretariat with Respect to the Beginning of the War, 8 September 1939, *KIVMV,* 88-89.

12. War and Tasks of Communists, end of September 1939, *KIVMV,* 117.

13. Memorandum of conversation between Stalin, Molotov, and Turkish foreign minister, 1 October 1939, *DVP,* 149. The Turks nonetheless signed an economic alliance with the British and French on October 19, but they remained neutral.

14. Bennett, *Roosevelt and Security,* 181-85.

15. FDR to Steinhardt, 11 October 1939, PSF, FDR Library; memorandum of conversation between Molotov and Steinhardt, 12 October 1939, *DVP,* 2:179-80. Molotov told Steinhardt that he was glad that U.S.-Finnish relations were "fine," but the problem was that Finland was holding Soviet territory around Lake Ladoga.

16. Steinhardt to Hull, 1 November 1939, *FRUS: Soviet Union,* 788.

17. Roosevelt to Hull and Welles, 22 December 1939, *FRUS: Soviet Union,* 868-69.

18. Gromyko to Molotov, 23 September 1939, *DVP,* 2:197-98.

19. Memorandum of conversation between V. P. Potemkin and Steinhardt, 17 October 1939, *DVP,* 2:197-98; D. S. Chuvakhin to Molotov, telegram, 30 October 1939, *DVP,* 2:245-46.

20. Memorandum of conversation between Molotov and Schulenburg, 19 October 1939, *DVP,* 2:201; Oumansky and K. I. Lukhashev to Molotov, telegram, 20 November 1939, *DVP,* 2:319-20; Oumansky to Molotov, telegram, 27 November 1939, *DVP,* 2:338-39.

21. Ulam, *Expansion and Coexistence,* 284.

22. Maisky to Molotov, telegram, 17 October 1939, *DVP,* 2:196-97; memorandum of conversation between Molotov and Schulenburg, 19 October 1939, *DVP,* 2:200-201; Molotov to Maisky, telegram, 19 October 1939, *DVP,* 2:210-12. Maisky also had conversations with Churchill and Anthony Eden about the war. See Maisky to Molotov, telegrams, 7 and 13 October 1939, 2:167-69, 183-84.

23. For Molotov's comment, see Ulam, *Expansion and Coexistence,* 284. For Stalin's comments to Hopkins, see memorandums by Hopkins, 30 and 31 July 1941, U.S. State Department, *Foreign Relations of the United States,* vol. 1, *General, the Soviet Union, 1941* (Washington: Government Printing Office, 1958), 803.

24. Steinhardt to Hull, 1 December 1939, no. 740.0016 European War/1939/108, RG 59, NA.

25. Memorandum of conversation between Molotov and Steinhardt, 12 October 1939, *DVP,* 2:179-80.

26. Steinhardt to Hull, 8 December 1939, no. 760D.61/681, RG 59, NA.

27. Steinhardt to Hull, 2 December 1939, no. 760D.61/585, RG 59, NA.

28. Steinhardt to Hull, 18 December 1939, no. 760D.61/790, RG 59, NA.

29. Steinhardt to Henderson, 13 December 1939, SP.

30. Steinhardt to Henderson, 6 January 1940; Steinhardt to Sumner Welles, 11 January 1940, SP.

31. Steinhardt to Henderson, 2 March 1940, SP.

32. Memorandum by Hull, 1 February 1940, and Hull to Amtrog Trading Corporation, 2 March 1940, *FRUS: 1940,* 3:250-51, 253.

33. Memorandum by Henderson, 7 June 1940, and memorandum by Hull, 12

June 1940; memorandum by Henderson, 22 May 1940; Oumansky to Hull, 12 June 1940, *FRUS: 1940*, 3:297-98, 311-21; Henderson to Steinhardt, 29 January 1940, SP. In *America and the Winter War, 1939-1940* (New York: Garland, 1980), Travis Beal Jacobs argues that Roosevelt's actions on behalf of Finland were strong and supportive.

34. Steinhardt to Henderson, 28 September 1939, 20 October 1939; and Henderson to Steinhardt, 29 January 1940, SP. Also see Mayers, *Ambassadors*, 128.

35. Hull to Steinhardt, 8 March 1940, no. 760D.61/1225, RG 59, NA; Steinhardt to Henderson, 16 March 1940, SP.

36. V. N. Barkov diary, 5 March 1940, AVP, col. 0129, reg. 24, file 4, pp. 12-15; Soloman A. Lozovsky diary, 27 March 1940, AVP, col. 0129, reg. 24, file 2, pp. 8-13. Note added stating that revised memorandum delivered to Steinhardt at 9 A.M. on March 28.

37. Barkov diary, 16 April 1940, AVP, col. 0129, reg. 24, file 4, pp. 21-23.

38. Winston S. Churchill, *Their Finest Hour* (Boston: Houghton Mifflin, 1949), 134-37.

39. Memorandum by Atherton to Welles, 26 November 1940, *FRUS: 1940*, 3:408.

40. Churchill, *Their Finest Hour*, 136. For a thorough study of the Cripps mission, see Steven M. Miner, *Between Churchill and Stalin: The Soviet Union, Great Britain, and the Origins of the Grand Alliance* (Chapel Hill: University of North Carolina Press, 1988), chaps. 1-4.

41 Welles to Lothian, 18 June 1940, *FRUS: 1940*, 3:322 (my italics).

42. Memorandum by Welles, 27 July 1940, *FRUS: 1940*, 3:329.

43. Memorandums by Henderson, 1 and 7 August 1940; *FRUS: 1940*, 3:340-62.

44. Welles to Oumansky, 21 January 1941, *FRUS: 1941*, 1:696.

45. Hull to Steinhardt, 3 October 1940, *FRUS: 1940*, 3:388-91.

46. Steinhardt to Henderson, 20 October 1940, Henderson Papers, Library of Congress.

47. Hull to Steinhardt, 3 October 1940, *FRUS: 1940*, 3:391; O'Connor, "Steinhardt and American Policy," 122; Mayers, *Ambassadors*, 128.

48. Steinhardt to Hull, 30 October 1940, *FRUS: 1940*, 3:401-3.

49. Steinhardt to Henderson, 20 October 1940, Henderson Papers; Steinhardt to Hull, 11 January 1941, *FRUS: 1941*, 1:121-22.

50. Welles to Roosevelt, 19 August 1940, no. 702.6111/334, RG 59, NA.

51. Information from NKVD reports on German military preparations, 6 November 1940, *OGBSSSR*, 278-79.

52. Miner, *Between Churchill and Stalin*, 99-100, 136-37. On the Soviet plan for Iran, see Robert Levine, *Flying in the Face of Uncertainty: Alternative Plans and Postures for Intervention in Southwest Asia* (Santa Monica, Calif.: Rand Graduate Institute, 1985), and Gerald Guensberg, *Soviet Command Study of Iran with Brief Analysis* (Falls Church, Va.: Delphic Associates, 1980).

53. *Documents on German Foreign Policy, 1918-1945*, series D (Washington, 1962), 12:195, 285. See also Ulam, *Expansion and Coexistence*, 306.

54. Conquest, *Stalin*, 234-35.

55. Miner, *Between Churchill and Stalin*, 137, 146; Urban, "Harriman," 26. Also see Louis Rotundo, "Stalin and the Outbreak of War in 1941," *Journal of Contemporary History* 24 (Apr. 1989): 277-99. R. C. Raack and a few Russian observers believe,

as mentioned, that there is enough evidence to investigate whether or not Stalin was planning an attack against Germany in July 1941—a strike motivated by Marxist-Leninist logic and only cut short by Hitler's preemptive invasion against Stalin. See Raack, "Stalin's Role," 198-211.

56. Steinhardt to Hull, 22 September 1940, no. 741.61/899, RG 59, NA; Steinhardt to Hull, 9 March 1941, no. 740.0011 European War 1939/8893, RG 59, NA; Steinhardt to Hull, 7 May 1941, *FRUS: 1941*, 1:613-15.

57. Steinhardt to Hull, 2 October 1940, no. 762.9411/93; Steinhardt to Hull, 31 October 1940, no. 761.62/769; and Steinhardt to Hull, 10 November 1940, no. 761.62/774, RG 59, NA.

58. Volkogonov, *Stalin*, 409. Volkogonov added in June 1991 that "the genetically flawed nature of our system was the major cause of the military failures at the start of the war." See *Izvestiia*, 22 June 1991. Radzinsky argues that Stalin's absence was a test à la Ivan IV to see who was loyal: *Stalin*, 471. Also see Michel Heller, "Mr. Stalin, I Presume?" *Survey: A Journal of East and West Studies* 30 (June 1989): 155-63.

59. Radio address by Foreign Minister Molotov, 22 June 1941; Ministerstvo inostrannyk del SSSR, *Sovetsko-Amerikanskie otnosheniia vo vremia velikoi otechestvennoi voiny 1941-1945* (Moscow: Izdatel'stvo politicheskoi literatury, 1984), 1:40-42 (hereafter cited as SAOVVOV).

60. *Novy mir*, December 1964, 163, 165; radio address by Stalin, 3 July 1941, SAOVVOV, 1:52. For the full text of radio address, see I. V. Stalin, *O velikoi otechestvennoi voine Sovetskogo Soiuza* (Moscow, 1948), 11-12.

61. Steinhardt to Hull, 7 June 1941, *FRUS: 1941*, 1:621. For a good account of the German invasion of the Soviet Union, see Alan Clark, *Barbarossa: The Russian-German Conflict, 1941-45* (New York: William Morrow, 1965), and John Erickson's two books, *The Road to Stalingrad: Stalin's War with Germany* (New York: Harper and Row, 1975) and *The Road to Berlin: Stalin's War with Germany* (Boulder, Colo.: Westview Press, 1983). Jews, of course, were caught between a rock and a hard place when it came to the Communists and the Nazis, but ultimately decided that the Soviets were "the lesser of two evils." The latter quote is taken from Dov Levin, *The Lesser of Two Evils: Eastern European Jewry under Soviet Rule, 1939-1941* (Philadelphia: Jewish Publication Society, 1995).

62. Molotov to Oumansky, 8 July 1941, Oumansky to Molotov, 10 July 1941, 11 July 1941, 12 July 1941, SAOVVOV, 1:56-65.

63. In his speech to the Soviet people on July 3, Stalin gave the same explanation for the Nazi-Soviet alliance. See Stalin, *O velikoi otechestvennoi voine Sovetskogo Soiuza*, 11-12.

64. Miner, *Between Churchill and Stalin*, 99-100, 136-39; Winston S. Churchill, *The Grand Alliance* (Boston: Houghton Mifflin, 1950), 391-92. Also see Raack, "Stalin's Role," 199-201.

65. Memorandum by Eden, 5-7 January 1942, Foreign Office 954/25, fols. 3-19, Public Records Office, Kew Green (hereafter cited as FO, PRO). Also see Steinhardt to Hull, 29 September 1941, *FRUS: 1941*, 1:836-37; Steinhardt to Hull, 30 September 1941, *FRUS: 1941*, 1:838; Harriman and Abel, *Special Envoy*, 88.

66. Rothschild, *Diversity*, 28.

67. Ibid., 35-38, 40-43, 49, 57, 63-64, 65-70.

68. Beneš visited Oumansky twice in June and July 1939 to discuss his views of

the European crisis. Later in London he worked closely with the Soviet embassy and visited Moscow in December 1943: Oumansky to Molotov, telegram, 1 July 1939, *DVP*, 1:519. Sudoplatov claims he became a Soviet agent: *Special Tasks*, 104, 235.

69. Oumansky to Molotov, 3 July 1941; Molotov to Oumansky, 8 July 1941, SAOVVOV, Oumansky to Molotov, 10 July 1941, SAOVVOV, 1:52-53, 56-57, 61-62.

9. "Comrade Stalin" Becomes "Mr. Stalin"

1. Roosevelt to Churchill, 28 October 1942, FO 954/30, fol. 459, PRO.

2. Perlmutter, *FDR and Stalin*, 194-95, 212-13. On isolationism, see Wayne S. Cole, *Roosevelt and the Isolationists, 1932-1945* (Lincoln: University of Nebraska Press, 1983). On FDR's struggle against isolationist critics and his determination to control and manipulate the media to support his objectives, see Richard W. Steele, "Franklin D. Roosevelt and His Foreign Policy Critics," *Political Science Quarterly* 94 (spring 1979): 15-35. On FDR's willingness to use Lend-Lease to keep England from its old sin of imperialism, see Warren F. Kimball, "Lend-Lease and the Open Door: The Temptation of British Opulence, 1937-1942," *Political Science Quarterly* 86 (Jan. 1971): 232-59. On the decision and its consequences to aid Soviet Russia, see Richard H. Dawson, *The Decision to Aid Russia, 1941* (Chapel Hill: University of North Carolina Press, 1959), and George C. Herring Jr., *Aid to Russia, 1941-1946: Strategy, Diplomacy, and the Origins of the Cold War* (New York: Columbia University Press, 1973). On British aid to Soviet Russia, see Joan Beaumont, *Comrades in Arms: British Aid to Russia, 1941-1945* (London: Davis-Poynter, 1980).

3. Perlmutter, *FDR and Stalin*, 72.

4. Hull, *Memoirs*, 2:967.

5. Molotov to Oumansky, 29 June 1941, SAOVVOV, 1:46; memorandum of conversation between Steinhardt and Molotov, 29 June 1941, SAOVVOV, 1:47-48; Molotov to Oumansky, 8 July 1941, SAOVVOV, 1:56-57.

6. Molotov to Oumansky, 24 July 1941, SAOVVOV, 1:75-77; Erskine Caldwell, "Behind Russian Lines," *Life*, 28 July 1941. Caldwell wrote *Tobacco Road* and *God's Little Acre*. His wife, Margaret Bourke-White, was a photographer for *Life* and was in Moscow to photograph the meeting between Hopkins and Stalin.

7. David McCullough, *Truman* (New York: Simon and Schuster, 1992), 262. The Soviet government highlighted the quotation in its publication of documents relating to American-Soviet relations during World War II. See SAOVVOV, 2:64.

8. *Time*, 7 July 1941, 11.

9. Perlmutter, *FDR and Stalin*, 72-76; Langer, "Red General," 214-15.

10. Perlmutter, *FDR and Stalin*, 102-8. There is no question that the U.S. public would have benefited from the embassy's and State Department's expert opinion about Stalin instead of being subjected to a totally unrealistic portrait of the Soviet dictator. See Maddux, "American Diplomats," 468, 486-87.

11. Kimball, *Juggler*, 7.

12. Oumansky to Molotov, 22 June 1941, SAOVVOV, 1:42-44; Molotov to Oumansky, 27 June 1941, SAOVVOV, 1:46.

13. George McJimsey, *Harry Hopkins: Ally of the Poor and Defender of Democracy* (Cambridge: Harvard University Press, 1987), 179, 261. For War Department reservations, see Edward M. Bennett, *Franklin D. Roosevelt and the Search for Victory:*

American-Soviet Relations, 1939-1945 (Wilmington, Del.: Scholarly Resources, 1990), 28. See also Dwight William Tuttle, *Harry L. Hopkins and Anglo-American-Soviet Relations, 1941-1945* (New York: Garland, 1985), 82-86.

14. Oumansky to Molotov, 12 July 1941, SAOVVOV, 1:65-66.

15. Langer, "Red General," 215. General Marshall believed that Faymonville was too pro-Soviet, but he was Hopkins's man, which meant that he had the support of the White House. See Forrest C. Pogue, *George C. Marshall: Ordeal and Hope, 1939-1942* (New York: Viking Press, 1965), 75; and Forrest C. Pogue, *George C. Marshall: Organizer of Victory, 1943-1945* (New York: Viking Press, 1973), 288-90.

16. Oumansky to Molotov, 17 July 1941, SAOVVOV, 1:72-73.

17. Oumansky to Molotov, 31 July and 1 August 1941, SAOVVOV, 1:87-94.

18. Lozovsky diary, 13 June 1942, AVP, col. 0129, reg. 26a, file (031)3, pp. 56-57.

19. Churchill to Stalin, 22 July 1941, FO 954/24, fol. 422, PRO.

20. McJimsey, *Hopkins,* 183. Litvinov emphasized Hopkins's access to Roosevelt. See Litvinov to Molotov, 11 December 1941, SAOVVOV, 1:145.

21. Burns, *Roosevelt,* 113; McJimsey, *Hopkins,* 184.

22. Steinhardt to Hull, 1 August 1941, *FRUS: 1941,* 1:815.

23. Berle to Welles, 30 July 1941; Steinhardt to Hull, 1 July 1941; Steinhardt to Hull, 26 July 1941; memorandum by Hopkins, 30 and 31 July 1941, *FRUS: 1941,* 1:798-99, 802-15, 889, 903. Molotov to Oumansky, 30 July 1941, SAOVVOV, 1:80-82. Steinhardt was included only in the initial meeting between Hopkins and Stalin.

24. Memorandum by Hopkins, 30 and 31 July 1941, *FRUS: 1941,* 1:803; Molotov to Oumansky, 30 July 1941, SAOVVOV, 1:81; Conquest, *Stalin,* 245. Edward Bennett mistakenly attributes the quoted passages in the Hopkins-Stalin conversation to Hopkins instead of Stalin: *Roosevelt and Victory,* 29-30.

25. Marshal Georgi K. Zhukov, *Vospominaniia i razmyshlenia* (Moscow: Novosti, 1992), 2:9. Khrushchev adds that Soviet troops were initially ordered not to fire back at the Germans in the forlorn hope that the invasion was a mistake: *Glasnost Tapes,* 166-68.

26. Volkogonov, *Stalin,* 484; Molotov to Oumansky, 30 July 1941, SAOVVOV, 1:80-81; Langer, "Red General," 215; McJimsey, *Hopkins,* 184. The Soviet government eventually allowed a limited consulate with a naval attaché in civilian clothes in Vladivostok in 1942. See Kemp Tolley, *Caviar and the Commissars: The Experiences of a U.S. Naval Officer in Stalin's Russia* (Annapolis, Md.: Naval Institute Press, 1983), 48, 51, 58.

27. Laqueur, *Stalin,* 204.

28. Hopkins to Sir Hastings Ismay, 7 August 1941, Hopkins microfilm, reel 19, as cited in McJimsey, *Hopkins,* 184-86, 432.

29. Bullitt, "Won the War and Lost the Peace," 94; Conquest, *Stalin,* 245.

30. Roosevelt and Churchill to Stalin, 15 August 1941, SAOVVOV, 1:101-2.

31. Steinhardt to Hull, 15 August 1941, *FRUS: 1941,* 1:822.

32. Oumansky to acting secretary of state, 2 August 1941, *FRUS: 1941,* 1:817.

33. Memorandum of conversation between Steinhardt and A. Vyshinsky, 2 November 1941, SAOVVOV, 1:134-35.

34. A. J. P. Taylor, *Beaverbrook* (New York: Simon and Schuster, 1972), 481-82, 487.

35. Harriman and Abel, *Special Envoy,* 213-14; McJimsey, *Hopkins,* 179, 189.

36. Langer, "Red General," 215-17.

37. Memorandum of conversation between Harriman, Beaverbrook, Stalin, and Molotov, 30 September 1941, SAOVVOV, 1:117-20; Secret Protocol of the Moscow Conference between Representatives of the USSR, USA, and Great Britain, 1 October 1941, SAOVVOV, 1:121-26; Molotov's Speech to the Moscow Conference, 1 October 1941, SAOVVOV, 1:127-29; Harriman's Speech to the Moscow Conference, 1 October 1941, SAOVVOV, 1:129-30; communiqué of the Moscow Conference, 2 October 1941, SAOVVOV, 1:131; Rudy Abramson, *Spanning the Century: The Life of W. Averell Harriman, 1891-1986* (New York: William Morrow, 1992), 292-93; Ismay quoted in Conquest, *Stalin,* 243, 246-47.

38. Miner, *Between Churchill and Stalin,* 252-56. The popular press in the United States also understood that Stalin had only agreed to support the Atlantic Charter for expedient reasons. See Demaree Bess, "What Does Russia Want?" *Saturday Evening Post,* 20 March 1943, and Demaree Bess, "The Cost of Roosevelt's 'Great Design,'" *Saturday Evening Post,* 27 May 1944.

39. Robert Sherwood, *Roosevelt and Hopkins: An Intimate History* (New York: Harper, 1948), 362-63.

40. Sumner Welles, *Seven Decisions That Shaped History* (New York: Harper, 1951), 136-37.

41. Stalin to Molotov, 5 December 1929, as found in Lih et al., *Stalin's Letters,* 183.

42. Milovan Djilas, *Conversations with Stalin* (New York: Harcourt, Brace and World, 1962), 73.

43. Khrushchev, *Glasnost Tapes,* 82.

44. Miner, *Between Churchill and Stalin,* 252. Sumner Welles believed that the United States should have accepted the minimal demands when the USSR was at its weakest: *Seven Decisions,* 125.

45. Oumansky to Molotov, 13 September 1941, SAOVVOV, 1:106.

46. The Soviet government itself came to appreciate the political influence of organized religion, and before long it was opening churches in the Soviet Union, reestablishing the Moscow Patriarchate, curtailing atheistic propaganda, and wistfully posturing toward the Vatican. Ambassadors Standley and Harriman closely monitored the change and viewed it as a positive fruit of American-Soviet collaboration. The Soviets were not unmindful of the American interest, and to that end, in April 1944, they invited an obscure Polish-American priest, Rev. Stanislaus Orlemanski from Springfield, Mass., to "report" on religious conditions in the Soviet Union and, capitalizing on his Polish background, on Soviet intentions toward Catholic Poles. Orlemanski returned to the United States and announced that the Soviet government wanted to cooperate with Catholics and rejected a policy of religious persecution. See Dennis J. Dunn, *The Catholic Church and the Soviet Government, 1939-1949* (New York: Columbia University Press, 1977), 120-21.

47. Another example came in September 1942, when FDR sent Wendell Willkie to Moscow to examine the Russian front, and he told the Soviets that they "could be sure if he saw something which he did not like or which made known in the United States might create an unfavorable impression, he would remain silent." Memorandum by Standley, undated (attached to letter to Hull dated 24 October 1942, no. 811.44 Willkie, Wendell L/9, RG 59, NA).

48. Dallek, *Roosevelt and Foreign Policy,* 298, 521; Dawson, *Decision to Aid Rus-*

sia, 258-69; Robert Murphy, *Diplomat among Warriors* (Garden City, N.Y.: Doubleday, 1964), 217; Dunn, *Catholic Church*, 90-91, passim.

49. The best book on the Katyn Forest massacre remains J. K. Zawodny's *Death in the Forest* (South Bend, Ind.: University of Notre Dame Press, 1962). A new book that uses some newly released information is Allen Paul, *Katyn: The Untold Story of Stalin's Polish Massacre* (New York: Macmillan, 1991). The Soviet government first admitted its responsibility for the massacre in 1990. For new material see *Mazhdunarodnaia zhizn,* May 1990; *Voprosy istorii,* no. 7, 1990; *Novaia i noveyshaia istoriia,* no. 1990; *Novoye vremya,* no. 52, 1990. Also see the *Observer,* 6 October 1991. New documents and information are also contained in Sudoplatov et al., *Special Tasks,* 276-78.

50. Burrows to War Office, 15 April 1944, FO 954/26, fol. 382, PRO.

51. Personal interview with W. Averell Harriman, 19 November 1981, Washington, D.C.

52. George F. Kennan, *Russia and the West under Lenin and Stalin* (Boston: Little, Brown, 1961), 355; Bullitt, "Won the War and Lost the Peace," 94.

53. Harriman and Abel, *Special Envoy,* 170.

54. Warren F. Kimball, ed., *Churchill and Roosevelt: The Complete Correspondence* (Princeton: Princeton University Press, 1984), 1:421.

55. Robert Nisbet, *Roosevelt and Stalin* (Washington, D.C.: Regnery Gateway, 1988), 97. The best book on the Churchill-Stalin relationship is Miner, *Between Churchill and Stalin.* Forrest Davis and Demaree Bess, two writers for the *Saturday Evening Post* who had ties to the White House, presented favorable views of Stalin. Davis called him after Teheran "the Georgian cobbler's son" and he called Churchill "a tough House of Commons controversialist." See Forrest Davis, "What Really Happened at Teheran?" *Saturday Evening Post,* 13 and 20 May 1944, as well as Demaree Bess, "What Does Russia Want?" and "The Cost of Roosevelt's 'Great Design.'"

56. Abramson, *Harriman,* 293; Harriman and Abel, *Special Envoy,* 346.

57. Harriman to Roosevelt, 3 October 1941, *FRUS: 1941,* 1:840-41.

58. Abramson, *Harriman,* 293.

59. Elliott Roosevelt, ed., *F.D.R.: His Personal Letters* (New York: Duell, Sloan, and Pearce, 1950), 2:1195, 1177.

60. MacLean, *Davies,* 81; McJimsey, *Hopkins,* 261; Dawson, *Decision to Aid Russia,* 13.

61. Oumansky to Molotov, 13 July 1941, SAOVVOV, 1:65.

62. William L. Langer and Everett S. Gleason, *The Undeclared War* (New York: Harper and Row, 1952), 540; see also Burns, *Soldier of Freedom,* 102.

63. MacLean, *Davies,* 81.

64. Gromyko to Molotov, 28 October 1941, SAOVVOV, 1:133, 186. See also Hugh Phillips, "Mission to America: Maksim M. Litvinov in the United States, 1941-43," *Diplomatic History* 12 (summer 1988): 267-72.

65. U.S. State Department, *Foreign Relations of the United States, Diplomatic Papers: 1943* (Washington: Government Printing Office, 1943), 3:654.

66. Davies, *Mission,* 357. Roosevelt's copy of *Mission to Moscow* can be found at the Roosevelt Library at Hyde Park, N.Y.

67. Yergin, *Shattered Peace,* 429.

68. Memorandum by Elbridge Durbrow, 3 February 1943, *FRUS* 3:500-505.

See also MacLean, *Davies,* 188; Richard H. Ullman, "The Davies Mission and United States-Soviet Relations, 1937-1941," *World Politics* 9 (Jan. 1957): 220-39.

69. Robert H. Ferrell, ed., *Off the Record: The Private Papers of Harry S Truman* (New York: Harper and Row, 1980), 35.

70. MacLean, *Davies,* 160-61.

71. David Remnick, former *Washington Post* correspondent in Moscow from 1988 to 1992, reported that by the 1980s Party awards were for sale. The Order of Lenin cost between $165,000 and $750,000. See Remnick, *Lenin's Tomb: The Last Days of the Soviet Empire* (New York: Random House, 1993), 184.

72. The British ambassador, Sir Stafford Cripps, agreed with Steinhardt. See Cripps to Eden, 15 November 1941, FO 954/24, fol. 506, PRO.

73. Gromyko to Molotov, 27 November 1941, SAOVVOV, 1:141-43.

74. Harriman and Abel, *Special Envoy,* 93. Abramson, *Harriman,* 293-94; interview with Harriman, 19 November 1981.

75. Conquest, *Stalin,* 246.

76. Gabriel Gorodetsky, *Stafford Cripps's Mission to Moscow, 1940-42* (Cambridge: Cambridge University Press, 1984), 240ff.; Miner, *Between Churchill and Stalin,* 160-61.

77. Roosevelt to Steinhardt, 5 November 1941, no. 123 Steinhardt, Laurence A/380 1/2, RG 59, NA.

78. Conquest, *Stalin,* 323.

79. In a note to Molotov on what had to be done to organize the revolution in Manchuria in 1929 Stalin wrote: "Send in the army, establish a revolutionary government (massacre the landowners, bring in the peasants, create soviets in the cities and towns, and so on). This is necessary. This we can and, I think, should do. No 'international law' contradicts this task." Stalin to Molotov, 7 October 1929, in Lih et al., *Stalin's Letters,* 182.

80. Harriman and Abel, *Special Envoy,* 95.

81. Davies diary, 29 September 1941, DP.

82. Gromyko, *Memories,* 26.

83. Faymonville to Hopkins, 4 November 1941, "book 4: Harriman-Beaverbrook mission" file, box 306, Hopkins Papers (HHP), FDR Library; Langer, "Red General," 217.

84. Hopkins to Burns, 7 November 1941, "book 4: Harriman-Beaverbrook mission" file, box 306, HHP; Spalding to Faymonville, 21 November 1941, "Hopkins memoranda," records of the president's Soviet protocol committee, FDR Library, as cited in Langer, "Red General," 218.

85. McJimsey, *Hopkins,* 192.

86. George C. Herring Jr., "Lend-Lease to Russia and the Origins of the Cold War, 1944-1945," *Journal of American History* 56 (June 1969): 93-114.

87. Hopkins to Marshall, 15 January 1942, "book 5: aid to Russia" file, box 309, HHP; Langer, "Red General," 218.

88. Pogue, *Ordeal and Hope,* 74-75; Pogue, *Organizer of Victory,* 288.

10. The Secret Message

1. Kimball, *Correspondence,* 1:616, 621.

2. Stalin to Roosevelt, 7 October 1942, SAOVVOV, 1:249-50; Roosevelt to Stalin, 12 October 1942, SAOVVOV, 1:250-51.

3. Kimball, *Correspondence,* 1:616; William H. Standley and Arthur A. Ageton, *Admiral Ambassador to Russia* (Chicago: Henry Regnery, 1955), 308-10, 238-39.

4. Langer, "Red General," 219; Standley and Ageton, *Ambassador,* 308-10; McJimsey, *Hopkins,* 262.

5. Miner, *Between Churchill and Stalin,* 140-41.

6. Standley and Ageton, *Ambassador,* 16, 21, 26.

7. Radio talk show, Westminster College, Fulton, Missouri, 27 February 1941, William H. Standley Papers (WSP), Library of Congress.

8. Standley and Ageton, *Ambassador,* 63-71, 73, 254.

9. Kennan, *Memoirs,* 195-96; Bohlen, *Witness,* 36; Langer, "Red General," 217; Abramson, *Harriman,* 352.

10. Standley and Ageton, *Ambassador,* 76, 69.

11. Speech by Standley, 1941 (no place, no specific date), WSP.

12. Radio broadcast by Standley, 26 October 1941, WSP.

13. Standley and Ageton, *Ambassador,* 92-93; Soloman A. Lozovsky diary, 6 and 7 February 1942, AVP, col. 0129, reg. 26a, file (031)3, pp. 19-20.

14. Personal interview with W. Averell Harriman, 19 November 1981, Washington, D.C.

15. Radio broadcast by Standley, 26 October 1941, WSP.

16. Standley and Ageton, *Ambassador,* 338.

17. Roosevelt to Stalin, 13 February 1942, and Stalin to Roosevelt, 18 February 1942, SAOVVOV, 1:153-55.

18. Sherwood, *Roosevelt and Hopkins,* 269.

19. Roosevelt to Churchill, 27 October 1942, FO 954/25, fol. 459, PRO.

20. Langer, "Red General," 218.

21. Standley and Ageton, *Ambassador,* 97, 111.

22. Ibid., 148; Tolley, *Caviar and Commissars,* 54, 61-65; Herring, *Aid to Russia;* Mayers, *Ambassadors,* 141.

23. Henderson to Welles, 9 April 1942, no. 861.20211/67, RG 59, NA.

24. Standley and Ageton, *Ambassador,* 96, 117-18, 152-53.

25. Kimball, *Correspondence,* 1:279.

26. Litvinov to Molotov, 8 December 1941, Molotov to Litvinov, 11 December 1941, and Litvinov to Molotov, 11 December 1941, SAOVVOV, 1:143-45.

27. Declaration of the United Nations, 1 January 1942, SAOVVOV, 1:146; Litvinov to Molotov, 12 January 1942, SAOVVOV, 1:147-48; Molotov's memorandum of conversation with Roosevelt, 1 June 1942, SAOVVOV, 1:194; Paul Fussell, *Wartime: Understanding and Behavior in the Second World War* (New York: Oxford University Press, 1989), 136-38.

28. Litvinov told Molotov that Roosevelt estimated that the United States would defeat Japan within nine to twelve months. Of course, he told him that before Germany declared war on the United States. See Litvinov to Molotov, 8 December 1941, SAOVVOV, 1:143.

29. Anthony Eden, *The Memoirs of Anthony Eden (Earl of Avon): The Reckoning* (Boston: Houghton Mifflin, 1965), 335, 339-42; Herbert Feis, *Churchill, Roosevelt,*

Stalin: The War They Waged and the Peace They Sought (Princeton: Princeton University Press, 1970), 26; memorandum by Eden, 5-7 January 1943, FO 954/25, fols. 3-19, PRO; Hull to Roosevelt, 4 February 1942, U.S. State Department, *Foreign Relations of the United States, Diplomatic Papers 1942, Europe* (Washington: Government Printing Office, 1961), 3:508; Conquest, *Stalin*, 250; Miner, *Between Churchill and Stalin*, 186-91.

30. Eden, *Memoirs*, 343; memorandum by Welles, 18 February 1942, *FRUS: 1942*, 3:515.

31. Miner, *Between Churchill and Stalin*, 110-11, 113-14, 194, 252-54. The popular press clearly outlined Stalin's demands in 1943. See Demaree Bess, "What Does Russia Want?" *Saturday Evening Post*, 20 March 1943.

32. Eden, *Memoirs*, 344; Miner, *Between Churchill and Stalin*, 191-93; Feis, *Churchill, Roosevelt, Stalin*, 27-28.

33. Eden, *Memoirs*, 370; Elisabeth Barker, *Churchill and Eden at War* (New York: St. Martin's Press, 1978), 236-37; memorandum by Welles, 18 February 1942, *FRUS: 1942*, 3:513, 515; Thurston to Hull, 5 January 1942, *FRUS: 1942*, 3:491; Gorodetsky, *Cripps*, 290; Taylor, *Beaverbrook*, 510-11; David Dilks, ed., *The Diaries of Sir Alexander Cadogan, 1938-1945* (New York: G. P. Putnam's Sons, 1972), 437; Miner, *Between Churchill and Stalin*, 115, 194-95, 205, 207-8, 214, 224; Kimball, *Correspondence*, 1:393-94; David Carlton, *Anthony Eden: A Biography* (London: Allen Lane, 1981), 184.

34. Kimball, *Correspondence*, 1:394; Miner, *Between Churchill and Stalin*, 9, 149-50, 211-13.

35. Eden, *Memoirs*, 370-71; Barker, *Churchill and Eden*, 233; Gorodetsky, *Cripps*, 47, 290.

36. Litvinov to Molotov, 8 December 1941, SAOVVOV, 1:143.

37. Litvinov to Molotov, 12 January 1942, SAOVVOV, 1:148.

38. Welles to Berle, 4 April 1942, *FRUS: 1942*, 3:542.

39. John Morton Blum, ed., *The Price of Vision: The Diary of Henry A. Wallace, 1942-1946* (Boston: Houghton Mifflin, 1973), 159-60.

40. Litvinov to Molotov, 12 March 1942, SAOVVOV, 1:155-56.

41. Kimball, *Correspondence*, 1:421.

42. Welles to Thurston, 2 March 1942, *FRUS: 1942*, 3:526-27.

43. Standley and Ageton, *Ambassador*, 107.

44. See John R. Deane, *The Strange Alliance* (Bloomington: Indiana University Press, 1973).

45. Report, 17 April 1943, "overseas missions" file, box 212, Records of the Foreign Economic Administration, RG 169, NA; Clark-Kerr to Foreign Office, 31 May 1943, file FO 371/N3255/22/38, PRO, as cited in Langer, "Red General," 217.

46. Thurston to Hull, 20 December 1941, *FRUS: 1941*, 1:201. Langer notes that the editors of the relevant *FRUS* volume were still confused over Faymonville's role in 1958: "Red General," 217n. 44.

47. Lozovsky diary, 13 June 1942, AVP, col. 0129, reg. 26a, file (031)3, pp. 56-57.

48. Standley and Ageton, *Ambassador*, 152-60; notes of conversation between Standley, Stalin, and Molotov," 23 April 1942, SAOVVOV, 1:166-72. On the Alsib operation, see Roosevelt to Molotov, 17 June 1942, SAOVVOV, 1:204; Roosevelt to Stalin, 7 July 1942, SAOVVOV, 1:217; Stalin to Roosevelt, 18 July 1942, SAOVVOV, 1:218; notes of conversation between Stalin, Standley, General Bradley, and Molotov, 6

October 1942, SAOVVOV, 1:244-47. The Soviets interned five Americans whose plane landed near Vladivostok after the Doolittle raid on Japan. The Soviets also held other American pilots in 1944 and 1945. See Richard Lukas, *Eagles East: The Army Air Force and the Soviet Union, 1941-1945* (Tallahassee: Florida State University Press, 1970), 103.

49. Lozovsky diary, 3 September, 3 October 1942, AVP, col. 0129, reg. 26a, file (031)3, pp. 84-85, 106-7; A. Y. Vyshinsky diary, 11 July 1942, AVP, col. 0129, reg. 26a, file (031)1, pp. 63-66.

50. Standley and Ageton, *Ambassador*, 202. The State Department eventually sent word to Standley on April 14. Hull to Standley, 14 April 1942, no. 740.0011 European War 1939/21011a, RG 59, NA.

51. Roosevelt to Stalin, 11 April 1942, *FRUS: 1942*, 3:543; Roosevelt to Stalin, 12 April 1942, SAOVVOV, 1:159-60.

52. Litvinov to Molotov, 12 January 1942, Molotov to Litvinov, 18 January 1942, SAOVVOV, 1:148-49. By implication, Molotov was signaling Roosevelt that Moscow did have "territorial ambitions" against Iran.

53. Molotov to Litvinov, 4 February 1942, Litvinov to Molotov, 12 February 1942, SAOVVOV, 1:150-52.

54. Litvinov to Molotov, 11 April 1942, Litvinov to Molotov, 11 April 1942, Roosevelt to Stalin, 12 April 1942, Molotov to Litvinov, 13 April 1942, Litvinov to Molotov, 14 April 1942, SAOVVOV, 1:158-63.

55. Churchill to Roosevelt, 18 December 1942, FO 954/25, fol. 514, PRO.

56. Memorandum of conversation by Acting Secretary of State Welles, 12 March 1942, *FRUS: 1942*, 3:532.

57. Welles to Assistant Secretary of State Berle, 4 April 1942, *FRUS: 1942*, 3:541-42; Litvinov to Molotov, 12 March 1942, SAOVVOV, 1:156-57.

58. Molotov to Litvinov, 23 March 1942, SAOVVOV, 1:158.

59. For a copy of the treaty dated 24 May 1942, see FO 954/25, fol. 33, PRO.

60. Memorandum by Samuel H. Cross, 1 June 1942, *FRUS: 1942*, 3:582-83; memorandum of conversation with Hopkins, 29 May 1942, SAOVVOV, 1:180-81; memorandum of conversation with Roosevelt, 30 May 1942, SAOVVOV, 1:181, 184-85, 191-93; Eubanks, *Teheran*, 51.

61. Memorandum by Samuel H. Cross, 29 May 1942, *FRUS: 1942*, 3:568; memo-randum by Hopkins, 29 May 1942, *FRUS: 1942*, 3:573; notes of conversation be-tween Hopkins and Molotov, 29 May 1942, SAOVVOV, 1:180-81. Also, notes of conversations between Roosevelt and Molotov, 29 and 30 May 1942, 1 June 1942, SAOVVOV, 1:175-80, 81-92.

62. Litvinov to Molotov, 12 March 1942, SAOVVOV, 1:155-57; notes of con-versation between Roosevelt and Molotov, 29 May 1942, SAOVVOV, 1:175-80; notes of conversation between Roosevelt and Molotov, 1 June 1942, SAOVVOV, 1:187-92; Dallek, *Roosevelt and Foreign Policy*, 342; Barker, *Churchill and Eden*, 238.

63. Notes of conversation between Roosevelt and Molotov, 29 May 1942, 1 June 1942, SAOVVOV, 1:176-77, 187, 190, 194; Stalin to Molotov, 4 June 1942, SAOVVOV, 1:197-98; Roosevelt to Molotov, 17 June 1942, SAOVVOV, 1:204.

64. Stalin to Molotov, 2 June 1942, SAOVVOV, 1:195; MacLean, *Davies*, 87; notes of conversation between Hull and Molotov, 3 June 1942, SAOVVOV, 1:195-96; Mark Stoler, *The Politics of the Second Front: American Military Planning and Diplo-macy in Coalition Warfare, 1941-1943* (Westport, Conn.: Greenwood Press, 1977), 42.

65. Winant to Hull, 10 July 1942, no. 740.0011 European War 1939/22839, RG 59, NA; notes of conversation between Standley and Molotov, 19 June 1942, SAOVVOV, 1:204-5.

66. Standley to Hull, 22 June 1942, *FRUS: 1942*, 3:598.

67. Winant to Hull, 10 July 1942, *FRUS: 1942*, 3:608.

68. Standley to Hull, 22 July 1942, *FRUS: 1942*, 3:612-14.

69. Litvinov to Molotov, 23 July 1942, 30 July 1942, SAOVVOV, 1:219-21.

70. Winston S. Churchill, *The Hinge of Fate* (Boston: Houghton Mifflin, 1950), 496-502.

71. Roosevelt to Molotov, 17 June 1942, SAOVVOV, 1:204; Roosevelt to Stalin, 23 June 1942, SAOVVOV, 1:206; Stalin to Roosevelt, 1 July 1942, SAOVVOV, 1:210; notes of conversation between Standley, Stalin, and Molotov, 2 July 1942, SAOVVOV, 1:211-14; notes of conversation between Standley and Molotov, 5 October 1942, SAOVVOV, 1:240-41; Miner, *Between Churchill and Stalin*, 152, 162.

72. Standley and Ageton, *Ambassador*, 214.

73. Harriman to Roosevelt, 13 August 1942, *FRUS: 1942*, 3:620; notes of conversation between Harriman and Molotov, 11 August 1944, SAOVVOV, 2:176.

74. Standley to Hull, 3 May 1942, *FRUS: 1942*, 3:551; Standley to Hull, 22 July 1942, *FRUS: 1942*, 3:612-16; Harriman to Roosevelt, 13 August 1942, *FRUS: 1942*, 3:618-24.

75. Notes of conversation between Willkie and Stalin, 23 September 1942, SAOVVOV, 1:232-39; Litvinov to Molotov, 13 October 1942, SAOVVOV, 1:251-52.

76. For details on the confrontation between Standley and Willkie, see Ellsworth Barnard, *Wendell Willkie: Fighter for Freedom* (Marquette: Northern Michigan University Press, 1966), 355-59; see also Bernard Asbell, ed., *Mother and Daughter: The Letters of Eleanor and Anna Roosevelt* (London: Sidgwick and Jackson, 1984), 149; *FRUS: 1942*, 3:637-50; Standley and Ageton, *Ambassador*, 282, 285, 291-93.

77. Notes of conversation between Stalin, Standley, General Bradley, and Molotov, 6 October 1942, SAOVVOV, 1:248; A. Y. Vyshinsky diary, 17 September 1942, AVP, col. 0129, reg. 26a, file (031)3, pp. 95-96.

78. Standley and Ageton, *Ambassador*, 308-9, 74-75; notes of conversations between Stalin, Standley, and Molotov, 2 July 1942, 5 October 1942, SAOVVOV, 1:211-16, 240-41; Isaacson and Thomas, *Wise Men*, 218.

79. Vyshinsky diary, 11 July 1942, 19 December 1942, AVP, col. 0129, reg. 26a, file (031)3, pp. 65-66, 135.

80. Letter to author from historian Vladimir Pozniakov, who wrote on 10 November 1995 that "judging by a number of memoirs, Soviet military trusted Brig. Faymonville more than any other American military official in the USSR, [and] tried to use him as a kind of super military envoy on many occasions."

81. Standley and Ageton, *Ambassador*, 313-14; Langer, "Red General," 219.

11. The News Conference

1. Roosevelt to Stalin, 2 and 6 December 1942, SAOVVOV, 1:262-63.

2. *Novy mir*, August 1965, 177; Eubanks, *Teheran*, 61.

3. Elliott Roosevelt, *As He Saw It* (New York: Duell, Sloan, and Pearce, 1946), 117; Kimball, *Juggler*, 76-77; Harriman and Abel, *Special Envoy*, 190. In the view of Kimball and A. E. Campbell, unconditional surrender was a given, operating assump-

tion in FDR's approach to the war. See Kimball, *Juggler,* 63, and A. E. Campbell, "Franklin D. Roosevelt and Unconditional Surrender," in *Diplomacy and Intelligence during the Second World War,* ed. Richard Longhorne (Cambridge: Cambridge University Press, 1985), 219-41. Roosevelt told General Sikorski on December 2, 1942, that he was going to demand unconditional surrender. See Weinberg, *World at Arms,* 439.

4. See Churchill, *Hinge of Fate,* 687-88. For more information on this controversy, see Pogue, *Organizer of Victory,* 32-35; Raymond G. O'Connor, *Diplomacy for Victory: FDR and Unconditional Surrender* (New York: W. W. Norton, 1971), 50-53; Dilks, *Diaries of Cadogan,* 506; and Kimball, *Juggler,* 76. See also Kimball, *Correspondence,* 2:119.

5. Kennan, *Russia and the West,* 384.

6. Kimball, *Correspondence,* 2:645-46; U.S. State Department, *Foreign Relations of the United States: The Conferences at Cairo and Teheran 1943* (Washington: Government Printing Office, 1961), 513, 554; Martin Gilbert, *Winston S. Churchill: Road to Victory, 1941-1945* (Boston: Houghton Mifflin, 1986), 581. Stalin made it clear from the beginning of the alliance that he was only at war with "Hitlerite Germany," not Germany sans Hitler. See Miner, *Between Churchill and Stalin,* 242.

7. Stalin to Roosevelt and Churchill, 30 January 1942, SAOVVOV, 1:283; notes of conversation between Standley and Molotov, 5 April 1943, SAOVVOV, 1:307.

8. Harriman and Abel, *Special Envoy,* 197-98.

9. Feis, *Churchill, Roosevelt, Stalin,* 117; Bullitt, *For the President,* 582, 592.

10. Spears to Eden, 7 October 1943, FO 954/25, fol. 159, PRO.

11. Standley and Ageton, *Ambassador,* 363; Langer, "Red General," 219; notes of conversation between Standley, Henderson, and Molotov, 29 January 1943, SAOVVOV, 1:282; notes of conversation between General Burns, Standley, and Molotov, 23 April 1943, SAOVVOV, 1:313.

12. Langer, "Red General," 209, 219-20. General Marshall and General John R. Deane thought that the charges against Faymonville were exaggerated, but Marshall was embarrassed by the division among the Americans in Moscow. See Pogue, *Organizer of Victory,* 288-90.

13. Notes of conversation between Standley and Molotov, 29 January 1943, SAOVVOV, 1:276-82.

14. PSF, Bullitt folder, Roosevelt Papers; Bullitt, *For the President,* 577-89, 591-99; Bullitt, "Won the War and Lost the Peace," 94.

15. Kennan, introduction to *For the President: Personal and Secret,* by Orville Bullitt, xiv.

16. Sudoplatov et al., *Special Tasks,* 115-16; Dunn, *Catholic Church,* 70-73, 89-90.

17. Eden to Churchill, 17 March 1943, FO 954/25, fol. 33, PRO.

18. Kennan, introduction to *For the President,* xiv; Miner, *Between Churchill and Stalin,* 9.

19. Standley and Ageton, *Ambassador,* 333.

20. Asbell, *Mother and Daughter,* 156-57.

21. Standley and Ageton, *Ambassador,* 341; Eubanks, *Teheran,* 60; Quentin Reynolds, *The Curtain Rises* (New York: Random House, 1944), 86-88; *FRUS: 1943,* 3:631-32.

22. Eubanks, *Teheran,* 60; Herring, *Aid to Russia,* 80-81.

23. Eubanks, *Teheran*, 67.

24. Notes of conversation between Standley and Molotov, 10 March 1943, SAOVVOV, 1:290-92; Alexander Werth, *Russia at War, 1941-1945* (New York: E. P. Dutton, 1964), 628.

25. Standley and Ageton, *Ambassador*, 347-48; Eubanks, *Teheran*, 67. Molotov sent Litvinov a list of citations that he could use as evidence of Soviet acknowledgment of U.S. aid. See Molotov to Litvinov, 10 March 1943, SAOVVOV, 1:292-93. Soviet commentary in SAOVVOV stated that Standley's position was not popular in Washington. See SAOVVOV, 1:488n. 44.

26. Paul Johnson, *Modern Times* (New York: HarperCollins, 1991), 384-85; Conquest, *Stalin*, 247. Dmitri Volkogonov said that western aid was "massive" and that this fact was "either consistently ignored or underestimated by Soviet historians": *Stalin*, 485. Khrushchev states that the USSR could not have defeated Germany without western aid: *Glasnost Tapes*, 84.

27. Standley to Hull, 10 March 1943, *FRUS: 1943*, 3:509-12.

28. Standley and Ageton, *Ambassador*, 232-34.

29. Notes of conversations between Standley and Molotov, 27 March 1943, 2 April 1943, 5 April 1943, 12 April 1943, 14 April 1943, SAOVVOV, 1:298-99, 1:302-4, 307-12.

30. Notes of conversation between Harriman, Stalin, and Molotov, 26 June 1944, SAOVVOV, 2:147-48.

31. Sherwood, *Roosevelt and Hopkins*, 705; Harriman and Abel, *Special Envoy*, 198; Isaacson and Thomas, *Wise Men*, 218; Eubanks, *Teheran*, 68-69.

32. Eden to Churchill, 17 March 1943, FO 954/25, fol. 33, PRO; Litvinov to Molotov, 29 and 31 March 1943, SAOVVOV, 1:299-302; Gromyko to Molotov, 19 July 1943, SAOVVOV, 1:352.

33. Burns, *Soldier of Freedom*, 368. Churchill was also working on Stalin to meet with him and FDR. He wrote him in December 1942 that FDR wanted to meet in North Africa. See Churchill to Stalin, 3 December 1942, FO 954/25, fol. 495, PRO. Churchill, of course, was adamantly opposed to a private meeting between Roosevelt and Stalin. Roosevelt also told Litvinov that he wanted to meet Stalin without Churchill. See Litvinov to Molotov, 5 May 1943, SAOVVOV, 1:314-15.

34. Eden to Churchill, 17 March 1943; Eubanks, *Teheran*, 72-73.

35. Litvinov to Molotov, 5 May 1943, SAOVVOV, 1:314-15; Gromyko to Molotov, 19 July 1943, SAOVVOV, 1:351-52.

36. Hull, *Memoirs*, 2:1248; McJimsey, *Hopkins*, 291.

12. Joseph Davies to the Rescue

1. Abramson, *Harriman*, 347; Urban, "Harriman," 24.

2. Eubanks, *Teheran*, 71-75, 84; Litvinov to Molotov, 5 May 1943, SAOVVOV, 1:314-15.

3. Kennan, *Memoirs*, 208; Winston S. Churchill, *Hinge of Fate*, 759.

4. Davies diary, 26 April 1943; Davies journal, 27 April 1943, DP. Robert Dallek claims that FDR believed the Soviets were responsible, which makes more sense and would be consistent with his position on Stalin's persecution of religion. See Dallek, *Roosevelt*, 400.

5. McJimsey, *Hopkins,* 293.

6. Standley to Hull, 28 April 1943, *FRUS: 1943,* 3:402; notes of conversation between Molotov and Standley, 6 May 1942, SAOVVOV, 1:316-17; Litvinov to Molotov, 7 May 1943, SAOVVOV, 1:318-19; Oumansky diary, 21 May 1943, AVP, col. 06, reg. 5, file 337, pp. 8-9. Gromyko recalled that the Soviets considered Davies to have a major influence on Roosevelt and "among influential American circles": *Memories,* 27-28.

7. Eubanks, *Teheran,* 79, 81-82; MacLean, *Davies,* 103.

8. Davies diary, 20 May 1943; Davies diary, 28 May 1943, DP.

9. Of course, Stalin knew that dissolving the Comintern and reestablishing the Patriarchate would be popular moves in the West and likely to fortify the alliance. See Volkogonov, *Stalin,* 486-87.

10. Notes of conversation between Molotov and Davies, 28 May 1943, SAOVVOV, 1:326; notes of conversation between Voroshilov and Davies," 22 May 1943, SAOVVOV, 1:320.

11. Davis to Hopkins and FDR, 28 May 1943, DP; Davies diary, 20 May, 1943, DP. The article appeared in *Life* on 29 March 1943, 49-55, under the title of "Joseph E. Davies Answers Problems on 'the Soviets and the Post-War.'" The Polish ambassador to the United States, J. Ciechanowski, protested the Davies article in a letter to the editor, *Life,* 19 April 1943, 6.

12. Davies diary, 12 April 1943, 3 June 1943, DP. Lend-lease aid to the USSR actually increased after Standley's outburst and the news about Katyn, so the Kremlin knew that it had not lost any leverage with the American government. See Weinberg, *World at Arms,* 420, 469.

13. Oumansky diary, 21 May 1943, p. 8.

14. Eubanks, *Teheran,* 61, 83-84, 493n. 8; Reynolds, *Curtain Rises,* 83-84; Kimball, *Correspondence,* 2:233. Also see Quentin Reynolds, "Diplomat on the Spot," *Collier's,* 24 June 1943.

15. Eubanks, *Teheran,* 84-85; Davies diary, 4 August 1943, DP; Gromyko, *Memories,* 29.

16. Eubanks, *Teheran,* 85-86; Stalin to Roosevelt, 26 May 1943, SAOVVOV, 1:346-47.

17. Eubanks, *Teheran,* 87; Standley and Ageton, *Ambassador,* 370 (his italics).

18. Davis to Hopkins and FDR, 28 May 1943, DP.

19. Davies journal, 24 May 1943, DP; Davies to wife, Marjorie, 28 May 1943, DP.

20. Kimball, *Correspondence,* 2:212, 214; Eubanks, *Teheran,* 92; McJimsey, *Hopkins,* 294.

21. Notes of conversation between Stalin, Molotov, Sulzberger, and Standley, 5 July 1943, SAOVVOV, 1:346-47.

22. Kimball, *Correspondence,* 2:214; Kimball, *Juggler,* 87; Martin J. Sherwin, *A World Destroyed: The Atomic Bomb and the Grand Alliance* (New York: Alfred A. Knopf, 1975); Timothy J. Botti, *The Long Wait: The Forging of the Anglo-American Nuclear Alliance, 1945-58* (Westport, Conn.: Greenwood Press, 1987); Richard Rhodes, *The Making of the Atomic Bomb* (New York: Simon and Schuster, 1986). For Litvinov's comment, see Vojtech Mastny, "The Cassandra in the Foreign Commissariat: Maxim Litvinov and the Cold War," *Foreign Affairs* 54 (Jan. 1976): 373. The United States

did not share all of its atomic secrets with the British, either. FDR decided, in the case of both the British and the Soviets, that Americans should be the main beneficiary of the research, because they were paying for it and its practical application would not likely affect the war but would be a postwar invention that the United States should control. See Weinberg, *World at Arms,* 572-73.

23. Stalin to Roosevelt, 11 June 1943, SAOVVOV, 1:330-31; Kimball, *Correspondence,* 2:244-45, 260, 285.

24. Kimball, *Correspondence,* 2:283-84, 290, 1:621; Eubanks, *Teheran,* 97-99.

25. Gromyko to Molotov, 19 July 1943, 30 July 1943, SAOVVOV, 1:351-52, 1:356.

26. Joachim Fest, *Hitler,* trans. Richard and Clara Winston (New York: Harcourt Brace Jovanovich, 1974), 1031; Johnson, *Modern Times,* 410-11; Eubanks, *Teheran,* 97.

27. Notes of conversation between Stalin, Molotov, Sulzberger, and Standley, 5 July 1943, SAOVVOV, 1:346-47; Gromyko to Molotov, 19 July 1943, SAOVVOV, 1:351-52.

28. Volkogonov, *Stalin,* 488; Eubanks, *Teheran,* 102-5.

29. Stalin to Roosevelt, 8 August 1943, SAOVVOV, 1:359-60; Eubanks, *Teheran,* 104-6, 109, 117.

30. Kennan, *Memoirs,* 521.

31. Arno Mayer argues that the failure of Hitler's campaign against Bolshevism triggered the Nazi "final solution" to exterminate the Jews. See his *Why Did the Heavens Not Darken? The "Final Solution" in History* (New York: Pantheon Books, 1989). There are many excellent books on the Holocaust. One of the most moving is Art Spiegelman, *Maus: A Survivor's Tale* (New York: Pantheon Books, 1986), and its sequel, *Maus II: A Survivor's Tale: and here my troubles began* (New York: Pantheon Books, 1991). Hitler consistently maintained that his movement was focused on anti-Communism. Kennan pointed out that the non-Communist German resistance to Hitler "received literally no encouragement from the Allied side." *Russia and West,* 367.

32. Eubanks, *Teheran,* 111-17. MacLean isn't sure if Davies gave away FDR's bargaining chip. See MacLean, *Davies,* 120-22. Davies, however, had indicated consistently since his May 1943 trip to Moscow and in numerous conversations with Soviet officials, especially Litvinov, that FDR would guarantee Soviet security needs if a meeting could only be held between Stalin and Roosevelt.

33. Vojtech Mastny, *Russia's Road to the Cold War* (New York: Columbia University Press, 1979), 108; Kimball, *Juggler,* 183.

34. Rothschild, *Diversity,* 74-75.

35. Murphy, *Diplomat,* 210-15. Also see Vaksberg, *Stalin's Prosecutor,* 242-49.

36. Welles, *Seven Decisions,* 144. In an article in the popular press that passed inspection at the White House, Forrest Davis argued that FDR was now moving away from welfare politics to power politics, that he was considering concrete ways by which aggressor states could be contained, and that he wanted to avoid the mistakes of the Congress of Vienna and the Congress of Versailles. The key for success was cooperation with Soviet Russia. The article states that Stalin was in the driver's seat and that "it is not too much to say that he can have the kind of world he desires." FDR should have been in the driver's seat because his power and influence were superior to Stalin's.

See Davis, "Roosevelt's World Blueprint," *Saturday Evening Post,* 10 April 1943, and Davis, "What Really Happened at Teheran?" *Saturday Evening Post,* 13 and 20 May 1944.

37. Herbert Feis, *From Trust to Terror: The Onset of the Cold War, 1945-1950* (New York: W. W. Norton, 1970), 17-18.

38. Langer, "Red General," 220.

39. McJimsey, *Hopkins,* 292-93.

40. Standley and Ageton, *Ambassador,* 497-99, 490; Abramson, *Harriman,* 350.

41. Isaacson and Thomas, *Wise Men,* 219.

13. "Uncle Joe"

1. Abramson, *Harriman,* 17; Jacob Heilbrunn, "The Playboy of the Western World," *New Republic,* 27 July 1992, 58.

2. Harriman and Abel, *Special Envoy,* 54.

3. Abramson, *Harriman,* 94, 97.

4. Ibid., 109-11, 164-85, 312-18, 677-78. For information on Pamela Harriman, see Sally Bedell Smith, *Reflected Glory: The Life of Pamela Churchill Harriman* (New York: Simon and Schuster, 1996).

5. Abramson, *Harriman,* 112-40.

6. Ibid., 140-41, 163.

7. Harriman and Abel, *Special Envoy,* 47; Abramson, *Harriman,* 207-8.

8. Harriman and Abel, *Special Envoy,* 44, 38.

9. Ibid., 54; Abramson, *Harriman,* 236, 243-44.

10. Harriman and Abel, *Special Envoy,* 13. "Cardinal Woolsey" remark is from Heilbrunn, "Playboy," 55.

11. Sherwood, *Roosevelt and Hopkins,* 269.

12. Kennan, "Comment," 30-31.

13. For the details of the Roosevelt-Churchill tie, see Joseph Lash, *Roosevelt and Churchill, 1939-1941: The Partnership That Saved the West* (New York: W. W. Norton, 1976).

14. Harriman and Abel, *Special Envoy,* 3.

15. Taylor, *Beaverbrook,* 487.

16. Dawson, *Decision to Aid Russia,* 256; Urban, "Harriman," 22-23.

17. Harriman and Abel, *Special Envoy,* 112; Abramson, *Harriman,* 297.

18. Isaacson and Thomas, *Wise Men,* 219; Abramson, *Harriman,* 348.

19. Bullitt, *For the President,* 588; Kennan, *Memoirs,* 224-25.

20. Cripps to Eden, 27 January 1943, FO 954/25, fol. 10, PRO. Roosevelt also told Gromyko that Litvinov was a major asset. See Gromyko to Molotov, 30 July 1943, SAOVVOV, 1:356.

21. Harriman and Abel, *Special Envoy,* 218, 226.

22. Halifax to Eden, 13 February 1944, FO 954/30, fol. 248, PRO; Asbell, *Mother and Daughter,* 141.

23. Harriman told Molotov that General Deane was the principal contact for the Soviet military. See notes of conversation between Molotov and Harriman, 5 November 1943, SAOVVOV, 1:426-27.

24. Hopkins met Bohlen at a cocktail party and asked him if he were "anti-So-

viet." Bohlen, who was always a diplomat, finessed the question and persuaded Hopkins that he had an open mind. Hopkins knew that Bohlen was indeed part of the anti-Stalin group at the State Department, but he liked Bohlen's charming personality and his willingness to support FDR's policy despite his personal opposition. Besides, the only people who knew anything about the Soviet Union were anti-Stalin, so if Hopkins wanted informed opinion, he had no choice but to accept someone from the so-called Riga School.

25. Kathleen was twenty-three when she went to Moscow. She eventually learned some Russian and proved herself to be an able hostess and companion for her lonely father. Harriman learned no Russian.

26. Notes of conversation between Molotov, Harriman, Hamilton, 21 October 1943, SAOVVOV, 1:386; Kennan, *Memoirs,* 231-33; Harriman to Stettinius, 9 November 1943, and Stettinius to Harriman, 12 November 1943, no. 861.24/1704, RG 59, NA.

27. Abramson, *Harriman,* 352.

28. Notes of conversation between Molotov, Harriman, and Hamilton, 21 October 1943, SAOVVOV, 1:389; G. N. Zarubin diary, American Section of the Foreign Ministry, meeting with Bohlen, 4 January 1944, AVP, col. 0129, reg. 28, file 6, pp. 5-6.

29. Abramson, *Harriman,* 352-60.

30. Kennan, *Memoirs,* 226-27.

31. Hull, *Memoirs,* 2:1288.

32. Harriman and Abel, *Special Envoy,* 249.

33. Harriman to Roosevelt, 4 and 5 November 1943, *FRUS: 1943,* 3:589; Harriman and Abel, *Special Envoy,* 249-50.

34. Secret Protocol of the Foreign Ministers of the USSR, USA, and Great Britain, 1 November 1943, SAOVVOV, 1:396-402; Supplements to the Secret Protocol of the Moscow Conference, nos. 1-10, 19-30 October 1943, SAOVVOV, 1:403-19.

35. Gromyko to Molotov, 2 November 1943, SAOVVOV, 1:425.

36. Notes of conversation between Molotov and Harriman, 6 November 1943, SAOVVOV, 1:432-34; Clark-Kerr to Eden, 7 November 1943, FO 954/25, fol. 196, PRO; notes of conversation between Molotov and Harriman, 16 November 1943, SAOVVOV, 1:436-37.

37. Churchill to Roosevelt, 11 November 1943, FO 954/25, fol. 199, PRO; Volkogonov, *Stalin,* 488.

38. Notes of conversation between Molotov and Harriman, 28 November 1943, SAOVVOV, 1:442-43; Winston S. Churchill, *Closing the Ring* (Boston: Houghton Mifflin, 1951), 343-44.

39. *FRUS: Conferences at Cairo and Teheran,* 463; personal interview with W. Averell Harriman, 19 November 1981, Washington, D.C.; Perkins, *The Roosevelt I Knew,* 84.

40. Ulam, *Expansion and Coexistence,* 587.

41. Notes of conversation between Roosevelt and Stalin, 28 November 1943, SAOVVOV, 1:446-51; Spears to Eden, 7 October 1943, FO 954/25, fol. 159, PRO.

42. Notes of conversation between Roosevelt and Stalin, 1 December 1943, SAOVVOV, 1:457; *FRUS: Conferences at Cairo and Teheran,* 594-95.

43. Perkins, *The Roosevelt I Knew,* 83-84; Eubanks, *Teheran,* 351; Bohlen, *Witness,* 146.

44. Memorandum by Bohlen, 26 May 1945, Bohlen Papers (BP), RG 59, NA.

45. Harriman to Hull, 18 December 1943, no. 860F.001/163, RG 59, NA.

46. Clark-Kerr to Eden, 16 July 1944, FO 954/30, fol. 438, PRO.

47. Clark-Kerr to Eden, 25 September 1944, FO 954/30, fol. 462, PRO.

48. Abramson, *Harriman*, 347.

49. Churchill, *Closing the Ring*, 373-74; *FRUS: Conferences at Cairo and Teheran*, 554. Also see Bullock, *Hitler and Stalin*, 816-17.

50. Feis, *Churchill, Roosevelt, Stalin*, 272.

51. Halifax to Eden, 13 February 1944, FO 954/30, fol. 248, PRO. The *Saturday Evening Post* reported that FDR was the mediator. See Davis, "What Really Happened at Teheran?" 13 May 1944.

52. Churchill, *Closing the Ring*, 363, 375-76.

53. Bullitt, *For the President*, 584. On the American plans for occupied Germany, see Warren F. Kimball, *Swords or Ploughshares? The Morgenthau Plan for Defeated Nazi Germany* (Philadelphia: J. B. Lippincott, 1976).

54. Churchill, *Closing the Ring*, 361-62; *FRUS: Conferences at Cairo and Teheran*, 599-604.

55. "Personal memorandum of conversations at London, May 2-May 5, 1944: Dinner with the Prime Minister at 10 Downing Street, Tuesday, May 2, 1944," Harriman Papers; William Larsh, "W. Averell Harriman and the Polish Question, December 1943-August 1944," *East European Politics and Societies* 7 (fall 1993): 537-42, 546-50. Harriman asked Molotov in June 1944 to arrange a meeting between him and the Moscow Poles. See notes of conversation between Molotov and Harriman, 3 June 1944, SAOVVOV, 2:125-26.

56. Notes of conversation between Roosevelt, Stalin, and Churchill, 30 November 1943, SAOVVOV, 1:455.

57. "Naval Operations in the Northwest Part of the Pacific Ocean," 29 November 1943, suppl. no. 3, SAOVVOV, 1:452-53; Khrushchev, *Glasnost Tapes*, 81; Bullitt, *For the President*, 582, 592-93.

58. Harriman and Abel, *Special Envoy*, 371; notes of conversation between Roosevelt and Stalin, 29 November 1943, SAOVVOV, 1:447-48; notes of conversation between Roosevelt, Stalin, and Churchill, 30 November 1943, SAOVVOV, 1:455-56.

59. Kimball, *Juggler*, 77, 96, 98, 103.

60. Notes of conversation between Roosevelt and Stalin, 29 November 1943, SAOVVOV, 1:449-51.

61. Marshall L. Miller, *Bulgaria during the Second World War* (Stanford: Stanford University Press, 1975), 171.

62. Notes of conversation between Roosevelt, Stalin, and Churchill, 30 November 1943, SAOVVOV, 1:453-55; "Military Resolution of Teheran Conference," 1 December 1943, SAOVVOV, 1:458-59; notes of conversation between Molotov and Harriman, 7 December 1943, SAOVVOV, 1:463-64, 466; Roosevelt to Churchill, 9 January 1944, FO 954/26, fol. 240, PRO.

63. William D. Hassett, *Off the Record with F.D.R., 1942-1945* (New Brunswick, N.J.: Rutgers University Press, 1950), 226.

64. Sherwood, *Roosevelt and Hopkins*, 798-99.

65. Harriman and Abel, *Special Envoy*, 283.

66. Kimball, *Juggler*, 103. Davis reported that FDR's dealings with Stalin at Te-

heran were considered by some as "appeasement." See Davis, "What Really Happened at Teheran?" 13 May 1944.

67. Roosevelt to Churchill, 10 January 1944, FO 954/26, fol. 240, PRO.

68. Kimball, *Juggler*, 100. For the comment of General Brooke, see Moran, *Churchill: Taken from the Diaries of Lord Moran* (Boston: Houghton Mifflin, 1966), 143.

69. Davis, "What Really Happened at Teheran?" 13 and 20 May 1944.

70. Volkogonov, *Stalin*, 488-89.

14. "The Russian Bear Is Biting"

1. See Kathleen Harriman's report on Katyn, 23 February 1944; John Melby's report on Katyn, 23 February 1944; Harriman to secretary of state, 25 January 1944, container 187, Harriman Papers (WAHP), Library of Congress; also see Abramson, *Harriman,* 362-63. Kathleen Harriman eventually recanted her conclusion, but her father did not. See Heilbrunn, "Playboy," 56.

2. Memorandum of conversation between Harriman and Molotov, 31 December 1943, *FRUS: 1943,* 3:736.

3. Harriman and Abel, *Special Envoy,* 295.

4. Harriman to Roosevelt and Hull, 9 January 1944, no. 711.61/968, RG 59, NA; Harriman to Hull and Stettinius, 20 April 1944, no. 861.911/507, RG 59, NA; Harriman to Hull, 18 January 1944, no. 760C.61/2173, RG 59, NA; "Memorandum of Conversation on January 16, 1944, Participants: Molotov, Harriman, Pavlov (interpreter), and L. Thompson," container 171, WAHP. Also see Edward J. Rozek, *Allied Wartime Diplomacy: A Pattern in Poland* (New York: John Wiley, 1958), 193-94. Also see notes of conversations between Molotov and Harriman, 25 December and 31 December 1943, SAOVVOV, 1:471-80.

5. "Memorandum of Conversation on January 16, 1944," container 171, WAHP; Larsh, "Harriman and Polish Question," 523-28; notes of conversation between Molotov and Harriman, 19 January 1944, SAOVVOV, 2:8-10.

6. "Memorandum of Conversation, February 2, 1944, Participants: Harriman, Stevens, Stalin, Berezhkov (interpreter), The Kremlin," container 171, WAHP; Larsh, "Harriman and Polish Question," 529-30; notes of conversation between Stalin, Molotov, and Harriman, 2 February 1944, SAOVVOV, 2:21-22.

7. "Conversation, March 3, 1944, Subject: Poland, Participants: Harriman, F. B. stevens, second secretary of the U.S. embassy, Stalin, Molotov, and Berezhkov (interpreter)," container 171, WAHP; Larsh, "Harriman and Polish Question," 532-33.

8. Hull to Harriman, 9 February 1944, no. 711.61/977A, RG 59, NA.

9. Memorandum by Elbridge Durbrow, 3 February 1944, no. 761.00/2-344; memorandum prepared by Division of European Affairs, 24 March 1944, no. 740.0011 Stettinius Mission/3-1944, RG 59, NA. Hull told Halifax that the "Soviet attitude is very unreasonable." Hull to Halifax, 5 April 1944, FO 954/30, fol. 366, PRO. Also see Halifax to Eden, 19 June 1944, FO 954/30, fols. 403-7, PRO.

10. Kimball, *Correspondence,* 2:694-95, 697-98, 3:14-15, 23-24, 27, 32; Nisbet, *Roosevelt and Stalin,* 53-55. Molotov had complained to Harriman on January 15 about the slow delivery of the Italian ships. See notes of conversation between Molotov and Harriman, 15 January 1944, SAOVVOV, 2:6-7; Stalin to Roosevelt and Churchill, 29 January 1944, SAOVVOV, 2:14-15.

11. Notes of conversation between Vyshinsky and Harriman, 30 March 1944, SAOVVOV, 2:70-71. Two additional cruisers were delivered in 1945. See Harriman to Molotov, 15 March 1945, SAOVVOV, 2:330-31.

12. "Personal Memorandum of Conversations at London, May 2-May 5, 1944: Dinner with the Prime Minister at 10 Downing Street, Tuesday, May 2, 1944," container 172, WAHP; Harriman and Abel, *Special Envoy*, 327-28; Larsh, "Harriman and Polish Question," 537-42, 546-50.

13. Churchill to FDR, 1 April 1944, FO 954/30, fol. 356, PRO.

14. "Secret and Personal Memorandum of Conversations with the President during Trip to Washington, D.C., October 21-November 10, 1944," container 175, WAHP; Memorandum by Stettinius, 23 May 1944, no. 123 Harriman, W. Averell/74, RG 59, NA; Harriman and Abel, *Special Envoy*, 311, 359-70; Larsh, "Harriman and Polish Question," 540-41, 545; Gromyko to Molotov, 10 May 1944, SAOVVOV, 2:104.

15. Kennan, *Memoirs*, 180.

16. Ibid., 190, 196-97, 224-25. Kennan, of course, had a high opinion of the Russian people and, as he told Vyshinsky, he hoped for "a strengthening of American-Soviet friendship." The Soviets also considered him competent. A. Y. Vyshinsky diary, 4 July 1944, AVP, col. 0129, reg. 28, file 5, p. 163; S. K. Tsarapkin diary, 23 June 1944, ibid., p. 26.

17. Kennan, *Memoirs*, 522.

18. "Paraphrase of Telegram May 29, 1944," container 172, WAHP; Larsh, "Harriman and Polish Question," 547-49.

19. Harriman to Roosevelt, 11 June 1944, PSF, FDR Library. Stalin had given tentative approval for the Poltava base in February. See notes of conversation between Stalin, Molotov, and Harriman, 2 February 1944, SAOVVOV, 2:16; notes of conversation between Molotov, General Deane, and Harriman, 5 February 1944, SAOVVOV, 2:23-29.

20. Churchill to Eden, 1 April 1944, FO 954/26, fol. 357, PRO.

21. Notes of conversation between Molotov and Harriman, 3 June 1944, SAOVVOV, 2:123-25; notes of conversation between Molotov and Harriman, 28 June 1944, SAOVVOV, 2:150-53; notes of conversation between Molotov and Harriman, 10 July 1944, SAOVVOV, 2:160; memorandum of agreement between USA and USSR, 22 July 1944, SAOVVOV, 2:170.

22. Notes of conversation between Molotov and Harriman, 25 April 1944, SAOVVOV, 2:94; notes of conversation between Molotov and Harriman, 3 June 1944, SAOVVOV, 2:124-25; notes of conversation between Molotov and Harriman, 11 August 1944, SAOVVOV, 2:173.

23. Notes of conversation between Molotov and Harriman, 3 June 1944, SAOVVOV, 2:123-24.

24. *Perepiska Predsedatelia Soveta Ministrov SSSR s prezidentami SSHA i prem'er-ministrami Velikobritanii vo vpremia velikoi otechestvennoi voiny 1941-1945 gg.*, 2 vols. (Moscow, 1957), 2:145-46; notes of conversation between Molotov and Harriman, 28 June 1944, SAOVVOV, 2:153. See also Hull to Harriman, 17 June 1944, no. 760C.61/2443a, RG 59, NA. Churchill had written FDR and asked him to receive Mikolajczyk in order to "show the Russians the interest which the United States takes in the fate and future of Poland," Churchill to FDR, 1 April 1944, FO 954/30, fol. 356, PRO.

25. Notes of conversation between Molotov and Harriman, 3 June 1944, SAOVVOV, 2:123; Larsh, "Harriman and Polish Question," 548-49.

26. *Perepiska,* 147. Also see notes of conversation between Molotov and Harriman, 28 June 1944, SAOVVOV, 2:153; notes of conversation between Molotov and Harriman, 11 August 1944, SAOVVOV, 2:174.

27. Larsh, "Harriman and Polish Question," 550; notes of conversation between Molotov and Harriman, 3 June 1944, SAOVVOV, 2:126-27.

28. Hull to Harriman, 17 June 1944, no. 033.60C11/80a, RG 59, NA. Also see Rozek's *Allied Wartime Diplomacy,* which is based on Stanislaus Mikolajczyk's papers.

29. Notes of conversation between Molotov and Harriman, 28 June 1944, SAOVVOV, 2:153-54.

30. Kennan, *Memoirs,* 206-7; notes of conversation between Molotov and Harriman, 11 August 1944, SAOVVOV, 2:172-73.

31. Kennan, *Memoirs,* 207-8.

32. In anticipation of the uprising, Churchill told Stalin: "I trust in you to make comradeship with the Underground Movement if it really strikes hard and true against the Germans." Churchill to Stalin, 20 July 1944, FO 954/30, fol. 420, PRO. For an excellent treatment of the uprising by the former Polish ambassador to the United States, see Jan M. Ciechanowski, *The Warsaw Uprising of 1944* (Cambridge: Cambridge University Press, 1974).

33. Ulam, *Expansion and Coexistence,* 363. Richard Lukas outlines the horror of the Nazi occupation for the non-Jews in his *Forgotten Holocaust: The Poles under German Occupation, 1939-1944* (Lexington: University Press of Kentucky, 1986).

34. Ulam, *Expansion and Coexistence,* 362; Abramson, *Harriman,* 382-83. Molotov even claimed that the Soviet commanders had no knowledge of the uprising on August 11. See notes of conversation between Molotov and Harriman, 11 August 1944, SAOVVOV, 2:173-74.

35. Notes of conversation between Stalin, Molotov, Harriman, and Clark-Kerr, 23 September 1944, SAOVVOV, 2:214.

36. Eden and the Polish government believed the Soviets wanted the Germans to destroy the Home Army so that they could avoid the onus of destroying a Polish force that would complicate their occupation of Poland as it had complicated the German occupation. See Eden to Churchill, 8 August 1944, FO 954/30, fol. 434, PRO; Abramson, *Harriman,* 382-84.

37. Notes of conversation between Stalin, Molotov, Harriman, and Clark-Kerr, 23 September 1944, SAOVVOV, 2:214; Stalin to Roosevelt and Churchill, 22 August 1944, SAOVVOV, 2:181-82; Ulam, *Expansion and Coexistence,* 362-63; notes of conversation between Molotov and Harriman, 11 August 1944, SAOVVOV, 2:175-76.

38. Kennan, *Memoirs,* 211.

39. Harriman and Abel, *Special Envoy,* 342; Abramson, *Harriman,* 382; Kennan, *Memoirs,* 210-11; Harriman to Harry Hopkins, 10 September 1944, box 157, HHP; Mayers, *Ambassadors,* 156.

40. Harriman and Abel, *Special Envoy,* 342; Nisbet, *Roosevelt and Stalin,* 57; Abramson, *Harriman,* 360, 383; Lukas, *Eagles East,* 195, 198-201, 207-11.

41. Isaacson and Thomas, *Wise Men,* 240-41.

42. Kennan, *Memoirs,* 206, 506-11, 521-22, 523-30.

43. Abramson, *Harriman,* 381.

44. Harriman and Abel, *Special Envoy,* 295; notes of conversation between Stalin, Molotov, Harriman, and Clark-Kerr, 23 September 1944, SAOVVOV, 2:214.

45. Harriman and Abel, *Special Envoy,* 309.

46. Harriman to Hopkins, 7 January 1944, no. 861.51/3019, RG 59, NA; also see Harriman to Stettinius, 16 November 1943, no. 861.24/1707, RG 59, NA.

47. Isaacson and Thomas, *Wise Men,* 233.

48. Roosevelt to Stalin, 9 September 1944, SAOVVOV, 2:205.

49. Kennan, *Memoirs,* 218-20, 222, 507-10, 521-22. Soviet historiography agrees with Kennan that all "economic levers" would have been futile. See V. L. Israelian, *Antigitlerovskaia koalitsiia* (Moscow, 1964), 574-75.

50. Kennan, *Memoirs,* 221, 510, 521-22.

51. Harriman to Hopkins, 10 September 1944, PSF, FDR Library. Also see Roosevelt to Churchill, 12 September 1944, Premier's File 3, fol. 195, PRO; Abramson, *Harriman,* 383. Also see notes of conversation between Molotov and Harriman, 11 August 1944, SAOVVOV, 2:175-76.

52. Burrows to War Office, 15 April 1944, FO 954/26, fol. 382, PRO.

53. Hull to Harriman, 18 September 1944, no. 740.0011 European War 1939/9-1844, RG 59, NA.

54. Harriman to Hull, 20 September 1944, no. 500.CC/9-2044, RG 59, NA.

55. Kennan, *Memoirs,* 521.

56. Memorandum of conversation by Welles, 7 May 1943, *FRUS: 1943,* 3:522-24; Mastny, "Cassandra," 368-71; Mastny, *Russia's Road,* 222; Remnick, *Lenin's Tomb,* 15. Historian Eduard Mark points out that the United States was willing as late as summer 1945 to accept a Soviet sphere of influence that was "open" and reasonable in terms of Soviet security needs. See his "Charles E. Bohlen and the Acceptable Limits of Soviet Hegemony in Eastern Europe: A Memorandum of 18 October 1945," *Diplomatic History* 3 (spring 1979): 201-13.

57. Harriman and Abel, *Special Envoy,* 364; Abramson, *Harriman,* 384, 387; Harriman to Hull and Roosevelt, 29 September 1944, no. 711.61/9-2944, RG 59, NA.

58. McJimsey, *Hopkins,* 359-60.

59. Feis, *Churchill, Roosevelt, Stalin,* 442-43; Warren F. Kimball, "Naked Reverse Right: From TOLSTOY to Yalta—and a Little Beyond," *Diplomatic History* 9 (winter 1985): 2. On the evolution of the Hopkins-Churchill tie, see Fraser J. Harbutt, "Churchill, Hopkins, and the 'Other' Americans: An Alternative Perspective on Anglo-American Relations, 1941-1945," *International History Review* 8 (May 1986): 236-62.

60. Winston S. Churchill, *Triumph and Tragedy* (Boston: Houghton Mifflin, 1953), 227.

61. Kimball, "TOLSTOY," 4; Urban, "Harriman," 36. Also see Joseph Siracusa, "The Night Stalin and Churchill Divided Europe: The View from Washington," *Review of Politics* 43 (July 1981): 381-409; and Joseph Siracusa, "The Meaning of TOLSTOY: Churchill, Stalin, and the Balkans, Moscow, October 1944," *Diplomatic History* 3 (fall 1979): 443-63.

62. Abramson, *Harriman,* 386. Published Soviet documents on the private conversations between Roosevelt and Stalin do not mention the Curzon Line agreement. See notes of conversations between Roosevelt and Stalin, 28 November 1943, 29 November 1943, 1 December 1943, SAOVVOV, 1:443-51, 456-58.

63. Gromyko to Molotov, 13 October 1944, SAOVVOV, 2:234-35.

64. Kimball, "TOLSTOY," 6-7; MacLean, *Davies,* 137.

65. Churchill, *Triumph and Tragedy,* 636. Eden had agreed to a formula of 80 percent influence for the USSR and 20 percent influence for England in Yugoslavia. See Martin Gilbert, *Churchill: A Life* (New York: Henry Holt, 1991), 797.

66. Barker, *Churchill and Eden,* 244.

67. Isaacson and Thomas, *Wise Men,* 243.

68. Kennan, *Memoirs,* 222.

69. Harriman and Abel, *Special Envoy,* 364, 389; Urban, "Harriman," 22; Gromyko to Molotov, 13 October 1944, SAOVVOV, 2:238.

70. Harriman and Abel, *Special Envoy,* 366, 370; Urban, "Harriman," 22-23.

71. Stalin to Roosevelt, 19 October 1944, SAOVVOV, 2:241; Roosevelt to Stalin, 25 October 1944, SAOVVOV, 2:244.

72. Roosevelt to Stalin, 19 November 1944, SAOVVOV, 2:264-65; Stalin to Roosevelt, 2 December 1944, SAOVVOV, 2:266-67; notes of conversation between Stalin, Molotov, and Harriman, 14 December 1944, SAOVVOV, 2:271-72, 274; notes of conversation between Molotov and Harriman, 26 December 1944, SAOVVOV, 2:283; Abramson, *Harriman,* 388.

73. Deane, *Alliance,* 84.

74. Harriman to Stettinius, 4 January 1945, no. 861.24/1-445, RG 59, NA. Stalin thought Jewish financiers in the West would provide postwar reconstruction aid. See Sudoplatov et al., *Special Tasks,* 296. Stalin, too, was convinced that the United States would go into another depression after the war. See his interview with Eric Johnston, president of the U.S. Chamber of Commerce: notes of conversation between Johnston, Harriman, Stalin, and Molotov, 26 June 1944, SAOVVOV, 2:143-44. Litvinov, with tongue in cheek, one must believe, told a skeptical Johnston that there was no evidence of Soviet interference in other countries' affairs; M. M. Litvinov diary, 19 June 1944, AVP, col. 0129, reg. 28, file 5, pp. 153-54.

75. Sudoplatov et al., *Special Tasks,* 228n; Roy Cohn, *McCarthy* (New York: New American Library, 1968), 56ff.

76. Roosevelt to Stettinius, 5 January 1945, no. 861.24/1-545, RG 59, NA.

77. Johnson, *Modern Times,* 458.

78. Sudoplatov et al., *Special Tasks,* 224-26; Urban, "Harriman," 23.

79. Kennan to Stettinius, 2 February 1945, no. 124.616/2-245, RG 59, NA.

80. Roosevelt to Stalin, 18 March 1944, SAOVVOV, 2:55-56; Sudoplatov et al., *Special Tasks,* 226; Urban, "Harriman," 23; Gromyko to Molotov, 13 October 1944, SAOVVOV, 2:234; Gromyko to Molotov, 10 November 1944, SAOVVOV, 2:255-57; notes of conversations between Stalin, Molotov, and Harriman, 14 December and 26 December 1944, SAOVVOV, 2:271, 280-82.

15. "The Russians Have Given So Much"

1. Kennan, *Russia and the West,* 384-85.

2. Roosevelt to Churchill, 27 September 1944, FDR Library; Kimball, "TOLSTOY," 2; Kimball, *Juggler,* 195. Kimball adds in a footnote that "even if the 'child' referred to by Roosevelt is obviously the postwar international organization, the President believed that the Russians had a good deal to 'learn' about proper international behavior." See *Juggler,* 275n. 33.

3. Harriman and Abel, *Special Envoy,* 391.

4. Kennan, *Memoirs,* 510.

5. Isaacson and Thomas, *Wise Men,* 227-28, 246-47.

6. Kennan, *Memoirs,* 510.

7. Stalin told Harry Hopkins in May 1945 that the USSR had been planning to thank the United States publicly for its Lend-Lease aid, but since the United States had temporarily discontinued the aid after Germany surrendered, the Soviet Union was angry and it was "impossible" now "to make a suitable expression of gratitude."

8. Sherwood, *Roosevelt and Hopkins,* 342.

9. Sudoplatov et al., *Special Tasks,* 210, 296. Some recent Russian scholarship is now critical of Stalin for breaking the anti-Hitler coalition. It blames him for the cold war and claims that it was a consequence of his class-based view of the world. He simply could not trust a capitalist like Roosevelt. See the polemical but nonetheless useful work of N. V. Zagladin, *Istoriia uspeckhori neudach sovetskoi diplomatii* (Moscow: Mezhdunarodnye otnosheniia, 1990), 132-48. On Stalin's conduct of the war, see the valuable interviews that Konstanin Simonov conducted with various Soviet military leaders: *Glazami chelovek moevo pokoleniia: razymyshleniia o I. V. Staline* (Moscow: Pravda, 1990), esp. 287-388.

10. Sudoplatov et al., *Special Tasks,* 227-29; also see Sam Tanenhaus, "Hiss: Guilty as Charged," *Commentary,* April 1993, 32-37; and Maria Schmidt, "The Hiss Dossier," *New Republic,* 8 November 1993, 17-20.

11. U.S. State Department, *Foreign Relations of the United States: Diplomatic Papers, The Conferences at Malta and Yalta, 1945* (Washington: Government Printing Office, 1955), 768-69, 896; Deane, *Alliance,* 182-201; Abramson, *Harriman,* 391. Also see the documents on the Yalta Conference in SAOVVOV, 2:290-311.

12. *FRUS: Malta and Yalta,* 768-69, 896.

13. Harriman and Abel, *Special Envoy,* 404; Sherwood, *Roosevelt and Hopkins,* 869-70. For information on the repatriation agreement, see Mark Elliott, *Pawns of Yalta: Soviet Refugees and America's Role in Their Repatriation* (Urbana: University of Illinois Press, 1982).

14. Kennan, *Memoirs,* 212-14.

15. Roosevelt to Stalin, 4 March 1944, and Stalin to Roosevelt, 5 March 1944, SAOVVOV, 2:322-24; *Perepiska,* 194-95. Also see Harriman to secretary of state, 11 April 1945, "Moscow Post Records," RG 84, NA; and Elliott, *Pawns of Yalta,* 248.

16. Harriman to secretary of state, 11 April 1945, "Moscow Post Records," RG 84, NA; Abramson, *Harriman,* 392-93.

17. Kimball, "TOLSTOY," 14-22. Also see Terry H. Anderson, *The United States, Great Britain, and the Cold War: 1944-1947* (Columbia: University of Missouri Press, 1981).

18. Harriman to Molotov, 12 March 1945, SAOVVOV, 2:327-29; Molotov to Harriman, 12 March 1945, SAOVVOV, 2:329; Harriman to Molotov, 15 March 1945, SAOVVOV, 2:331-32; Molotov to Harriman, 16 March 1945, SAOVVOV, 2:332-33; Harriman to Molotov, 21 March 1945, SAOVVOV, 2:337-38; Molotov to Harriman, 22 March 1945, SAOVVOV, 2:338; Roosevelt to Stalin, 25 March 1945, SAOVVOV, 2:340-41; Stalin to Roosevelt, 1 April 1945, SAOVVOV, 2:341-42; Stalin to Roosevelt, 3 April 1945, SAOVVOV, 2:344-45; Abramson, *Harriman,* 393; *Perepiska,* 204. Also see memorandum by Bohlen for the secretary, 13 March 1945, BP, RG 59, NA.

19. Roosevelt to Stalin, 5 April 1945, SAOVVOV, 2:346-47; *Perepiska*, 205-6.

20. Harriman to Stettinius, 4 April 1945, no. 840.50/4-445, RG 59, NA; Harriman to Stettinius, 6 April 1945, no. 711.61/4-645, RG 59, NA.

21. Stalin to Roosevelt, 7 April 1945, SAOVVOV, 2:350-51; Abramson, *Harriman*, 394; Kimball, "TOLSTOY," 18-22.

22. Isaacson and Thomas, *Wise Men*, 248; Harriman and Abel, *Special Envoy*, 432.

23. Personal interview with W. Averell Harriman, 19 November 1981, Washington, D.C.; Kennan to secretary of state, 22 February 1946, no. 861.00/2-2246, RG 59, NA; memorandum by Bohlen, 15 May 1945, BP, RG 59, NA.

24. Isaacson and Thomas, *Wise Men*, 263, 266.

25. Abramson, *Harriman*, 395; Harry S Truman, *Memoirs: Year of Decisions* (Garden City, N.Y.: Doubleday, 1955), 71.

26. Isaacson and Thomas, *Wise Men*, 277-78, 280.

27. Ibid., 278, 294-96; Weinberg, *World at Arms*, 807, 836.

28. Memorandum by Bohlen, 23 April 1945, BP, RG 59, NA; notes of conversation between Truman, Stettinius, Harriman, Molotov, Gromyko, and Bohlen, 22 April 1945, SAOVVOV, 2:367-69.

29. Isaacson and Thomas, *Wise Men*, 269, 273; Harriman and Abel, *Special Envoy*, 454.

30. Truman resumed Lend-Lease aid to the USSR within a few days after the USSR and pro-Soviet advisers in Washington bitterly complained. Truman had also discontinued Lend-Lease aid to Britain because the United States was doing the bulk of the fighting in the Pacific and needed transport ships. As with the Soviets, he resumed it after London objected.

31. Bohlen, *Witness*, 216; Isaacson and Thomas, *Wise Men*, 279; Harriman and Abel, *Special Envoy*, 460. For an excellent study of the decision and its consequences, see Herring, "Lend-Lease."

32. Isaacson and Thomas, *Wise Men*, 270.

33. Memorandum by Bohlen, 15 May 1945, BP, RG 59, NA; Isaacson and Thomas, *Wise Men*, 276-80.

34. Notes of meeting between Truman, Stettinius, Harriman, Molotov, Gromyko, and Bohlen, 22 April 1945, SAOVVOV, 2:368.

35. Isaacson and Thomas, *Wise Men*, 279-83; Feis, *Trust to Terror*, 35. Truman stated that even he was pro-Soviet at the time. See Ferrell, *Off the Record*, 348.

36. Churchill, *Triumph and Tragedy*, 577. For Davies's role in advising Truman and meeting with Churchill, see MacLean, *Davies*, 139-46.

37. Memorandum by Bohlen for secretary of state, 19 April 1945, BP, RG 59, NA.

38. Harriman has claimed that he actually did most of the talking for the American side at the meeting because Hopkins wanted him to. He explained that Chip Bohlen, the translator, recorded the minutes as if Hopkins were the principal speaker because in Bohlen's mind that was "proper protocol," since Hopkins was the head of the mission. Personal interview with W. Averell Harriman, 19 November 1981, Washington, D.C.

39. Notes of conversations between Stalin, Hopkins, Harriman, Molotov, and Bohlen, 26 and 28 May 1945, SAOVVOV, 2:397-411. Professor Lange became the ambassador of the Polish Communist government in Washington.

40. Memorandums by Bohlen, 26 and 27 May 1945, BP, RG 59, NA; McJimsey, *Hopkins,* 392.

41. Memorandum by Bohlen, 22 April 1945, BP, RG 59, NA; notes of conversation between Truman, Stettinius, Harriman, Molotov, Gromyko, and Bohlen, 22 April 1945, SAOVVOV, 2:367-69.

42. Memorandum by Bohlen, 28 May 1945, BP, RG 59, NA.

43. Isaacson and Thomas, *Wise Men,* 305.

44. See Odd Arne Westad, *Cold War and Revolution: Soviet-American Rivalry and the Origins of the Chinese Civil War* (New York: Columbia University Press, 1993).

45. Kennan, *Memoirs,* 212-13.

46. Isaacson and Thomas, *Wise Men,* 289-91, 292, 299, 303-4.

47. MacLean, *Davies,* 160-61. For Soviet documents relating to the Potsdam Conference, see "Protocol of the Berlin Conference," 1 August 1945, SAOVVOV, 2:442-60; and "Communication of Berlin Conference," 2 August 1945, SAOVVOV, 2:460-72.

48. Notes of conversation between Stalin, Molotov, Truman, and Byrnes, 17 July 1945, SAOVVOV, 2:439; MacLean, *Davies,* 125-30; Isaacson and Thomas, *Wise Men,* 309.

49. David Holloway proves that Moscow's first atomic bomb resulted from espionage within the Manhattan Project. See his *Stalin and the Bomb* (New Haven: Yale University Press, 1994). Also see Isaacson and Thomas, *Wise Men,* 309-11; Volkogonov, *Stalin,* 498. Sudoplatov maintains, without proof, that the western science team of Robert Oppenheimer, Enrico Fermi, and Leo Szilard provided the Soviet government with the atomic secrets in the belief that world peace would be best served if no one power or group of powers had an atomic monopoly. See Sudoplatov et al., *Special Tasks,* 172.

50. Isaacson and Thomas, *Wise Men,* 310-11.

51. Notes of conversation between Molotov, Harriman, and Clark-Kerr, 8 August 1945, SAOVVOV, 2:478; Isaacson and Thomas, *Wise Men,* 316-17.

52. Harriman and Abel, *Special Envoy,* 512-22; Harriman to secretary of state, 27 November 1945, "Moscow Post Records," RG 84, NA; Isaacson and Thomas, *Wise Men,* 342. Pavel Sudoplatov maintains that Harriman never did get to see Stalin: *Special Tasks,* 226.

53. Vladimir O. Pechatnov, "The Big Three after World War II," Cold War International History Project Working Paper No. 13, Woodrow Wilson International Center, 1995, 17. Litvinov, Maisky, and Gromyko all shared strong ties to the West (Litvinov and Gromyko were stationed in the United States and Maisky was in London) and were not decisionmakers.

54. Kennan, *Memoirs,* 284; Harriman and Abel, *Special Envoy,* 525; Isaacson and Thomas, *Wise Men,* 344-45.

55. Kennan to Byrnes, 22 February 1946, U.S. State Department, *Foreign Relations of the United States 1946,* vol. 6: Eastern Europe; The Soviet Union (Washington: Government Printing Office, 1969), 696-709; Isaacson and Thomas, *Wise Men,* 352-53.

56. Mastny, "Cassandra," 373-74; *Washington Post,* 21-26 January 1951.

57. Sir Llewellyn Woodward, *British Foreign Policy in the Second World War* (London: Her Majesty's Stationery Office, 1970), 1:xliv.

58. Urban, "Harriman," 28.

59. Norman Naimark reveals that Stalin was flexible on East Germany's future. See his *Russians in Germany: A History of the Soviet Zone of Occupation, 1945-49* (Cambridge: Harvard University Press, 1995).

60. Isaacson and Thomas, *Wise Men,* 346, 352-56, 372.

Epilogue

1. Perkins, *The Roosevelt I Knew,* 86.

2. Kennan, *Memoirs,* 233.

3. MacLean, *Davies,* 185.

4. See, for example, Adam Hochschild, *The Unquiet Ghost: Russians Remember Stalin* (New York: Viking, 1993), 193-94. Also see Kathleen E. Smith, *Remembering Stalin's Victims: Popular Memory and the End of the USSR* (Ithaca, N.Y.: Cornell University Press, 1996).

5. Bullitt to FDR, 1 July 1941, PPF, FDR Library.

6. Kennan, "Comment," 31.

7. Kimball, *Juggler,* 185-200.

8. This is not to say, of course, that the United States was a perfect society. Ironically, Roosevelt's moral relativism did push the United States closer to convergence with the Soviet Union. While recognizing that there is much that is right with the United States, it is also true that there is much that needs improvement, and at the end of the twentieth century with the cold war over, maybe the best that can be said is that the United States was less evil than the "evil empire." Interestingly, Russian intellectuals today think of the former Soviet Union as "evil" and "totalitarian." For a judicious examination of this development and the use of the term *totalitarianism* in the cold war, see Abbott Gleason, *Totalitarianism: The Inner History of the Cold War* (New York: Oxford University Press, 1995), and Abbott Gleason, "Totalitarianism and the Cold War: A Personal View," *Newsnet: Newsletter of the American Association for the Advancement of Slavic Studies,* September 1995, 1, 3.

9. Weinberg, *World at Arms,* 288.

10. Samuel P. Huntington, "The West and the World," *Foreign Affairs* (Nov./Dec. 1996): 39.

Bibliography

Archives and Manuscript Collections

Arkhiv vneshnei politiki R F (Archive of Foreign Affairs, Russian Federation), Moscow, Collection 06 (Molotov's Secretariat) and Collection 0129 (U.S. Desk)
Bohlen, Charles. Papers. Record Group 59, National Archives.
Bullitt, William C. Papers. Yale University.
Bullitt, William C. Papers. Franklin D. Roosevelt Library.
Davies, Joseph. Papers. Library of Congress.
Foreign Office. Papers. Public Record Office, Kew Green, London.
Harriman, W. Averell. Papers. Library of Congress.
Henderson, Loy W. Papers. Library of Congress.
Hopkins, Harry. Papers. Franklin D. Roosevelt Library.
Moore, R. Walton. Papers. Franklin D. Roosevelt Library.
Morgenthau, Henry Jr. Papers. Franklin D. Roosevelt Library.
Records of the Division of Eastern European Affairs, 1917-1941, Record Group 59, National Archives.
Roosevelt, Franklin D. Official File; President's Personal File; President's Secretary's File. Franklin D. Roosevelt Library.
Rossiiskii tsentr khraneniia i izucheniia dokumentov noveishei istorii (Russian Center for the Preservation and Study of Contemporary Historical Documents, formerly known as the Central Party Archive), Moscow.
Standley, William. Papers. Library of Congress.
State Department Records, 1917–1945. Record Groups 59, 84, and 169. National Archives.
Steinhardt, Laurence. Papers. Library of Congress.

Interviews

Personal interview with Elbridge Durbrow, November 10, 1981, Washington, D.C.
Personal interview with W. Averell Harriman, November 19, 1981, Washington, D.C.
Telephone interview with George Kennan, November 17, 1981, Princeton, N.J.
Personal interview with Thomas Pickering, September 26, 1993, Moscow.

Documents and Memoirs

Asbell, Bernard, ed., *Mother and Daughter: The Letters of Eleanor and Anna Roosevelt.* London: Sidgwick and Jackson, 1984.

Baer, George M., ed. *A Question of Trust: The Origins of U.S.–Soviet Diplomatic Relations, the Memoirs of Loy W. Henderson.* Stanford, Calif.: Hoover Institution Press, 1986.

Blum, John Morton, ed., *The Price of Vision: The Diary of Henry A. Wallace, 1942–1946.* Boston: Houghton Mifflin, 1973.

Bohlen, Charles E. *Witness to History, 1929–1969.* New York: W. W. Norton, 1973.

Bourne, Kenneth, and D. C. Watt, eds., *British Documents on Foreign Affairs: Reports and Papers from the Foreign Office.* Vol. 14, *The Soviet Union.* Frederick, Md.: University Publications of America, 1983.

Bullitt, Orville H., ed., *For the President: Personal and Secret.* With an introduction by George F. Kennan. Boston: Houghton Mifflin, 1972.

Bullitt, William C. *The Bullitt Mission to Russia.* New York: B. W. H. Huebsch, 1919.

Cassidy, Henry C. *Moscow Dateline.* Boston: Houghton Mifflin, 1943.

Churchill, Winston S. *Their Finest Hour.* Boston: Houghton Mifflin, 1949.

———. *The Grand Alliance.* Boston: Houghton Mifflin, 1950.

———. *The Hinge of Fate.* Boston: Houghton Mifflin, 1950.

———. *Closing the Ring.* Boston: Houghton Mifflin, 1951.

———. *Triumph and Tragedy.* Boston: Houghton Mifflin, 1953.

Chuyev, Feliks. *Sto sorok besed c Molotovym: Iz dnevnika F. Chuyeva.* Moscow: Terra, 1991.

Ciechanowski, Jan M. *The Warsaw Uprising of 1944.* Cambridge: Cambridge University Press, 1974.

Coulondre, Robert. *From Stalin to Hitler: Memoirs of Two Embassies, 1936–39.* Paris, 1950.

Davies, Joseph E. *Mission to Moscow.* New York: Simon and Schuster, 1941.

Dilks, David, ed., *The Diaries of Sir Alexander Cadogan, 1938–1945.* New York: G. P. Putnam's Sons, 1972.

Djilas, Milovan. *Conversations with Stalin.* New York: Harcourt, Brace and World, 1962.

Documents on German Foreign Policy, 1918–45, series D, vol. 4. From the archives of the German Foreign Ministry. Washington: Government Printing Office, 1956.

Eden, Anthony. *The Eden Memoirs: The Reckoning.* Boston: Houghton Mifflin, 1965.

Federal'naia sluzhba kontrrazvedki Rossiiskoi federatsii, *Organy gosudarstvennoi bezopasnosti SSSR v Velikoi Otechestvennoi voine.* Vol. 1, *Nakanune.* Nov. 1938–Dec. 1940. Moscow: Kniga i Biznes, 1995.

Ferrell, Robert H., ed., *Off the Record: The Private Papers of Harry S Truman.* New York: Harper and Row, 1980.

Gromyko, Andrei. *Memories.* Translated by Harold Shukman. London: Hutchinson, 1989.

Harriman, W. Averell, and Elie Abel, *Special Envoy to Churchill and Stalin, 1941–1946.* New York: Random House, 1976.

Hassett, William D. *Off the Record with F.D.R., 1942–1945.* New Brunswick, N.J.: Rutgers University Press, 1950.

Herwarth, Hans von. *Against Two Evils: Memoirs of a Diplomat-Soldier during the Third Reich.* New York: Rawson, 1981.

Hull, Cordell. *The Memoirs of Cordell Hull.* 2 vols. New York: Macmillan, 1948.

Kennan, George F. *Memoirs, 1925–1950.* Boston: Little, Brown, 1967.

Khrushchev, Nikita. *Khrushchev Remembers: The Glasnost Tapes.* Translated by Jerrold L. Schechter and Vyacheslav Luchkov. Boston: Little, Brown, 1990.

Kimball, Warren F., ed., *Churchill and Roosevelt: The Complete Correspondence.* 3 vols. Princeton: Princeton University Press, 1984.

Lih, Lars T., Oleg V. Naumov, and Oleg V. Khlevniuk, eds. *Stalin's Letters to Molotov.* Translated by Catherine A. Fitzpatrick. New Haven: Yale University Press, 1995.

Litvinov, Maxim. *Notes for a Journal.* New York: William Morrow, 1955.

Lyons, Eugene. *Assignment in Utopia.* New York: Harcourt, Brace, 1937.

Ministerstvo inostrannyk del Rossiiskoi federatsii. *Dokumenty vneshnei politiki 1939 god.* 2 vols. Moscow: Mezhdunarodnye othnosheniia, 1992.

Ministerstvo inostrannyk del SSSR. *Sovetsko-Amerikanskie otnosheniia vo vremia velikoi otechestvennoi voiny 1941–1945.* 2 vols. Moscow: Izdatel'stvo politicheskoi literatury, 1984.

Moran, Lord [Charles Wilson]. *Churchill: The Struggle for Survival, 1940–1965, Taken from the Diaries of Lord Moran.* Boston: Houghton Mifflin, 1966.

Murphy, Robert. *Diplomat among Warriors.* Garden City, N.Y.: Doubleday, 1964.

Nixon, Edgar B., ed., *Franklin D. Roosevelt and Foreign Affairs.* 3 vols. Cambridge, Mass.: Harvard University Press, 1969.

Perepiska Predsedatelia Soveta Ministrov SSSR s prezidentami SSHA i prem'er-ministrami Velikobritanii vo vremia velikoi otechestvennoi voiny, 1941–1945 gg. 2 vols. Moscow, 1957.

Perkins, Frances. *The Roosevelt I Knew.* New York: Viking Press, 1946.

Procacci, G., et al., eds. *The Cominform: Minutes of the Three Conferences, 1947/1948/1949.* Milan: Feltrinelli, 1994.

Roosevelt, Elliott. *As He Saw It.* New York: Duell, Sloan, and Pearce, 1946.

———. ed., *F.D.R.: His Personal Letters, 1928–1945.* 3 vols. New York: Duell, Sloan, and Pearce, 1950.

Rossiiskaia akademiia nauk institut vseobshchei istorii. *Komintern i vtoraia mirovaia voina.* Moscow: Pamiatniki istoricheskoi mysli, 1994.

Schewe, Donald B., ed. *Franklin D. Roosevelt and Foreign Affairs.* Vol. 13. New York: Clearwater, 1979.

Sherwood, Robert. *Roosevelt and Hopkins: An Intimate History.* New York: Harper, 1948.

Simonov, Konstantin. *Glazami chelovek moevo pokoleniia: razmyshleniia o I. V. Staline.* Moscow: Pravda, 1990.

Stalin, I. V. *O velikoi otechestvennoi voine Sovetskovo Soiuza.* Moscow, 1948.

———. *Sochineniia.* 13 vols. to date. Moscow, 1946–.

Standley, William H., and Arthur A. Ageton. *Admiral Ambassador to Russia.* Chicago: Henry Regnery, 1955.

Sudoplatov, Pavel, et al., *Special Tasks: The Memoirs of an Unwanted Witness—A Soviet Spymaster.* Boston: Little, Brown, 1994.

Thayer, Charles W. *Bears in the Caviar.* Philadelphia: J. B. Lippincott, 1950.

Truman, Harry S. *Memoirs: Year of Decisions.* Garden City, N.Y.: Doubleday, 1955.

U.S. State Department, *Foreign Relations of the United States: Diplomatic Papers: The Soviet Union, 1933–1939.* Washington: Government Printing Office, 1952.

———. *Foreign Relations of the United States: Diplomatic Papers: The Conferences at Malta and Yalta, 1945.* Washington: Government Printing Office, 1955.

———. *Foreign Relations of the United States 1940.* Vol. 3, *The British Commonwealth, the Soviet Union, the Near East, and Africa.* Washington: Government Printing Office, 1958–59.

———. *Foreign Relations of the United States.* Vol. 1, *General, the Soviet Union, 1941.* Washington: Government Printing Office, 1958.

———. *Foreign Relations of the United States, Diplomatic Papers 1942.* Vol. 3, *Europe.* Washington: Government Printing Office, 1961.

———. *Foreign Relations of the United States: Diplomatic Papers: The Conferences at Cairo and Teheran, 1943.* Washington: Government Printing Office, 1961.

———. *Foreign Relations of the United States, Diplomatic Papers 1943.* Vol. 3, *The British Commonwealth, Eastern Europe, and the Far East.* Washington: Government Printing Office, 1963.

———. *Foreign Relations of the United States 1946.* Vol. 6, *Eastern Europe; The Soviet Union.* Washington: Government Printing Office, 1969.

Woodward, Sir Llewellyn. *British Foreign Policy in the Second World War.* Vol. 1. London: Her Majesty's Stationery Office, 1970.

Welles, Sumner. *Seven Decisions That Shaped History.* New York: Harper, 1951.

———. *Where Are We Heading?* New York: Harper, 1946.

Zhukov, Marshal G. K. *Vospominaniia i razmyshleniia.* 3 vols. Moscow: Novosti, 1992.

Books

Abramson, Rudy. *Spanning the Century: The Life of W. Averell Harriman, 1891–1986.* New York: William Morrow, 1992.

Anderson, Terry H. *The United States, Great Britain, and the Cold War, 1944–1947.* Columbia: University of Missouri Press, 1981.

Aronson, Michael. *Troubled Waters: The Origins of the 1881 Anti-Jewish Pogroms in Russia.* Pittsburgh: University of Pittsburgh Press, 1990.

Barker, Elisabeth. *Churchill and Eden at War.* New York: St. Martin's Press, 1978.

Barnard, Ellsworth. *Wendell Willkie: Fighter for Freedom.* Marquette: Northern Michigan University Press, 1966.

Bassow, Whitman. *The Moscow Correspondents: Reporting on Russia from the Revolution to Glasnost.* New York: William Morrow, 1988.

Beaumont, Joan. *Comrades in Arms: British Aid to Russia, 1941–1945.* London: Davis-Poynter, 1980.

Bennett, Edward M. *Recognition of Russia: An American Foreign Policy Dilemma.* Waltham, Mass.: Blaisdell, 1970.

———. *Franklin D. Roosevelt and the Search for Security: American-Soviet Relations, 1933–1939.* Wilmington, Del.: Scholarly Resources, 1985.

———. *Franklin D. Roosevelt and the Search for Victory: American-Soviet Relations, 1939–1945.* Wilmington, Del.: Scholarly Resources, 1990.

Beschloss, Michael R. *Kennedy and Roosevelt: The Uneasy Alliance.* New York: W. W. Norton, 1980.

Bishop, Donald G. *The Roosevelt-Litvinov Agreement: The American View.* Syracuse, N.Y.: Syracuse University Press, 1965.

Bohlen, Charles E. *The Transformation of American Foreign Policy.* New York: W. W. Norton, 1966.

Botti, Timothy J. *The Long Wait: The Forging of the Anglo-American Nuclear Alliance, 1945–1958.* Westport, Conn.: Greenwood Press, 1987.

Brands, H. W. *Inside the Cold War: Loy Henderson and the Rise of the American Empire.* New York: Oxford University Press, 1991.

Browder, Robert P. *The Origins of Soviet-American Diplomacy.* Princeton: Princeton University Press, 1953.

Brownell, Will, and Richard N. Billings. *So Close to Greatness: A Biography of William C. Bullitt.* New York: Macmillan, 1987.

Bullock, Alan. *Hitler and Stalin: Parallel Lives.* New York: Vintage Books, 1993.

Burns, James McGregor. *Roosevelt: The Soldier of Freedom.* New York: Harcourt Brace Jovanovich, 1970.

Carlton, David. *Anthony Eden: A Biography.* London: Allen Lane, 1981.

Ciechanowski, Jan M. *The Warsaw Uprising of 1944.* Cambridge: Cambridge University Press, 1974.

Clark, Alan. *Barbarossa: The Russian-German Conflict, 1941–45.* New York: William Morrow, 1965.

Cohn, Roy. *McCarthy.* New York: New American Library, 1968.

Cole, Wayne S. *Roosevelt and the Isolationists, 1932–1945.* Lincoln: University of Nebraska Press, 1983.

Conquest, Robert. *Harvest of Sorrow: Soviet Collectivization and Terror-Famine.* New York: Oxford University Press, 1986.

———. *The Great Terror: Stalin's Purges of the Thirties.* New ed. New York: Macmillan, 1990.

———. *Stalin: Breaker of Nations.* New York: Penguin Books, 1991.

———. *Stalin and the Kirov Murder.* New York: Oxford University Press, 1989.

Crowl, James William. *Angels in Stalin's Paradise: Western Reporters in Soviet Russia, 1917–1937: A Study of Louis Fischer and Walter Duranty.* Washington: University Press of America, 1982.

Dallek, Robert. *Franklin D. Roosevelt and American Foreign Policy, 1932–1945.* New York: Oxford University Press, 1979.

Davis, Nathaniel. *A Long Walk to Church: A History of Contemporary Russian Orthodoxy.* Boulder, Colo.: Westview Press, 1995.

Dawson, Raymond H. *The Decision to Aid Russia, 1941.* Chapel Hill: University of North Carolina Press, 1959.

Deane, John R. *The Strange Alliance.* Bloomington: Indiana University Press, 1973.

DeSantis, Hugh. *The Diplomacy of Silence: The American Foreign Service, the Soviet Union, and the Cold War, 1933–1947.* Chicago: University of Chicago Press, 1980.

Divine, Robert. *Roosevelt and World War II.* Baltimore: Johns Hopkins University Press, 1969.

Djilas, Milovan. *Conversations with Stalin.* New York: Harcourt, Brace and World, 1962.

Dunn, Dennis J. *The Catholic Church and the Soviet Government, 1939–1949.* New York: Columbia University Press, 1977.

Eagles, Keith. *Ambassador Joseph E. Davies and American-Soviet Relations, 1937–1941.* New York: Garland, 1985.

Elliott, Mark. *Pawns of Yalta: Soviet Refugees and America's Role in Their Repatriation*. Urbana: University of Illinois Press, 1982.

Erickson, John. *The Road to Stalingrad: Stalin's War with Germany*. New York: Harper and Row, 1975.

———. *The Road to Berlin: Stalin's War with Germany*. Boulder, Colo.: Westview Press, 1983.

Eubanks, Keith. *Summit at Teheran*. New York: William Morrow, 1985.

Farnsworth, Beatrice. *William C. Bullitt and the Soviet Union*. Bloomington: Indiana University Press, 1967.

Feis, Herbert. *Characters in Crisis*. Boston: Little, Brown, 1966.

———. *Churchill, Roosevelt, Stalin: The War They Waged and the Peace They Sought*. Princeton: Princeton University Press, 1957.

———. *From Trust to Terror: The Onset of the Cold War, 1945–1950*. New York: W. W. Norton, 1970.

Ferrell, Robert H., ed., *Off the Record: The Private Papers of Harry S Truman*. New York: Harper and Row, 1980.

Fest, Joachim. *Hitler*. Translated by Richard and Clara Winston. New York: Harcourt Brace Jovanovich, 1974.

Filene, Peter. *Americans and the Soviet Experiment, 1917–1933*. Cambridge, Mass.: Harvard University Press, 1967.

Fischer, Louis. *Men and Politics: An Autobiography*. New York: Duell, Sloan, and Pearce, 1941.

Gaddis, John Lewis. *Now We Know: Rethinking Cold War History*. New York: Oxford University Press, 1997.

———. *Russia, the Soviet Union, and the United States: An Interpretative History*. New York: John Wiley, 1978.

———. *The United States and the Origins of the Cold War, 1941-1947*. New York: Columbia University Press, 1972.

Gardner, Lloyd C. *Architects of Illusion*. Chicago: Quadrangle Books, 1972.

Gilbert, Martin. *Winston S. Churchill: Road to Victory, 1941–1945*. Boston: Houghton Mifflin, 1986.

———. *Churchill: A Life*. New York: Henry Holt, 1991.

Gleason, Abbott. *Totalitarianism: The Inner History of the Cold War*. New York: Oxford University Press, 1995.

Gorodetsky, Gabriel. *Stafford Cripps's Mission to Moscow, 1940–42*. Cambridge: Cambridge University Press, 1984.

Gross, Jan T. *Revolution from Abroad: The Soviet Conquest of Poland's Western Ukraine and Western Byelorussia*. Princeton: Princeton University Press, 1987.

Guensberg, Gerald. *Soviet Command Study of Iran with Brief Analysis*. Falls Church, Va.: Delphic Associates, 1980.

Gunther, John. *Roosevelt in Retrospect: A Profile in History*. New York: Harper, 1950.

Haslam, Jonathan. *The Soviet Union and the Search for Collective Security in Europe, 1933–1939*. New York: St. Martin's Press, 1984.

Herring, George C. Jr. *Aid to Russia, 1941–1946: Strategy, Diplomacy, and the Origins of the Cold War*. New York: Columbia University Press, 1973.

Hochman, Jiri. *The Soviet Union and the Failure of Collective Security, 1934–1938*. Ithaca, N.Y.: Cornell University Press, 1984.

Hochschild, Adam. *The Unquiet Ghost: Russians Remember Stalin*. New York: Viking, 1993.

Hoff-Wilson, Joan. *Ideology and Economics: U.S. Relations with the Soviet Union, 1918–1933*. Columbia: University of Missouri Press, 1974.

Hollander, Paul. *Political Pilgrims: Travels of Western Intellectuals to the Soviet Union, China, and Cuba, 1928–1978*. New York: Oxford University Press, 1981.

Holloway, David. *Stalin and the Bomb*. New Haven: Yale University Press, 1994.

Isaacson, Walter, and Evan Thomas. *The Wise Men: Six Friends and the World They Made*. New York: Simon and Schuster, 1986.

Israelian, V. L. *Antigitlerovskaia koalitsiia*. Moscow, 1964.

Jacobs, Travis Beal. *America and the Winter War, 1939–1940*. New York: Garland, 1980.

Johnson, Paul. *Modern Times*. New York: HarperCollins, 1991.

Kennan, George F. *Russia and the West under Lenin and Stalin*. Boston: Little, Brown, 1961.

Khlevniuk, Oleg V. *1937: Stalin, NKVD, i Sovetskoi obshchestvo*. Moscow, 1992.

Kimball, Warren F. *Swords or Ploughshares? The Morgenthau Plan for Defeated Nazi Germany*. Philadelphia: J. B. Lippincott, 1976.

———. *The Juggler: Franklin Roosevelt as Wartime Statesman*. Princeton: Princeton University Press, 1991.

Langer, William L., and Everett S. Gleason. *The Challenge to Isolation: The World Crisis of 1937–1940 and American Foreign Policy*. New York: Harper, 1952.

———. and Everett S. Gleason. *The Undeclared War*. New York: Harper and Row, 1953.

Laqueur, Walter. *Stalin: The Glasnost Revelations*. New York: Scribner, 1990.

Lash, Joseph. *Roosevelt and Churchill, 1939–1941: The Partnership That Saved the West*. New York: W. W. Norton, 1976.

Levin, Dov. *The Lesser of Two Evils: Eastern European Jewry under Soviet Rule, 1939–1941*. Philadelphia: Jewish Publication Society, 1995.

Levine, Robert. *Flying in the Face of Uncertainty: Alternative Plans and Postures for Intervention in Southwest Asia*. Santa Monica: Rand Graduate Institute, 1985.

Libbey, James K. *Alexander Gumberg and Soviet-American Relations, 1917–1933*. Lexington: University Press of Kentucky, 1977.

Litvinov, Maxim. *Vneshniaia politika SSSR*. Moscow, 1937.

Lukas, Richard. *Eagles East: The Army Air Force and the Soviet Union, 1941–1945*. Tallahassee: Florida State University Press, 1970.

———. *Forgotten Holocaust: The Poles under German Occupation, 1939–1944*. Lexington: University Press of Kentucky, 1986.

McCullough, David. *Truman*. New York: Simon and Schuster, 1992.

McJimsey, George. *Harry Hopkins: Ally of the Poor and Defender of Democracy*. Cambridge, Mass.: Harvard University Press, 1987.

MacLean, Elizabeth Kimball. *Joseph E. Davies: Envoy to the Soviets*. Westport, Colo.: Praeger, 1992.

Maddux, Thomas R. *Years of Estrangement: American Relations with the Soviet Union, 1933–1941*. Tallahassee: University Presses of Florida, 1980.

Mastny, Vojtech. *The Cold War and Soviet Insecurity: The Stalin Years*. New York: Oxford University Press, 1996.

———. *Russia's Road to the Cold War*. New York: Columbia University Press, 1979.

Mayer, Arno. *Why Did the Heavens Not Darken? The "Final Solution" in History*. New York: Pantheon Books, 1989.

Mayers, David. *George Kennan and the Dilemmas of U.S. Foreign Policy*. New York: Oxford University Press, 1988.

———. *The Ambassadors and America's Soviet Policy*. New York: Oxford University Press, 1995.

Medvedev, Roy. *All Stalin's Men*. New York: Anchor/Doubleday, 1984.

Miller, Marshall L. *Bulgaria during the Second World War*. Stanford, Calif.: Stanford University Press, 1975.

Miner, Steven M. *Between Churchill and Stalin: The Soviet Union, Great Britain, and the Origins of the Grand Alliance*. Chapel Hill: University of North Carolina Press, 1988.

Morris, M. Wayne. *Stalin's Famine and Roosevelt's Recognition of Russia*. Lanham, Md.: University Press of America, 1994.

Naimark, Norman. *The Russians in Germany: A History of the Soviet Zone of Occupation, 1945–49*. Cambridge, Mass.: Harvard University Press, 1995.

Nisbet, Robert. *Roosevelt and Stalin*. Washington, D.C.: Regnery Gateway, 1988.

O'Connor, Raymond G. *Diplomacy for Victory: FDR and Unconditional Surrender*. New York: W. W. Norton, 1971.

Paul, Allen. *Katyn: The Untold Story of Stalin's Polish Massacre*. New York: Macmillan, 1991.

Perlmutter, Amos. *FDR and Stalin: A Not So Grand Alliance, 1943–1945*. Columbia: University of Missouri Press, 1993.

Phillips, William. *Ventures in Diplomacy*. Boston: Beacon Press, 1953.

Pogue, Forrest C. *George C. Marshall: Ordeal and Hope*. New York: Viking Press, 1966.

———. *George C. Marshall: Organizer of Victory*. New York: Viking Press, 1973.

Pope, Arthur U. *Maxim Litvinoff*. New York: L. B. Fischer, 1943.

Raack, R. C. *Stalin's Drive to the West, 1938–1941: The Origins of the Cold War*. Stanford, Calif.: Stanford University Press, 1995.

Radzinsky, Edvard. *Stalin*. Translated by H. T. Willetts. New York: Doubleday, 1996.

Read, Anthony, and David Fisher. *Deadly Embrace: Hitler, Stalin, and the Nazi-Soviet Pact, 1939–1941*. New York: W. W. Norton, 1989.

Remnick, David. *Lenin's Tomb: The Last Days of the Soviet Empire*. New York: Random House, 1993.

Reynolds, Quentin. *The Curtain Rises*. New York: Random House, 1944.

Rhodes, Richard. *The Making of the Atomic Bomb*. New York: Simon and Schuster, 1986.

Richman, John. *The United States and the Soviet Union: The Decision to Recognize*. Raleigh, N.C.: Camberleigh Hall, 1980.

Rosenfeldt, Niels Erik. *Stalin's Secret Chancellery and the Comintern*. Copenhagen: C. A. Reitzels, 1991.

Rosenstone, Robert A. *Romantic Revolutionary: A Biography of John Reed*. New York: Vintage Books, 1975.

Rothschild, Joseph. *Return to Diversity: A Political History of East Central Europe since World War II*. 2d ed. New York: Oxford University Press, 1993.

Rozek, Edward J. *Allied Wartime Diplomacy: A Pattern in Poland*. New York: John Wiley, 1958.

Rubin, Nancy. *American Empress: The Life and Times of Marjorie Merriweather Post.* New York: Villard Books, 1995.

Ruddy, Michael T. *The Cautious Diplomat: Charles E. Bohlen and the Soviet Union, 1929–1969.* Kent, Ohio: Kent State University Press, 1986.

Schlesinger, Arthur M. Jr. *The Age of Roosevelt.* Vol. 1, *The Crisis of the Old Order, 1919–1933.* Boston: Houghton Mifflin, 1957.

Sherwin, Martin J. *A World Destroyed: The Atomic Bomb and the Grand Alliance.* New York: Alfred A. Knopf, 1975.

Smith, Kathleen E. *Remembering Stalin's Victims: Popular Memory and the End of the USSR.* Ithaca, N.Y.: Cornell University Press, 1996.

Smith, Sally Bedell. *Reflected Glory: The Life of Pamela Churchill Harriman.* New York: Simon and Schuster, 1996.

Spiegelman, Art. *Maus: A Survivor's Tale.* New York: Pantheon Books, 1986

———. *Maus II: A Survivor's Tale: and here my troubles began.* New York: Pantheon Books, 1991.

Stoler, Mark. *The Politics of the Second Front: American Military Planning and Diplomacy in Coalition Warfare, 1941–1943.* Westport, Conn.: Greenwood Press, 1977.

Sword, Keith, ed. *The Soviet Takeover of the Polish Eastern Provinces, 1939–41.* New York: St. Martin's Press, 1991.

Taylor, A. J. P. *Beaverbrook.* New York: Simon and Schuster, 1972

Taylor, S. J. *Stalin's Apologist: Walter Duranty, the New York Times's Man in Moscow.* New York: Oxford University Press, 1990.

Thurston, Robert W. *Life and Terror in Stalin's Russia, 1934–1941.* New Haven: Yale University Press, 1996.

Tolley, Kemp. *Caviar and Commissars: The Experiences of a U.S. Naval Officer in Stalin's Russia.* Annapolis, Md.: Naval Institute Press, 1983.

Tucker, Robert C. *Stalin in Power: The Revolution from Above, 1929–1941.* New York: W. W. Norton, 1990.

Tugwell, Rexford G. *In Search of Roosevelt.* Cambridge, Mass.: Harvard University Press, 1972.

Tuttle, Dwight William. *Harry L. Hopkins and Anglo-American-Soviet Relations, 1941–1945.* New York: Garland, 1985.

Ulam, Adam B. *Expansion and Coexistence: The History of Soviet Foreign Policy, 1917–1973.* 2d ed. New York: Praeger, 1974.

Vaksberg, Arkday. *Stalin's Prosecutor: The Life of Andrei Vyshinsky.* New York: Grove Weidenfeld, 1991.

Volkogonov, Dmitri. *Stalin: Triumph and Tragedy.* Translated by Harold Shukman. New York: Grove Weidenfeld, 1991.

Wehle, Louis B. *Hidden Threads of History.* New York: Macmillan, 1953.

Weil, Martin A. *A Pretty Good Club: The Founding Fathers of the U.S. Foreign Service.* New York: W. W. Norton, 1978.

Weinberg, Gerhard L. *A World at Arms: A Global History of World War II.* Cambridge: Cambridge University Press, 1994.

Werth, Alexander. *Russia at War, 1941–1945.* New York: E. P. Dutton, 1964.

Westad, Odd Arne. *Cold War and Revolution: Soviet-American Rivalry and the Origins of the Chinese Civil War.* New York: Columbia University Press, 1993.

Williams, Robert C. *Russian Art and American Money, 1900–1940.* Cambridge, Mass.: Harvard University Press, 1980.

Yergin, Daniel. *Shattered Peace: The Origins of the Cold War and the National Security State*. Boston: Houghton Mifflin, 1978.

Zawodny, J. K. *Death in the Forest*. South Bend, Ind.: University of Notre Dame Press, 1962.

Zubok, Vladimir, and Constantine Pleshakov, eds. *Inside the Kremlin's Cold War: From Stalin to Khrushchev*. Cambridge, Mass.: Harvard University Press, 1996.

Articles

Bess, Demaree. "The Cost of Roosevelt's 'Great Design.'" *Saturday Evening Post*, 27 May 1944.

———. "What Does Russia Want?" *Saturday Evening Post*, 20 March 1943.

Bullitt, William C. "How We Won the War and Lost the Peace." *Life*, 30 August 1948, 88–97.

Campbell, A. E. "Franklin D. Roosevelt and Unconditional Surrender." In *Diplomacy and Intelligence during the Second World War*, ed. Richard Langhorne, 219–41. Cambridge: Cambridge University Press, 1985.

Dallek, Robert. "Franklin Roosevelt as World Leader." *American Historical Review* 76 (Dec. 1971): 1503–13.

Davis, Forrest. "Roosevelt's World Blueprint." *Saturday Evening Post*, 10 April 1943.

———. "What Really Happened at Teheran?" *Saturday Evening Post*, 13 and 20 May 1944.

Di Biagio, Anna. "The Establishment of the Cominform." In *The Cominform: Minutes of the Three Conferences, 1947/1948/1949*, ed. G. Procacci et al., 11–34. Milan: Feltrinelli, 1994.

Dunn, Dennis J. "Religion, Revolution, and Order in Russia." In *Christianity after Communism: Social, Political, and Cultural Struggle in Russia*, ed. Niels C. Nielson Jr., 15–28. Boulder, Colo.: Westview Press, 1994.

Gaddis, John Lewis. "The Tragedy of Cold War History." *Foreign Affairs* (Jan./Feb. 1994): 142–54.

Grant, Natalie. "The Russian Section: A Window on the Soviet Union." *Diplomatic History* 2 (spring 1978): 107–15.

Harbutt, Fraser J. "Churchill, Hopkins, and the 'Other' Americans: An Alternative Perspective on Anglo-American Relations, 1941–1945." *International History Review* 8 (May 1986): 236–62.

Harrington, Daniel. "Kennan, Bohlen, and the Riga Axioms." *Diplomatic History* 2 (winter 1978): 423–37.

Heilbrunn, Jacob. "The Playboy of the Western World." *New Republic*, 27 July 1992.

Heller, Michel. "Mr. Stalin, I Presume?" *Survey: A Journal of East and West Studies* 30 (June 1989): 155–63.

Herndon, James S., and Joseph O. Baylen, "Col. Philip R. Faymonville and the Red Army, 1934–43." *Slavic Review* 34 (Sept. 1975): 483–505.

Herring, George C. Jr. "Lend-Lease to Russia and the Origins of the Cold War, 1944–1945." *Journal of American History* 56 (June 1969): 93–114.

Huntington, Samuel. "The West and the World." *Foreign Affairs* (Nov./Dec. 1996): 28–46.

Kennan, George. "Comment." *Survey: A Journal of East and West Studies* 21 (winter/spring 1975): 29–36.

Kimball, Warren F. "Lend-Lease and the Open Door: The Temptation of British Opulence, 1937–1942." *Political Science Quarterly* 86 (Jan. 1971): 232–59.

———. "Naked Reverse Right: Roosevelt, Churchill, and Eastern Europe from TOLSTOY to Yalta—and a Little Beyond." *Diplomatic History* 9 (winter 1985): 1–24.

Langer, John Daniel. "The 'Red General': Philip R. Faymonville and the Soviet Union, 1917–1952." *Prologue* 8 (winter 1976): 209–21.

Larsh, William. "W. Averell Harriman and the Polish Question, December 1943–August 1944." *East European Politics and Societies* 7 (fall 1993): 513–54.

Leffler, Melvyn P. "Inside Enemy Archives: The Cold War Reopened." *Foreign Affairs* (July/Aug. 1996), 120–35.

Luce, Clare Boothe. "The Ambassadorial Issue: Professional or Amateurs." *Foreign Affairs* (Oct. 1957), 105–21.

Maddux, Thomas R. "American Diplomats and the Soviet Experiment: The View from the Moscow Embassy, 1934–1939." *South Atlantic Quarterly* (autumn 1975), 468–87.

———. "Watching Stalin Maneuver between Hitler and the West: American Diplomats and Soviet Diplomacy, 1934–1939." *Diplomatic History* 1 (spring 1977): 140–54.

Mark, Eduard. "Charles E. Bohlen and the Acceptable Limits of Soviet Hegemony in Eastern Europe: A Memorandum of 18 October 1945." *Diplomatic History* 3 (spring 1979): 201–13.

———. "October or Thermidor? Interpretations of Stalinism and the Perception of Soviet Foreign Policy in the United States, 1927–1947." *American Historical Review* 94 (Oct. 1989): 937–62.

Mastny, Vojtech. "The Cassandra in the Foreign Commissariat: Maxim Litvinov and the Cold War." *Foreign Affairs* 54 (Jan. 1976): 373.

Matlock, Rebecca B. "Backdrop to History: Spaso House." *Foreign Service Journal,* April 1989, 41–44.

Miner, Steven M. "Revelations, Secrets, Gossip, and Lies: Sifting Warily through the Soviet Archives." *New York Times Book Review,* 14 May 1995, 19–21.

Pechatnov, Vladimir O. "The Big Three after World War II." Cold War International History Project Working Paper, no. 13, Woodrow Wilson International Center, 1995.

Propas, Frederic L. "Creating a Hard Line toward Russia: The Training of State Department Soviet Experts, 1927–1937." *Diplomatic History* 8 (summer 1984): 209–26.

Raack, R. C. "Stalin's Role in the Coming of World War II." *World Affairs* 158 (spring 1996): 198–211.

———. "Stalin's Role in the Coming of World War II: The International Debate Goes On." *World Affairs* 159 (fall 1996): 47–54.

Reynolds, Quentin. "Diplomat on the Spot." *Collier's,* 24 June 1943.

Rotundo, Louis. "Stalin and the Outbreak of War in 1941." *Journal of Contemporary History* 24 (Apr. 1989): 277–99.

Schmidt, Maria. "The Hiss Dossier." *New Republic,* 8 November 1993, 17–20.

Siracusa, Joseph. "The Meaning of TOLSTOY: Churchill, Stalin, and the Balkans, Moscow, October 1944." *Diplomatic History* 3 (fall 1979): 443–63.

———. "The Night Stalin and Churchill Divided Europe: The View from Washington." *Review of Politics* 43 (July 1981): 381–409.

Steele, Richard W. "Franklin D. Roosevelt and His Foreign Policy Critics." *Political Science Quarterly* 94 (spring 1979): 15–35.

Tanenhaus, Sam. "Hiss: Guilty as Charged." *Commentary,* April 1993, 32–37.

Ullman, Richard H. "The Davies Mission and United States–Soviet Relations, 1937–1941." *World Politics* 9 (Jan. 1957): 220–39.

Urban, George. "Was Stalin (the Terrible) Really a Great Man? A Long Conversation with Averell Harriman." *Encounter* 57 (Nov. 1981): 20–40.

Unpublished Material

O'Connor, J. E. "Laurence A. Steinhardt and American Policy toward the Soviet Union, 1939–1941." Ph.D. diss., University of Virginia, 1968.

Index